THE HISTORY OF THEATER IN IRAN

Willem Floor

MAGE PUBLISHERS
WASHINGTON, DC

Library of Congress Cataloging-in-Publication Data

Floor, Willem M.
The history of theater in Iran / Willem Floor.
p. cm.
Includes bibliographical references and index.
ISBN 0-934211-29-9 (pbk. : alk. paper)
1. Theater--Iran--History. 2. Performing arts--Iran--History. 3.
Persian drama--History and criticism. I. Title.
PN2951.F56 2005
792'.0955--dc22
2005014686

ISBN 0-934211-29-9

Mage books are available through bookstores
or directly from the publisher toll-free 800.962.0922 or 202.342.1642
www.mage.com • as@mage.com

CONTENTS

TABLE OF FIGURES

FOREWORD

When a friend asked me some questions in 2003 about theater in Iran I had to admit my ignorance of the subject. My friend then asked me whether I would be willing to find the answers to the queries raised, to which I optimistically reacted that I would do so. I found that although there were a number of studies in Persian, there was no study available on Iranian Theater in English.

In other Western languages the harvest was likewise poor. Thus, when digging for information I found that rather than being able to do a quick search to satisfy my friend's curiosity, I had to dig for the data and, as a result, all of a sudden, I found that I had written a book. I hope that those who read this book will find as much pleasure in doing so as I found in researching and writing it, and that they feel they have been enriched and will even want to read more about the subject or go to a theater and see one or more of the plays that have been mentioned here.

As usual, I have to express my thanks to John Emerson (Widener Library, Harvard), whose perseverance to find some very hard-to-find articles has enriched the material available to me and thus allowed me to offer a richer fare to the reader. Also, many thanks are due to Mr. Sadegh Sajjadi of the Greater Islamic Encyclopedia (*Dayerat al-Ma`aref Bozorg Eslami*) in Tehran for sending me other hard-to-find Persian articles. Anneke Floor (chapters 1-3) and Eric Hooglund (chapters 4-5) were so kind to apply their editorial skills and make it seem as if I know my way around the English language and consequently my gratitude is boundless. Finally, I have to thank Dr. Gholam Reza Vatandoust (Shiraz University) and Mr. Rahim Hudi, the doyen of theatrical activities in Shiraz—the former because he reacted to my question to find me material on theatrical activities in Shiraz by asking Mr. Hudi to write an article about what he knew about the subject matter, which the latter was so kind to do.

CHAPTER ONE

COMIC IMPROVISATORY DRAMA

INTRODUCTION

Dramatic performance has existed in Iran throughout history, although some Iranian and Western scholars say differently.[1] Drama in Iran is generally thought to be of recent date and of European origin. It is further believed that the development of formal theatrical institutions is of an even more recent date. Religious Islamic opposition against frivolous entertainment of any kind in general, and the impersonation of living beings in particular, is sometimes cited as an explanation for the slow development of theatrical drama in Iran and elsewhere. This certainly was the case, but as will be clear from the discussion in this book, despite opposition and warnings from conservative Moslems it never stopped dramatic artists from performing and from Moslems enjoying their performances. Although Western-style drama was indeed introduced in Iran in the nineteenth century, this did not mean that indigenous dramatic art did not exist in Iran prior to the nineteenth century; it was, however, not necessarily of the kind that Westerners identify as theater, as much of Iran's dramatic art took the form of folk theater. Not much is known about the manifestations of these early art forms, but I discuss what is known about them and how they grew into art forms that are more recognizable to the modern reader as dramatic art.

Many people may not necessarily recognize these early art forms as theatrical performance, because most people in the twenty-first century have been divorced from their ancient cultural roots and have no or little inkling that dramatic performances usually were not staged in a theater. It also depends, of course, how you define drama. Therefore I state upfront what I mean by the term 'drama' when I use it in this study. Drama is the writing, acting, or producing of a portrayal of life characters or the telling of a story, usually involving conflicts and emotions exhibited through action and dialogue. In short, it is an art form, usually

---

[1] See, for example: Bahar, Mohammad Taqi. *Bahar va Adab-e Farsi.* ed. Mohammad Golbon (Tehran, 1351/1972), p. 285 ("Theater and acting did not exist in Iran."); Khanlari, Parviz Natel. "Teyatr va Adabiyyat," *Sokhan* 23 (1352/1973), p. 141 ("We know that it its special sense theater is not an Iranian art."); Chelkowski, Peter. "Dramatic and Literary Aspects of Ta'zieh-Khani—an Iranian Passion Play," *Review of National Literatures*: Iran 2 (Spring, 1971), p. 121 ("There is evidence that Ta'zieh Khani is, indeed, the only indigenous drama ever developed on the Iranian plateau in twenty-five centuries of written literature."). See also de Bruijn, J.T.P. "Masrah" *Encyclopedia of Islam*[2] and Ghanoonparvar, M. R. "Drama" *Encyclopedia Iranica.*

in dialogue, that centers on the actions of characters. Taking this as my starting point means that drama is not necessarily only a written text that is performed by actors in a building often specifically built for that purpose. The definition explicitly includes minstrels, mimes, dancers, story-tellers, in fact anyone acting out the action of characters in song, spoken words, or gesture.

Iran is unique in that within its borders the only form of Islamic religious drama (*ta`ziyeh-khvani*) came into being. What is characteristic for traditional Iranian drama is that with the exception of religious and narrative drama written texts were seldom used. Dramatic art in Iran was strong on improvisation emphasizing the limited role that written text played. The difference between high and low culture was a rather artificial one; all traditional forms of Iranian dramatic art were expressions of popular culture. Those artists who were attached to the royal court and sponsored by the rich were just better and more competent than their less fortunate colleagues, who performed for the public at large.

Theater was initially of a ritual nature, a dramatization of man's relationship with nature, the gods, and other human beings. Theater was born out of sacred rites performed by priests and lay actors dramatizing myths and legends at fixed times and often in fixed locations. As such the dialogues of the Avesta (ca. 1000 BCE) may be considered as a source for, if not a form of, this ritual religious drama as may *ta`ziyeh-khvani* or Shi`ite religious tragedy. Folk theater—mime, puppetry, farce, juggling—also had a ritual context in that it was performed at religious and/or social high days such as days of naming, circumcisions, and marriages. Often these plays were seasonal due to the agricultural calendar that made peasants 'available' as an audience and as actors only at certain times of the year. Over time some of these contextual ritual enactments became divorced from their religious meaning and they were performed throughout the year. However, until this day many of these dramatized rites are still performed at the times and for the (watered-down) purposes for which they originally had come into being.

For example, Georg Goyan has argued that Armenian theater grew out of the funeral rites for the gods Anahita-Gisane, the Armenian counterpart of the contemporary Ishtar-Tammuz and the Anahita-Ahura Mazda cult in the Iranian Empire and other parts of the Middle East.[2] The Armenian god Gisane was the son of the Mother Goddess Turan. Like the other gods, Gisane also had an astronomical symbol that represented his divinity in the celestial firmament. In his case it was a comet that appeared and disappeared on the horizon, symbolizing the god's death

---

[2] Goyan, Georg. *Teatr Dvernei Armenii* 2 vols. (Moscow, 1952), vol. 1, p. 67f. The same is also argued by other Russian scholars, who submit that rock inscriptions in Caucasian Albania near Gabala (Kabala) show that primitive magic gave rise to drawings, paintings, folk dances and theater, music, and oral folk. See the article "Albania" *The Great Soviet Encyclopedia*, 3rd edition (Moscow, 1973).

and resurrection. Because of the tail of the comet and its form it was called the "hairy star" and the meaning of Gisane in Armenian literally is "the long haired one." The priests or ministrants of Gisane were called *gusan*s; they let their hair grow long in honor of their god. This hair was then combed high to resemble the tail of the comet. To achieve this effect the priests supported their hair with a cone-shaped *gisakal*, which over time developed into the *onkos* triangles such as worn in ancient Greek tragic theater. This is the origin of the *onkos* and the cone-shaped hats worn by the actors in antiquity. As stated above, the cult of Anahita-Gisane had its parallels elsewhere in the Middle-East and Eurasia: the funerary rites of, for example, Adonis with the god's resurrection and his return into the arms of Decreta Aphrodite had its counterpart in Armenia. The resurrection of Gisane was also accompanied by bacchanals dedicated to celebrate nature's fertility in which the priestesses of the Armenian goddess of fertility (Anahita) played a prominent role. These priestesses were known as *vartzak*, about whom later.

Figure 1: Statuettes of dzainarku-gusans

Over time, the funerary rites for the god were also enacted for his human descendants, the semi-divine Armenian kings, and later for the Armenian nobility as a kind of ancestor worship. Like in the case of the rites for Gisane, the funerary rites for the Armenain kings and nobility also were performed by the *dzainarku-gusans* or the *gusan-voghbergaks*, singing mourners and wailers, who sang the praises of the deceased and his family. They rhapsodized the "immortal" heroic deeds of the deceased and thus the *gusans* were initially bards and minstrels and the ceremonial was not yet a play. Gradually, to more vividly portray the heroic deeds of the deceased, mimicry and dance were added to singing lamentation, which resulted in a presentation on stage and in the transformation of *gusans* into actors. Moses of Khorene mentioned that Armenians honored the memory of their departed kings with songs, pageantry and dancing. According to Goyan, this practice evoked that of Roman funeral rites where masked actor-dancers represented the deceased with motions and gestures mimicking those of the deceased while singing the praise of his life. Because it was difficult for one actor-dancer to enact the life of the deceased one or more were added and thus tragic theater came into being.

Similarly comic Armenian theater developed out of the spring rites related to the Gisane cult, celebrating fertility and the return of life. Aristotle also opined that comedy originated with "the conceivers of phallic songs." The revelry and the comic-singing (*kataker-gutiun*) in connection with the Gisane rites were indeed fertility rites in which both *gusans* (the Gisane priests) and the *vartzaks* (priest-esses of Anahita) participated. For a long time it was comic theater rather than tragic theater that dominated life in Armenia.

Thus, both tragic and comic Armenian theater originated in the funerary and resurrection rites of Gisane-Ara. The funerary rites were characterized by lamentation and wailing called *voghbergutiun* or song of lamentation in ancient Armenian. The resurrection rites that were characterized by laughter, banter and wild rejoicing were called *katakergutiun*, literally jesting or joyous singing. The modern Armenian word for tragic theater is *voghbergutiun* just like the old Armenian word for actor (*vartzak*) is a reminder of the original religious role of the actor-dancer as the word *vartzak* is derived from the word *vartz*, meaning a bundle of young budding twigs tied with a ribbon, which symbolized spring and was an emblem of the resurrected god. Finally, the *gusans*, who originally were ministrants of Gisane, over time turned into bards and mimes; thus along with the terms *vartzak* and *voghbergutiun*, clearly establishing the link between funerary rites and theater.[3]

---

[3] Goyan, *Teatr*, vol. 1, pp. 205-80, 349-88.

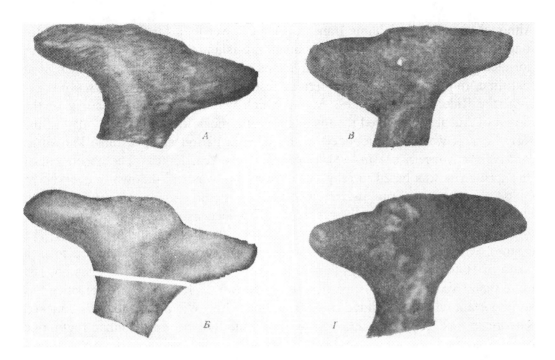

Figure 2: Heads of arazel, the dog-headed Armenian divinities

Goyan not only based his analysis on historical and literary written evidence, but also on archeological evidence to strengthen his analysis. He mentioned statuettes of divinities represented by dog heads, called *aralez*, who resurrected Gisane as well as fallen warriors and therefore played a major role in Armenian funeral rites. They were depicted wearing human-like bird masks symbolically ornamented with coxcombs associated with the sun-god Mithra, and horns in the form of half-moons, signifying the newly risen moon. This form allegedly gave rise to the jesters' hats in Europe. The hats on the statuettes found in Serekamish usually are elongated and cone-shaped in form, suggesting the tail of the "long-haired" comet, symbolizing the god Gisane. These are also the type of hats which Armenian *gusan*s wore until recent times, as do European clowns, and, as I discuss later, were also worn by comedians in Iran. The conic cap, the symbolic phallus, the image of the canine head, and the mask constitute the four elements of Armenian classic tragedy and of its interpreters, the *dzainarku-gusans*. These symbols continued to be characteristic for Armenian actors in later centuries. The phallus was transformed in medieval times into a triangular apron, and later into a hanging belt with a ball or tassel at the end. The canine head, the mask of the god *Aralez*, was transposed from the hand to the end of the stick. Later the stick was replaced by a snake with a canine head, which was used in Armenian theater till the eighteenth century.[4]

---

[4] Goyan, *Teatr*, vol. 1, pp. 349-453.

Although data on pre-Islamic Iran proper are fewer than for Armenia, which for long periods formed part of the subsequent pre-Islamic Iranian Empires, that does not mean that there were not similar forms of dramatic performances in Iran at that time. In pre-Islamic Iran a religious festival existed, known as *kuseh bar ne-shin* (the Ride of the Beardless Man), which was held at the beginning of the month of Adhar. It involved the installation of a mock king on the 13th day of the New Year. It was also celebrated in the Islamic period and was also known as *Padeshah-e Nowruzi* or *Mir-e Nowruzi* (the New Year King).[5] The enactment of this spring rite was based in religious custom that was well-known to everybody. Given the nature of rite, which involved the enthronement of the king (and queen), interaction between the king and his subjects as well as comical behavior, imply the existence of dialogue, stage directions and dramatic conventions. The custom, which recalls that of the May King in Europe, is also referred to in a poem of Hafez, where he says that the reign of the New Year King does not last more than five days.[6] The institution of the New Year King was also practiced as an important religiously-tinted ritual in political life. When the Mongols attacked Khvorezm in 1220 "it was deserted by [both] the Sultans, but Khumar Tegin, one of the leaders of the army [and] by reason of his relationship to the royal house, was with one voice elected Sultan and made a *Nauruz* king."[7] A very serious off-shoot of the custom was the installation of a political opponent as a mock king by Shah `Abbas I in 1593. This ritual was even more refined in 1668, when Safi I was re-enthroned under the new name of Soleyman to propitiate Fate.[8] The installation of a mock king continued to be practiced in parts of Iran until quite recently, and in fact may still be practiced. Qazvini provides a description of this event as witnessed by a friend of his in 1923 at Bojnord (Khorasan).[9] Through

[5] Biruni, Abu Reyhan. *Al-Tafhim li ava'il sana`at al-tanjim* ed. Jalal Homa'i (Tehran, 1362/1983), pp. 256-57; `Emad al-Din Dhakariya Mahmud Qazvini, *`Aja'eb al-makhluqat va ghara'eb al-mowjudat* (Lucknow, 1912), pp. 128-29; Qazvini, Mohammad. "Mir-e Nowruzi," *Yadgar* 1/3 (1323/1944), pp. 13-16; Ibid., "Shahedi-ye digar baraye 'Mir-e Nowruzi'," *Yadgar* 1/10 (1323/1944), pp. 57-66. The custom of *Emir-e Nowruz* also was celebrated in Egypt in the tenth century CE and was only suppressed around 1380. Mez, A. *Die Renaissance des Islams* (Heidelberg, 1922), pp. 400-01.

[6] Hafez-e Shirazi, Khvajeh Shams al-Din. *Lesan al-Gheyb* ed. Pazhman Bakhtiyari (Tehran, 1362/1983), p. 446.

[7] Juvaini, `Ata-Malik. *The History of the World-Conquerer.* Translated by John Andrew Boyle 2 vols. (Manchester, 1958), vol. 1, p. 124. For another example see Qazwini, "Mir-e Nowruzi," p. 15 quoting the *Tadhkereh-ye Dowlatshah.*

[8] Monshi, Eskander Beg. *Tarikh-e `Alamara-ye `Abbasi.* Iraj Afshar ed. 2 vols. (Tehran, 1350/1971), p. 474-76; Ibid., *History of Shah `Abbas the Great,* tr. R.M. Savory, 2 vols. (Boulder, 1978); Natanzi, Mahmud b. Hedayatollah Afushteh-ye. *Naqavat al-athar fi dhekr al-akhyar,* ed. Ehsan Eshraqi. (Tehran, 1350/1971), pp. 522-23; Chardin, Jean. *Voyages,* ed. L. Langlès, 10 vols., (Paris 1811), vol. 10, p. 94.

[9] Qazwini, "Mir-e Nowruzi," pp. 13-16. In the 1890s, the three-day festival of the "false emir" was still being celebrated each year in the spring in the Kurdish town of Sowj-Bulagh. De Morgan, J. *Mission Scientifique en Perse.* 5 vols. (Paris, 1895), vol. 2, pp. 39-40 (with one drawing and one picture showing the 'false emir' and his court).

their fieldwork in the 1970s, Anjavi Shirazi and Ilhan Başgöz have been able to collect data of the continued celebration of this festival in Kermanshah, Fars, Azerbaijan, and Khuzestan.

> The ceremony is performed by a group of actors whose main figures are a *kuseh* (beardless or thinly bearded man), a bride, and an antagonist. They all wear special costumes and are joined by a band of musicians (usually a drum and *surna* [flute] players). Followed by children, they go to visit the houses of the village, performing a dance in front of each house. The dance is a dramatic representation of the death and resurrection of the *kuseh*. The head of each household donates some food, which is shared and eaten by the members of the group.

> A variant is *Kuseh* and *Nagaldi*.[10] This is performed on the 41st morning of winter. *Kuseh* wears a felt coat, hangs bells around his legs and arms, powders his face with flour, covers his head with a goatskin, and wears a wide belt on which are sewn many bells. On his head he ties two bushes to form a pair of 'horns,' and from his waist he hangs an axe. In his hand he carries a long stick. The second character is *Kuseh*'s bride, a young boy disguised as a girl, who wears a long robe, artificial breasts, rouge and mascara. She also wears bells on her wrists and neck. ... Turkish-speaking peoples call the ceremony '*Ne qaldeh*,' and name the first character 'Male *Kuseh*' and the bride "Female *Kuseh*.' [In Fars] *Kuseh* wears a dress made of felt and walks on stilts, with bells hung about his neck and wearing two horns on his head. ... This ceremony is performed on the fourth Tuesday night preceding the vernal equinox (March 21), which is called the New Year. Among the Turks living in the Caspian Sea region, *Kuseh* wears a coat inside out and has a tail attached to his back. His face is covered with a mask and his head is ornamented with a high cap, to which bells are attached. The second character is a doctor, who wears a fantastic dress, a hat inside out, a mask on his face, and he also carries a stick in his hand.[11]

The description of this festival very much resembles that of similar celebrations in pre-Christian Armenia. These festivities in both Iran and Armenia were dramatic enactments of "the renewal" of the world, in particular at the occasion of the beginning of the New Year and they are all religious fertility ceremonies in origin, of a pre-Zoroastrian nature. They have their equivalents throughout Eurasia where the main figures were 'the king', 'the queen,' 'the clown', 'the wild man' etc., in

---

[10] *Nagaldi* derives from the Turkish *ne kaldi*, meaning 'how much is left,' or 'how many days are left?' It is a reference to the remaining number of days of winter.

[11] Başgöz, Ilhan. "Marasem-e tamanay-e baran va baran-sazi dar Iran," *Ketab-e Jom`eh* 1/19 (29 Adhar 1358), pp. 130-41; Anjavi Shirazi, Sayyed Abu'l-Qasem. *Baziha-ye Namayeshi* (Tehran: Amir Kabir, 1973); Ibid., *Jashnehha va Adab va Mo`tadiqat-e Zamestan* (Tehran: Amir Kabir, 1973).

which one easily recognizes their Iranian and Armenian counterparts. Anthropomorphic masks or representations usually were part of these events. Typically also were the ritual fights at that time, which symbolized the struggle of the resurrection, the renewal of the world. It may well be that the ritual fights during Moharram hail back to this same religious substratum. Similar pre-Islamic rites continued to be enacted in Islamic Iran, some of them even to this day. What it shows is that neither Zoroastrianism nor Islam has been able to supplant these older beliefs, which each year gave rise to the enactment of a series of dramatic scenes signaling the passing of the old and the rebirth of the New Year.[12]

There was also Greek mimic drama in pre-Islamic Iran. The first recorded dramatic performance in Iran was noted by Xenophon in around 400 BCE:

> After this [a dance by Thracians] some Aenianians and Magnesians [both Aeolian groups from Thessaly] got up and fell to dancing the Carpaea, as it is called, under arms. This was the manner of the dance: one man lays aside his arms and proceeds to drive a yoke of oxen, and while he drives he sows, turning him about frequently, as though he were afraid of something; up comes a cattle-lifter, and no sooner does the ploughman catch sight of him afar, than he snatches up his arms and confronts him. They fight in front of his team, and all in rhythm to the sound of the pipe. At last the robber binds the countryman and drives off the team. Or sometimes the cattle-driver binds the robber, and then he puts him under the yoke beside the oxen, with his two hands tied behind his back, and off he drives. After this a Mysian came in with a light shield in either hand and danced, at one time going through a pantomime, as if he were dealing with two assailants at once; at another plying his shields as if to face a single foe, and then again he would whirl about and throw somersaults, keeping the shields in his hands, so that it was a beautiful spectacle. Last of all he danced the *Persian dance*, clashing the shields together, crouching down on one knee and springing up again from earth; and all this he did in measured time to the sound of the flute.[13]

At the end of the Acheamenid Empire there is evidence of the existence of theater, although it may be of the kind that the conquering Macedonian army brought with it rather than already existing constructions. Plutach reported that:

> When he [i.e, Alexander] came to Ecbatana in Media, and had despatched his most urgent affairs, he began to divert himself again with spectacles and public entertainments, to carry on which he had a supply of three thousand actors and artists, newly arrived out of Greece. But

---

[12] For a detailed discussion of these and other related issues see Eliade, Mircea. *Traité d'Histoire des Réligions* (Paris, 1964), chapter viii. For other examples see Anjavi Shirazi, *Baziha-ye Namayeshi*; Ibid., *Jashnehha va Adab*.
[13] Xenephon, *Anabasis*, Book VI, section 1.

they were soon interrupted by Hephaestion's falling sick of a fever, in which, being a young man and a soldier, too, he could not confine himself to so exact a diet as was necessary; for whilst his physician, Glaucus, was gone to the theater, he ate a fowl for his dinner, and drank a large draught of wine, upon which he became very ill, and shortly after died.

Alexander the Great attended a show at Gedrosia (Carmania) in which a dance contest was performed.[14]

> As soon as he came to the royal palace of Gedrosia, he again refreshed and feasted his army; and one day after he had drunk pretty hard, it is said, he went to see a prize of dancing contended for, in which his favourite Bagoas, having gained the victory, crossed the theater in his dancing habit, and sat down close by him, which so pleased the Macedonians that they made loud acclamations for him to kiss Bagoas, and never stopped clapping their hands and shouting till Alexander put his arms round him and kissed him.

Greek theaters were established in the Seleucid Empire after Alexander's conquest of Iran and they still existed and were frequented in Parthian times. This is not only known from written classical sources, but also "from excavations of theaters and a form for the making of a comedy mask from Nisa."[15] There also were theaters in Armenia; the first one in Tigranakerta was destroyed by the Roman general Lucullus in 69 BCE, and a second one was built at Artashet, which had a professional group of actors attached to it. In 53 BCE the Parthians under Surena defeated the Romans under Crassus. To celebrate his victory Surena put on a show ridiculing Crassus in the theater of Artashet. The Parthian king Orodes II was received in Armenia where he was entertained by Armenian actors. The tragedy *The Bacchanals* by Euripides was played and the mask of Penteus was replaced by that of Chrassus to mock the defeated Romans.[16] According to Plutarch,

> Surena sent the head and hand of Crassus to Hyrodes, the king, into Armenia, but himself by his messengers scattering a report that he was bringing

---

[14] Plutarch, *Lives* (Alexander). According to Rezvani, M. *Le théâtre et la danse en Iran* (Paris, 1962), p. 29 and Beyza'i, Bahram. *Namayesh dar Iran* (Tehran, 1344/1965), pp. 26-27 this theater was built prior to Alexander's arrival.

[15] Frye, Richard N. *The Heritage of Persia* (Cleveland, 1963), p. 188. Greco-Roman theater masks were among the decorations of the Jewish synagogue of Dura-Europos, which may indicate that the building originally was a non-Jewish building. Kelley, Christopher Pierce. "Who Did the Iconaclasm in the Dura Synagogue?" *Bulletin of the Amercian Schools of Oriental Research* 295 (August 1994), 59; Moon, Warren G. "Nudity and Narrative: Observations on the Frescoes of the Dura Synagogue," *Journal of the American Academy of Religion* LX, 4 (Winter 1992), p. 603.

[16] 'Ata'i, Abu'l-Qasem Jannati. *Bonyad-e Namayesh dar Iran* (Tehran: Mihan, 1333/1954), p. 15; Goyan, *Teatr*, vol. 1, p. 113-16.

Crassus alive to Seleucia, made a ridiculous procession, which by way of scorn, he called a triumph. For one Caius Paccianus, who of all the prisoners was most like Crassus, being put into a woman's dress of the fashion of the barbarians, and instructed to answer to the title of Crassus and Imperator, was brought sitting upon his horse, while before him went a parcel of trumpeters and lictors upon camels. Purses were hung at the end of the bundles of rods, and the heads of the slain fresh bleeding at the end of their axes. After them followed the Seleucian singing women, repeating scurrilous and abusive songs upon the effeminacy and cowardliness of Crassus. This show was seen by everybody; but Surena, calling together the senate of Seleucia, laid before them certain wanton books, of the writings of Aristides, the Milesian; neither, indeed, was this any forgery, for they had been found among the baggage of Rustius, and were a good subject to supply Surena with insulting remarks upon the Romans, who were not able even in the time of war to forget such writings and practices. But the people of Seleucia had reason to commend the wisdom of Aesop's fable of the wallet, seeing their general Surena carrying a bag full of loose Milesian stories before him, but keeping behind him a whole Parthian Sybaris in his many wagons full of concubines; like the vipers and asps people talk of, all the foremost and more visible parts fierce and terrible with spears and arrows and horsemen, but the rear terminating in loose women and castanets, music of the lute, and midnight revellings. Rustius, indeed, is not to be excused, but the Parthians had forgot, when they mocked at the Milesian stories, that many of the royal line of their Arsacidae had been born of Milesian and Ionian mistresses.

Whilst these things were doing, Hyrodes had struck up a peace with the king of Armenia, and made a match between his son Pacorus and the king of Armenia's sister. Their feastings and entertainments in consequence were very sumptuous, and various Grecian compositions, suitable to the occasion, were recited before them. For Hyrodes was not ignorant of the Greek language and literature, and Artavasdes was so expert in it, that he wrote tragedies and orations and histories, some of which are still extant. When the head of Crassus was brought to the door, the tables were just taken away, and one Jason, a tragic actor, of the town of Tralles, was singing the scene in the Bacchae of Euripides concerning Agave. He was receiving much applause, when Sillaces coming to the room, and having made obeisance to the king, threw down the head of Crassus into the midst of the company. The Parthians receiving it with joy and acclamations, Sillaces, by the king's command, was made to sit down, while Jason handed over the costume of Pentheus to one of the dancers in the chorus, and taking up the head of Crassus, and acting the part of a bacchante in her frenzy, in a rapturous impassioned manner, sang the lyric passages,

> We've hunted down a mighty chase to-day,
> And from the mountain bring the noble prey;

to the great delight of all the company; but when the verses of the dialogue followed,

> What happy hand the glorious victim slew?
> I claim that honor to my courage due;

Pomaxathres, who happened to be there at the supper, started up and
would have got the head into his own hands, "for it is my due," said he,
"and no man's else." The king was greatly pleased, and gave presents,
according to the custom of the Parthians, to them, and to Jason, the actor,
a talent. Such was the burlesque that was played, they tell us, as the
afterpiece to the tragedy of Crassus's expedition.[17]

Despite the presence of Greek theater in the Iranian Empire, with the advent of
the Arab Empire this theatrical tradition disappeared seemingly without leaving
any trace. From the above it is clear that the origins of traditional Iranian drama
are lost in the mists of history and only by combining the snippets extant in literary texts, chronicles, still existing folk traditions and foreign travel accounts may
we arrive at a better understanding and reconstruction of the earliest forms of
drama. Traditional drama in Iran manifested itself through a range of artistic expressions. There was (a) puppet drama, (b) comic improvisatory drama, (c) narrative drama and dramatic storytelling, and (d) religious epic drama. Finally,
modern European theater joined this traditional foursome in the nineteenth century, with its emphasis on a written play.

WHO WERE THE ENTERTAINERS?

Before discussing the different dramatic forms of expression that developed in
Iran throughout the ages, it is necessary to have a look at the entertainers. Relatively little is known about them, because polite society and thus literary sources
paid little attention to them. Entertainers were identified with the popular type of
performances, generally referred to as *ma`rekeh*, *hengameh*, or *tamasha*. As these
terms already imply, the performances of these entertainers took place mostly in
public places. The performer (*ma`rekeh-gir*) could be a storyteller, an acrobat, a
magician, a performer with dancing animals, or a musician. In fact, as I discuss in
what follows, often these male entertainers were skilled in more than one art form
so as to enhance their earning power or of that of their troupe. Each one could
usually play more than one instrument, could sing, and play one or more role in
one of the theatrical performances that the troupe might enact. The younger members of the troupe were the dancers, and had to be handsome, young boys, as convention required. This held especially for those members of the troupe who were
dancers and played female roles. All roles, male and female, were played by boys

---

[17] Plutarch, *Lives* (of Crassus).

and men. The specialty of the adept dancers in the troupe was playing female roles. They imitated female voices in song and speech in falsetto.

There also were female musicians as well as dancers, but they were not part of the 'normal' troupes of entertainers. These usually performed inside harems. In Safavid times, however, it was quite normal for female dancers to perform in public, in particular at official occasions. They also, of course, performed in private. However, in the Qajar period this was not the case any longer, although the female members of gypsy troupes still performed in public.

Like other trades in Iran, professional entertainers tended to be family, i.e. they were recruited from among the families of troupe members or their acquaintances. According to Beyza'i, actors used the oral method for teaching roles, although narrators also had written texts since medieval times. The young members learned their art on-the-job, and over time grew into new roles and skills, starting with minor ones and slowly learning more demanding skills and roles. The troupes, although urban based, traveled around the countryside and followed a performance route that might take them hundreds of kilometers from their home base. That also held for those who were individual performers, who did not necessarily join a troupe, but struck out on their own. They were usually storytellers and animal handlers; in short they had skills that allowed them to make a living as an entertainer.[18]

The various kinds of entertainers often performed together, where one or the other performed in a supporting role, either as an introductory or intermission act. Over time, as discussed in what follows, some of these supportive acts became the main acts. This did not mean that these artists did not perform alone. They did, but whether by design or chance they were often found to be performing either simultaneously or consecutively in the same public and private space. The career of the Tehrani puppet player Luti Ramazan is instructive in this context. Galunov writes that he was the son of a storyteller (*naqqal*). He learnt many verses from his father. Under influence of dervishes he also participated in contest-recitation (*sokhanvari*). This was also described in popular Azeri-Turkish popular tales such as `Asheq Gharib; and also by the traveling dervishes singing pseudo-religious verses. Then he became a prestidigitator and became an apprentice (*shagerd*) to a puppeteer in Tehran, under whose guidance he learnt the craft. Then he became an independent performer and traveled around.[19] Similarly, the actors for the religious drama in Tehran were recruited in Ramazan from among the best actors and singers of the country, most of

---

[18] Beyza'i, *Namayesh*, p. 203; Shahri, *Tarikh*, vol. 6, pp. 19-44.
[19] Galunov, R.A. "Pakhlavan Kachal-Persidskii Teatr Petrushki," *IRAN* II (1928, Leningrad), pp. 26-27.

whom played comic popular theater during the remainder of the year.[20] Thus, it would seem that although there was specialization the actors might switch between categories.

ENTERTAINERS IN THE PRE-ISLAMIC PERIOD

In Achaemenid times, "There were also jesters, jugglers, clowns, and musicians. The last played an important part in Court life and were likewise divided into three grades, according to their skill and the instruments on which they performed."[21] There were also story tellers, many of which were itinerant, who narrated stories and legends about gods and heroes. There was also the staging of tragedy as suggested by a depiction on an ornamented cup from the second century BCE. This is further confirmed by similar depictions in subsequent centuries such as on a cup in the Hermitage that shows scenes from *Alcestis, Alope, Bacchantes* and *Ion*, all plays by Euripides. Some of the dancers and actors may have worn masks as they did in contemporary Greek and Roman theater as well as later in the Islamic period. At Bishapur there is a building (D) which has a court with floor mosaics that depict nobles, musicians and garland bearers, and isolated human heads reminiscent of Roman theater masks.[22] Central Asian towns were centers of the fine arts (dance, music, theater). One of them, the Greek-Bactrian town of Aï Khanom (on the border between Afghanistan and Tajikestan), had the usual installations of a Greek city—a theater, a gymnasium, and a fountain. In the royal treasury two extracts of theatrical plays have been found.[23] Theater in Armenia was Hellenistic in nature, although built upon Armenian traditions. The theater buildings also clearly were modeled after those elsewhere in the Hellenistic region, which, given the fact that these amphitheaters were built by imported architects and master builders is not a surprise. The Roman emperor Nero sent actormimes as a present to the Armenian king Tiridates I, while companies of Roman mimes continued to visit Armenia during the first to third century CE. During the Arsacid period a new theater was built taking its cue from models in Asia Minor. According to Goyan, the educational role of theater was changed to one of amusing the masses. In Parthian theater performances by mimes dominated. Initially the Greek word μίμοσ (*mimos*) was translated as *gusan* in Armenian, but later it

---

[20] Aubin, Eugène. *La Perse d'aujourd'hui* (Perse, 1908), pp. 230-33; *Revue du Monde Musulmane* 4 (1908), p. 486; see also chapter five.

[21] Ghirshman, Roman. *Iran* (Hammondsworth: Penguin, 1961), p. 312.

[22] Ghirshman, Roman, *Parthes et Sassanides* (Paris: Gallimard, 1962), pp. 141-46, 215-16, 268, 274-77.

[23] Litvinsky, B. A., Guang-da, Zhang and Samghabadi, R. Shabani eds. *History of the Civilizations of Central Asia, Volume III: The Crossroads of Civilizations: A.D. 250 to 750.* (Paris: UNESCO Publishing, 1996), p. 490; Rapin, Claude. *Fouilles d'Aï Khanoum*, vol. VIII: La *trésorerie du palais hellénistique d'Aï Khanoum. Mémoires de la Délégation archéologique française en Afghanistan* XXXIII. (Paris, 1992), pp. 3 n.9, 115-30, 192-94, 278.

was retained as an Armenian loanword and it became a synonym of the Armenian words *vartzak* and *gusan* over time.[24]

Whereas under the Parthians the minstrels (*goshan*) in the Iranian homeland were rhapsodists and storytellers they were not so anymore in Armenia, although they originally had been. Likewise the *vartzak*s were not professional dancers at funeral rites any longer, but like the *gusan*s they had become mimes. The acting of these mimes was very popular and of Nazenik, the actress-mime, Moses of Khorene (Khorenats'i) wrote that she "sang with her hands."[25] The Armenian king Pap (r. 368-374) was murdered in 374 CE when he was engrossed watching the "multitude of gusans" on the stage, accompanied by music. The mimes had a large repertory of farces and they sported a phallus as an integral part of their costume. This suggests that these plays were rooted in the ancient rites of phallic cults, which had thrived in the area as attested by archeological evidence. The phallus was such a normal part of the *gusan*'s costume that it is still found as late as 1401 CE in a drawing of an actor in the margin of an Armenian bible. A special kind of comic acting was that of the *kataks* or comedians. The actors were called *katakagusans* or *kheghkataks*, while the playwrights of these comedies were called *katakergaks*, as were Aristophanes and Menander in ancient Armenian. From the few brief references to these comedies Goyan has concluded that this type of repertory differed radically from that of the mimes. In fact, Goyan suggests that the comedians often were an outlet for social criticism, or an early form of *baqqal-bazi*, which I discuss in what follows. In addition to mime (*mimos-gusan*) and comedy (*katak*[-*gusan*]), there was dramatic presentation (*dzainarku-gusan*). This was the Armenian rendition of Greaco-Roman tragedy, which drew heavily on Armenian myths, legends and history. In this kind of theater the use of human-like masks and of usually elongated and cone-shaped hats became a standard attribute of the actors.[26]

These theatrical acts were not only to entertain, but as in the case of Soghdia also to enact religious rites. According to Chinese sources, "On the eleventh month, the Sughdians, tambourine in hand, danced, asking for rain or warmth. In their happy mood, they sprinkled water on each other." Such were the skills of the artists of the Iranian culture area, in particular of Central Asia, that they were quite popular at the imperial court of T'ang China. Songs, singers, mimes, musicians, acrobats, conjurors, contortionists, and prestidigators were imported from Soghdia and Tokharistan. "Shows of illusion, including apparent self-maiming, were regularly given at the temples of Ahura-Mazda in Liang-chou and Lo-yang." Many of

---

[24] Goyan, *Teatr*, vol. 1, pp. 234-70.
[25] Moses Khorenats'i. *History of the Armenians* translated by Robert W. Thomson (Cambridge, 1978), p. 207, n. 5-6.
[26] Goyan, *Teatr*, vol. 1, pp. 220, 241, 268, 301-88; Garsoïan, Nina G. translator. *The Epic Histories Attributed to P'awstos Buzand* (Cambridge, 1989), pp. 94, 199, 214, 529.

these artists were sent as presents to the imperial Chinese court by the rulers of Samarqand (713 CE), Kumadh (719 CE), Kish, Samarqand (727 CE), and Maimargh (733 CE). According to Schafer, the Chinese classified Soghdian dances as "pliant" and "vigorous" dances. Of the former the "Thrill of the Spring Marbler" is mentioned, which was described as poetic, graceful and refined. The vigorous dances include the "Western Prancing Dance" danced by Soghdian boys in typical Iranian dress, crouching, whirling, and leaping to the accompaniment of lutes and transverse flutes. The "Dance of Chach" named for a place near Tashkent, was danced by young girls. It was an amorous dance; they emerged from artificial lotus flowers, danced vigorously to the beat of the drum, made eyes at the spectators, "and, at the end pulled down their blouses to reveal their bare shoulders." Most popular were the Western Twirling Girls sent as a present by the rulers of Kumadh, Kish, Maimargh, and in particular Samarqand. "These Soghdian girls, clad in crimson robes with brocaded sleeves, green damask pantaloons, and boots of red deerskin, skipped, tripped, and twirled on the tops of balls rolling about on the dance platform."[27]

It may be inferred from these Chinese descriptions that similar performances also must have taken place at the Sasanid court, where allegedly 12,000 maidens served at the court of Parviz as singers, dancers. Similarly, Parviz's wife, beautiful Shirin, had gathered dancers and singers like Borbad, Sarkash, and Khushazarvak around her. The directorship of the activities of these performers, singers, composers, and clowns at Shirin's "White Pavilion" was entrusted to Borbad.[28] The importance and size of the artistic establishment at the Sasanid court was still 'remembered' some 500 years later when Nezami-Ganjavi wrote of Parviz Khosrow's court with some poetic license:

> Six thousand master narrators
> Musicians, dancers, and puppeteers
> Gathered from the quarters of each city
> And distributed around the land
> So that wherever they live
> Entertain the people and themselves.[29]

In Sasanid times actors/dancers were called *pat-vaz-guy* and their performance *pat-vaz-guftan*.[30] The official in charge of the artists at the Sasanid court was the *khorram-bakhsh* (the joy-giver), who was responsible for all entertainment, including minstrels, story tellers, musicians, acrobats, and what not.[31]

---

[27] Schafer, Edward H. *The Golden Peaches of Samarkand* (Berkeley, 1953 [1962]), pp. 52-56.
[28] Ata'i, *Bonyad-e Namayesh*, p. 19.
[29] Nezami Ganjavi (ca. 1165) quoted by Ata'i, *Bonyad-e namayesh*, p. 19.
[30] Ata'i, *Bonyad-e namayesh*, p. 19.
[31] Mary Boyce, "The Parthian gosan professional singer and the Iranian Minstrel Tradition," *Journal of the Royal Asiatic Society*, 1957, vol. Pt 1 & 2," pp. 18, 25.

ENTERTAINERS IN THE EARLY ISLAMIC PERIOD

Like the Sasanid kings the new Islamic rulers of and in Iran also amused themselves with the performances of minstrels, singers and musicians, as well as acrobats, magicians and animal trainers. The Arab caliphate and the courts of its
provincial governors drew heavily on Iranian models of amusements, culture and
court protocol.[32] Both the court at Damascus and later at Baghdad sent for both
male and female singers from Iran, and Iranian singing and theatrical art dominated those courts.[33] Around 980, farcical plays (*shamajat*) were performed before
the caliph in Baghdad on the occasion of *Now-ruz* (New Year). The performers
wore different kinds of masks.[34] Thus, the system of pre-Islamic entertainment
continued in Islamic Iran. From a bureaucratic, if not societal, point of view, there
were two broad categories of entertainers, i.e. (i) musicians and (ii) actors and acrobats. This twofold division of the entertainment class dates back to at least the
Seljuq period (eleventh century), if not earlier. In those days the *amir-e motreb*
was responsible for the musicians and singers as well as the storytellers (*qavvalan*).[35] It is quite likely that he was the 'successor' of the Sasanid *khorram-
bakhsh*.

As in the pre-Islamic period singing, acting and dancing were among the principal
amusements during social events at court and in private homes. The audience wanted
to be stirred by past deeds of valor and prowess in war, or by moving and romantic
heroic love stories, whether borrowed from history or legend. Or it wanted to be simply amused by comical events. Dramatic narration of a versified story was empha-
sized by stirring music and clearly pleased the listeners. Mas'ud Sa'd-e Salman
mentions in a short *mathnavi* the presence of musicians playing various instruments,
singers and dancers at a local court about the end of the eleventh century.[36] He was
but one of the many poets of the eleventh and twelfth century who referred to music
making, singing, and dancing. The detailed information about musical instruments
and styles (dancing, singing, playing) in those poetical verses are an indication of
their importance in daily life.[37] The main performer was the minstrel (*khunyagar*) and
the singer-musician (*motreb*), in addition to the narrator (*naqqal*), about whom there

---

[32] Hodgson, Marshall G.S. *The Venture of Islam: conscience and history in a world civilization.* 3
vols. (Chicago, 1974) vol. 1, pp. 280-84; Morony, Michael G. *Iraq After the Muslim Conquest*
(Princeton, 1984), pp. 27-98.

[33] Spuler, Berthold. *Iran in früh-Islamischer Zeit* (Wiesbaden, 1952), p. 290.

[34] Mez, *Die Renaissance*, p. 400.

[35] Heribert Horst, *Die Staatsverwaltung der Grossseljuqen und der Khorazmshahs (1038-1231)*
(Wiesbaden: Steiner, 1964), p. 102.

[36] Mas'ud Sa'd-e Salman *Divan*, ed. Rashid Yasimi (Tehran 1339/1960), pp. 562-79.

[37] Mallah, Hoseyn'Ali. *Hafez va Musiqi* (Tehran, 1351/1972); Ibid., *Manuchehri Damghani va
Musiqi* (Tehran, 1363/1984); Eqbal, 'Abbas et alii, *She'r va Musiqi dar Iran* (Tehran, 1366/1987).

will be more in the next section.[38] They are more frequently mentioned in classical Persian literature than other entertainers. Minstrels, like actors of comic drama, adapted their texts to the nature of the audience and thus switched from the serious and solemn to light and merry tunes. Kay Ka'us b. Eskandar, prince of Gorgan, advised in his chapter 'On Being a Musician':

> If you see that the audience is military or given to living by freebooting, sing them quatrains of Turkestan, songs about battle and bloodshed and in praise of an adventurous life. Do not be sad, nor play all your melodies in the 'Royal' mode, claiming it is the rule of minstrelsy." […] "You must understand that musicians are hired by topers, who refuse to pay quarrelsome musicians." … Furthermore, it has been said that a minstrel should be deaf, blind and dumb. That is to say, he should not turn his ears in any direction that is not meant for him, nor look in any direction in which he should not look, nor report anything which he has seen or heard in a particular company. The minstrel with those qualities will never lack a host.[39]

Thus, the minstrel played to the audience, and adapted his performance to the mood of the audience; in short, he had to create a sense of drama. It was not always the sounds of battle the listeners wanted; often they wanted satire, or lewdness, and/or comedy. The minstrel and his troupe gave them all that and more. This versatility of the minstrel "required much committing to memory of verses of all types—narrative, lyrical, laudatory, elegiac, satirical, gnomic—so that they had a store of traditional vocabulary, imagery, and themes by drawing on which they could create new compositions of their own; and they would also thus have learnt a quantity of familiar and well-loved poetry with which to please listeners on demand."[40]

Not only men sang, but so did women and children, although this is usually not reported. In the mid-twelfth century, an Islamic 'Book of Mirrors' points out that singing should not be done by women and children, not be accompanied by the harp, lute and Iraqi flute, and not contain any obscenities. This means that this situation existed and that everything the author preached against was practiced and probably widely. In fact, he confirms this indirectly elsewhere when he writes: "the *Bayt al-Mal* rightfully belongs to the `ulama, the judges, the Koran readers, the poor, the orphans, and the *ghazis*. But they have taken it all, and have established a treasury for astronomers, physicians, musicians, buffoons, cheats, winesellers and gamblers."[41]

---

[38] According to the *Mojmal al-Tawarikh* ed. Bahar, p. 69, partially tr. by Jules Mohl, as "Extraits du *Modjmel al-Tewarikh*, relatifs à l'histoire de la Perse," *Journal Asiatique*, 1841, pp. 514-15, in the Parthian language *khonyagar* was *goshan*.
[39] Levy, *Mirror*, pp. 189-90.
[40] Boyce, Mary. "Goshan," *Encyclopedia Iranica*.
[41] Meisami, Julie Scott. *The Sea of Virtues (Bahr al-Fava'id) A Medieval Islamic Mirror for Princes* (Salt Lake City: Utah UP, 1991), pp. 138, 171, 216.

ENTERTAINERS IN THE TIMURID PERIOD

Although Timur allegedly "by nature spurned actors and poets" he loved musicians, singers and dancers. Just prior to his death he was "amid zithers, harps, lyres, organs and pipes; amid dances, zither-players, singers and things wonderful. … And when he was in the midst of dancing, he tottered among them because of his age and lameness."[42] Other forms of entertainment were also found at his court. In 1404-05, Clavijo, the Spanish ambassador to the court of Timur, observed the performance of various kinds of entertainers such as jugglers who performed before Timur's women as well as before the court in general.[43] Of great interest was the display on October 9, 1405 when Timur "ordered that each trade should play a game, and go through the camp, that his people might be amused. … each trade played a game, and went through the horde, for the amusement of the people."[44] More detail is provided by `Ali Yazdi, who reported: "On this occasion Timour caused all sorts of amusement to be enjoyed. An amphitheater was covered with carpets, where there were masquerades. The women were dressed like goats, others like sheep and fairies, and they ran after each other. The skinners and butchers appeared like lions and foxes, and all other tradesmen contributed specimens of their skills"[45] This information shows that in addition to the usual suspects (jugglers, musicians, etc.) acting also had its place. For Yazdi referred to masked dancing and mime acting, which, as is clear from later more detailed descriptions, was the dramatic enactment of various kinds of stories.

In the fifteenth century, the so-called *mehtar* of the *naqqareh-khaneh* was not only responsible for the *naqqarehchi*s or the musicians, but in addition to the following groups: itinerant entertainers (*gharibzadehgan*), story tellers (*qavvalan*), prestidigitators (*fart-malan*), and traveling musicians (*luliyan*) as well as bath attendants, masseurs, barbers, washers of the dead. The official's responsibility meant that these groups had to pay 'protection money' to this official, who, in turn, would extend his patronage to them and thus provide them some measure of protection against less influential officials. Other entertainers such as puppeteers, illusionists, and wrestlers are not mentioned and it is not known what official, if any, controlled these groups, unless they were grouped under the term *gharibzadehgan* and *luliyan*, which seems likely.[46] The variety was much larger as is

---

[42] Arabshah, Ahmed ibn. *Tamerlane or Timur the Great Amir* translated by J.H. Sanders (Lahore, n.d.), pp. 221, 298, 300. Musicians were much appreciated at his court above all "Abdul Qader Maraghi, his son Safi al-Din, his son-in-law Nashrin, Qotb of Mosul, Ardashir Janki and others." Ibid., p. 314.

[43] De Clavijo, Ruy Gonzalez. *Narrative of the Embassy of Ruy Gonzalez de Clavijo to the Court of Timour at Samarcand A.D. 1403-06* translated by Clements R. Markham (London, 1859), pp. 147, 154.

[44] De Clavijo, *Narrative*, p. 149.

[45] De Clavijo, *Narrative*, p. 149, n. 1.

[46] Roemer, Hans Robert. *Staatsschreiben der Timuridenzeit. Das Sharafnama des `Abdallah Marwarid in kritischer Auswertung* (Wiesbaden 1952), pp. 90-01, 174-75.

clear from an unexpected source, a literary one. Literary sources rarely paid attention to the lower classes, let alone performing artists. A notable exception is the *Fotovvat-nameh-ye Soltani* by Hoseyn Va`ez Kashefi, who mentioned that the entertainers (*ahl-e ma`rakeh*) were part of the *fotovvat* movement, a kind of religious brotherhood to which mostly people from the laboring class belonged and that was attached to one or more dervish orders. The entertainers were divided into three categories, to wit:

(i)   the category of declaimers (*ahl-e sokhan*) and actors (*ma`rakeh-giran*), which was itself subdivided into three groups
   a. elegists (*maddahan*), poem declaimers (*ghazal-khvanan*) and water carriers (*saqqayan*);
   b. tellers of tales (*khavass-guyan*) and carpet-spreaders, i.e. story-tellers who sat on a carpet (*besat-andazan*);
   c. story-tellers (*qesseh-khvanan*) and tellers of fables (*afsaneh-guyan*).

(ii)   the category of strong-men (*ahl-e zur*), which consists of eight groups: wrestlers, weight lifters (*sang-giran*), plasterers (*naveh-giran*), basket-carriers (*salleh-keshan*), porters (*hammalan*), mace-wielders (*maghir-giran*), rope-dancers (*rasan-bazan*), strong-men (*zurgaran*).

Figure 3: A gusan-mime with a wolf mask (Armenian miniature 13th century)

(iii)   the category of acrobats (*ahl-e bazi*), which consists of three groups: jugglers (*tas-bazan*), puppet-players (*lo`bat-bazan*) and conjurors (*ho-qqeh-bazan*).[47]

The performing artists (*ahl-e ma`arek*) or the entertainers are also mentioned in the so-called *shahr-e ashub* literature,[48] as are wrestlers (*pahlavan*) and jugglers (*hoqqeh-baz*), and storytellers (*qesseh-khvan*).[49]

ENTERTAINERS IN THE SAFAVID PERIOD

A similar type of administrative structure as under the Timurids existed under the Safavid dynasty (1501-1736). The master of musicians depended on the chief torch-holder (*mash`aldar-bashi*), because the latter was in charge of the music band (*naqqarah-khanah*). The involvement of musicians with actors and the like automatically involved the *mash`aldar-bashi*, who probably was in charge of not only the master of musicians (*qalichi-bashi*), but also of the *moqalled-bashi* (chief comedian), the *maskhareh-bashi* (chief jester), the *geda-bashi* (chief beggar), the *luti-bashi* (chief clown), and the *pahlavan-bashi* (chief wrestler).[50] Under the Safavids it would seem an innovation was introduced, i.e. a second official (the chief clown or *luti-bashi*) who was in charge of what Aubin later would call the department of entertainers (*luti-khaneh*). This official was the chief of the sayyeds or *naqib al-molk* or, as he was known towards the end of the Safavid dynasty, the *naqib al-mamalek* who was appointed by the shah.[51] He assisted the mayor of the town (*kalantar*) in administrating the tax burden of the town's guilds. The chief of the sayyeds (*naqib*) also appointed the elders of dervishes, the street artists (*ahl-e ma`arek*), the passion play actors (*ta`ziyeh-khvan*s), the *rowzeh-khvan*s, and the like. The *naqib*'s jurisdiction with regards to the appointment of the elders of the street performers touched closely upon that of the chief of the royal lighting department (*mash`aldar-bashi*).[52]

---

[47] Kashefi, Hoseyn Va`ez. *Fotovvat-nameh-ye Soltani* ed. Mohammad Mahjub (Tehran, 1350/1971), pp. 280-343.

[48] Ma`ani, Ahmad Golchin. *Shahr-e Ashub dar she`r-e farsi* (Tehran, 1346/1967).

[49] Keyvani, Mehdi. *Artisans and Guild Life in the later Safavid period* (Berlin 1982), p. 290 (*Divan-e Rezvan* of Mirza Taher Vahid).

[50] Asaf, Mohammad Hashem. 'Rostam al-Hokoma', *Rostam al-Tavarikh*, ed. Mohammad Moshiri (Tehran, 1348/1969), pp. 100-101; Monajjem, Molla Jalal al-Din. *Ruznameh-ye `Abbasi ya Ruznameh-ye Molla Jalal*, ed. Seyfollah Vahidniya (Tehran 1366/1967), p. 66; for more information about the antics of the court buffoons see Nurbakhsh, Hoseyn. *Delqakha-ye mashur-e darbari va maskharahha-ye dowrehgerd* (Tehran, 1354/1975).

[51] Tabataba'i, *Bargi*, p. 188, 299; Bafqi, Mohammad Mofid Mostowfi-ye. *Jame`-ye Mofidi*. 3 vols. ed. Iraj Afshar (Tehran 1340/1961), vol. 3, p. 62. On the function of *naqib* see Floor, Willem. "The Secular Judicial System in Safavid Persia," *Studia Iranica* 29 (2000), pp. 49-50.

[52] Mirza Rafi`a, *Dastur al-Moluk*. ed. Mohammad Taqi Daneshpazhuh. Zamimeh-ye shomareh-ye 5 va 6 sal-e 16 Majalleh-ye Daneshkadeh-ye Adabiyat va `Olum-e Ensani (Tehran 1347/1967), pp. 121, 123; *The Tadhkirat al-Muluk, A Manual of Safavid Administration.* (Cambridge, 1980), p. 81, 83,

Scanty as it is, there is much more information about entertainers during the Safavid period (1501-1732) than for earlier times. From this information it is clear that performing artists were not only present at the royal court in Tabriz, Qazvin, and Isfahan, but also at the court of regional rulers. For example, the court and people of the island-kingdom of Hormuz were diverted by buffoons, jugglers, goat handlers, trained monkeys, and fights between goats. This was accompanied by betting, storytellers, singers, musicians, narrators of legends and other artists.[53] Similarly, in sixteenth century Seistan all kinds of entertainers were to be found entertaining the ruler and his court as well as the public in general. "In those days there were classes of people [such as]: epic story reciters (shahnameh-khvan), story tellers (qesseh-khvan) and performers (ma`rekeh-gar) like conjurors (hoqqeh-baz), jugglers (tas-baz), puppeteers (khayal-baz), and other kinds of these arts in Rashak ... and most days they diverted the community in the place of [in front of] Government House (dowlat-khaneh) towards the end of the day." Although the ruler had banned these activities he was such drawn to them that he nevertheless wanted to enjoy their company. Among them was Mir Hasan Khayalbaz who was peerless in juggling (sho`bdeh-bazi) and in archery second to Sa`d Vaqqas.[54] Similarly, Khan Ahmad Khan, ruler of Gilan, gave 400 tumans to Ostad Zeytun Tanbur-navaz and ordered that puppet players (shab-baz), sword dancers (shamshir-baz), fighting rams (quch-baz), performing lions (shir-baz), wrestlers (keshti-gir) and all kinds of other main artists be brought from `Iraq and Khorasan.[55] Shah Esma`il I had many minstrels and musicians at his court. His son Tahmasp I also employed many until he found religion in 1565. He then dismissed most of them, but kept the singer Ostad Hoseyn Shushtari Baliyani. The born-again Moslem Tashmasp I believed that the royal princes and the emirs might corrupt their morals by associating with minstrels and musicians, leading to a demand for forbidden pleasures. At the same time, minstrels and other artists continued to be employed at regional courts, however. After Tahmasp I's death musicians were once again welcome at court. One of them, the singer Hafez Jalalel Bakharzi, who excelled at both singing and chanting, was even appointed master of the musicians

148; Atabay, Badri. *Fehrest-e Ketabkhaneh-ye Saltanati, fehrest-e tarikh, safarnameh, siyahatnameh,* etc. (Tehran 2537/1977), p. 55.

[53] Felix de Jesus, "Chronica da Ordem de S. Augustinho nas Indias Orientais," *Analecta Augustiniana* 30 (1967), p. 24; Huan, Ma. *Ying-yai Sheng-lan: The Overall Survey of the Ocean's Shores [1443]* (trans. & ed. by J.V.G. Mills (Cambridge, 1970), pp. 167-69, 172; Tenreiro, António. *Viagens por terra da India a Portugal* Neves Aguas ed. (Lisbon 1991), pp. 24-25; Castanheda, Fernão Lopes. *História do descobrimento e conquista da India peolos Portugueses,* 4 vols. Ed. Pedro de Azevedo (Coimbre, 1924-33), vol. 2, ch. 58, pp. 337-39; Orta Rebelo, N. de. *Un voyageur portugais en Perse au debut du XVII siecle* ed. J. Verissimo Serrao (Lisbon 1972), p. 94.

[54] Seystani, Malek Shah Hoseyn b. Malek Ghayath al-Din Mohammad b. Shah Mahmud. *Ehya al-Moluk.* ed. Manuchehr Setudeh (Tehran 1344/1966), p. 254.

[55] Fumeni, `Abd al-Fattah. *Tarikh-e Gilan dar vaqaye`-ye salha 923-1038 hejri qamari,* ed. Manuchehr Setudeh (Tehran 1349/1970), p. 41; for a picture of a *zurgar,* the strongman and a *kuzeh-baz,* the juggler see Dickson, M.B. and Welch, S.C. Introduction. *The Houghton Shahnameh.* 2 vols. (Cambridge 1981), vol. 1, p. 114, fig. 160.

(*chalichi-bashi*).[56] A bald clown by the name of Kal `Enayat was an entertainer at the court of Shah `Abbas I, according to Chardin.[57]

Figure 4: Drawing of a masked mime-dancers and musicians (1519)

To make musical performance more attractive the shah also paid for female dancers, female singers, comics, storytellers (*naqqal*), actors, poets, narrators, wrestlers, etc. "I will not go into the morals of these people," Kaempfer piously remarks.[58] From the very beginning of the Safavid period women performed song and dance in public. Around 1510 a Venetian merchant reports that "during the sports, music is played and dancing girls perform after their manner, singing the praises of Ismael."[59] In 1651, during the entry of the Dutch ambassador in Shiraz, music and dance were part of the amusements offered in the streets. Dancing boys were seen

---

[56] Monshi, *Tarikh*, vol. 1, p. 190; Savory, *History*, vol. 1, pp. 280-81.

[57] Chardin, *Voyages*, vol. 8, 124-30.

[58] Kaempfer, Engelbert. *Am Hofe des persischen Grosskönigs (1684-85). Das erste Buch der Amoenitates exoticae in deutscher Bearbeitung*, hrsg. v. Walter Hinz. (Leipzig 1940), p. 87; Della Valle, Pietro. "Extract of the Travels of Della Valle", in John Pinkerton, *A General Collection of Voyages and Travels*, (London, 1811), vol. 9, p. 19. There were also *shahnamah-khvan*s. Nasrabadi, Mirza Mohammad Taher. *Tadhkereh-ye Nasrabadi*. Ed. Vahid Dastgerdi (Tehran 1361/1982), p. 307. For a picture with dancing girls and musicians see Honarfar, Lotfollah. *Ganjineh-ye athar-e tarikhi-ye Esfahan*. (Tehran 1350/1971), p. 570 of reception of Homayun by Tahmasp I in the Chehel Sotun.

[59] Stanley, Lord. *Travels to Tana and Persia by J. Barbaro and A. Contarini* 2 vols. in one (London: Hakluyt, 1873), p. 202. In 1602 the dancing and singing of women in public is also mention by San Bernardino, Gaspar de. *Itinerario da India por terra ate a ilha de Chipre* (Lisboa, 1842), p. 144.

as well as "7 to 8 public women of Venus demonstrated their lame dancing art."[60]
There also were female minstrels as is clear from contemporary paintings.[61]

Not only the shah and his courtiers enjoyed the antics of the entertaining class, but
so did the public at large. In 1624, when in Isfahan, the Russian merchant Kotov
observed, "Here too on the maidan they have all sorts of entertainments and throw
dice in large pots, and they divide the earth with little reeds, and play, and they tell
fortunes out of books." … "on the old maidan … they have all kinds of shows, they
let out big snakes and tell fortunes."[62] On the square of Tabriz around 1670 people
come to divert themselves, according to Chardin. "There are games, legerdemain,
and farce, and also mountebanks, wrestlers, bull and goat fighting, recitation of
verses and prose, and dancing wolves."[63]

Figure 5: Drawing of masked actors and musicians by Soltan Mohammad (1594)

---

[60] Hotz, *Reis*, p.87.

[61] For a drawing of female minstrel commisisoned by Kaempfer, see Titley, Norah M. *Miniatures
from Persian Manuscripts* (London, 1977), nrs. 227 (12, 37 Iraqi entertainers); also nrs. 404, 140-
41, 263. For Armenian pictures see Female Troubadour with Saz, M6288, Horomos, 1211. Photo:
Matenadaran 267. Troubadour, Marriage at Cana, Matenadaran, XVIth century. Photo: Matenadaran 268. Group of Musicians, Matenadaran, XVIth or XVIIth century. Photo: Matenadaran. [ar-
menianstudies.csufresno.edu/arts_of_armenia/captions.htm]

[62] Kotov, F.A. *Khozhenie kuptsa Fedota Kotova* ed. N.A. Kuznetsova (Moscow, 1958) translated
by Kemp, P.M. as *Russian Travellers to India and Persia [1624-1798] Kotov-Yefremov-Danibegov*
(Delhi, 1959), pp. 20-21.

[63] Chardin, *Voyages*, vol. 2, p. 326.

Figure 6: Rural amusements (around 1800)

Chardin further noted that in Isfahan, among

> the Diversion of the Persians, they have of those who Dance upon the
> Ropes, Poppet-Shows, and doing Feats of Activity as adroit and nimble
> as in any Country whatever. [...] The Puppet-shows and Juglers ask no
> Money at the Door as they do in our Country, for they play openly in the
> publick Places, and those give 'em that will. They intermingle Farce, and
> juggling, with a thousand Stories and Buffooneries, which they do some-
> times Mask'd, and sometimes Un-mask'd, and this lasts two or three
> Hours: And when they have done, they go round to the Spectators and
> ask something; and when they perceive any one to be stealing off before
> they go to ask him for any thing, the Master of the Company cries out
> with a loud Voice, and in an Emphatical manner, That he who steals
> away, is an Enemy to Ali. As who should say among us, An Enemy to
> God and his Saints. For two Crowns the Juglers will come to their
> House. They call these sort of Diversions Mascare [*maskhareh*], that is to
> say Play, Pleasantry, Raillerie, Representation; from whence comes our
> word Masquerade.[64]

Du Mans, Tavernier and Chardin mention a variety a public performers such as
the sword-player (*shamshir-baz*), who put on mock-fights. Further the rope-
dancers, who were as good as in France, as well as *hoqqeh-baz* or jugglers who
also were good. They used eggs instead of balls.[65] The performing artists were

---

[64] Chardin, Sir John. *Travels in Persia 1673-1677* (London, 1927), p. 203.
[65] Du Mans, Raphael. *Estat de la Perse*. ed. Ch. Schefer (Paris: Leroux, 1890), pp. 212-13; Chardin,
Voyages, vol. 3, pp. 180-81 (wrestlers, sword fighters and fighting animals at Isfahan); Tavernier,
Les six voyages ... en Turquie, en Perse et aux Indes (Amsterdam, 1678), vol. 1, pp. 442-43
(performances at the *meydan* of Tabriz).

also used as political instruments. Not only to sing the shah's praises, but also, for example, to mock a conquered foe, who was led through the bazaar, while story-tellers (*qavvalan*), jokers (*mokhannethan*), buffoons (*mozhekan*) and jesters (*maskharehha*) welcomed him with their derisory mockeries such as in 943/1536-37.[66]

Karim Khan Zand, the ruler of most of Iran during the 1760-70s, also had a jester at court. His own Zand tribe was known for its distinct dialect, which was there-fore referred as "the barbarous dialect" (*kaj-zaban* or crooked tongue). When the very loud barking of a dog disturbed the serenity of the royal court Karim Khan sent his jester to find out what it wanted. After some time the jester returned and said: "Your Majesty must send one of the chief officers of your own family to re-port what that gentleman says: he speaks no language except 'the barbarous dia-lect,' with which they are familiar, but of which I do not understand one word." Karim Khan is said to have laughed heartily at the ridicule of the rude dialect of his tribe and gave the jester a present as a reward for his witticism.[67]

ENTERTAINERS IN THE QAJAR PERIOD

In the nineteenth century, the Qajar shahs also had jesters. The royal court was never without a jester, "who enjoys a very extraordinary latitude of speech, and assumes, both in his dress and manner, the habit and appearance of folly. It is usual to laugh at the witticisms of those jesters, even when they are most severe; and the sovereign himself profess to respect their privilege."[68] Even the last Qajar Shah had a jester, who had already been employed by his grandfather Mozaffar al-Din Shah, and was described in 1910 as "a fat, jovial little hunchback."[69] Jesters were also found at regional courts as well as in the retinue of leading tribal chiefs. "Buffoonery and jokes of all sorts are very much in favour amongst the Koords, every chief having a buffoon whose duty is to keep the company merry."[70] More-over, buffoonery and the like were above all found in public places, both urban and rural, and even among tribal groups. Benjamin described "the baboons dancing to the beat of tambourines, … a poor chained lioness put through her paces, … But one of the most ordinary sights in Teheran at this hour [i.e. the evening]—a sight which always draws a crowd—is a match of trained wrestlers or athletes exercising with clubs, at which the Persians are experts."[71] In 1907, for example, Grothe saw jug-

---

[66] Rumlu, Hoseyn Beg. *Ahsan al-Tavarikh.* ed. `Abdol-Hoseyn Nava'i (Tehran 1357/1978), p. 356.
[67] Malcolm, John. *The History of Persia.* 2 vols. (London, 1820 [Tehran: Imp. Org. f. Soc. Ser-vices, 1976]), vol. 2, pp. 551-52.
[68] Malcolm, *History*, vol. 2, p. 551.
[69] Lorey, Eustache and Sladen, Douglas. *The Moon of the Fourteenth Night* (London, 1910), p. 60.
[70] Millingen, Frederick. *Wild Life Among The Koords* (London: Hurst and Blackett, 1870), p. 255; Mostowfi, *Sharh*, vol. 2, p. 33.
[71] Benjamin, S. G. W. *Persia and the Persians* (London: John Murray, 1887), p.p. 100-01, with pic-ture on p. 150.

glers, bear players and other entertainers perform in Lurestan.[72] Around the same time, Moore observed in Samnan, in the open square, "a mountebank … preparing to swallow glass."[73] People loved music and dancing, despite the fact the fact that it was very much frowned upon. Although musicians and dancers were at the bottom of social ranking they were much sought after and well paid. Those who played well and had a good repertoire traveled around the country each year and earned a good living. Even among the tribes they were invited, well regaled and paid. Most of the heroic and war songs were in Turkish, which Höltzer considered fitting. The tambourine, zither, and two singers accompanied dancers; the musicians' modulations were in harmony with the movements of the dancers. These performers were referred to as *luti*.[74] These and similar forms of entertainment continued well into the twentieth century, although not as often as one might think, for "the poor people seldom have such wholesome amusement."[75]

Aubin, writing in 1907, referred to the two-fold division of the entertainers as the musical department (*naqqareh-khaneh*) and the department of entertainers (*luti-khaneh*).[76] Like Aubin, Tahvildar, an Iranian official who wrote a social geography of his home town of Isfahan in 1890, also distinguishes two broad categories of performers: the entertainers (*luti*s sing. or *alvat* pl.) and the musicians and members of the royal music band (*ahl-e tarabeh va 'amaleh-ye naqqareh-khaneh*), which indeed concurs with Aubin's *luti-khaneh* and *naqqareh-khaneh*. It would therefore seem that the dividing line was between actor-entertainers and musicians.[77]

The *luti*s (*alvat*)

In Isfahan there are several kinds of *luti*s. The kind consists of those who keep a lion (*lutiha-ye shiri*) and tour around the province. These form one troupe. Their number is neither in- nor decreasing. The second kind are those *luti*s who carry a drum (*tonbak*) on their back (*lutiha-ye tonbak bedush*); some have bears and monkeys who dance. They form three to four troupes. The third kind consists of the jugglers (*lutiha-ye hoqqe-hbaz*) who perform unusual tricks like jugglery and legerdemain. Formerly there were many of them in Isfahan, but now they left this town

---

[72] Grothe, Hugo. *Wanderungen in Persien* (Berlin, Alg. Verein f. Deutsche Literatur, 1910), p. 63. For a picture of a trained bear and goat and their handler see Shahri, Ja`far. *Tarikh-e ejtema`i -Tehran dar qarn-e sizdahom*, 6 vols. (Tehran: Farhang-Rasa, 1368/1989), vol. 6, pp. 41-42.

[73] Moore, Benjamin Burges. From *Moscow to the Persian Gulf*. (New York: G.P. Putnam's Sons, 1915), p. 208.

[74] Höltzer, Ernst. *Persien vor 113 Jahren* ed. Mohammad Assemi (Tehran: Vezarat-e Farhang va Honar, 2535/1976), pp. 65-66.

[75] Koelz, Walter N. *Persian Diary, 1939-1941* (Ann Arbor, Michigan, 1983), pp. 223, see also p. 210.

[76] Aubin, *La Perse*, pp. 231, 233

[77] Tahvildar, Mirza Hoseyn Khan. *Joghrafiya-ye Isfahan*, ed. M. Setudeh. (Tehran: Daneshgah, 1342/1963), pp. 86-87, 126.

for Tehran and other cities. In the province of Isfahan you do not see them anymore. The fourth kind consists of the ropedancers (*lutiha-ye bandbaz va chubini pa*). They form one troupe. Sometimes they come to the province of Isfahan, but most of the time they are in the other provinces. The fifth kind consists of the puppeteers (*lutiha-ye kheymeh-shab bazi*), who perform on nights of a party or a marriage. This kind of entertainment seems to have fallen into disuse nowadays, because one does not see these *luti*s in Isfahan anymore. The sixth kind of *luti*s consists of the satirists (*lutiha-ye sar-khvancheh-ye ostad baqqal*).

There is another kind of *luti*s [rowdies]. They are cruel, bloodthirsty, rebellious, drinkers of wine, slanderers, gamblers, pederasts, adulterers, and thieves. The number of this kind of lutes has always been large in Isfahan. These *luti*s have largely been responsible for the ruin of the province of Isfahan. A description of their harsh, rough, and ignorant deed here is not appropriate. God be praised, they have all been exterminated by the might of the everlasting empire so that no trace of them has remained.[78]

The group of musicians and performers of the official band (*ahl-e tarab va `amaleh-ye naqqareh-khaneh*). There are seven troupes of dancers and musicians, of which one is Jewish, the six other troupes are composed of Moslems. Their leader (*bozorg*) is called Fath `Ali Khan.[79]

---

[78] On these rowdies see Floor, Willem. "The Lutis, a social phenomenon in Qajar Persia," *Die Welt des Islams* 13 (1971), pp. 103-120; Ibid., "The political role of the lutis in Qajar Iran," in: G. Schweizer ed., *Interdisziplinaere Iran-Forschung, Beitrage aus Kulturgeographie, Ethnologie, Soziologie und Neuerer Geschichte*, (Beihefte zum Tuebinger Atlas, reihe B, no. 40) (Wiesbaden: Reichert, 1978), pp. 179-88; and Ibid., "The political role of the lutis in Iran," in: *Modern Iran, the dialectics of continuity and change*, M.E. Bonine & N.R. Keddie eds. (Albany: SUNY, 1981), pp. 83-95.

[79] Tahvildar, *Joghrafiya*, pp. 125-26. In Qajar times this terminology as well as `amalah-ye tarab refers to musicians and singers who were attached to the royal court or to the establishments of grandees, while the term *motreb* was used for unattached musicians and singers who performed for the public in general. Mallah, *Hafez*, p. 191, n. 1.

Figure 7: A *luti* with his monkey (19th century miniature)

The artists of the *luti-khaneh* were in the charge of the *luti-bashi*, who was appointed by the shah. He received 10-15% of their income, such as from the snake charmers. The music band was under the Ehtesham al-Khalvat, according to Aubin, while Mostowfi reports that he was under the chief of the royal workshops. This official appointed the chief of the music band, called *na'eb* or deputy. One of these *na'eb*s was the famous Karim Shireh'i. In 1907, it was Qasem Khan Bashi, whose father also had held this position. The *na'eb* was also a musician, and supervised all musicians in the country, and not only of the royal band. He further had artists such as *ghowl biyabanha*, fire-eaters, and strolling players (*dowri gardanha-ye `eyd*) in his charge. He allowed them to perform in exchange for a fee, settled their quarrels, punished misbehavior and acted as intermediary between them and the government.[80] These two officials were not in charge of the storytellers, however. These fell under the *naqib al-mamalek*, which was a continuation of Safavid practice.

TAMASHA AND TAQLID

According to Beyza'i, popular theater gradually expanded from the middle of the Safavid period onwards, and comedy (*tamasha*) and mime (*taqlid*) started to take form. It is more likely, however, that this movement had started much earlier, evolving from pre-Islamic forms of theater. This is suggested by the existence of both mime and comedy in pre-Islamic times as well as the existence of the so-called comical street theater (*maydan-oyun*, *tiulaat* and *tamasha*) in Armenia under Iranian and Turkish overlordship. The Armenian entertainers (*vartzaks* and *gusans*) performed "dressed in their traditional ancient Armenian costumes, with their masks, symbols of the *aralez*, the phallus, and the rest."[81] In Safavid times, itinerant groups of musicians and dancers performed at private houses, usually during the night. Their repertoire consisted of ballets featuring local dances as well as some element of mime, e.g. a piece called *qahr va ashti* (quarrel and reconciliation). The so-called curtain raisers (*pish-pardeh*) introducing such performances gave rise to more elaborate farces, called *mazhakeh*.[82]

According to Fryer, Iranians liked the buffoonery and acrobatic performances, but "within doors they chuse the other, where the Stage-players, Tumblers, and dancing Wenches usher in their Interludes by Songs, Tabers, and Flutes."[83] This implies that people made a distinction between farce (*maskhareh*) or comedy (*tamasha*) and danced-mime (*taqlid*) at that time. Probably the most advanced form of danced-mime was found at the royal court. According to Beyza'i, the early *lal-baz* or mime had two or three characters one of which stood for a tree, another represented a gardener, and a third one was a passerby. The conflict between the gardener and the passerby over the fruit of the tree gave rise to much laughter. Also, laughter was provoked when the gardener slept in the shade of the tree and the tree moved to another place.[84] Chardin reported that mimic dancing combined with singing, which constituted a kind of bawdy opera was one of the main amusements of the Iranian elite.

---

[80] Massé, Henri. *Croyances et Coutumes Persanes* 2 vols. (Paris: Maisonneuve, 1938), vol. 1, p. 147; Aubin, *La Perse*, pp. 213, 230-33, 238, 247; Mostowfi, `Abdollah. *Sharh-e Zendegani-ye Man* 3 vols. (Tehran: Zavvar, n.d.), vol. 1, pp. 239, 354-57, 359.
[81] Goyan, *Teatr*, vol. 2, pp. 365-75
[82] Beyza'i, *Namayesh*, p. 168.
[83] Fryer, John. *A New Account of East India and Persia Being Nine Years' Travels, 1672-1681*, 3 vols. (London: Hakluyt, 1909-15), vol. 3, p. 94
[84] Beyza'i, *Namayesh*, p. 52.

The musicians and the female dancers are the mimes and the comedians of the Orientals, or better said, these are their *opera*; because they only sing verses, and prose does not figure at all in their chants. ... The pieces that they represent are always amatory subjects. The newest actresses open the scene, which begins with a description of love, of which they enact the endowments (sex appeal) and enchantment of the opposite sex, and then represent passion and furor, which they intermix with episodes that contain portraits of handsome boys and beautiful girls, more alive and touching than you can imagine, and that is usually the first act. In the second act you see the group split in two choirs, representing, one, the pursuit of a passionate love, the other, the refusal by a proud mistress. The third contains the agreement of the lovers, and it is here that the actresses outdo themselves and wear out their voices and gestures. The singers and instrumentalists get up at the passionate moment, and come close to them more or less, sometimes even to cry in their ears to enthuse them, in doing so they become as if they have been transported beyond themselves; but it is right there where the eyes and ears, where some prudery remains, are obliged to turn away, not being able to support neither the effrontery nor the lasciviousness of these last acts.[85]

From Chardin's description it is clear that danced-mime (*taqlid*) was not a different trade and was performed by the same entertainers that performed comedy (*tamasha*). However, these entertainers apparently did not perform mime in public, but as Fryer also observed only in private. The fact that many of the entertainers were women may have something to do with this, but not so much that their performance was highly sexually seductive. After all, the stand-up comics, buffoons and other entertainers also were often quite explicit about sexual matters. This is clear from the dances that were meant to arouse sexual desires, which the dancers were more than willing to gratify, for a fee, of course. Chardin remarked on this matter:

Persian dancing, as elsewhere in the Orient, is a representation; there are comical and playful, serious and introvert moments; passion is represented by it in all its force, but which is detestable, are the lascivious and indecent postures, the delights and inabilities of which these representations are rife with, and where they are able to do in manner contrary to what is virtuous, because they cannot think of anything more touching. A dance lasts sometimes three to four hours, without pause; the heroine performs herself the main acts; the others, numbering four to five, join her from time to time. Ordinarily, after the dance, the women and the musicians make dangerous leaps. These people do not perform at all at public places, as our comedians, but you send for them at your own home, and in addition to the present that you send it is customary that at

---

[85] Chardin, *Voyage*, vol. 2, pp. 207-08 (for a description of the organization of the royal female dancing troupe see Ibid., pp. 208-11).

the end of the dance, an old lady, who is like the troupe's mother, or the main actress, stretches out her hand to everybody in the assembly, to get something. Because these girls make more money by prostituting themselves than with dancing they make an effort to touch the people [present].[86]

In this connection it is also of interest to mention what Dr. John Covel saw on May 25, 1675 in Istanbul as part of the festivities staged during prince Mustafa's circumcision. It not only shows that Ottoman Turkey 'imported' Iranian actors, but also that they performed mime, thus confirming its importance as a form of dramatic art.

> There were many actors of little plays or interludes, all in the most beastly brutish language possible, as I was sufficiently informed by my companions, and their action fully confirmed it. The actors of men were Armenians, and Turks that came from the borders of Persia, and several times acted certain conceits in Persian habit which was very becoming, being far more rich and gaudy than the Turks wear." ... "In Persian habit, with every one his plume of feathers in his Turbant, they acted an [sic] humor which pleased mightily. They begin in a ring, and what the chief does all the rest are to imitate, or run the gauntlet. If he turns to the right, left, forward or around sculk down, starts up, etc. they immediately do the like. [87]

Not everybody was pleased with these kinds of theatrical performances. Conservative religious groups opposed them. The very bigoted Shah Soltan Hoseyn (r. 1694-1722) shortly after he had acceded to the throne issued an edict in 1703-04 stating that everybody who was engaged in frivolous performances (*namayeshha-ye khoshhal-konandeh*) had to be punished.[88] Needless to say that this and other religiously inspired edicts of this monarch, such as the banning of drinking alcohol, remained a dead letter.

During the eighteenth century the art of buffoonery, comedy and mime also thrived in elite society. Some of these artists were so much appreciated that the early Qajar author Asef even commemorated their names for posterity. He wrote:

---

[86] Chardin, *Voyage*, vol. 4, pp. 61-62, 309-10. On prostitution during that period see Floor, Willem. *A Fiscal History of Iran in the Safavid and Qajar Period* (New York: Bibliotheca Persica, 1999), pp. 155-59.

[87] Bent, Theodore ed. *Early voyages and travels in the Levant. I. The diary of Master Thomas Dallam, 1599-1600. II. Extracts from the diaries of Dr. John Covel, 1670-1679. With some account of the Levant company of Turkey merchants* (London: Hakluyt society, 1893) pp. 215-16; And, Metin. *A History of Theatre and Popular Entertainment in Turkey* (Ankara, 1963-64), p. 25.

[88] Osku'i, *Mostafa. Pazhuheshi dar tarikh-e te'atr-e Iran* (Moscow, 1992), p. 247.

In those cheerful, merry, and carefree days there were many funny, jocular, witty and comical mimes (*moqalledan*) and jesters (*maskheran*). One of them was Najaf Mir Hasan Khan, whom the Jamshid-like regent (*vakil al-dowleh*), the illustrious Karim Khan Zand had sentenced to pay 1,500 *tu-mans*, because he had mimicked him. The money collector pressured him, but he bribed him [saying]: 'If you please would allow me to go once again to the Jamshid-like Vakil al-Dowleh to discuss [the matter] with him then I will give you 100 *tuman*s for the respite." He allowed it. Then he went to the great [Karim Khan] and said courteously and respectfully: "May I be your sacrifice. You have ordered that the money collector take some *tuman*s from me to the benefit of the supreme graced royal domains." Karim Khan said: "Fifteen hundred *tuman*s." He then replied: "May I be your sacrifice, I am a rich and respectable man. Give orders that the money collector take the money from me in your presence." The great one said: "You poor devil, you do not have anything that you could give." Then he said: "By the unhal-lowed head of your enemies, by the beard and face of those who hate you, I swear that my belly is my treasury and that it contains sparkling jewels as well as gold and silver in large quantities." The great one, being in his cups, said in jest to the money collector: "Take the hem of his coat with two hands and collect the money from him." The said money collector angrily cuffed the ears of the said Najaf and said to him in Zand dialect: "You rascal, you rapscallion, give me immediately the money that you owe to the divan." Then the said Najaf stepped suddenly forwards, took the moustache of the money collectors and let go exactly 1,500 farts in deep and high tones, like the bang of guns and pistols; yes, he even extorted the bribe from the money collector. The Jamshid-like Vakil al-Dowleh, the illustrious Karim Khan and his courtiers were senseless and motionless from laughter. Then Karim Khan gave the witty comedian a long robe of honor and forgave him his miscon-duct.[89]

As discussed in the preceding section, farce or slap-stick comedy was known as *tamasha*, while the term *taqlid* originally referred more in particular to mime, which was a prominent element in most plays. Both terms gradually became a general designation for comical improvisatory drama; it is called *ru-howzi* or *tak-hteh-howzi* in modern times. According to Thalasso, these kinds of entertainments that at first were only offered as an extra to the buffoonery show slowly became longer and more important so that in the end they themselves became the main offering. They supplanted the genre from which they originated and became a genre of its own, totally differing from puppet plays. Thus, comedy plays were a mixture of pantomime, dance, song and dialogue. It was performed by so-called *luti*s, who were the only professional dancers and musicians in Iran. They traveled through the country and a complete troupe also had monkeys, bears, and other

---

[89] Asaf, *Rostam al-Tavarikh*, pp. 410-11.

animals. When they performed their comedy shows their tumblers, mountebanks, and their animals assisted them.[90]

Figure 8: Dancing girl at court (late 18th century)

There was no décor. A simple carpet hung in the back served as such. The stage was often a slightly elevated wooden platform (*takhteh*), and because it often was put over the pond (*howz*) in the courtyard of the house where the performance took place this type of theater became known as "planks-over-the pond" (*ru-howzi* or *takhteh-howzi*). More often than not there was no platform at all and the actors performed in a room of the house without even a curtain. The actors usually did not don special clothes and performed in the clothes that they daily wore. Make-up was kept to a minimum, often the use of a piece of cotton or of goatskin as a beard sufficed for the public.

The usual course of the performance was that it started with a musical prologue, which was followed by an intro. After this the play itself would be performed, followed by an interval. Then the second phase would begin with once again a musical prologue, followed by intro, and a second play, and the entire performance was

---

[90] Chodzko, Aleksander B. *Théatre Persan. Choix de Tèaziès* (Tehran, 1976), p. x; Thalasso, *Le Théatre Persan*, p. 876.

concluded by an epilogue. It was a kind of variety show that presented acts of individual performers of different types. The shows took place in the open air, during the day, in public places and access to the show was gratis. Dance and music preceded dramatic art.[91] Typically, a show would start with a prologue of circus type activities such as musicians, dancers, acrobats, and jugglers. Larger groups also had handlers of animal such as monkeys and bears. The noise of the music and the allure of the dancing aimed to alert and attract the people of the city quarter or the village where the troupe had arrived. Seated on a donkey, dressed up in a clownesque manner, the entertainers would enter a village or city quarter; then they made their rounds and announced their presence with fifes and drums.

> The names of the main characters were borrowed from the puppeteers. Thus the strong, muscular man was called Rostam. The comics of the troupe were called Panj and Kechel. They were very much like Footit and Chocolat in France (?) for one powdered his face with flour and the other with soot. While the strong man did his calisthenics on the trapeze, the greasy pole and the double ladder, Panj and Kachal had as task to amuse the gallery, which they did very well, though shticks, sparkling repartees, and trying to imitate the acrobat. These grimaces, these somersaults, and drops on the ground each time whenever they wanted to get the trapeze, to climb the mast or to climb the ladder. Their very saucy replies were always larded with references to current events. After them came the singer, jongleurs, bear fighters, cat, dog and monkey players.[92]

Just like the Turkish *orta-yunu* the play had no décor and the spectators formed a circle. The notables were seated upfront, the rest in 2nd and 3rd row seated or standing. In the center was the place reserved for the actors on an elevated platform.

After the 'warming-up' phase there followed an intro during which the entertainers played some forward pieces or a light-hearted dialogue with the musicians and other members of the troupe. Then followed pantomime; the one that Chodzko saw he named "The Day of a Fashionable Lady" with the following plot. A young wife fought with her husband, she was miffed, then she sulked, after which she dressed to leave the house, and next arrived at one of her friends. There was much flirtation and charm.[93] At the end of the mime there was a musical interval and then came the comedians.

> What is called comedy in Persia are bad farces played in gardens or homes (there are no theaters) by wretches, who often have been taken by chance from among the day laborers. These pieces remind you of the Italians slapstick; it is only about fast and smart rogues, who use all kinds of disguises

[91] De Gobineau, A. *Trois Ans en Asie* 2 vols. (Paris, 1923), vol. 1, p. 251.
[92] Thalasso, M.A. "Le Théatre Persan," *La Revue Théatrale* (1905), p. 875.
[93] Chodzko, *Théatre Persan*, p.xi.

and language to steal from herders or merchants, and in particular cream and sweetmeats. This results in rather burlesque scenes larded with witticisms. These actors, though no professionals, would be in Europe rather good bas-comics. They use gestures to emphasize their words, and it suffices for them to have a plot, if the master of the house does not himself supply them with one that he wants them to play. Then it is up to them to make it up and to say whatever they want, but they would never be lost in the public opinion, if their subject matter moves too far from the agreed plot. The thieves always have to be smarter than the merchants and to have a ready answer to any question, often embarrassing those who pose them. What makes it quite piquant is that they keep secret their manner of attack or defense; everything is improvised on the spot. They still have to be very slick to find excuses to get into the shops or the herder camps that are supervised by their masters, because if they make a mistake they are really chased away with beating of the stick, to the great pleasure of the public that cries, 'hur, hur, strike, strike, to make it clear to them that their inaptitude merits punishment. The thief always resumes the attack in new disguises. I have seen those who put on 30 costumes during one play that they change with a surprising agility by passing quickly behind a screen and talking each time in a different jargon. At any rate, no play ends without [the thieves] having found the means to steal a sheep and some jars of cream and sweetmeats."[94]

At the end of the show the entrepreneur came around with the 'hat' with his assistants. You were free to give what you wanted.

The actors played popular scenes in the dialect of Isfahan or of some other town. "One was obliged to correct and abridge much, because that kind of sketches, that normally represents the ruses of mollahs, the peculations of judges, the perfidy of women, the cheating of merchants and the fights of the rowdies, was composed with a verve that was untempered and with no holds barred. The most virulent chapters of Rabelais were rosewater in comparison. The host did not allow the performance to go out of hand and when he noticed that the actors were getting to lay into it he intervened so that all remained within bounds."[95] These *lutis* performed with a dressed-up monkey and also played *siyah-bazi*. They blackened their face with soot, spoke with a funny accent and said peculiar and even offensive words or sentences. They also sang songs and danced in a ridiculous way. The number of their songs was rather large and in Yazd, for example, had been imported from all over Iran due to the fact that Yazd was a commercial town and its traders brought these songs back with them.[96]

---

[94] Drouville, Gaspard. *Voyage en Perse pendant les années 1812 et 1813.* 2 vols. (Paris, 1819 [reprint Tehran: Imp. Org. f. Social Services, 1976), vol. 2, pp. 50-52.

[95] De Gobineau, *Trois Ans*, vol. 1, pp. 252-53.

[96] Shari`ati, `Ali Akbar, "Sargarmiha va Baziha-ye Pishin-e Yazd," in Afshar, Iraj ed. *Yazdnameh.* 2 vols. (Tehran, 1371/1992), vol. 1, pp. 507-09 (with list of 44 titles of these songs).

Tänzerinnen und Musikanten aus dem Stamme der Ssusmani bei Kermanschah
Suzmani dancing girls and musicians
near Kirmanshah   مطربان سوزمانی   Danseuses et musiciens souzmanis
                                                                                      près de Kirmanchah

Comical theater also found its way into the royal palace and that of the power elite. Fraser reports that in 1833, a show was put on in Tehran for Fath `Ali Shah Shah (r.1797-1834). After a performance of jugglers, rope dancers etc., "came a very stupid and indecent pantomime, consisting of an old man and two old women, strangely masked-very miserable editions of our clown and pantaloon. This again was followed by as vile an imitation of Punch and Judy, with other despicable buffooneries, equally deficient in wit, humor, and decency."[97] Comic drama took its cues from real life and therefore most of its themes addressed human folly and weakness. Neither the plot nor the substance was very well developed, for a typical piece consisted mainly of witticisms, allusions to local situations and personalities. They were very much like Thespis and Mousarion pieces. Their real art was in action, i.e. gestures. They used all kinds of unseemly gestures, if not worse. The farce was an improvisation and difficult to write down. Because it was the actors' aim to amuse people, serious passion was excluded. The actors (lutis) exposed the hypocrisy of Islamic sanctimoniousness and presented daily life as it really was. They revealed details about affairs that were public knowledge, but which nobody dared to

[97] Fraser, J.B. *A Winter's Journey from Constantinople to Teheran*, 2 vols. in one (London, 1838 [New York: Arno, 1973]), vol. 2, pp. 94-95.

mention let alone criticize in public. This was the strength of this art form, telling the truth in a dramatic manner with a well-developed sense of reality. The spoken word was accompanied usually by singing, music and dancing.[98]

Unlike the "planks-over-the pond" or *ru-howzi* type of comedy or its Ottoman equivalent known as *orta-yuni* that are organized around the central role of the main comic figure, the clown, *taqlid* had several comic characters. The idea was the same, i.e. in each play there was one central figure around which the entire dialogue was woven, but in each play there was a different one. There was not just one clown. One of the main characters was the *baqqal* (the grocer), hence called "the grocer's play" (*baqqal-bazi*), while another time it could be his black servant (*siyah*), in which case the play would be called "the black-man's play" (*siyah-bazi*). There were always two players, which, according to Marr, may be due to influence of the puppet show, where the number of players was limited. Whereas one character was always the fool or clown the other supporting character denoted conventional morality and respectability.[99]

To provide variety and maintain the action the device of stock characters was used to support the main story. The main stock figures were: (i) *Hajji-Agha* (the master); (ii) *Nokar* (the wily servant) known as Hajji Firuz, a clown with a blackened face; (iii) *Khanom* (the lady); (iv) *Kaniz* (the lady's maid); and (v) *Fokuli* or *Ferangi-Ma'ab* (the Westernized Iranian). He favored Europeans (*ferangi*) and wore a badly cut jacket, a homemade white paper high detachable collar (*faux-colle*, hence *fokoli*), a light cane and glasses or eye-piece with dark glass.[100] However, the portrayed characters could be anybody (women, courtiers, ethnic groups), and would be chosen depending on the patron's wishes, the geographic location, the political situation. This also may explain why the *luti* actors powdered their faces with flour or with soot (in case of playing the role of *siyah*), egg yellow, etc. Furthermore, the actors imitated accents and personal characteristics, and improvised their text adapting it to the need of the day and place. There was, for example, one comedy called *yahud-bazi* that probably had ethnic characterization as its main theme. This required, of course, that the actors concerned had the skill to imitate voices, accents (e.g., Kashani and Qazvini, both favorite stock-groups) and typical phrases. The strange masks that the actors put on their face served to make these acts interesting and amusing. These hairless and invariably sad masks counteract so comically with the *lazze* (shticks) of the artists who they appear to be.[101] Marr

---

[98] Bertel's, E. "Persidskii teatr," *Vostotsnyj teatr* IV (Leningrad, 1924), pp. 81-82; Chodzko, *Théatre Persan*, p. 875.

[99] Marr, Y.N. "Koje-shto Pehlevan Kechel i drygikh vidakh narodnogo teatre v Persii." *IRAN* II (Leningrad, 1928), pp. 75-80 (see Appendix for a translation of this artcle).

[100] Rezvani, *Le théatre* p. 111.

[101] Bertel's, *Persidskiy teatr*, pp. 11-12, 63-65; Massé, *Croyances*, vol. 1, 146ff.; Ettinghausen, R. "The dance with zoomorphic masks," in G. Makdisi, ed., *Arabic and Islamic studies in honour of*

saw a piece "Bloody Love" (`Eshq-e khunin`) in Enzeli and *Mashti `Ebad* in Isfa-han, which he considered to constitute a transitional form, because some of the actors still wore masks.[102] These shticks or comic routines were a vital element in the comic plays. They were interspaced with the normal story line, and involved pratfalls, acrobatics, gross and obscene gestures or movements as well as risqué verbal humor. People might even appear in Adam's costume with just a cover for the private parts. Just as the jester could get away with saying offensive things to and/or about his patron, so could the *luti* playing *taqlid*. Playing the role of a fool to a certain extent took away the venom of his attacks on authority, on morality, and sanctimony. He could say things about sexual and political matters that others could not, because it was presented in a mocking, distorted manner.[103]

Those who wanted to have a show at home, such as leading merchants and for-eign consuls, addressed themselves to the entrepreneur. The *luti*s believed that in the latter case they had to show off by dressing young actors with female clothes and amazing toilettes which they pretended were European, thus ridiculing Euro-pean customs, which costumes, according to Thalasso, were "in truth grotesque, false and pretentious."[104] Chodzko has provided the following description of such a comical performance:

The gardener, a Persian farce

The scene is supposed to represent a garden; it is summer. Two gardeners appear in Adam's costume dressed only in some sheepskin covering their mid-section. The oldest one is called Baqer, he is rich, father of a young beautiful daughter, that he guards in his harem. The younger one is called Najaf, he is poor, but active and smart. The two neighbors start to discuss the excellence of their fruit. "The pulp of this one makes the whitest sugar candy pale from jealousy." Etc. The gardeners get into a scuffle. They fight with their fists and pick-axes, making the spectators laugh. Finally Baqer is overcome and he admits defeat. They make peace, and Baqer proposes his neighbor "to extinguish the root of discord in seas of alcohol that some bad jokers pretend has been banned by the prophet." They ridicule the local mollah by declaiming the distich: "you drink the blood of your kin; me, I drink the blood of the grape' admit, on your con-

---

H. A. R. Gibb (Leiden 1965), pp. 211-24. Rezvani, *Le théatre*, p. 132-33 writes that this kind of theatre was called *ruband-bazi* (masked theatre), but he was unable to find much information about it beyond the fact that each actor used more than one mask, the names of two stock character (*Tajer-e kashi*; a bearded mask, and Jamileh: a wife wearing a long dress), it was a coarse play, but much appreciated and it went out of fashion by the end of the eighteenth century. See also Goyan, *Teyatr*, vol. 2, p. 369.
[102] Marr, "Koje-chto," pp. 79, n-80; Menzel, Theodor. *Meddah, Schattentheater und Orta Ojunu* (Prague, 1941), p. 27.
[103] Chodzko, *Théatre Persan*, pp. xi-xii; Thallaso, *Le Théatre Persan*, p. 875
[104] Thalasso, *Le Théatre Persan*, p. 875.

science, say, which one of us is the prevaricator?" Baqer gets his purse and gives some money to pay for the cost of the banquet. Najaf hurries to get the wine. Baqer calls him back and tells him not to forget some lamb kebabs. Najaf leaves, but Baqer calls him again to add some tidbits to the meal. When he has gone some distance Baqer again calls after him, and this act continues till Najaf falls from exhaustion, still not having received the orders of the host and not being able to resist the temptation to receive more, finally decides, just like Ulysses, to close his ears and run for it. Baqer, left alone, prepares himself for the meal as a good Moslem. He makes his ablutions very seriously while parroting the rites the mullahs usually apply prior to their meal. The scene ends with a meal that Najaf enlivens with guitar playing. Both neighbors drink much. The comical aspect is enhanced by their play-acting that shows increasing levels of drunkenness. In Persia, there are no public cabarets and the people are very sober, this scene is very piquant for the spectators. Baqer falls asleep. Najaf, whose drunkenness was but a lover's ruse, runs towards the young daughter to sing her his victory song, with obligatory accompaniment of the guitar.[105]

Figure 9: Boys-dancers dressed as girls with musicians at Orumiyeh (ca. 1900)

None of the farcical plays were printed. The actors therefore had to know their text, and its variations, by heart, which was achieved by frequent rehearsal and

---

[105] Chodzko, *Théatre Persan*, pp. xii-xiv.

interaction with other members of the troupe. The *luti*s were not really inspired by the moment, even if they acted as if they were. Although their performance was not spontaneously improvisatory, there were planned variations of a prepared text with an eye on the situation where they were playing. It may be assumed that all these variations were as rehearsed as the main text and that these were improved upon and refined based on experience and interaction with the public. Given the absence of a written text, the actors relied on one basic story line that allowed a large variety of stock characters to be added on to it. A play could last from half an hour to three hours, depending on the situation. According to Thalasso, the golden age of the *tamasha* was the 1860s for which he does not provide any argument other than stating that this decline was due to new theatrical developments. However, as I discuss in the last chapter, the major interest in modern theater only acquired some importance after the first decade of the twentieth century and therefore this, as so many of Thalasso's other observations, have to be disregarded.[106]

Only the mime-dancers used masks and make-up. Those performing female dances would thicken and exaggerate their eyebrows and henna their hands. The dancers made the masks themselves either from skins, starched cloth, or from cardboard. The latter kind had no expression and they were made as follows. After having put oil onto one's face a thin cover of cardboard was applied to the face and pressed on it to make it assume the form of the face. Next, holes were made for the eyes and mouth. Later imported carnival masks were used. Each dance had a name indicating its theme. For example, for the dance "The farm-girl goes to the market" the dancer wore a farm-girl's mask with red cheeks and a kerchief of the same color on his head. Furthermore, a shawl around the shoulders and a long red skirt with flowers. For the dance named "Betrothed" the dancer wore the mask of a young girl with a headdress that was typical for betrothed girls.[107] Dance was also an integral part of the comical theater. Dancers also used their voice and to express grief would cry. One piece called "The Future Doctor" (*Aqa-ye Doktor min bedezin*) was a true ballet, according to Rezvani. The main character, to make money, becomes a quack who treats unsuspecting patients. The scene of the dance is the doctor's office. Each dancer has freedom of interpretation of his role and they all interact with different turns, leaps, pirouettes and gestures to express themselves. The mime dances are interspersed with dialogue and songs, and the result is a comical ballet.[108]

In short, actor-dancer-buffoons were professionals who led an itinerant life to make a living. They performed everywhere, at court, the homes of the rich and in the streets. They acted masked and unmasked. In case they were 'masked' they

---

[106] Thalasso, *Le Théatre Persan*, p. 867 (see also pictures).
[107] Rezvani, *Le Théatre*, pp. 196-97.
[108] Rezvani, *Le Théatre*, pp. 198-99.

used flour or egg-yolk as materials as well as masks made from animal hide or other materials. Typically, they also wore a long conical hat and goat skins. The buffoon shows were a mix of farce, puppet shows and juggling, while the organizers of these shows also used animals to attract an audience. Although the actors stuck to a standard routine, they improvised during show, depending on location, patron and reactions from the public. The show lasted about two hours and during and after the show the actors collected money.

> In a room called *rakhtkan* (dressing room) or *surat-khaneh* (make-up room) … each actor put on his own make-up according to known conventions and from simple materials. The materials they used consisted of flour which before the availability of sufficient light was put on faces to help visibility, or was put on hair to show age; red dye with which they painter flowers on their faces, cotton or sheep and goat hair with which they made beards, and moustaches; horse's mane with which they made long tresses, coal with which they darkened their faces, herbal dyes with which they painted colorful circles on the bodies and faces of the clowns, a few masks which were put on by a few giants, and 'chaspt' (sticky stuff), which was made of glue, cotton and a few other materials. Exaggeration was a natural aspect of masks and make-up, since the characters themselves were exaggerated. … It seems that the colors were used to make up for insufficient light.[109]

One of the most distinguishing characteristics of the buffoons was indeed their attire. The masks were already used in pre-Islamic Iran and originally may have had religious meaning. Later, they became part of the routine and increased recognition and attraction. In the 1660-70s Chardin noted that the entertainers "intermingle Farce, and Juggling, with a thousand Stories and Buffooneries, which they do sometimes Mask'd, and sometimes Unmask'd, and this lasts two or three Hours."[110] Also, very characteristic was the long conical felt hat worn by clowns. A 1621 painting by Soltan Mohammad Naqqash shows a clown with a long hat and a few men wearing goat skins, entertaining a party.[111] The same attire was worn by clowns during the Qajar period. For example, Karim Shireh'i, Naser al-Din Shah's leading buffoon and comical actor "put on a long felt hat, a shabby robe, a flour mask, a wool and skin beard and moustache, rode a small donkey, and surrounded by his troupe, he entered the stage."[112] Buffoons used their attire to represent the age, sex, status etc. of each character and in particular that of stock characters. They also employed other elements such as size and deformities to create character-recognition and laughter. The phallus and in general sex was

---

[109] Beyza'i, *Namayesh*, p. 212 (the make-up room was a temporary space and often also served as living space for the actor); Mostowfi, *Sharh*, vol. 1, p. 340.

[110] Chardin, *Travels*, p. 203.

[111] Beyza'i, *Namayesh*, p. 55. For other examples see Ettinghausen, "The dance."

[112] Beyza'i, *Namayesh*, p. 177-78.

also a strong source for humor. Finally, the use of archetypes, in particular of natural opposites, the so-called stock characters, was a characteristic of Iranian folk drama.[113]

Figure 10: Court jester of Naser al-Din Shah (left picture); two actors, on the left Karim Shireh'i (right picture)

Mostowfi in his auto-biography not only reminds us of the versatility of the actors (buffoon, juggler, singer, musician, etc. at the same time), but also of the importance of their attire to represent their stock characters. In this case he described a play performed by a group of rural musicians/actors, whom he considered to be quite good.

> These musicians performed plays too. In one of their plays, a man painted eyes, a nose, and mouth on his stomach with coal. He put a sieve upside down on his head, and covered it with a piece of sheep hide, and tied its ends around his chest which formed a big hat. He placed a stick through the sleeves of a shirt on his waist. Thus he made a short man

---

[113] Beyza'i, *Namayesh*, pp. 174, 210.

with a big head and face, a thin waist, thick neck, and ugly appearance and came on the stage and danced.[114]

Despite the use of masks and make-up the actors did not conceal their real identity, whether on or off stage. According to Beyza'i, "The actors neither forget nor hide their extra-theatrical relations with each other and with the audience. It is conceivable that at times on the stage they converse among themselves as their 'real selves,' or after their roles in a play, they sit in the audience and talk with them"[115]

BAQQAL-BAZI

A very popular kind of dramatic satirical comedy was known as *baqqal-bazi* because the play's main character was a rich grocer (*baqqal*) who claimed to be a *hajji* or pilgrim and was made fun of by his insolent servant. The latter was often represented as a negro. If the latter had a major role this type of plays was also called *siyah-bazi*. The aim of this kind of drama was formulated as follows by Tahvildar in 1890.

> The sixth kind of *luti*s consists of the satirists (*lutiha-ye sar-khvancheh-ye ostad baqqal*).
>
> Old master invented *baqqal-bazi*, because of its various public benefits. On the outside it seems that the only function of this entertainment is the causing of joy and laughter during amusements, but, in reality, it has many useful advantages for the administration of the cities.
>
> The basic idea of the aforementioned play was like this, that someone's unlawful actions should become public in the most shameful way, by presenting a similar situation in the foulest language and by ridiculing it, so that these shameful acts were witnessed and felt in all their reality and perplexity and so that using this way of exaggerating and thus exposing depravity would make even the most unscrupulous deviator feel ashamed. Truly, these *luti*s are in fact the mirror of the villainies of man; their ridicule bears fruit most of the time.
>
> All these *luti*s are witty, facetious, subtle and saucy. Each one of them has become famous to the extent that their witty remarks were even written down. Formerly, they were numerous [in Isfahan] and constituted several troupes. Now they are few in number and are dispersed over Tehran and other cities.[116]

---

[114] Mostowfi, *Sharh*, vol. 1, p. 340.
[115] Beyza'i, *Namayesh*, pp. 206, 207-08.
[116] Tahvildar, *Joghrafiya*, p. 125.

Such was the fame of *baqqal-bazi* that it was also regularly played for Naser al-Din Shah,[117] in particular by his favorite court-jester Karim Shireh'i and his group. Eyn al-Saltaneh noted in is Diary:

> Half an hour after night had fallen they brought the acting implements [props?]. Karim Khan came and danced a bit. Then the acting implements were ready. First there was *pahlavan-kachal*; second there was *baqqal-bazi*. The acting of the play (*bazi-ye baqqal-bazi*) was very flat. Third there was *bazi-ye yahudi*; it was very comical unlike the *baqqal-bazi*; I laughed so much that my insides hurt. Everbody laughed. It was a very good play. Four hours after night fall the show ended. It was a good show.[118]

Baqqal-bazi thus was not a separate form of comic drama, but just a character routine that seems to have been a very, if not the most, popular one of other similar comedies. *Siyah-bazi* has been mentioned as another related off-shoot, while *yahud-bazi* was another one, presumably a comedy with a Jewish character as the main role. Just as in the case of the storytellers, who were named after the piece that they narrated (*shahnameh-khvan* or *hamzeh-khvan*) in the same way comical plays each became known by the name of the main routine. Another play that belongs to this category of comedy is the "Priest's Tale" (*bazi-ye keshish*) that Esma`il Bazzaz, another well-known comedy actor, performed for Amin al-Soltan and other members of the elite.[119] He also performed other similar comedies. For example, on 13 August 1887 there was a marriage in one of Tehran's quarters where many artists of Esma`il Bazzaz's troupe performed. "The musicians (*motreb*) played "The Physician and his mute servant" (*Hakim va Nokar-e Lal-e u*) and then the "The Old Police Chief and His Behavior" (*bazi-ye kalantari-ye qadimi va soluk-e ishan*)."[120]

Rezvani nevertheless maintains that *kachaleh-bazi* or *baqqal-bazi* or *baqqal-oyini* (Azerbaijan) was indeed a separate category of comical theater. He ascribes its origin to ancient times and sees Aristophanes's Greek bald hero and his *kordax* dance as its forerunner. The main character of this type of theater is a bald hero called *Pahlavan Kachal*. Between the theatrical pieces the actors did comical dances or buffoonery. There were usually only two, rarely three or four persons. The play was rather primi-

[117] E`temad al-Saltaneh, Mohammad Hasan Khan. *Ruznameh-ye Khaterat*. ed. Iraj Afshar (Tehran: Amir Kabir, 1345/1967), p. 484.

[118] `Eyn al-Saltaneh, Qahraman Mirza Salur. *Ruznameh-ye Khaterat*. 10 vols. eds. Mas`ud Salur and Iraj Afshar (Tehran: Asatir, 1376/1997), vol. 1, p. 56 (11 Safar 1302 or 30/11/1884).

[119] Mostowfi, *Sharh*, vol. 1, p. 340; Basir al-Molk Sheybani. *Ruznameh-ye Khaterat*. eds. Iraj Afshar and Mohammad Rasul Daryagasht (Tehran: Donya-ye Ketab, 1374/1995), pp. 282, 454 (Amin al-Soltan and Sayyed Shushtari), 465.

[120] Sheykh-Reza'i, Ensiyeh and Azari, Shahla ed. *Gozareshha-ye Nazmiyyeh az Mahallat-e Tehran* (Tehran: Sazman-e Asnad-e Melli, 1377/1998), vol. 2, pp. 561-62 (10 Dhu'l-Hejjeh 1304).

tive and coarse. The hero had a stick (*chomaq*) in his hands, which had been cut up lengthwise. When he beat somebody it made a very loud noise, but it was not hurtful at all. Because of its never failing effect actors made often made use of it. Some of their acts were performed entirely in mime. Rezvani personally saw two performances one in Baku and the other in Gorgan in 1923.[121]

As noted previously these troupes or individual entertainers also performed in the rural areas.[122] Shari`ati reported that comical plays were seldom performed at Yazd, but were very popular in its rural areas, where they were mostly performed in spring and summer. The artists mostly performed in gardens and played in the evenings with the help of illumination provided by candles, oil lamps, or an open fire. The repertory of these plays was rather large and those played in Yazd province numbered at least 35.[123] In Mazandaran and Gilan these types of plays were still performed in the rural areas as late as the 1978. The actors were mostly villagers, who did this as a side-activity, because they all had regular, usually non-farming, jobs. They normally did not ask money for their performances, unless they performed outside their village, in which case they might. They performed both in the open village square as well inside with a minimum of décor. In case of inside performances the women usually stayed outside, unless it was in very small village where relations were very close. The actors dressed up for the occasion and wore different kinds of masks for the different roles. The masks were home-made from various kinds of fabrics as well as of goatskin. All of these plays were of the traditional kind such as cock-fighting (*khorush jangi*), bear-fighting (*khors-bazi*), `arusi-ye galleh, pir-a babu, a'ineh takom, ahu chereh, kheymeh shab-bazi, shab-bazi, terek gun terek (a Torkoman play), etc. Whereas in the past the village chief and the small land-owners would underwrite and organize these plays during slack time in the agricultural cycle, nowadays it is done by shopkeepers and middlemen.[124]

Ru-howzi or *takht-e howzi*, as comedy is known nowadays, also was such a variety show under a different name that included various and different kinds of entertainment. The term derived its name from the stage where it was commonly performed: a platform on a pond in the courtyard of a house. Shari`ati relates that in Yazd in the 1920s when musicians were invited to come and perform at weddings and circumcisions the owner of the house put on a platform over the pond (literally: *ru-howzi*)

[121] Rezvani, *Le Théatre*, pp. 112-14; he also provides a description of the play seen at Gorgan as performed by two actors from Damghan.

[122] MacKenzie, Charles Francis. *Safarnameh-ye Shomal* tr. Mansureh Ettehadiyeh (Nezam-Mafi) (Tehran: Gostareh, 1359/1980), p. 18.

[123] Shari`ati, "Sargarmiha," vol. 1, pp. 509-10.

[124] Mir Shokra'i, Mohammad. Paygah-e ejtema`i-ye namayeshha-ye `amiyaneh dar Mazandaran va Gilan," *Honar va Mardom* 129-130 (1358/1979), pp. 52-65. See also Setudeh, Manuchehr. "Namayesh-e `arusi dar jangal," *Yadgar* 1/8 (1324/1945), pp. 41-43.

in the courtyard. These musicians also would come when they had not been invited, if they knew there was a party somewhere. The owner of the house then either sent them away or invited them in. In addition to playing, they also performed dances, jest and mountebanks.[125] The practice of having entertainers perform on a wooden platform put over the pond existed already in the nineteenth century and thus was not a twentieth century innovation.

Ru-howzi was reportedly first performed in Kermanshah by `Ali Chini Bandzan, who did only solo performances at private homes during the first decade of the twentieth century. Later he formed a troupe with several actors and played at parties. Bandzan developed a comical routine that included, amongst other things, the use of a spoon and plate as musical instruments, while singing humorous songs of his own making taking themes from daily life. He also mimicked people from other regions and dialects. Most of his co-actors were gainfully employed and their acting was a hobby, not a full-time job.[126] A group, known as Hoseyn Arbab, followed Bandzan's example a few years later. Arbab's group had three permanent actors and the others did it part-time. They usually performed at house parties. Another Kermanshahi comedian (*moqalled*) was known as Faraj Lal, because of his stammer. He performed also at coffeehouses; further there was `Ali Naqi Nava'i. The most famous of them all was Hoseyn Kharrazi, who also got a group together. In winter he performed inside, but otherwise in outside spaces. Kharrazi took ideas for his dramas from little-known stories and his improvisations were well-known.[127] Famous actors from Tehran sometimes traveled to other towns, such as Sheikh Sheypur.[128]

When modern Western-style plays were introduced the old theatrical forms continued to co-exist. There was even some influence of traditional Iranian drama on Western-style theater. In Tehran some play-houses were even established to perform traditional comedy (*taqlid*). One by Hoseyn Chubi in the *Meydan-e Amin al-Soltan*; it was a temporary one for summer performances only. In its place came one that was housed in a warehouse of a wood seller, which became known as the *Bongah-e Tirforushi*. It was established in 1900. One of its plays was that of "The Four Boxes" (*Chahar Sanduq*) and "The Cobbler's New Year" (*Nowruz-e Pinehduz*). In 1901, Tiyarat `Ali Beg through `Ali Beg Qavqazi established a playhouse in Khiyaban-e Shahpur. He moved in 1903 to a carriage-house in Khiyaban-e Naseriyeh, which became known as *Tamasha-khaneh-ye Naseriyeh*. The creators of these theaters all came from the farcical tradition and thus the stage of comedy theater (*takhteh*) was

[125] Shari`ati, "Sargarmiha," vol. 1, pp. 506-07.
[126] Soltani, Mohammad `Ali. *Joghrafiya-ye Tarikhi va Tarikh-e Mofassal-e Kermanshahan*. 3 vols. (Tehran: author, 1370/1991), vol. 1, p. 350 citing Mansur Khalaj, *Tarikhcheh-ye Namayesh dar Kermanshah* (Tehran, 1364/1985).
[127] Soltani, *Joghrafiya*, vol. 1, p. 351.
[128] Soltani, *Joghrafiya*, vol. 1, pp. 351-52.

their model. This meant a square wooden stage, but this design was later transformed under the influence of European theater models and they built stages that were open on three sides. Later they even added a curtain. These theaters had no good repute with the modernizing reformers.[129]

Comical plays were also staged in coffeehouses and in small theaters, particularly in Tehran. In spite of its great popularity, orthodox religious groups had always criticized popular drama, but in the late 1920s it also came under attack from the side of the modernizing Pahlavi government. The police had orders to suppress anything that might be considered vulgar; it thus exercised censorship. An interesting example is that of the Mo'ayyed Company that had to stop its activities several times due to a police ban. The Mo'ayyad Company was the only one in Tehran if not in the entire country that still performed farcical comedy, according to Galunov. It preserved "the old theater tradition and was not affected by European theater. In none of the other theaters of Persian comedy that I visited traditional Persian gestures were not as preserved as amazingly as by the Mo`ayyad company." It was also an interesting phenomenon for other reasons, in particular for its internal organization. The company consisted of amateur actors, artisans, craftsmen, small merchants and traders who during the day worked in the shops and workshops and in the evening played in the theater that they rented or in private homes by invitation. In summer the Mo'ayyed Company moved from village to village and did performances very often by invitation during family celebrations and holidays. Mirza Hasan Mo'ayyed wrote the scripts of the plays for the theater, but the actors had large discretion for improvisation. The Mo'ayyed theater was frequented almost exclusively by traders, artisans, small merchants and workers and was completely ignored by the Iranian intelligentsia, who found it too vulgar and very often did not even know about its existence. Because of the general government policy this theatrical genre is also doomed to extinction and it has not been studied yet, Galunov opined. The character of this theater was discussed in the newspaper *Nahid*. The paper considered that these plays staged in a theater were no good. For the plays did not promote the improvement of life, with the exception of plays translated from European languages and adapted to the Iranian stage. In short, the usual plots were: (i) a man had 2-3 wives and there are serious misunderstandings between them or (ii) an adulterous husband being engaged in adultery hiding it from his wife or doing it in her presence. The paper demanded that the government and police pay more attention to the content of plays on stage so that the traditional genre of comedy would not be resurrected.[130]

---

[129] Malekpur, Jamshid. *Adabiyyat-e Namayeshi dar Iran* 2 vols. (Tehran, 1363/1994), vol. 2, pp. 55-56; Osku'i, *Pazhuheshi*, pp. 159-62.

[130] Galunov, R. A. "Neskol'ko slov o perspektivakh sobiraniya materialov po fol'kloru i teatru v Persii," *Doklady Akademii Nauk* 17 (1929), p. 309; Monshi-bashi-ye Nahid, "Valedeh-ye Te'atr Mireh." *Nahid* nr. 47, 11 Dey 1307, pp. 1-2.

FEMALE PLAYS

Thalasso was the first who drew attention to the existence of exclusive female theater, which he considered proof of the total exclusion of Iranian women from society.[131] Galunov, some 25 years later, was the second person to discuss this form of theater, which he called theater of the Iranian women's quarters (*anderun*). He noted that that was rapidly disappearing from every day life. He described these plays as follows:

> It means the presentation of small every day life scenes played by middle-class women in their *anderun*s [female quarters]. This is absolutely not studied and unknown to Europeans and Persians themselves. It is necessary to take into consideration that the female theater of Persia appeared as the result of the limited role of Persian women and their impossibility to participate in social life. Disappearance of this theater will be fast, because of the possibility given to Persian women now to go to the theater, cinema and concerts with men which was absolutely impossible even one year ago. As a result of disappearance of the old theatrical genres it would be hardly possible to reconstruct the old Persian theater especially when we consider the scarcity of iconographic material and the almost complete lack of the mention of theater in Persian literature. It may seem that as a result of a gradually earned emancipation of Persian women, the European researcher will receive broader opportunity to talk to them and write down the wealth of old folklore material. In reality, it is not like that at all. Persian women, even more than men, are ashamed of giving Europeans examples of oral folklore or share old customs and beliefs. They do not consider it worth of any mention, for they expect European to look down on them. The ongoing Europeanization increases this attitude.[132]

Since then one or two authors have alluded to this practice, but they did not provide many details. Shari'ati, for example, only reported that women had their separate, exclusive amusements where they accompanied themselves with drums, bells, castanets, and handclapping, but since it happened behind closed doors, and no men were admitted, he had no other information. He only added that the *rowzeh-ye 'Omar-koshan* was one of those exclusive female activities.[133] These "plays" could be simple or more elaborate. A simple entertainment, as described

---

[131] Thalasso, "Le Théatre Persan," pp. 867, 874.

[132] Galunov, "Neskol'ko slov," pp. 310-11. He also noted in the same article: "The true guardians of the folklore poetry, Persian women, are ashamed to share examples of this folk poetry and to talk about customs and beliefs and to show Europeans how backward they are. Attempts to write down oral art of expression or beliefs and customs by Persians are very rare. In the best case the European is met with an attitude of sympathetic tolerance."

[133] Shari'ati, "Sargarmiha," vol. 1, pp. 510-11. For a discussion of *'Omar-koshan* performances see chapter five.

in the case of the village of Davarabad (Khorasan) around 1960, concerned a form of dancing, which was:

> generally confined to small and intimate female groups. This is pro-grammatic and is the only important departure from the individual dance. Here simple stories are acted out by several dancers to some rhythmic accompaniment and chanted continuity by the onlookers. The story scenes are largely heroic or domestic, usually with many a raucous and bawdy element depicting seduction, rape and the strategies thereof. In these the women may hoist their skirts up into their pajama tops and por-tray the men as insatiably virile. The dance has more pretext than context and the choreography is largely incidental.[134]

`Ali Bolukbashi has provided the best description of this form of entertainment. He reported that he had assisted himself to many of these plays as a young boy, while he further interviewed a large number of old women about this custom and its plays. Based on that information he reported that many of these exclusive fe-male plays were performed during marriages, *pa-takhti*, *pagoshakonan*, *shesh shab*, naming ceremony, circumcision, and `Omar-koshan*. They took place be-hind closed doors and no males (i.e. above the age of seven) were allowed. These plays represented scenes from real life with much zest and poignancy. The women also dressed up as men, spoke as men by changing their voice, and walked as men, which they did in a very convincing manner. Apparently there were seven of these plays whose titles were: (i) *khaleh ruru*, (ii) *zan-e ashikh*, (iii) `arus va madar-e shohar*, (iv) `amu-ye sabzi-forush*, (v) *naneh-ye gholam hoseyni*, (vi) *gandom gol-e gandom*, and (vii) *khaleh-ye ghorbali* also named *khaleh-ye dig beh sar*. The last two are special dances, but the others are plays, in which the actors shed light on people's bad deeds and thoughts in a sharp witty manner and then make fun of them. The play usually took place in a large room without a décor. The actors played in one corner and the spectators either sat in another corner or in a circle around them. The plays were accompanied by rhythmic music with the help of small drums, bells, castanets, hand clapping, etc.; the women themselves played the instruments. Either an invited person or one of the participating women did simple make-up (*chehreh-gardan*) to make the actors look ridiculous. Some-times the actors just did the make-up themselves. The costumes of the actors were normal contemporary women's or male clothes depending on the role.[135]

---

[134] Alberts, Robert Charles. *Social Structure and Culture Change in an Iranian Village* 2 vols. (unpublished dissertation; University of Wisconsin, 1963), vol. 2, pp. 1086-87.
[135] Bolukbashi, `Ali. "Namayeshha-ye shadi-avar-e zananeh dar Tehran," *Honar va Mardom* 27 (1343/1964), pp. 26-28 (with a short description of the content of the *Khaleh-ye ghorbali* play). Rezvani, *Le théatre*, p. 167 also mentions "Goli-Gendom, Ami-Sebze-Fooch, Ro-Ro-Khalaro" and classifies the first two as dances accompanied by singing and music and the last one as a panto-mime dance. The themes of these dances he characterizes as being often indecent.

CHAPTER TWO

PUPPET DRAMA

INTRODUCTION

Three kinds of puppet theater were played in Iran. One, where puppets were moved by gloved hands. Two, where they were moved by strings (marionettes). Three, where two-dimensional puppets cast their shadows on a screen (shadow theater). It is unknown where the puppet theater originated. It may have been introduced from neighboring countries and it may have been developed independently in Iran itself. Although we have no data showing the existence of puppet theater in Iran before the eleventh century CE, puppets were already commonly known as early as 421 BCE. The *Symposium of Xenophon* describes a dinner party. A performer from Syracuse who entertained the guests, said, when asked by Socrates what he was most proud of, "Fools, in faith. For they give me a livelihood by coming to view my puppets."[1] Although the entertainer was not putting on a puppet show, his remark implies that puppets must have been common entertainment at that time. In the *Deipnosophists*, Athenaeos reproaches the people of Athens because they had handed over the theater of Dionysos to the puppets of Potheimos and took more delight in these than in the plays of Euripides.[2] Marcus Aurelius also mentions puppets ("no longer be pulled by the strings like a puppet"). He, like Horace, made a comparison between the puppets strings and man's free will. It is of further interest that the puppets of Iranian and Turkish marionette theater use "the traditional attributes of classical theater in ancient Armenia (the use of the symbol of *aralez*, the phallus, and the cone-shaped hats of Gisane.)"[3] This makes the case of a Greek or W. Asian origin of puppet theater a strong one.

Not to forget the possible Indian connection, the Indian *Mahabharata* also mentions string-controlled marionettes, and compares their servile condition to human beings, and thus an Indian origin cannot be ruled out. George Speaight mentions that: "In the sixth century the Bishop of Alexandria [of the Byzantine Empire] referred to little wooden figures that were shown at weddings, and were moved by some kind of remote control in the actions of dancing."[4] Since there were close

---

[1] *Xenophon's Symposium*, with notes by Samuel Ross Winans (Boston, 1881), p. 28.
[2] Athenaeus of Naucratis, *The Deipnosophists*, translated by Charles Burton Gulick (Cambridge: Harvard UP, 1926-57), I, 1, 19E.
[3] Goyan, *Teatr*, vol. 2, pp. 265-66; Speaight, George. *The History of the English Puppet Theatre* (London, 1955), p. 24-26.
[4] Speaight, *The History*, p. 28.

contacts between Iran and all these countries concerned it is quite likely that puppet drama was known in Iran as well at an early period.

SHADOW THEATER

The Persian terms for the puppet show include *khayal*, *khayal bazi*, *bazi-khayal*,
khass sayeh-bazi; further, the cloth (*na't*) on which the plays were performed, and
the puppeteer or *khayal-baz*. However, it is not clear whether shadow theater was
actually performed in Iran despite some literary evidence that seems to demonstrate its existence there. For example, Asad-e Tusi (ca. 999-1073) in his *Geraspnameh* wrote:[5]

> How dexterous is the player
> In putting images on the screen
> He hands on this Lapis Dome
> Two screens, now black and now yellow
> And as a play on these screens
> Of various creatures He brings images

The poet Khaqani mentioned puppet shows (*lo'bat-bazi*) as well as shadows (*khayal*), shadow theater (*khayal-bazi*) and screen (*pardeh*). Nezami referred in his
works to these same elements (*pardeh, khayal, khayal-bazi, bazi-ye khayal,
lo'bat-bazi*).[6] All these terms appear to refer only to shadow theater rather than the
other two forms of puppet theater. However, beyond the occurrence of these
terms, which also may refer to marionettes there is no mention of shadow theater
in Iran at all. Elsewhere in the Middle East, such as in Egypt, shadow theater was
wildly popular. In 1024 CE, farces (*samajat*), narration (*hekayat*) and shadow
theater (*khayal*) were performed there.[7] It is only at the beginning of the twelfth
century that once again reference is made to shadow theater by an Iranian poet.
One of Omar Khayyam's (c. 1050-1123) verses in his *Rob'ayat* reads:

> We are no other than a moving row
> Of magic shadow-shapes that come and go
> Round with Sun-illumined lantern held
> In Midnight by the Master of the Show

Khayyam speaks of a *fanus-e khayal*, referring to a rotating magic lantern with
shadow figures propelled by hot air generated by the heat from a candle inside the
lantern. However, there is no further mention of or evidence for the use of a magic
lantern in Iran.

---

[5] Beyza'i, *Namayesh*, p. 48; *Geraspnameh* ed. Habib Yaghma'i (Tehran, 1939), p. 6.
[6] Beyza'i, *Namayesh*, pp. 84-86.
[7] Mez, *Die Renaissance*, p. 399 quoting Maqrizi's *Khitat*.

Although the term *zell-e khayal* is generally used in the Middle East to denote shadow theater there is general unanimity among scholars that in Iran the term *khayal* did not refer to shadow theater. Nezami's use of the term *khayal* refers, according to Menzel, not to puppet shadows, but rather to shadows in the Platonic sense,[8] while others maintain that the term *khayal* only refers to three-dimensional string puppets, and according to again other scholars it is uncertain whether any of the known references may be interpreted as evidence of the existence of shadow play in medieval Iran.[9] Menzel also adduces as a clinching argument that shadow theater had never existed in Central Asia, a region that culturally was very closely intertwined with Iran. Whatever the truth of the matter, there is agreement that in Iran the shadow play never gained the prominence which it had other countries of the Middle East.[10] It probably disappeared in the twelfth century without leaving many traces.

However, there seems to be some evidence that shadow thater persisted, at least in some locations in Iran. *Qaragöz* (black eye) under which name the two-dimensional puppet show was known in Turkey, may have been played in nineteenth century Iran. In 1907, Aubin mentioned that prior to the recent introduction of marionettes it was the only kind of puppet theater in Iran,[11] although he does not provide any information as to how and where it was played. If true, this suggests that rather than having faded away without leaving a trace, as has been suggested, it was continued in Iran, albeit in a very limited way. Thalasso also confirmed that shadow theater was played in Iran. He further noted that "puppets in Iran are modeled after those in Turkey, and are of colored goldbeater's skin (*baudruche*) and are moved by a large stick through a large hole pierced right in the breast. The play is like that of Karaguez. The same disposition of the puppet, play of lights, same curtain behind which the comical silhouettes are created."[12] However, much of what Thalasso writes is suspect, because he did not provide this information based on his own observations. Rezvani maintains that shadow theater existed in Iran at the beginning of the twentieth century, and even was to be found at some locations until the 1960s, but he does not provide any evidence either.[13] Menzel argues that there is no shred of evidence for the existence of shadow theater in the Caucasus and Azerbaijan, that scholars from those regions who had studied the matter confirmed this, and that it probably never existed in

---

[8] Menzel, Theodor. *Meddah, Schattentheater und Orta Ojunu* (Prague, 1941), pp. 13-14
[9] Boratav, P. N. "Qaragöz," *Encyclopedia of Islam*[2].
[10] Landau, J.M., "Khayal al-Zill," *Encyclopedia of Islam*[2]. The 'invention' of the Qaragöz puppet show is, however, ascribed to an itinerant dervish coming from Tabriz, Iran. Beyza'i, *Namayesh*, p. 92; quoting Jacob, Georg. *Geschichte des Schattentheater* (Berlin, 1907); see also Ibid., *Die Herkunft der Silhouettenkunst (ojmadschylyk) aus Persien* (Berlin, 1913).
[11] Aubin, *La Perse*, p. 234.
[12] Thalasso, *Le Théatre Persan*, p. 869.
[13] Rezvani, *Le théatre*, p. 123.

Iran.[14] An unrelated and new development was that the British Church Missionary Society showed slide pictures to villagers in the early twentieth century using a lantern.[15]

GLOVE PUPPETS

Given the apparent near absence of shadow theater in Iran it follows that the two other forms of puppet-play (glove and string puppets) were the most common ones. They were played in public and private in Iran until quite recently. The terms lo`bat and surat may also have referred to glove puppets, although we do not know for certain. It is only as of the early sixteenth century that we have solid evidence that glove puppets were used in Iran. Hoseyn Va`ez Kashefi mentioned kheymeh, the puppet theater that is played during the day, where the player moves the puppets directly by hand and improvises.[16] Handheld puppet shows were played in two ways, one without and the other with the use of a tent. The first way was a very simple and inexpensive way of staging a puppet drama. Hoseyn Va`ez Kashefi wrote in 1502:

> One day I was present at the time of a performance. I saw a person seated with a shawl pulled over his head. Two faces appeared from under the shawl. Sometimes, he would ask a question in the tongue of one face in a loud, mature male voice; then he himself would reply as through from the other face in the soft voice of a little girl. The he would speak in such a way that their questions and answers in their two distinct voices could be heard from him. During the dialogue affairs rose to anger. They attacked each other and then made peace. And all this was the voice and action of the one person who was under that covering![17]

A variant of this type of easy-to-mount glove puppet theater was called `arusak or puppet, which was still performed in the early twentieth century. The puppeteer, according to Rezvani, stretched out on the floor and raised his legs. His feet then were enveloped with white cloth on which a comical face was drawn in colors with pronounced features. Alternatively, he put masks on his feet. After having done this, the puppet's head (i.e. the masks or the two pieces of cloth with the drawing of a face) was covered with a handkerchief. Then the puppeteer donned a jacket by putting his hands through the sleeves and buttoning the jacket over his knees. In each hand he held a wooden spoon, while a sheet covered his head and

---

[14] Menzel, *Meddah*, pp. 13, 33, 35.

[15] Howard, R. W. *A Merry Mountaineer. The Story of Clifford Harris of Persia* (London: CMS, 1931), pp. 52, 55, 57.

[16] Kashefi, *Fotovvat-nameh-ye Soltani*, p. 342.

[17] Kashefi, Hoseyn Va`ez. *Fotovvatnameh-ye Soltani* ed. Mohammad Mahjub (Tehran, 1340/1971), pp. 340-41, translated by Jay R. Crook as *The Royal Book of Spiritual Chivalry* (Chicago, 2000), p. 330.

upper body. The result was a kind of robed puppet. An assistant sat next to the puppeteer and chanted. The puppet beat the spoons against one another as if applauding, and then it bowed, turned from one side to the other and then danced.[18]

Figure 11: A glove-puppet player with a 'walking' tent at a rural fair (1637)

The other way of staging glove puppets was one that used a kind of rudimentary tent and which seems to have been common in the fifteenth century, if not earlier. One form was that of a kind of 'walking' tent (*kheymeh-ye kamar*), which Olearius described in 1637. In his travelogue there is a picture of a juggler, a sleight-of-hand performer, and of a puppeteer in Russia. He performed "comic drama or *klucht* as the Dutch say with the puppets." The puppeteer bound a coverlet around his body that stuck out above his head and shoulders and thus he had made a portable theater that allowed him to walk the streets and to play the puppets at the same time. In Shamakhi the governor had invited the Holstein embassy to a tent where all kinds of entertainments were performed. There were mountebanks and dancers, and a monkey player as well as a performer who played puppets in the manner described

---

[18] Rezvani, *Le théatre*, p. 131.

in the case of Russia.[19] This kind of puppet show was called *khom-bazi*, according to Beyza'i. The doll was set in a wooden cylinder or cup (like pestle in a mortar) with a hole through which it is tied to the puppeteer's thumb but concealed from the audience by a curtain. By moving his thumb, and synchronizing the movements of the dolls to his conversation, the puppeteer created an atmosphere of magic, which required much skill and dexterity.[20] Chardin also mentioned the occurrence of puppet-shows, which often were performed in collaboration with jugglers and other similar entertainers. He does not specify the nature of the puppet-show booth, unfortunately.[21]

The other variant was that of using a fixed tent with an opening in front similar to that used by string puppet theater. This was used by a very popular form of glove puppetry theater known as Pahlavan Kachal ("the bald wrestler or hero"), so named because it was the name of its leading character. I will return to this character later, because it was also popular in comic drama. It was allegedly sometimes also called *panj* or 'five' because five puppets constituted the basic cast of the play. It was normally performed during the day. The puppeteer made the head and neck of the puppets (*surat*) from wood, cardboard or rags. He also made their clothes. The handheld puppets only had a head and clothes, because the puppeteer moved them with his fingers. He moved the head with his middle or index finger, and the arms with the thumbs, the ring and small finger. This meant that the puppeteer could only move two puppets at a time. This required a frequent change of puppets, for usually only one or two puppeteers were play-acting. Usually one player (*shagerd*; assistant) was behind the curtain and played two puppets at a time and let them speak. The owner-manager (*ostad*) of the theater stood beside the curtain, or even among the public, and participated actively in the course of events. Musical accompaniment was played on the small hand-held drum (*tonbak*), flute (*ney*) and a string instrument (the *tar* or the *kamancheh*). The basic plot of the plays was always the same. Strictly speaking there was only one play on which the puppeteers made improvisations depending on where they were, the political situation, new events and inventions.[22]

Kachal Pahlavan (meaning the bald wrestler) had no special dress and was the stock-character of puppetry in Iran. His baldness was his trademark. He had received a religious education and he is a major hypocrite and unscrupulous trickster. He acts very piously, is widely read, even a poet. His main occupation is to make a fool of mullahs and to court ladies and sometimes pretty boys. Because of

---

[19] Olearius, Adam. *Vermehrte newe Beschreibung der moscowitischen und persischen Reyse*, ed. D. Lohmeier (Schleswig, 1656 [Tübingen, 1971]), pp. 193-94, 437.

[20] Beyza'i, *Namayesh*, p. 105.

[21] Chardin, *Travels*, p. 203.

[22] Menzel, *Meddah*, p. 32.

his wide reading and pretense piety he gains the trust of the Akhund, and finally, when he is found out, he always gets away.[23]

The beginning of the Kachal Pahlavan puppet-show was announced by a buffoon, who, in front of the puppet-box, directs a small band, of which he himself is a part, consisting of three players: a flute player (*ney*), a player of the drum (*tombak*) and a *tar* (kind of violin) player. The number of puppets is limited. This number depends on the means of the puppeteer. But to give a presentation he needs at least five puppets. Hence the name *panj*, which means five in Persian, and which, according to Thalasso, often replaces the term Kachal to refer to the puppets. These persons are: Kachal Pahlavan, *Shaytan*, *Rustam*, *Akhond*, and *Zan*. To these five puppets, the puppeteer usually adds that of *Osmanli*, the Turk, who plays the role of a butt, just like the Iranian does in the Turkish *Qaragöz* show. Thalasso is the only person who mentions the five characters and the use of the term *panj*, while Menzel rejects that this term was ever used in Iran. Marr, who spent a number of years researching popular theater in Iran around 1920 wrote that he had never heard the term mentioned in that context.[24] In the absence of further data to determine the truth of the matter I have decided to mention Thalasso's account, including his short description of the five main puppets, although his account may not be correct.

> *Shaytan* or the devil, who represents the tempter. He is the symbol of evil, and all his actions aim to make evil triumph. After having aroused a bad desire in Kechel's heart he continues to press his case. He does not let up, and continues to press Pahlavan Kechel to attain his goal, which is to do evil for evil's sake. *Shaytan*'s language like that of Kechel is refined Persian, and, if need be, degenerates in magisterial duplicity.

> *Rustam* is the name of the famous Persian hero, who personifies power and virility. His role consists in giving support to Kechel and to share the women's favors with him.

> The *Akhund* is the village mullah, the semi-theologian. In addition to his religious functions he also is often mayor of the village. He is variously called Hasan Khvajeh or Mehmed Khvajeh. He allows himself to robbed, to have his wife and daughter taken, to be kicked out of his house, not out of stupidity but of the goodness of his heart. His philosophy is counterbalanced by his manias and his important studies. The public is elated when Akhund has been subverted by the smarts of Kechel, and starts

---

[23] Papazian, V. "Teatr v Persii: Iz vospominanij V. Paziana," *Kavkazskij Vestnik* 3/8-9 (Tiflis, 1902), pp. 152-60; Chodzko, *Théatre persan*, pp. xv, xviii (for a description of a play); Thalasso, *Le Théatre persan*, pp. 869.

[24] Menzel, *Meddah*, p. 30; Marr, "Koje-shto," p. 76.

drinking, singing, and dancing, all things that are forbidden in Moslem law, of which he is the upholder.

Zan or the wife, represents all womanhood, and is *Akhund*'s daughter, sometimes also a dancing–girl, or a courtesan without any relationship to *Akhund*. *Zan* is Kechel's object of desire and of *Rustam*'s lust and thus the theatrical story spins around her. *Zan* is innocent and chaste. As a young girl she is chaste; as a wife, she adores her husband and her only purpose is to make him happy. But this modesty and virtue are only the spice in the morsel for the two libertines, who go out of their way to sway her their way. There are some cheeky scenes, with some refined rejoinders in polished, contrived and natty language. Never an indecent word or an obscene gesture, but always innuendos, hints, double meanings, puns which say more than all the coarseness of *Qaragöz*.

The scripts of the puppet shows were never printed. Although somewhat daring, their form never offended the listener. The eyes and ears of the chaste could see and listen to them and take pleasure in it. In Tehran, Shiraz and Tabriz the puppets were not called Kachal Pahlavan, but Shah Selim. The spirit of the two plays is the same, with the difference that Shah Selim puppets instead of being in *baudruche* (gold-beater's skin) were made of wood, and also moved as real marionettes. Kachal Pahlavan was allegedly less popular in Iran than *Qaragöz* was in Turkey. Presentations of Kachal Pahlavan were extremely rare, according to Thalasso, who further maintained that since 1860 this type of theater faded away. In 1904 he wrote that in Tehran and Tabriz there had not been a show since 30 years. The only performer of Shah Selim allegedly had died of cholera in the winter of 1903. There was only one Kachal Pahlavan performer left in Iran, according to Thalasso. Depending on his mood, he shuttled between Isfahan and Yazd, and established his base of operations in a suburb of these two towns, towards New Year (*Nowruz*). Always ambulatory, he installed his small tent, mounted in an eye-wink, in a field, garden, or public place, lighted when needed by some resinous wooden torches. One of the puppeteer's aides, in clown's dress, his face done up with egg-yolk, went through the streets on a donkey, while tapping a small drum, and announced the show. The show lasted about two hours. Usually two to three pieces were played. During intermissions the puppeteer and his aides offered a show of a totally different nature. Thalasso has suggested that the diversions of these intermissions, since half a century, have become so important that they gave birth to comedy (*taqlid*). He further opined that the new nature of this amusement undoubtedly contributed to the artistic decadence of the Kachal Pahlavan, which it was replacing. Given the fact, as I have shown above, that *taqlid* already existed prior to 1800, Thalasso supposition is just that, an unsubstantiated supposition. The puppeteers also gave performances in the surrounding villages. To have the puppeteers at your own house cost only one *tuman* around 1890. The women of the harem saw the show from behind a wooden trellis. Thalasso further remarked that due to lack of operators, Kachal Pahlavan was not, as in the past, invited to private parties such as circumcisions, betrothals, and marriages any more. Comedians with their clowneries had replaced them.[25] As is clear from other authors and Appendix 1, which describes the entertainment during a private party in the 1920s, Thalasso was wrong.

STRING PUPPETS OR MARIONETTES.

A show with marionettes was referred to as *shab-bazi, pardeh-bazi, lo`bat-bazi,* which was performed by a *lo`bat-baz* or a *surat-baz,* both meaning a puppeteer. Puppets were also called *peykar* as well as *surat* or *suvar.*[26] Schafer reported that "Marionette plays are thought to have been brought to Ch`ang-an in the seventh century from Turkestan."[27] Omar Khayyam mentions the existence of the string puppet theater in one of his other quatrains. He used the terms puppet (*lo`bat*) and puppeteer (*lo`bat-baz*) as well as the box (*sanduq*) in which the puppets were stored after the end of the play.[28] There is `Omar Khayyam's verse that states:

> We are but puppets. Heaven is the puppet player
> In the literal, not figurative sense
> We are but here 2-3 days; we have played
> And have returned, one after the other, into the box of Nothingness

It was not Khayyam's intention to tell the reader or listener something about string puppetry, but rather to use it as a similitude for his idea that the existence of this world and its inhabitants is dependent entirely on God's will. The same idea was expressed by his Roman forerunners and his contemporaries who referred to it as *khayal,* as discussed above. Be that as it may, this verse (*mathnavi*) also gives the clue as to the nature of the puppet play referred to. There was the tent or *kheymeh* and the puppet box (*pardehlik*). The tent was generally used to play the puppets during the day. One single player moved the puppets by hand. Nezami Ganjavi wrote:[29]

> There is a puppeteer behind this curtain
> Otherwise, who made all these puppets?

In poems in the *Oshtornameh,* which is attributed to `Attar (d. 1221), the poet has a master puppeteer belonging to a Turkish tribe with had seven paid apprentices, who performed a number of shows (*pardeh-bazi*) using multi-colored dolls (*surat*)

---

[25] Thalasso, *Le théatre persan,* pp. 870-72.
[26] Beyza'i, *Namayesh,* p. 84.
[27] Schafer, *The Golden Peaches,* p. 54.
[28] Beyza'i, *Namayesh,* p. 88.
[29] Nezami Ganjavi, *Nameh-ye Makhzan al-Asrar* (Tehran, 1955), p. 98.

behind a curtain. In another verse `Attar describes a performer manipulating various dolls tied to strings. The theme of the plays is about good and evil; his characters are humans and animals; at the end of the show he puts his puppets in a box. The poet's intention was to present the Turkish puppet-player as a symbol of divine rule over human destiny.[30] The *Bahr al-Fava'id*, written in the mid-twelfth century, states that, "playing the drum, harp, or lute, rope dancing, and puppetry are unlawful, for they amount to self-destruction," thus indicating that all of these arts were practiced.[31] Juvayni mentioned the performance of a troupe from Khitay at the court of Oktay Khan (1227-47):

> Moreover, there had come some puppeteers from Khetay who showed strange Chinese puppets which no one had ever seen before. Among them were imitations of different peoples in which they brought a grey-bearded old man with a turban on his head, and tied to the tail of a horse which pulled him on his face. He asked, 'Whose imitation is this?' They answered, 'It is the imitation of a revolting Muslim whom armies drive out of the cities in this fashion.' He ordered, 'Stop the play.' [...] The sin you committed deserves punishment. But I grant you your lives, and be happy with it, and leave my presence, and from now on do not go after this play.[32]

Rashid al-Din reported its performance as well in 1310.[33] Hafez also refers to the puppet shows and Assar Tabrizi (15th century CE) in one of his *mathnavi*s explicitly mentions the marionette show (*kheymeh shab-bazi*).[34] Around 1500, Hoseyn Va`ez Kashefi mentions that glove puppetry was done during the day and string puppetry at night. He wrote: "What is the special token of puppeteering? Say: The tent (*kheymeh*) and the proscenium (*pishband*). They can perform with the tent by day and the proscenium at night. The trunk (*sanduq*) in front of which they they perform the play is called the proscenium (*pishband*). By day, they move the puppets by hand, and at night, the puppets are moved by strings."[35] The term *pishband* clearly referred to the box in which the puppets were kept after the performance. The fact that the term *kheymeh shab-bazi* also occurs further confirms Kashefi's statement about puppet shows at night.

In the sixteenth century there were many kinds of entertainers in Seistan, amongst whom Mir Hasan *Khayal-baz* (the puppet player) who was peerless in juggling (*sho`bdeh-bazi*) and in archery second to Sa`d Vaqqas. His art was so

---

[30] Beyza'i, *Namayesh*, pp. 89-91. *Osthornameh* ed. Mahdi Mohaqqeq (Tehran, 1962), pp. 20, 171.

[31] Meisami, *The Sea of Virtues*, p. 139.

[32] Joveyni, `Ata al-Molk. *Ketab-e Tarikh-e Jahangosha* ed. Mirza Mohammad Qazvini 3 vols. (London-Leiden, 1916-37), vol. 1, pp. 163-64; Beyza'i, *Namayesh*, p. 92.

[33] Rashid al-Din, *The Successors of Genghis Khan*. Translated by John Andrew Boyle (New York: Columbia UP, 1971), p. 78.

[34] Beyza'i, *Namayesh*, p. 93-94.

[35] Kashefi, *Fotovvat-nameh-ye Soltani*, p. 342.

much appreciated that the local ruler made him a member of his courtly entourage.[36] This confirms other information that entertainers were polyvalent, i.e. they had mastered more than one of the entertaining arts. Just like a dervish could tell epic, religious and ribald stories so could a puppeteer juggle, declaim, act and what not at the same time. Puppeteers also were found at regional courts as well at the court of the king of kings himself. Khan Ahmad Khan of Gilan (ca. 1575), for example, ordered that puppet players (*shab-baz*) be brought from `Iraq and Khorasan to his court.[37]

The Russian merchant Kotov mentioned puppets when he arrived in Qazvin in 1624. "On the *maidan* there are all manner of sports, wrestlers wrestle and puppets dance [my emphasis] and they let out live snakes and carry them in their hands and tell fortunes out of books."[38] Du Mans likewise describes puppet players (*lo`bat-baz*) as part of a larger show by public entertainers. He did not appreciate them very much, because the marionette players, in his opinion, had "rather coarse and vulgar puppets on sticks that they moved to portray various postures and events in accordance with their deformed unpleasant prose." Du Mans had a laugh at his despised subject, nevertheless. He recounted that,

> In 1659 it happened that an Indian walked an elephant over the Meydan who lifted with its trunk both the player and his puppets, uprooting the stakes and the tent and carried it away as would a villager an armful of straw; this made for additional pastime, because it did not cost anything but the preceding show. The poor blighter, feeling himself lifted up with his tent just like a spider with its web, started to fight like a fish in a net and in such a way that he fell on the ground, and then, out of fear, he ran away, and gave more cause to laughter to the spectators than he had done with his marionettes.[39]

Chodzko stressed that the marionette theater was national in nature, and was popular in particular among the Turkic speaking tribes. He further pointed out that the play's main characters loved all good earthly matters; they were big eaters, big drinkers, and *bon vivants*, but they were not bad. He called the marionette show "karaguez" (black eye) and its main hero Kachal Pahlavan.[40] As I have discussed above, other authors have used that term to denote glove puppets.

---

[36] Seystani, *Ehya al-Molk*, p. 254.

[37] Fumeni, *Tarikh*, p. 41; for a picture of a *zurgar*, the strongman and a *kuzehbâz*, the juggler see Dickson and Welch, *Houghton Shahnama*, vol. 1, p. 114, fig. 160.

[38] Kemp, *Russian Travellers*, p. 14; see also Olearius, *Vermehrte newe Beschreibung*, p. 486 (Qazvin).

[39] Du Mans, *Estat de la Perse*, p. 214.

[40] Chodzko, *Théatre Persan*, pp. xix-xv.

Рис. 1.

Рис. 2.

Figure 12: Master puppeteer and his assistant with their tent and puppets (1920s)

Baba Allah (1818-92) the son of an Iranian Minister, wrote in a letter to the Otto-man Soltan `Abd al-`Aziz (1871-76):

> When this slave [i.e. Baba Allah] was a child, and had not reached the age of maturity, his father proposed to the daughter of a rich man from Tehran. As was the custom of that city, they were celebrating for one week. On the last day they said, "Today there will be the play of Shah Soltan Salim," and many of the officials, courtiers and celebrities came.

> This slave was sitting in one of the booths in the building and watched un-til a tent was fixed in the middle of the compound. Humanlike puppets, one handspan tall, started coming out of the tent and calling, "Set the chairs! The king is coming." The other puppets came out and started sweeping, and other puppets began spreading water to settle the dust. The chief herald (*jarchi-bashi*) called everyone to rise for the salute to the king. Then a group with shawls and hats as is the custom of the Persians (*`Ajam*) a group with axes, a group of interior decorators, and the chief executioner (*mir ghazab-bashi*) with sticks and a *falak* came and took positions.

> Then a man with the dignity of a king taking jaunty steps, putting one forward while leaning on the other, came and with full grandeur placed himself in front of the throne. He was sitting down, gunfire and music were heard and smoke surrounded the tent. After the smoke went away, it was noticed that the king was sitting and the ministers, officials, and courtiers were standing in his presence. At this time a thief was brought in. The king ordered that he should be beheaded. Immediately, the execu-tioner cut his neck, and a red liquid that resembled blood gushed forth. Then the king talked with those who were in his presence. At this time news arrived that the subjects near such and such a border had rebelled. Then the king reviewed his army and assigned a few regiments with in-fantry to pacify the rebellion. After a few minutes cannon fire was heard from the back of the tent and they said, "Now the war is on."

> This slave was wondering what was happening. Then the final salute was given and the curtain in front of the tent was dropped. After twenty min-utes, a real person with a box under his arm came out of the tent. I asked him, "What is this box and what are all these objects?" He replied, "All the detailed instruments and object seen, the king, the ministers and offi-cials and the greatness and power that you saw are in this box."[41]

String puppet-shows were performed in a simple small and tight booth made out of four curtains attached to four poles; the entire contraption was called tent (*kheymeh*). The puppeteer stood on an elevated podium that was erected anywhere behind a cur-tain. This seems to have been the general manner of performance during the nineteenth

---

[41] Beyza'i, *Namayesh*, p. 98 quoting *Majmu`eh-ye Alvah-e Mobarakeh* (Cairo, 1920), p. 107-09.

century. Therefore, the term *kheymeh shab-bazi* (evening-tent show) or just *shab-bazi* (evening show) referred to the use of marionettes moved by strings. According to Aubin, *kheymeh shab-bazi* was a recent importation into Iran. Until about 1850 they only knew shadow theater and the Turkish *Qaragöz*. The marionettes allegedly were imported from Kurdistan and adopted by the *lutis*.[42] However, as shown above, marionettes were known in Iran already in early medieval times, if not before.

String puppet shows would mostly be shown in the evenings when the strings attached to the puppets cannot be seen. The number of black strings fixed to the joints of the puppets varied and depended on the complexity of the movements of each one. The main string was attached to the head and shoulders. The strings going to the joints of each puppet were fixed to the small stick that the puppeteer held in his hands. The number of puppets in a show was 70-80. The size of the puppets was from 20 to 35 cm. Most of the puppets had a head made of china; some were made of wood and cloth. The puppeteer himself mostly made the head and neck of the puppets (*surat*) from wood, cardboard or rags. The puppets' clothes were sown at his home.[43]

The performance was on ground level in a large square tent fixed on the ground by ropes fixed with iron stakes. The height of the tent walls was 170-190 cm. The back and the sides of the tent as well as the top have no openings. The front wall facing the audience has an opening along the entire width of 55 cm. The spectators were all sitting on the ground and could not see the players due to the darkness. There was a screen inside the tent at 60 cm from the front wall made of fabric, the height of which was about 80 cm. This screen was covered with white cloth embroidered with colorful silk.[44]

The puppet show took place against the dark background to hide the movement of the strings. The interior of the tent, where the puppeteer was standing, there was a box with the puppets. The audience could not see it, because it was hidden behind the screen. From the front wall to the screen was covered by a piece of cloth over which the show was happening. The puppets were brought to the stage from behind the screen. Here two persons played. The puppeteer was behind the curtain and moved the marionettes and talked. For the convenience of the puppeteer the puppets were hung in the interior of the tent in the order of appearance. During the show a small band was playing consisting of a tambourine player, a drummer, a fiddler and a boy with castanets. The puppeteer inside the booth moved the puppets and talked

[42] Aubin, *La Perse*, p. 234. According to Beyza'i, *Namayesh*, p. 105 the term *kheymeh shab-bazi* is from Isfahan, while the same entertainment was called *Jiji va Yaji* in Shiraz, probably because the player gave the puppets high and shrill voices, almost like a scream.

[43] Shahri, *Tarikh*, vol. 6, p. 37 (with pictures of a performance and of puppets on pp. 44-46); Beyza'i, *Namayesh*, p. 96 (puppets the size of a hand span).

[44] Galunov, R. A. "Kheime shab bazi—persidskii teatr marionetok," *Iran* III, p. 1.

like the dolls and to imitate high-pitched voices he kept a whistle (*pishchik* or *sutak*) in his mouth. As was the case with glove puppets, here also another player, often the owner-manager, sat next to the booth or among the public and played a small drum in the shape of a cup or *tombak*. He also participated actively in the dramatic events by starting a dialogue with the puppets by asking leading questions.

> I saw Morshed Azim play the puppets and Morshed Taqi played the drum and used his voice. A square tent is the puppet-show in the room. The carpet of the planks is the stage. The puppets are moved by strings. Morshed Azim plays the role of the master of the tent where they make the puppets while squatting. He calls them, asks them the reason for their existence, comments on their deeds and gestures. On their behalf the aide replies in a high falsetto voice aided by a whistle in his mouth. Morshed Taqi, aside, plays the drum, marks the rhythm while singing appropriate verses. The verses have been chosen from the well-known *Bayaz* (notebook), and dealt with Shirin and Farhad.[45]

The puppeteers sang romances or *tasnif* during the show that varied in contents. There were folk songs, historic songs, songs of the Tehran red-light district (*shahr-e payeh-now*), and romances that had only been just released. Like in the Iranian theater that used hand-held puppets or Pahlavan Kachal the puppeteers improvised. Words and gestures were characterized by a large measure of indecency. The most well developed part of Iranian puppet theater in terms of technique were dances and acrobatic acts by the puppets, which were much appreciated by the audience.

Every day life themes were represented by the puppet theater in a realistic way. These themes included: dances, very much like Iranian dances for women, the bastinado, participation in mourning processions; somebody who is jumping with a lantern (*fanar*) on his head; or exercises with conical sticks (*zurkhaneh*); or acrobatic exercises with a pole and a bottle; or a wedding; or the delivery of child, etc. The accessories and themes were adapted to current affairs. Galunov saw a Cossack puppet that wore a hat that only had been introduced into the Cossack Brigade three years before. He also saw the shah and diplomats in a toy car. This probably refers to the occurrence of political puppet shows towards the end of Qajar period. The marionettes wore European (English) clothes and also showed Ahmad Shah. The message they wanted to show was that foreigners ran the country. The representation of these scenes was very true to life, and, to be up-to-date, the texts were highly improvised. The language used was rich with indecent puns and vulgarities, and Galunov considered it a wonderful example of popular speech with its phonetic peculiarities.[46]

---

[45] Aubin, *La Perse*, pp. 234-35. Beyza'i, *Namayesh* p. 110 reports that the buffoon put the reed (*safir* or *pustak*) is his mouth and through it he talked.
[46] Galunov, "Kkeime shab bazi," pp. 2-3; Beyza'i, *Namayesh*, p. 98.

The marionettes show was mostly performed in public. A police report of March 25, 1887 stated, "Yesterday near the old Shah `Abdol-`Azim Gate *kheymeh shab-bazi* was performed. There were many spectators"[47] The puppet shows also often were performed in private homes by invitation. They even performed before the shah. E`temad al-Saltaneh noticed in his Diary on April 1, 1886, "To-night they arranged for juggling (*hoqqeh-bazi*) and marionettes (*kheymeh shab-bazi*) for the shah."[48] Our diarist even had a puppet show at his own house. He had never seen it before; everybody of his family showed up. He paid the players 14 *tumans*.[49] `Eyn al-Saltaneh, Naser al-Din Shah's nephew, noted: "Tomorrow I hope they will have *shab-bazi-ye baqqal-bazi*. The next night they had dance, followed by *pahlavan-kachal*; then *baqqal-bazi*."[50]

Apart from the negotiated payment of the puppeteers with the host of the party there was a collection of money from the spectators during the show, and there were several interruptions of the show during which they made a collection. To make the audience pay the puppeteers were very inventive, because people were not very willing to part from their money. For example, the puppeteers collected tips for the driver of the car who drove the shah or the diplomats on the stage. The show was stopped, and the car did not move until the audience showed its generosity. The show also would stop for the umbilical cord to benefit the midwife after the delivery of the baby and the cutting of the cord. There was also a collection after the execution of some complex acrobatic exercises or a good dance.[51]

The *Pahlavan Kachal* show only used nine puppets at most, while the marionette player might use no less than 66 puppets in his Shah Selim play. The plot for the plays was basically the same and simple. It was constantly adjusted to political and social events, the type of public, and always by daily improvisation. The large number of marionette puppets was, of course, much more impressive than the few glove puppets. There were marionettes of acrobats, dervishes, gypsies, wrestlers, ghosts, officials, officers, soldiers, courtiers, Europeans, etc. Invariably Shah Selim or Shah Afzal appeared with envoys, dancers, both male and female. What held all these characters together was a comical situation of fights, punishments, marital and divorce scenes. It was a series of loosely related scenes and did not really have a dramatic presentation and development.[52]

---

[47] Sheikh-Reza'i, and Azari, *Gozareshha*, vol. 1, p. 404 (28 Jomadi II 1304/24 March 1887).

[48] E`temad al-Saltaneh, *Ruznameh*, p. 481.

[49] E`temad al-Saltaneh, *Ruznameh*, p. 646

[50] `Eyn al-Saltaneh, *Ruznameh*, vol. 1, p. 56.

[51] Galunov, "Kheime shab bazi," p. 3.

[52] Menzel, *Meddah*, p. 32; Beyza'i, *Namayesh*, p. 108 also confirms the large number of puppets for the Selim Khan show.

Figure 13: Marionettes (1920s)—1. Sarv-e Naz Khanom with baby; 2. Korapet; 3. Div; 4. Thief; 5. Mobarak; 6. Jew; 7. Pahlavan (see appendix)

The marionette show that Aubin saw in 1907 dealt with two subjects: Soltan Selim and Pahlavan Kachal. The latter's house had been enriched with a new wife, whom a slave had brought from India. The wife is the sister of a *Div*. Furious about this audacity, the latter starts to ensorcel Pahlavan Kachal, but relents when he promises to repent. Pahlavan Kachal waiting for a favorable occasion then strangles the *Div*. Seven of the *Div*'s brothers share the same fate. The wife weeps because of the loss of her family; she consoles herself by marrying Pahlavan Kachal; a mollah draws up the marriage act; the wife becomes pregnant, the child is born; end of story.

The play about the court of Soltan Selim that Aubin saw performed offers a more varied spectacle, but no real plot. Prior to the appearance of the marionettes Morshed Taqi started to sing verses of Hafez, evocating the idea of the unity of God. Then the first marionette presents itself. "Greetings to everyone. Greetings to you," replies Morshed Azim, the puppeteer. "Who are you?" I am the herald of the camp of Soltan Selim Yemeni. It is his command that we should not make any noise, because he is coming. Guards placed themselves at the entrance of the camp and Cossacks were stationed at the entry of the harem. Water carriers sprinkled the tent; servants swept it. Then arrived the members of the royal household; mace-bearers, porters, valets (*farrash*), the general of the infantry, the commander of the Turkish soldiers, the musicians (*naqqarachi*s), the flute players, the standard-bearer, the royal messengers, and then the Soltan himself accompanied by the ambassadors of Turkey and Russia. Next the amusements began, showing wrestlers, monkey players, guitar players, acrobats, dancers, Kurds, Turks, Afghans, Arabs and a few Europeans.

The *luti*, the monkey player, complained about the manner in which his royal salary had been fixed. "The shah nevertheless has given you a present," said Morshed Azim. "Yes," replied the *luti*, "a note drawn on Najis al-Tojjar (the unclean of the merchants) who took a 10% fee." The Soltan immediately had the guilty merchant appear before him; the *farrash*es put his feet to a wooden bar to give him the bastinado. This act of justice was immediately applied. Then thieves were placed in front of the mount of a cannon. A hunter brought a sheep; the chief equerry brought a horse. The puppets were very ingenious and their articulations were sometimes excessive, according to Aubin. Many more appeared, including a *div*. It was a large puppet with white feathers on its head and very large arms. "Who are you? I am the *div* of the desert. What do you want to do? I want to grab all those who have betrayed the trust of the shah." The *div* then started to grab several persons who had not acted well in the interest of the shah. Once the clean-up was accomplished, the morality of the play, the *div* prostrated himself before the shah and rose into the air. End of the play.[53]

The puppet show felt the heavy hand of the Pahlavi regime just like other forms of popular theater, for it frowned upon the satirical and vulgar nature of this art form, which did not fit the modernizing image that the new regime wanted to project.

---

[53] Aubin, *La Perse*, pp. 235-37. For a description of another, but similar, Soltan Selim play see Beyza'i, *Namayesh*, p. 98.

Puppet shows therefore were forced to perform in private homes, because police regulations made public performances difficult.[54] As a result, puppet shows, like so many other forms of traditional culture faded away. It was still performed, but with ever declining frequency and geographic distribution. Between 1941 and about 1950, a marionette show (*kheymeh shab-bazi*) was still played at a fixed locality such as the Municipal Coffeehouse (*kafeh-ye shahrdari*) in Tehran.[55] But that was their swan song, for puppet shows became only a vague memory. In a recent book, for example, the author confuses *pahlavan kachal* and *kheymeh shab-bazi* with monkey and bear players.[56] According to Rezvani, by 1960 string puppet theater had been forgotten in Iran and he hoped for its revival.[57] His wish came true as soon as he had published his book. For in 1962, the Fine Arts Administration staged the first performance of puppet theater on Iranian TV with Marina Khodadad, Mohta-ram Sobhi, and Shahla Hirbod under the direction of Parviz Kardan.[58] Puppet theater was also again performed at the major art festivals in Iran. From about 1970, there was a Puppet Theater Course, held by Oscar Batek at the Dramatic Arts College in Tehran. It also trained directors of theater for children. The Faculty of Fine Arts in Tehran University still does so and so do all major universities.[59] Puppet theater is still supported by the government, now of the Islamic Republic of Iran, which, in collaboration with UNESCO, organizes a bi-annual International Puppet-Drama Festival in Tehran.

---

[54] Menzel, *Meddah*, p. 31; Galunov, "Neskol'ko slov," p. 309/
[55] Beyza'i, *Namayesh*, p. 110 f.
[56] Soltani, *Joghrafiya*, vol. 1, p. 352.
[57] Rezvani, *Le théatre*, p. 130.
[58] Echo of Iran, *Iran Almanac* 1963, p. 470.
[59] [http://www.qoqnoos.com/body/arosak/vafadari.y/resume.htm]

Рис. 1.

Рис. 2.

Figure 14: Marionettes (1920s)

CHAPTER THREE

NARRATIVE DRAMA OR DRAMATIC STORYTELLING

INTRODUCTION

Narrative drama is represented by the minstrel or *goshan* tradition and includes both secular and religious narration. The bard-minstrel occupied an important place at the court of pre-Islamic kings. There were already storytellers in Iran during the Median and Achaemenid period, many of whom were itinerant. They narrated stories and legends about gods and heroes. Ctesias mentioned the Median bard Angares who was invited by the Median king Astyages to sing at a banquet and then foretold that his successor would be Cyrus, the Persian.[1] Under the Parthians, the *goshan* (storytellers and minstrels) would sing and narrate epic tales such as that of the "Memorial of Zarer" or the "Death of Siyavosh." Both stories, as has been pointed out by Yarshater, like the later Islamic passion play (*ta`ziyeh-khvani*), had the basic elements of "a devoted warrior, inspired by the fire of his faith, faces a large army and a treacherous adversary. He is killed in battle and he is bitterly lamented. His death, however, fulfills a prophecy."[2] What is known about the Siyavosh cult confirms that songs were sung in his praise as well as to mourn him. In the tenth century CE, "The people of Bokhara have many a lament (*nowheh*) on the slaying of Siyavosh, which is known in all regions, and the minstrels have made them into song which they chant, and the singers (*qavvalan*) call them 'the weeping of the Magi' (*geristen-e Magi*)."[3] These mourning rites were also held in Khvorezm. Other sources also confirm the religious character of the Siyavosh cult, which was still in existence well into the tenth century CE.[4] In Parthian and Sasanid Armenia, a similar practice of funerary rites, lamentations for the dead and eulogies of their heroic deeds existed and these lamentations and praises were sung by a *voghbergak* or a *dzainarku-gusan*.[5]

Thus, storytelling and music seem to have gone naturally together. The *goshan* or minstrel of Parthian times was entertainer to king and commoner alike and

---

[1] Athenaus, *Detpnosophstae*, pp. 633-34; Ghirshman, *Parthes et Sassanides*, p. 274.
[2] Yarshater, Ehsan. "Ta`ziyeh and Pre-Islamic Mourning Rites in Iran," Peter J. Chelkowski, *Ta`ziyeh: Ritual and Drama in Iran* (New York, 1979), p. 90. [88-94] On the 'Memorial of Zarer' see Boyce, Mary. "Ayādgār ī Zarērān," *Encyclopedia Iranica*.
[3] Narsakhi. *The History of Bukhara*. Translated by Richard N. Frye (Cambridge, 1954), p. 23.
[4] Yarshater, "Ta`ziyeh," p. 91.
[5] Goyan, *Teatr*, vol. 1, pp. 349f.

performed at high days; he was eulogist, satirist, storyteller, musician, recorder of past achievements, and commentator of his own times."[6] Under the Sasanids the minstrels likewise were held in very high regard at court, and were always present. "They were called on at the discretion of the xurrambash."[7] According to al-Nadim, the rulers were regaled with stories, in particular from *Hazar Afsan*, a Sasanid prose work that formed the basis for the later *Thousand and One Nights*.[8] The stories of the feats of Rostam also were known in Armenia, for Moses Khorenats'i mentions Rostam without even feeling the need to explain who he was. This indicates that although his work dates from the eighth century that these tales of Rostam were already well-known in Armenia prior to that time.[9]

Figure 15: Mourning ceremony of Siyavosh [?] or a real person. Fresco from Panjkent (Khvarezm) 8th century CE. Note the uprooting of plants and the cutting of hair.

[6] Mary Boyce, "The Parthian gosan professional singer and the Iranian Minstrel Tradition," *Journal of the Royal Asiatic Society*, 1957, vol. Pt 1 & 2," pp. 18, 25; see also Ibid., "Some Remarks on the Transmission of the Kayanian Heroic Cycle," *Serta Cantabrigensia*, Studies presented to the XXIII International Congress of Orientalists, Mainz 1954, pp. 45-52; Ibid., "Zariadres and Zarer," *BSOAS* 17/4 (1955), pp. 463-77; Nöldeke, Th. *The Iranian National Epic or THE SHAHNAMAH*. Translated by L. Th. Bogdanov (Philadelphia, 1979), pp. 23-25.

[7] Boyce, "The Parthian gosan," pp. 18, 25.

[8] Al-Nadim. *The Fihrist of al-Nadim. A Tenth Century Survey of Muslim Culture*. Translated by B. Dodge 2 vols. (New York: Columbia UP, 1970), vol. 2, p. 714.

[9] Khorenats'i, Moses. *History of the Armenians*. Translated by Robert W. Thomson (London-Cambridge: Harvard UP, 1978), p.141.

The Iranian epic tradition with its narration of tales such as that of Siyavosh, Zarer, and Rostam was reinforced by the development of Islamic epic story telling. After the prophet Mohammad's death in 632 CE, his companions and early followers provided informal religious education through preaching and storytelling (*qāss*, pl. *qossās*), which was an Islamicized form of the practice of pre-Islamic Arab poets to rouse battle fever through rhymed prose (*saj`*). These companions and followers used Bible stories and legends to explain the Koran and provide moral guidance to the believers, especially the new ones. These storytellers seem to have first been observed during the strife between `Othman and `Ali (ca. 650 CE); the latter allegedly even banned them from the mosques.[10] Although the storytellers (*qass*) later became known in Persian as *qesseh-gu*, i.e. a narrator of imaginary and frivolous stories and tales, this was clearly not the case originally. The narration of Moslem religious stories became a profession after the caliph Mo`aviyeh's reign. In general this kind of religious narration was rejected by Moslem orthodoxy.[11]

Despite this religious opposition public demand for religious narration and epic storytelling was stronger than religious strictures. In the Islamic period the storyteller was known under various names, but generically as *naqqal*, *qavval*, *ravi*, and *qesseh-gu*. Dramatic storytelling concerns the telling of a story, which is history-based or is just a mythical tale or legend. It was done either in verse or prose and accompanied by gestures and movements appropriate to the events related. The purpose was to captivate and arouse the audience and transport them for a moment to ancient heroic times and events. In early Islamic times this art form was given impetus by sermons and public recitations, be it now in Islamized form. Ebn Qoteybah (213-267 Q) in his `*Oyun al-Akhbar* wrote in the ninth century CE that: "In Merv we had a story teller (*qass* or a *qesseh-gu*), who told stories and made us weep; then he took his *tanburi* from his breast and started to play and said: *Apa*, with all this grief we need some fun."[12] This sudden transformation from a tragic dramatic situation to a lighter, if not outright comical one, continued to be a characteristic of tragic religious drama in Iran (see chapter five). It was also a phenomenon that was found in other cultures, both in Europe and Asia. It seems to have been a natural step for elegists and *rowzeh-khvan*s to begin recitation of popular drama after having finished their

[10] Moroni, *Iraq*, p. 437; see also Pellat, Ch. "Qissa," *Encyclopedia of Islam²*. The reason for this may have been *sura* 31:6-7 which states: "There is one person who purchases frivolous stories so as to lead people away from the path of God." The person referred to may be a certain al-Harith who told stories about the Iranian kings in Mecca in the early 7th century CE. See Yamamoto, Kumiko. *The Oral Background of Persian Epics: Storytelling and Poetry* (Leiden: Brill, 2003), pp. 56-57 and literature cited.
[11] Ja`fariyan, Rasul. "Naqsh-e Qessehpardazan dar Tarikh-e Eslam," *Keyhan-e Andisheh* 30 (Khordad-Tir 1369/1990), p. 121; Moqaddasi, Mohammad b. Ahmad. *Ahsan al-Taqasim fi ma`rifat al-aqalim* (Leiden, 1967) pp. 236, 182, 327.
[12] Beyza'i, *Namayesh*, p. 61; see also Bahar, Mohammad Taqi. *Sabkshenasi ya tarikh-e tattavor-e nathr-e farsi* 3 vols. (Tehran, 1331/1952), vol. 2, pp. 133-34.

threnodies. In Turkey, this dramatic art form became known as *maddah* or eulogy, and in Iran as *qavvali* and later more often as *naqqali*. To differentiate between the various kinds, or rather specializations within the profession of narrator these were known by distinct terms. The two main categories of this dramatic art form are: (a) *naqqali* or *qavvali*, i.e. the narration of epic stories, and (b) *marthiyeh-khvani* or the narration of religious epic stories. Picture narration (*pardeh-dari* or *shamayel-gardani*) was a special variety of both art forms, while it also happened that the same narrator told both secular and religious epic stories.

NON-RELIGIOUS EPIC DRAMA OR *NAQQALI*

There were two kinds of performers: (i) the epic narrator (*naqqal, qavval*) and (ii) the short storyteller (*qesseh-gu*). The difference between the two is one of subject matter, technique, and objective, and the same person might perform either one. The epic storyteller had a repertory of heroic and romantic epic tales (*Eskander-nameh*; *Rustam-nameh*; *Shah-nameh*; *Romuz-e Hamzeh*; *Hoseyn-e Kord*, etc.) the telling of which might take a few days, if not a few weeks. The *qesseh-gu* only told short stories, just like the elegist (*maddah*). Those narrators telling the stories of the *Shah-nameh* were called *shahnameh-khvan*. When a storyteller was specialized in another epos such as the *Romuz-e Hamzeh* he was called *hamzeh-khvan*. The latter, therefore, was not a different kind of epic narrator, just one with a different tale to tell. The term *shahnameh-khvan* already occurred around the year 1,000 CE while a related term *karnameh-khvan* refers to the teller of the *Karnameh*.

According to Hanaway, "Story tellers used the non-metrical form, although earlier versified forms also existed as is clear from the Firuz Shah-nameh. The popular romances are linear, open-ended, flexible, and unsophisticated in structure." Because of this the stories were both often anecdotal in nature and very conventional as to themes. Also, there was no convention concerning pacing, climax, etc. These characteristics made the role of the story teller crucial. Given the conventional nature of the stories and the fact that most people had heard them before just telling the stories would scarcely keep people's attention. The story therefore was but a basic outline of the plot, the characters, the setting and the motivation, and the ending. George Orwell's maxim that the best books are the ones that tell us what we already know also holds for stories. Thus, the challenge for the storyteller was to flesh out the basic story and bring it to life by introducing sub-plots and new characters.[13] The best of the storytellers were indeed able to captivate and transport their audience by their art and skill, such that even foreigners who did not even know Persian fell under their spell. Malcolm told the following in this regard:

---

[13] See for a detailed discussion Hanaway, William L. "Formal Elements in the Persian Popular Romances," in *Review of National Literatures—Iran*, vol. 2/1 (1971), p. 142 and Yamamoto, *The Oral Background*, pp. 20-52.

Derveish Suffer, of Shiraz, is one of the best narrators of stories, as well as reciter of verses, that I have known in Persia. In 1800, when he was one day on the point of commencing a tale, two gentlemen rose to go away. On seeing him look disappointed, I observed to him, that the cause of their wishing to depart was owing to their inability to enjoy his story, from being unacquainted with the language in which it was to be told. "I beg they will stay,' he exclaimed, 'and you will see my power will reach them in spite of their want of knowledge of Persian.' They remained; and the changes of his countenance, and the different tones in which he spoke, had the effect he expected. They were delighted with the humorous part of his narrative, and moved with the pathetic.[14]

There was no interruption in story telling because of the fall of the Sassanid Empire and the slowly changing religious situation. There are unfortunately only scattered references to storytellers in Persian texts before the Safavid period. Mas`udi wrote in the tenth century CE, "In Baghdad, there was a street storyteller who amused the crowd with all sorts of tales and funny stories. His name was Ibn Maghazili. He was very amusing and could not be seen or heard without provoking laughter. As he told his stories, he added many jokes which would have made a mourning mother laugh and would have amused a serious man."[15] Beyhaqi condemned popular storytellers because they related tales of absurdities to please only the ignorant.

Most of the commoners are such that they prefer the absurdly improbable such as tales of *div*s, *pari*s and ghouls in a desert, mountain or sea. A fool gathers an audience (*hengameh sazad*) and others like himself come around and he says, 'In such and such a sea I saw an island and landed there with five hudred men. We cooked a meal and put a pan on the fire. When the fire flared up its tongue touched the ground, the island moved away. We saw it was a fish'; 'In a mountain I saw this or that,' and 'an old sorceress turned a man into an ass and another sorceress put ointment into his ears to change him back into a man' and such a kind of fables that would put the innocent to sleep when told at night.

What Beyhaqi referred to was probably a *qesseh-gu* who told fables (*khorafat*) rather than a *naqqal*, for he also without critcism relates the telling of epic and heroic tales. They seem to have been of a lesser station than poets, but nevertheless were part of the court of the Buyid and the Ghaznavid court. In fact, one of the storytellers named Karasi was such a favorite of Soltan Mahmud that a night he preferred to listen to Karasi's stories rather than those of the poet `Onsori. Storytellers (*mohaddeth*) performed at religious festivals and state banquets and were

[14] Malcolm, *History*, vol. 2, p. 553.
[15] Wiet, Gaston. *Baghdad: Metropolis of the Abbasid Caliphate* (Norman, Oklahoma UP, 196?), chapter 5 [http://www.fordham.edu/halsall/med/wiet.html].

always in attendance of the ruler, in case they were needed, just as the musicians were. They also performed privately for the shah just prior to his withdrawal for the night.[16]

Initially the repertoire of the tellers of epic tales was mainly pre-Islamic in nature. According to al-Nadim the following epic tales were told in Iran during the tenth century: "*Rustum and Asfandiyadh; Bahram Chubin; al-Karnamak*, about the life of Anushirwan; *Dara and the Golden Idol; the Book of Lords (Khuday namah); Bahram and Narsi; Abushirwan*."[17] Later Islamicized epic tales were added to the repertory such as that of the "Travails of Abu Moslem", the leader who began the revolt against the Ommayad caliphs and who made it possible for the `Abbasids to replace them. The original *Abu Moslem-nameh* is ascribed to Abu Taher Tusi, one of the storytellers (*qesseh-khvan*) of Mahmud of Ghazna.

Thus, epic storytelling tradition which had been very strong in pre-Islamic Iran continued to be so after the Islamization of the country. Like the Sasanid kings the new Islamic rulers of Iran also amused themselves with the performances of minstrels, singers and musicians. This model withstood the test of the ages, for the manner in which polite and popular society enjoyed itself was basically the same and hardly changed until the mid-twentieth century. Because the epic storyteller was a person of some education and with literary skills, and, in a mainly oral society, the repository of ancient traditions and stories, he was appreciated at all levels of society. In fact, what we know about these epics is partly due to these minstrels through the intermediary of poets and prose writers. The latter, therefore, acknowledge their debt to these storytellers. In some cases they even mention their names.

Rudaki called the storytellers *ravi* and so did Nezami `Aruzi, who mentions a *ravi* of Ferdowsi, and Beyza'i is correct to call him the first known *shahnameh-khvan*.[18] Other Iranian legends, tales and histories were also told, because these had been preserved by the rural landowner (*dehqan*) class. Asad-e Tusi in his *Gershapnameh*, Nezami Ganjavi in his *Leyla va Majnun, Khosrow va Shirin* and *Eskandernameh*, Fakhr al-Din As`ad-e Gorgani's *Vis va Ramin* and Tarsusi's *Darabnameh* at several occasions state that they got their stories from the landed gentry (*dehqan*s) and/or narrators of stories (*raviyan-e akhbar*). The role of story tellers and of their preservation of the epic tradition in Iran is still an unresolved issue, however. Ferdowsi, the versifier of the greatest Iranian epic, the

---

[16] Yamamoto, *The Oral Background*, pp. 54-55, 58-59 citing Beyhaqi, Abu'l-Fazl Mohammad b. Hoseyn. *Tarikh-e Beyhaqi*. ed. Fayyazi (Mashhad, 1340/1971).

[17] Al-Nadim. *The Fihrist*, vol. 2, p. 716; see further Yamamoto, *The Oral Background*, p. 57, n. 17.

[18] Beyza'i, *Namayesh*, p. 62; Nezami al-Samarqandi. *Ketab-e Chahar Maqaleh* ed. Mohammad Qazvini (Berlin: Iranschär, 1927), pp. 10, 78

Shah-nameh, states that many of his stories were collected from landowners (*dehqan*s) of whom he named a few. He also, however, mentions that he relied on written sources. Amin Mansur `Abdol-Razzaq, governor of Tus (ca. 957 CE) instructed his vizier to compile a *Shahnameh* to which end he sent for wise men from the various towns of Khorasan and to bring all four of them together so that they would produce their books (*namehha*) and epics (*karnamehha*) of the ancient Iranian kings. This book was probably Ferdowsi's main source of inspriration; together with other materials discussed by Yamamoto they seem to indicate that written sources were also used to compose the epic tales in Islamic times.[19] It seems therefore likely that both oral and written sources were used by these artists, the more so since both made use of formulaic and thematic structure as a literary device.[20]

In 1189 CE the *Samak-e `Ayyar* was collected and written down by Faramarz son of Khodadad b. `Abdollah al-Kateb al-Arrajani; his source probably was a storyteller (*ravi-ye qesseh*) named Sadaqeh b. Abu'l-Qasem Shirazi. The style of the text makes it clear that it was written to be recited. For example, many words were written as they were pronounced in popular usage rather than in the literate form, which is still a characteristic of recitation. From this book it is also clear that the storytellers asked and received money from the audience.[21] `Obeyd-e Zakani also mentioned storytellers as did some other well-known poets, amongst whom Hafez.[22] In fact, the designation dervish often was the synonym for storyteller. For example, Mowlana Dervish Divaneh Sham`-riz was a storyteller known for his sarcastic wit and very popular in Herat.[23] When discussing picture narration in what follows I demonstrate the important role that dervishes played in religious and secular epic recitation.

Above I stated that with the establishment of Shi`ism as the state religion in Iran elegies and lamentations became an important part of the diffusion of Shi`ite ritual through the telling of stories. One of the stories told was that of Abu Moslem, the

---

[19] Beyza'i, *Namayesh*, p. 63; Yamamoto, *The Oral Background*, p. 4.

[20] See on the issue of the oral or written origin of the various tales as well as the technique of story telling Yamamoto, *The Oral Background*, pp. 2-19, and in particular 60-80. As to the applicability of the oral-formulaic theory, as developed by Lord, A.B. *Singer of Tales* (Cambridge, 1991), see also Benson, I.D. *The literary character of anglo-saxon formulaic poetry* (n.p., 1966), p. 81 who argues that the application of the oral-formulaic theory is not as universal as suggested, because ancient traditional literature like oral tradition also consists of a large number of similar 'formulas.'

[21] Safa, Fathollah. *Tarikh-e Adabbiyat dar Iran* 3 vols. (Tehran: Ebn Sina, 1339/1960), vol. 2, pp. 988-90; Faramarz Fils de Khodadad. *Samak-e Ayyar* translated by Razavi, Frédérique (Paris: Maisonneuve, 1972), p. 8. Beyza'i, *Namayesh*, p. 64.

[22] Beyza'i, *Namayesh*, p. 67.

[23] Vasefi, Zeyn al-Din Mahmud. *Badaye` al-Vaqaye`* 2 vols. ed. A. N. Boldyreva, (Moscow, 1961), vol. 1, p. 249f.

leader of the revolt against the Ommayads in 750. Because Shah Esma`il I wanted to temper the extremism of his Turkoman supporters he invited Sheykh `Ali Karaki, a strict orthodox Emami scholar from Lebanon, to Iran. As one of the results of the latter's influence, the narration of extremist *Abu Moslem-Nameh*s was banned under Esma`il I (r. 1501-24) and Tahmasp I (r. 1524-76), but increasingly so in the seventeenth century. Sheykh `Ali Karaki issued a religious injunction (*fatva*) against those believing in and feeling attracted to Abu Moslem, which injunction ended with the exhortation: "So do not listen to the false stories about Abu Moslem, for these stories have been concocted by the *qesseh-khvan*s." In fact, these stories about Abu Moslem were ascribed to "the Sunni-tempered fairy tale tellers," who were said to have made them up prior to the rise of Shah Esma`il I. Due to the unsettled political times it was impossible to enforce these bans, and religious stories including those of Abu Moslem continued to be told.[24]

These stories about Abu Moslem and Mohammad b. Hanifah had thrived prior to the rise of the Safavids and were the standard fare offered by dervishes of the Safavid order throughout the reign of the Safavid dynasty.[25] Many of the Arab olama who had come to Iran were against dervishes and their storytelling, but other olama were not. Because the Safavid shahs did not really need their Sufis anymore they did nothing to protect them, in fact, they often supported their suppression.[26] The antis continued to state that storytelling, in particular of the *Abu Moslem-Nameh*, was forbidden (*haram*). These included also heavyweights such as Mir Damad and Sheikh Baha'i. There were, of course, also many leading olama who disagreed and who praised the virtues of such religious epic stories and their narration.[27] One of them was Mohammad Taqi Majlesi, the father of the even more famous son, Mohammad Baqer Majlesi. In response to a question whether it was permitted or not to go and see a show of entertainers (*tamasha-ye ma`rekeh-giran*) and listen to the stories of storytellers (*qesseh-khvanan*) and eulologists (*maddahan*) he wrote: "to look at the dancing of boys and the curly haired ones without apprehension is forbidden; other forms of show are of great apprehension and we have it [on the authority of] a link of sheikhs that they all are forbidden, except for the stories of the eulogizers where lie and truth are mixed and where it is not clear where the truth lies and what is false. The former should be avoided and the rest some consider as forbidden, while others do not. Proving this [i.e. what is false] is

---

[24] Babayan, Kathryn. *The Waning of the Qizilbash: The Spiritual and the Temporal in Seventeenth Century Iran* (unpublished dissertation, Princeton University, 1993), pp. 202-03; Zoveyri, Mahjub. *Abu Moslemnameh va naqsh-e an dar tarikh-e ejtema`i-ye `asr-e Safavi* (Tehran, 1382/2003), pp. 143-55.

[25] Zarrinkub, `Abdol-Hoseyn. *Donbaleh-ye josteju dar tasavvof dar Iran* (Tehran, 1357/1978) pp. 228-29.

[26] Ja`fariyan, Rasul. "Qesseh-khvani dar Iran `asr-e Safaviyyeh," in Ibid., *Safaviyyeh dar `arseh-ye din, farhangi va siyasat*. 3 vols. (Qom, 1379/2000), vol. 2, pp. 861-62. [858-78]

[27] Ja`fariyan, "Qesseh-khvani," vol. 2, pp. 862-73.

difficult for any one, and God knows best."[28] However, most leading olama seem to have been against the storytelling. Mohammad Baqer Majlesi forbade story telling, citing Traditions and Sayings, because they were inventions and lies, which were forbidden (*haram*) in and by themselves. He declared in particular the popular *Hamzeh-nameh* to be a pack of lies. Mohammad Baqer Majlesi made, however, an exception for the *Shah-nameh* and other epic tales.[29] The writings of the olama to ban storytelling tell a story by itself, to wit, that storytelling was thriving and very popular.

More favored than even the *Abu Moslem-nameh* was the *Shah-nameh*, the national epos as versified by Ferdowsi. It generated separate categories of epic narrators such as the *shahnameh-khvan*. These narrators were very popular, and the best of them had their own poetic outbursts and were deemed to be of sufficient quality to be collected in Nasrabadi's anthology and to be listed among the notable people of Shah Tahmasp I's reign. He wrote:

> Of the class of professional storytellers, Shah-nameh reciters, and the like, there was a considerable number, but I will just mention two or three: Mowlana Heydar Qesseh-khvan, who was unequalled in his art; Mowlana Mohammad Khorshid Esfahani, also a good story teller, but not better than Mowlana Heydar; Mowlana Fathi, the brother of the preceding, unrivaled Shah-nameh reciter whose peerless voice carried-without exaggeration-for several miles, without any loss of quality.[30]

Shah `Abbas also liked the recitation of the royal epic or *Shahnameh-khvani*. He invited Molla Bikhodi Jonabadi, who was one of the best *Shahnameh* narrators, to perform for him at court. Shah `Abbas I settled an annual income of 40 *tuman*s on him in appreciation, which was a considerable sum in those days.[31] One of the most famous ones was `Abdol-Razzaq Qazvini a calligrapher who had a salary of 300 *tuman*s per year. Storytellers not only performed for the elite, but also in the streets and squares and other public places, in particular the coffeehouses, which came into being in the beginning of the seventeenth century. Both epic narration (*naqqali*) and story-telling in the praise of Imam `Ali (*maddah-e `Ali*) were performed in coffeehouses. The storytellers would be standing on a four-legged pedestal while reciting or they recited with a stick (*metraq, chubdasti*) in their hand, possibly to point to a painted screen with pictures that they used.[32] Molla Mo'men a.k.a. Yekeh Savar was a famous *Shahnameh-khvan* and was idiosyncratic in that he

---

[28] Ja`fariyan, "Qesseh-khvani," vol. 2, p. 873.

[29] Ja`fariyan, "Qesseh-khvani," vol. 2, pp. 874-75.

[30] Monshi, *Tarikh*, vol. 1, p. 191; Savory, *History*, vol. 1, p. 282

[31] Nasrabadi, *Tadhkereh*, p. 307.

[32] Falsafi, Nasrollah. "Tarikh-e Qahveh va Qahvehkhanrh dar Iran" in Ibid., *Chand Maqaleh-ye Tarikhi va Adabi* (Tehran 1342/1963), p. 297-81; Ma`ani, Ahmad Golchin. *Karvan-e Hend* (Mashhad, 1369/1991) vol. 1, p. 305 (Jamshid *qesseh-khvan*).

dressed in a printed calico overcoat with a *tomar* on his head when he came to the coffeehouse and recited the *Shah-nameh*. Whatever he earned he gave to the dervishes after deduction of his expenses. Moqima Zargar started out as a *Shahnameh-khvan*, which was also his father's profession, but later became a goldsmith.[33] There also were storytellers who were specialized in other epics, such as the *Hamzeh-nameh* and were therefore known as *Hamzeh-khvan*. Some knew both epics. Hoseyna, who started as a dervish and then became an excellent guitar (*tar*) player, was a good *Shahnameh-* and *Hamzeh-khvan*.[34] Another specialty was an *Eskander-khvan*.[35] Anandraj'e Dictionary lists also the *Sowgand-nameh* by Mir Hashem Qesseh-khvan.[36] A *daftar-khvan* was somebody who just read stories to their patrons at court and thus was not a narrator like the others who have been mentioned.[37] All these storytellers were listed in Nasrabadi's anthology of Safavid poets, indicating that they also had poetic qualities, of which he provides the reader with some samples. Epic narrators were also mentioned in other literary works, such as the *Divan-e Khaki*[38] as well as in the literary *Shahr-e Ashub* genre. Mirza Taher Vahid, a major representative of this genre, said of the storytellers in his *Divan-e Rezvan*: "How can the kindness of the storyteller be described? His horoscope has made him the king of the empire of kindness."[39] They also performed in the provinces such as in Shamakhi in 1637, when a storyteller performed during the *Nowruz* celebration.[40]

Story tellers not only performed in coffeehouses, but apparently also in a kind of opium den, at least that is suggested by Nasrabadi, when he writes that Mir Zahir was a story teller (*qesseh-khvan*) who performed in a *koknar-khaneh*, i.e. an establishment where people drank a beverage made of the skin of the poppy plant (*koknar*).[41] Fryer, in the mid-1670s, reported that they told epic stories with the help of pictures. Also that in addition to epics they had a book like Aesop's fables, which was preferred to all others. "They have Romances of Famous heroes and their Deeds; among which are pleasant Rancounters, Huntings, Love-Intrigues, Banquetings, descriptions of Flowers and delightful groves, emphatically set down, with Cuts and Pictures represented lively enough, would their colours endure; for which Skill, otherwise than for hitting the Life, their Limmers are to be reckon'd defective,

---

[33] Nasrabadi, *Tadhkereh*, pp. 145, 357, 379.

[34] Nasrabadi, *Tadhkereh*, p. 401 (Mirza Mohammad).

[35] Ja`fariyan, "Qesseh-khvani," vol. 2, p. 859.

[36] Bayza'i, *Namayesh*, p. 71.

[37] Ja`fariyan, "Qesseh-khvani," vol. 2, pp. 859-60. Timur, who was illiterate, "loved the reading of annals and histories ... in Persian. [...] His reader of histories and annals was Maulana Abid." Arabshah, *Tamerlane*, pp. 299, 312.

[38] Ivanow, W. *An Abbreviated Version of the Diwan-e Khaki* (Bombay, 1933), p. 12.

[39] Keyvani, *Artisans*, p. 290.

[40] Olearius, *Vermehrte Newe Beschreibung*, p. 440 (*kasiechuan* or *qesseh-khvan*).

[41] Nasrabadi, *Tadhkereh*, p. 414; Gemelli-Careri, *Giro*, vol. 2, p. 198.

not knowing how to mix their Colours."[42] This type of picture narration was the same that I discussed in the preceding, but with the emphasis on the narration of religious epical stories.

What was new during the Safavid period was the composition and their narration of epic stories about Shah Esma'il I and Shah Tahmasp I. These stories were about their life, their wars, and their great deeds. Itinerant storytellers, who also performed in coffeehouses, told these stories.[43] Gemelli-Careri wrote that he went to a coffeehouse in 1694 to rest and have a smoke. He saw a mullah, but without the usual robe and bareheaded, who started in a serious voice to recite the threnodies of Shah 'Abbas the Great and Shah Safi I. He praised their actions and wars up to the heavens; he then became so animated and worked up that he cried like a madman or at least like an animal, in particular when he narrated their feats of arms, which earned him applause from the audience who beat their hands and stamped their feet. This performance lasted two hours, after which the mullah received alms of one or two *qazbegi*s (small copper coin) of each listener and went home with a total of two *'abbasi*s (small silver coin).[44]

In the Safavid era the shah also had his court storyteller, and often more than one. In the Qajar period there also was such a royal narrator. According to Malcolm:

> In the Court of Persia there is always a person who bears the name of 'story-teller to his majesty;' and the duties of his office require a man of no mean requirements. The Persians, though passionately fond of public exhibition, have none that merit the name of theatrical entertainments: but, though strangers to the regular drama, the frame of their stories are often dramatic; and those whose occupation is to tell them, sometimes display so extraordinary a skill, and such varied powers, that we can hardly believe, while we look upon their altered countenances, and listen to their changed tones, that it is the same person, who at one moment relates, in his natural voice, a plain narrative, then speaks in the hoarse and angry tone of offended authority, and next subdues the passions he had excited by the softest sounds of feminine tenderness. But the art of relating stories is, in Persia, attended both with profit and reputation. Great numbers attempt it, but few succeed. It requires considerable talent, and great study. None can arrive at eminence in this line except men of cultivated taste and retentive memory. They must not only be acquainted with the best ancient and modern stories, but be able to vary them by the relation of new incidents, which they have heard or invented. They must also

---

[42] Fryer, *A New Account*, vol. 3, pp. 82-83. The book referred to was the *Anvar-e Soheyli* (Emanation of the star Canopus) by Hoseyn Va'ez Kashefi, the Persian version of the folk-tales of Bidpai.

[43] On coffee-houses see the article on "Coffee-house" in the *Encyclopedia Iranica* and Floor, Willem. *The Economy of Safavid Persia* (Wiesbaden, 2000), p. 141.

[44] Gemelli-Careri, *Giro*, vol. 2, p. 153. According to Du Mans, *Estat*, p. 214 only the most eloquent story tellers (*qessas*) performed in coffee-houses.

recollect the finest passages of the most popular poets, that they may aid the impression of their narrative by appropriate quotation. The person whose peculiar office it is to amuse his majesty with these stories, is always in attendance. It is equally his duty to beguile the fatigue of a long march, or to sooth the mind when it has been disturbed by the toils of public affairs: and his tales are artfully suited to the disposition of the monarch, and the humor he is in at the moment. Sometimes he recites affable of the genii; at others, he speaks of the warlike deeds of the former Sovereigns of Persia, or recounts the love of some wandering prince. A story of more coarse materials is often framed, and the ear of the king is entertained with a narrative of low and obscene adventures."[45]

As Malcolm makes clear in this quote a good narrator stood out by certain qualities, which also makes it understandable why historians or other literati recorded their deeds as a sign of outstanding cultural, dramatic and literary quality. Not only did you have to know your stories well, but you had to update them, and, to keep it interesting, improvise on stories already known to the audience. Delivery was, of course, everything, for a narrator who could not captivate his audience would not remain in that line of business for long. Even foreigners such as Malcolm were impressed by the excellence and skills of these royal narrators. Malcolm wrote: "When I last visited Persia in 1810, I had the good fortune to be accompanied, during a part of my journey to court, by Moollah Adenah, the story-teller to the king. He proved to be a most agreeable companion; and the fatigue of the longest marches was forgotten in listening to his tales."[46] Naser al-Din Shah also had a court narrator who told him stories prior to sleeping.[47]

Folk tales were almost always in prose, and the narrator used much leeway in adapting, improvising and embellishing the tale depending on his skills and the circumstances. Professional storytellers often were people out-of-luck, who had held a normal trading or artisan job. Often they would occasionally enlarge their income by doing odd jobs in the bazaar. In fact, anybody who felt like it could be a story-teller; the audience determined whether you actually were one or not, according to Korf. "They paid or not or laughed at you and left. Anyone who wants to unload his troubles or who feels he has to tell a tale can stand in the street and get a number of people around him."[48] Among the wandering storytellers there were *charvadar*s or mule-drivers and above all dervishes. Iranian Jews were also among them, and had stories that others had forgotten. The good storytellers had a fairly large store of knowledge and told episodes from the *Shahnameh* (Rostam, Bizhan and Manizha, etc) or part of old Iranian romances of chivalry. The storytellers knew their tales by

[45] Malcolm, *The History of Persia*, vol. 2, pp. 552-54.

[46] Malcolm, *The History of Persia*, vol. 2, p. 554.

[47] Naqib al-Mamalek, Mohammad `Ali. *Amir Arsalan* (Tehran, 1966).

[48] Korf F. *Pro'ezd' chrez' Zakavkaskii krai* (St. Petersburg, 1838) translated by Eskander Dhabihan as Kurf, Barun Fyudur. *Safarnameh* (Tehran: Fekr-e Ruz, 1372/1993), p. 204.

heart, but they also made notes and wrote their repertory of tales in *ketabcheh*s or *tumar*s. Later some of these also were lithographed.[49] The simple short story teller (*qesseh-gu*) mostly narrated stories about animals and magic. In practice, the best storytellers, apart from having a knack for that art, also had received some kind of training. There were even 'schools' for storytellers. A group of young men attached themselves to an old and experienced narrator of high repute, usually a dervish, to learn the technique and practice of storytelling by listening and watching.[50] In 1907, Aubin observed the following:

> The `Ajam dervish Hoseyn is the *nakkal* [sic; *naqqal*]; he is currently tour- ing the neighboring villages that he amuses with his engaging stories, be- fore edifying them with short sermon about the martyred Imams. In his absence we had to do with his apprentice dervish Darab, who was studying with his [master's] *morshed*, Qashqul Ali Shah of Golpaygan and timidly tried his hand at the art. His master has not yet taught him how to detail the episodes, contained in a certain famous book; his memory classes the tales by category: virtue recompensed, vice punished, vengeance, marriage, death. Dervish Darab still wears normal peasant clothes; he crouches on his kneels and starts his tale with as many changes of face and gestures as he can manage. First he begins chanting some verses of Sa`di, then starts his tale, chosen from a well-known source.[51]

Most of the storytellers were dervishes, and of the dervishes in particular the Khaksar and their affiliated off-shoot of `Ajam dervishes stood out.[52] Their gov- ernmental overseer was, as discussed above, the royal storyteller. At Tehran there were 3,000 dervishes, of which 600 were Khaksar. The largest group was that of the `Ajams. They numbered 5,000 to 6,000 in Iran, 10,000 if you added the ap- prentices. The largest group was at Tehran, then Isfahan and Gilan. They were to be found at the mosques, seated below the pulpit where they told the peasants, while sobbing, the life of the martyrs of Karbala; they were the *rowzeh-khvan*s of the rural areas. Also, they transformed themselves into an elegist (*maddah*) to cry loudly the praise of `Ali in the bazaars, or they acted as storyteller, and made their audience laugh with stories from the *Eskandernameh* or the *Romuz-e Hamzeh*. Some even performed as snake charmers.[53] They operated under license of the chief of the storytellers, who traditionally held the title of *naqib al-mamalek*, but

---

[49] Yamamoto, *The Oral Background*, pp. 25-52 with an analysis of the text of one published *tumar*.

[50] Cejpek, Jiři. "Iranian Folk-Tales and Problems Arising From Them," in Jan Rypka ed. *History of Iranian Literature* (Dodrecht, 1986), p. 654; Aubin, *La Perse*, pp. 307-08; Nikitine, *Les Kurdes*, pp. 273-74; Shahri, *Tarikh*, vol. 5, pp. 506-09.

[51] Aubin, *La Perse*, pp. 307-08, 309 (summary of the tale).

[52] On the various dervish groups see Gramlich, Richard. *Die Schiitischen Derwischorden Persiens* 3 vols. (Wiesbaden, 1981); see also Afshari, Mehran ed. *Haft Lashkar ya Shahnameh-ye Naqqalan* (Tehran: Ketab-e Haftom, 1369); Ibid., *Ayin-e Qalandari* with Mir `Abedini (Tehran: Fararavan, 1374/1995), and Ibid., "Ferqeh-ye `Ajam va Sokhanvari," *Hasti* 3/1 (1374/1995), pp. 142-52.

[53] Aubin, *La Perse*, pp. 238, 241-42

E`temad al-Saltaneh referred to him as *naqib-e naqqal*.[54] Mirza Gholam Hoseyn Khan Naqib al-Mamalek was the favorite storyteller of Naser al-Din Shah and the chief administrator of the dervishes, but only of the Khaksar and the `Ajams. He had a delegate in each province and received a share of their income. His father had an even more important role; he was in charge of 17 professions, such as the washers of the dead and sellers of water pipes.[55]

Around 1909, Moore saw a dervish in Isfahan, "telling tales beside a tea-house below. His audience is smoking, seated on their heels on platforms with low railings, placed in rows along the walls and beside the conduit running round the square. ... He recites with a dramatic and highly inflected voice, and a profusion of gesture not unworthy of an actor."[56] Sometimes the story tellers were known under other names. In Kermanshah, for example, there was a kind of performers that were engaged in entertaining acts that were called *shamurti*. Such an entertainer usually performed at the outskirts of town and spread his carpet there. A boy, known as *bachcheh-ye darvish*, assisted him, which is clear indication that the storyteller was a dervish assisted by his pupil. The master or *morshed* when he was ready to begin called out loudly and clapped his hands for people to come and see. They often had snakes with them in a sack, did sleights of hand, etc.[57] Among the Kurds there were so-called *goranibech*s, reciters of songs, who moved from house to house chanting their poems; during the day they did their normal job, in he evening they became musicians.[58] Jewish storytellers were much in demand in Kurdistan.[59] According to Sabar, describing the style and technique of Jewish storytellers in Kurdistan, "the style is literary, often vivid and humorous. The vocabulary is rich and includes expressions referring to local cultural life, as well as onomatopoeia, imitative expressions, and other vocal effects. The general theme of the tale may well be familiar to the audience, but a skillful teller can still captivate his listeners with it again and again. The tales vary in length from an hour's telling to installments filling several long winter nights."[60]

De Gobineau observed that *the 1001 nights* were considered a classical collection of tales; certainly beautiful, but antiquated. The storytellers preferred the *Secrets of Hamzeh*, a vast collection in seven volumes, containing very colorful recitations, but all of them to the glory of the Imams. It is the source that they drew upon by preference. But they also looked for pleasant anecdotes, ingenious rejoinders, tales

---

[54] E`temad al-Saltaneh, *Ruznameh*, p. 16.

[55] Aubin, *La Perse*, p. 238. On these 17 groups see below.

[56] Moore, Benjamin Burges. *From Moscow to the Persian Gulf* (New York: G.P. Putnam's Sons, 1915), p. 287.

[57] Soltani, *Joghrafiya*, vol. 1, p. 352.

[58] Aubin, *La Perse*, pp. 87, 91-92.

[59] Sabar, Yona. *The Folk Literature of the Kurdistani Jews: An Anthology* (New Haven, 1982), p. xxxvii

[60] Sabar, *The Folk Literature*, p. xxxvii-xxxviii.

that contain some negative observations regarding mollahs and women; all of it mixed with verse and sometimes with chanting. The people passed much of their life listening to the tales, because it did not cost much to the idlers, if it costs them something at all.[61] "According to Romaskevich, the storyteller Juhunvaz from Ardakan, near Shiraz, used to hold sessions lasting several evenings during which he recited various tales, mostly related to each other through the main plot and common personages, interrupting the sequence with appropriate songs. This narrative style, in which the main story is interspersed with episodes and poetical interludes, is still alive."[62] They often brought some pictures with them to better explain and visualize the story during the narration. The stories were usually told at high speed and thus difficult to write down for European scholars in the absence of modern recording techniques.[63]

These tales and stories were not only fascinating in and by themselves, but they also taught culture, moral principals, and devotion to the Imams. The miracles, martyrdom, and the promise of salvation gave comfort, hope and strength to endure in this hard life on earth. In 1869, there were 30 storytellers (*naqqal*) in Tabriz, and a total of 225 minstrels (`asheq*), singers and dancers (*khvanandeh va raqqas*) and musicians (*motreb*).[64] They also sang songs as part of their repertory, but foreigners, unlike the Iranians, appreciated these less than the stories. According to Binning, the songs of oriental nations "are characterized by "silliness, sensuality and brutality. There is not a spark of honour or chivalry in the hero of an Eastern romaunt-he is either a piece of superhuman extravagance; or, if resembling ordinary mortal men, a treacherous, sensual ruffian."[65] The songs were often satirical and political in nature. According to de Gobineau, "they have to be new to become popular; many were produced by royal harem and from there they spread through city and country."[66]

The normal place for most story tellers in the nineteenth century was, of course, not the royal or a provincial court, but private homes as well as public spaces (*ma`rekeh*) such as squares, gardens, and the like. Storytellers were a familiar sight in the bazaar, while they also circulated in all the streets.[67] In 1828, Buckingham visited Isfahan and saw in the *Meydan-e Naqsh-e Jahan*,

> A party of nearly three hundred people had collected round a professed
> story-teller, who, when we first saw him, was disclaiming with all the dig-

---

[61] De Gobineau, A. *Trois Ans en Asie* 2 vols. (Paris, 1923), vol. 2, p. 215-16; Amir Hamzeh. *Ketab-e Romuz-e Hamzeh* 7 vols. (Tehran: `Ali Akbar Basmachi, 1273/1856).

[62] Cejpek, "Iranian Folk-Literature," p. 642.

[63] Cejpek, "Iranian Folk-Literature," p. 652.

[64] Javadi, Shafi`. *Tabriz va Peyramun* (Tabriz: Bonyad-e Farhang-e Reza Pahlavi, 1350/1971), pp. 227-28.

[65] Binning, R.B. M. *A Journal of Two Years' Travel in Persia, Ceylon, etc.* 2 vols. (London: Wm. H. Allen & Co, 1857), vol. 2, p. 183.

[66] De Gobineau, *Trois Ans*, vol. 2, p. 183.

[67] De Gobineau, *Trois Ans*, vol. 2, pp. 182, 215.

nity and warmth of the most eloquent and finished orator. We halted here without a murmur from any of our party, as they seemed to enjoy this species of exhibition as much as Englishmen would do the pleasures of the drama. It might itself, indeed, be called a dramatic representation; for although but one person appeared on the stage, there were as great a variety of characters personated by this one, as appears in any of our best plays. The subject of his tale was from the wars of Nadir Shah, more particularly at the period that his arms were directed against Bagdad; and in it he breathed forth the haughty fury of the conquering warrior; trembled in the supplicating tone of the captive; allured by the female voice of love and desire; and dictated in the firmer strain of remonstrance and reproach. I could understand this orator but imperfectly, and was unwilling at the moment to disturb the fixed attention of my companions, by soliciting their interpretation; but, as far as gestures and attitudes were explanatory of the passions and incidents on which they were exercised, I certainly had never yet seen any thing more complete. Bursts of laughter, sensations of fear, and sighs of pity, rapidly succeeded each other in the audience, who were at some periods of the tale so silent, that the fall of a pin might have been heard. Money was thrown into the circle by those whose approbation the story-teller had strongly won. This was gathered up by one of the boys who served the caleoons [sic; *qalyan* or water pipe], without charge, to those engaged in listening, and no money was at any time demanded; though, as far as our short stay there would warrant a judgment, I should conceive the gains of the performer to have been considerable.[68]

The same phenomenon could be seen elsewhere in the country, in towns, big and small, and villages. In 1840, in Dowlatabad, it was "a feast day, as all the inhabitants were congregated under some trees outside the village, listening to storytellers, and amusing themselves in various other ways."[69] In 1851, on his way from Shiraz to Isfahan, Binning reported that, "At Yezdikhaust I encountred, for the first time, a *kissa-goo* or professional storyteller-a character much the same as the 'disour' of Europe in former days."[70] In 1883 Safa al-Saltaneh saw in Kashan a narration of the *Tale of Nader Shah* in the compound of the tomb of Molla Mohsen Feyz. He noted that the dervish who narrated the story moved his female audience to tears.[71] In Baluchistan around 1905, Tate observed, "The people have few or no amusements. A clever story-teller draws large audiences, and these assemblies are held on the comfortable side of the walls, according to the season and the weather

---

[68] Buckingham, J.S. *Travels in Assyria, Media and Persia* (London, 1829 [Westmead: Gregg Int., 1971]), p. 203.

[69] Mitford, Edward Ledwich. *A Land March from England to Ceylon Forty Years Ago.* 2 vols. (London: Allen & Co, 1884), vol. 1, p. 20.

[70] Binning, *A Journal*, vol. 2, p. 351.

[71] Safa al-Saltaneh, Mirza `Ali Khan Na'ini. *Safarnameh-ye Safa al-Saltaneh* ed. Mohammad Golbon (Tehran, 1382/2003), p. 86.

that prevails."[72] The storytellers came to annual fairs and moved around to make a living, and traveled each year hundreds of kilometers. Binning met such a wandering minstrel in 1851:

> In the afternoon, a wandering minstrel visited the place where the Shahzadeh and I lodged, and insisted on entertaining us. He was a native of Marand in Azerbaijan, and was now on his way to Sheerauz. He carried a rude kind of guitar, the notes of which were not unpleasing, and his voice was remarkably good, but he often spoiled the effect by squalling in falsetto. He sang several of the lays of the famous bandit-minstrel Kurroglou; but as these songs are in the Toorkee language [Azeri], I could not understand them. Kuruglou was a real individual, who lived in the north-west of this country, during the reigns of Suffee and Abbas the Second. He was a chief of a formidable horde of seven hundred and seventy-seven banditti; and united in his own person, the somewhat opposite characters of robber and troubadour; being not less famous for his skill in improvisatory minstrelsy, than for his adventurous exploits, courage, and giant strength.[73]

Sometimes an entertainer would travel even farther. Aubin in 1907 met a dervish who was traveling to Mekka and en route made his living with story telling. He performed on the hay market and in coffeehouses. One of them was taken up by the prince-governor of Shiraz to tell stories to the prince's harem.[74]

The public storytellers continued their trade also in the twentieth century. Vita Sackville-West saw one in action in Isfahan during her visit in 1925, and she described her experience as follows:

> In the Meidan a dervish was sitting on the ground telling a story to the crowd; they sat around him in a circle with lips parted and eyes popping nearly out of their heads as the holy man worked himself into a state of frenzy over the exploits of his hero. (for Persian stories are usually heroic, and Firdusi's epic of the Kings their favourite recital) With his long beard, high hat, and orange nails, and fierce little eyes flashing out of his hairy face, he seemed indeed wild and inspired, as though he had been spinning his tale for the last five hundred years and was only now working up to the climax.[75]

---

[72] Tate, G. P. *The Frontiers of Baluchistan. Travels on the borders of Persia and Afghanistan* (London 1909 [Lahore: East & West Publishing Comp, 1976]), p. 226.
[73] Binning, *A Journal*, vol. 2, pp. 182-83.
[74] Aubin, *La Perse*, p. 248.
[75] Sackville-West, V. *Passenger to Teheran* (London, 1926 [New York, 1990]), pp. 110, 155 (photo of a story teller). For another picture taken around the time see Shahri, *Tarikh*, vol. 6, p. 38.

Figure 16: A storyteller in Isfahan (1925)

In addition to the public squares and streets (*ma`rekeh*), they also performed in coffeehouses that served the neighborhood and where the quarter elders came to re-solve disputes.[76] But the government sometimes closed down these coffeehouses, because there was too much talk of politics and people were too much engaged in opposition. When the coffeehouses were closed around 1858, some people built a kind of hangar from planks, open to all sides and equipped with steps, in quite large a location near the Sabz-e Meydan so that it could contain about 300 people who would squat on their heels. At the end of the hangar there was a stage. It was there that from morning till evening story tellers and listeners succeeded one another. The closure of the coffee-houses was temporary and soon the narrators entertained its clientele once again.[77] Benjamin, the first US ambassador to Iran wrote:

> What offers more attraction to a European in these tea-houses than the dances, are the recitation from the poets. The songs of Hafiz may be heard there, and entire cantos from the great epic of Firdoüsee, chanted with resonant modulations and listened to with enthusiastic rapture.

---

[76] Najmi, Naser. *Dar al-Khelafeh* (Tehran: Amir Kabir, 2536/1977), p. 190.

[77] De Gobineau, *Trois Ans*, vol. 2, p. 215. About the temporary closure of the coffee-houses as well as their role in general see Floor, Willem. "Tea Consumption and Imports into Qajar Iran," *Studia Iranica* 33/2004, pp. 53-62.

> Here, too, one may here the "Arabian Nights Tales" repeated without any
> attempts to expurgate passages offering a peculiarly oriental flavor.[78]

The presence of a regular storyteller was good for business and some coffee-houses are still remembered because of a certain storyteller. The owner hired some of the famous storytellers. A contract was drawn up stipulating mutual obligations, wages, advances, duration and time of performance.[79] The members of the audience were not obliged to pay the narrator. In the early twentieth century payment was in the order of two-three to ten *shahi*s and up to one *qran*. Payment was higher during the narration of "The Death of Siyavosh" and "The Death of Sohrab," when the coffee-house owner also decorated the interior lavishly and lighted more candles and lamps. On that occasion the lowest payment was five *qran*s and increased up to two *tuman*s. The coffeehouse owner would give the narrator a shawl as a present. During these two nights the narration would last at least one up to two hours.[80]

The Tehran coffeehouses were of a special design; they all had a wide space, which was filled with brick-lime platforms (*saku*) on which people would sit, and drink their coffee, tea or smoke a pipe. The water pipe (*qalyan*) was for the middle and upper class, the 'normal' pipe (*chepoq*) for the lower class.[81] Many a coffeehouse was a regular hang-out (*patuq*) for a guild. The best and most famous coffeehouse was behind the Shams al-`Emarat, which was known as *Yuzbashi*. Here princes, officers, ministers, etc, came. If a poet had a laudatory verse (*naghzi*) he went there to recite it. The most famous one was Morshed Barzu. Another famous coffeehouse was that of Qanbar in Khiyaban-e Naseriyeh. Here newspaper reading was banned. Every evening, sometimes all day, Dervish Marhab staged a story telling event. Luti `Azim and Luti GholamHoseyn often performed in the back. The Pahlavan Kachal theater (*Gol badan khanom*) also was performed there with much glee and fun. The Tambal coffeehouse in the cross roads of Moscow Street was the meeting place was of the *lutis* and their leaders (*baba shamal*s). Other well-known coffeehouses were *Bagh-e Anari* and

---

[78] Benjamin, *Persia*, p. 100. The walls of many coffee-houses were also covered with paitings depicting scenes from the Shahnameh and the Karbala tragedy. Most coffee house paintings are anonymous, but there are also some signed ones such as by Mohammad Modabber, Hoseyn Qollar-aghasi, his son Fathollah Qollar-aghasi and Hasan Esma`il. See H. Seyf. *Naqqashi-ye Qahvakhaneh* (Tehran 1369/1990); E. Nabavi. "Naqqashi-ye Qahvakhaneh'i." *Honar va Mardom* 12/38 (1353/1974), pp. 63-9; Kalantari, M. *Catalogue Exhibition*, Iran-American Society; Emami, K. "Naqqashiha-ye qahveh va qahvakhaneh'i," *Rahnama-ye Ketab*, 10/6 (1346/1967) pp. 557-63; B. Beyza'i, "Namayesh dar Iran," *Musiqi* 3rd. series, 66 (1341/1962) pp. 15-33; Kalantari, Manutcher. "Le Livre de Roi et les peintures des maison de thé," *Objets et Mondes* 9/1 (1971), pp. 141-58.
[79] Cejpek, "Iranian Folk-Literature," p. 653.
[80] Shahri, *Tarikh*, vol. 5, p. 517.
[81] On smoking and smoking implements see Floor, Willem. "The Art of Smoking in Iran and other uses of tobacco," in *Iranian Studies* 35 (2002), pp. 47-86.

Sar Godhar. The coffeehouse owners were much respected in those days, so much so that one of the crossroads is known as Sayyed `Ali after Sayyed `Ali *qahvehchi*.[82] Among the most famous *shah-nameh* narrators of the early twentieth century were Sayyed `Ali Hamadani, of whom it was said that he could resurrect a corpse with his story telling; Morshed Hasan, Hoseyn Asmal Chorak, and Morshed Gholam-Hoseyn Ghul-bachcheh.[83]

The same held true for other towns. In Kermanshah the *shahnameh-khvan*s also performed in coffeehouses where visiting rural Kurds also went to hear them. Some of them were famous and are still remembered for their voice and performance such as Morshed Khodadad and `Ali Akbar Zargar-bashi.[84] Story telling was quite well-known in Ardabil and was also performed in coffeehouses or in public places. The audience mostly consisted of peasants who had come to town to sell their products and who wanted to relax after having sold it. The Ardabilis themselves frowned upon frequenting coffeehouses, for it was frivolous and undignified. The storytellers (*naqqalan*) most wore dervish garb and played in public places in town.[85]

The telling of stories was restricted to certain times of the day and often the year. If such a taboo was not respected it was believed that it would bring ill-luck. Musical instruments also were often restricted. The best season for story telling was Ramazan, just after the fast was broken, and winter evenings. Further at *Nowruz*, and family parties such as marriages, births and circumcisions. There also were story telling parties organized among neighbors in a street, where everybody who had been invited would come to the neighbor's house, who also provided snacks.[86] A popular saying among Kurdish Jews was "Two things are necessary in winter, fire and folktale: fire, to warm the body, and folktale, to warm the heart."[87] Storytelling usually took place during idle periods and never before noon, when people were working. To attract an audience some of the storytellers also often had animals, usually various snakes whose fangs had previously been taken out. After the animal show they started to read or narrate and stories. The narration was appropriately paced and dramatized by pauses, gestures, intonation, and other features to create tension and keep the audience captivated for it knew the story already. The stories were short and fast-paced, for the narrator needed to attract an audience and keep it. He often had a colleague who sometimes raised a question or made a remark to boost people's attention and interest. Halfway and just before the climax of the

---

[82] Najmi, *Dar al-Khelafeh*, pp. 189-90; Mahdjoub, Mohamad Ja`far. "Le conteur en Iran," *Objets et Mondes* 9/1 (1971), pp. 159-70. On coffee-houses in the nineteenth century see Floor, "Tea Consumption," pp. 56-62.

[83] Shahri, *Tarikh*, vol. 5, p. 513.

[84] Soltani, *Joghrafiya*, vol. 1, p. 350.

[85] Safar, Baba. *Ardabil dar Godhargah-e Tarikh* 3 vols. (Tehran, 1350-62/1971-83), vol. 3, pp. 254.

[86] Shahri, *Tarikh*, vol. 5, p. 505-07.

[87] Sabar, *The Folk Literature*, p. xxxvii, n. 138.

story, the storyteller would stop and ask for money, which was called *niyaz* or *nadhr*. These short story tellers moved around in the town from one quarter to another and after having exhausted the "market" the storyteller moved on to a different town or village. There also were itinerant entertainers outside the town, also with animals. These were mostly bears and monkeys. But in the past, according to Ibn Bazzaz, they also had lions and elephants.[88]

Among the epic tales that of the *Shahnameh* was the most popular. According to Shahri, there were three categories of *Shahnameh* narrators. The first category consisted of those who knew the *Shahnameh* almost by heart and who narrated it in their fashion for the listeners. The second category consisted of those who mixed the verses of the *Shahnameh* with that of other stories, which also included the mixing of verse, prose, main and affiliated story. The third category consisted of those who added materials of their own or others to the stories of the *Shahnameh* to make it more interesting for the public. This type of narrator of stories marginal to the main one (*hashiyeh-khvani*) was known as *tumar-khvani*, because the narrator made use of a scroll (*tumar*) on which he had written the additional materials.[89] Binning, who traveled in Iran in 1851 left an interesting description of the performance of a *shahnameh-khvan*.

> One evening, at Shiraz I was entertained with a Shah-nameh-khoon, or reciter of the Shah Nameh-a professional the house of an acquaintance character who attends people's houses for the purpose of reciting aloud, and acting (as it may be termed) passages and episodes of Ferdousee's great poem. Of this description of entertainment the Persians are very fond. I had previously, at Ispahan, heard one or two of these performers; but this man, who was a Gabr (fire-worshipper) from Yezd, was considered a very superior artists. He possessed a powerful, clear, and melodious voice, and chanted the fine poetry with great emphasis, accompanied with appropriate action. At times he worked himself into a positive frenzy. Every kind of different verse-whether heroics, anacreontics, elegy, satire, &c.-is recited in an appropriate tone or chant. That of the Shah Nameh is expressive of *niheeb* (awe or terror). The Persian soldiery, when about to engage in combat, are accustomed to sing aloud certain passages of this epic poem, which practice has the effect of inspiring them to absolute fury.[90]

It is of interest to note here that Soltani mentioned the fact that *shahnameh-khvani* and knowledge of the epic was very popular and strong among the Kermanshah Kurds, who played an important military role in guarding the border and being

[88] Safar, Baba. *Ardabil*, vol. 3, pp. 255; Cejpek, "Iranian Folk-Literature," p. 653. For picture of a snake-charmer see Shahri, *Tarikh*, vol. 6, p. 40.
[89] Shahri, *Tarikh*, vol. 5, pp. 511-12.
[90] Binning, *A Journal*, vol. 2, pp. 383-84.

engaged in other warlike exploits. Each tribal unit had their own *shahnameh-khvan*s, who were much respected in tribal assemblies. Many verses were therefore adapted for popular consumption and translated into Kurdish.[91]

But also the less war-like had a passion for the epic. Colonel Pelly, the British Political Agent in Bushire, observed in 1860, or thereabouts the following:

> In Bushire there is a man who *daily* [my emphasis] in the afternoon takes his high arm-chair out and places it against the wall of a terraced tea and coffee shop. Women come and sit like crows immediately above along the edge of the flat roof, and male auditors crowd round and squat in the street below. Then he commences his recitative [of the Shahnameh] in a loud and authoritative voice. All sit rapt in interest, and will sit so for hours scarcely moving a limb. Surely one should in part judge a literary or poetical work by the effect it produces on the nation in general to which it was addressed.[92]

IMPACT OF MODERNIZATION

The modernization policy of the Pahlavi regime resulted in tough measures against many expressions of folk customs and folk medicine. Art. 276 of the new penal law stated that it is punishable to practice soothsaying (*ramal*), dream interpretation (*ta`bir-e shab*), snake conjuration (*afsungari*), magic (*jadugari*), jinn conjuration (*jenn-gari*), oracles (*fal-giri*), prognostication (*pish-bini*), and fortune telling using a scapula (*katef-giri*) whether in the street or in a shop as a business. Needless to say that any activity contrary to Islamic religious law (*shari`ah*) was also banned as well as those that were against the country's culture, which seems to have given the authorities much leeway. In 1928, the Municipality of Tehran issued local rules for coffeehouses (*tarz-e bina-ye kafeh*). These had to be entirely transformed after the European model. Instead of the traditional arrangement of benches covered with carpets, which made lengthy stays there more comfortable, they needed to have tables and chairs. The wall paintings with the display of the national epos and other stories with *div*s, dragons, Farhad and Shirin, Leyla and Majnun, Rustam, etc. had to go, for the walls had to be white-washed. The most dramatic and radical rule was the ban on all artistic activities that already had been banned in the streets, such as the performance of storytellers, the poetry contests (*sokhanvari*), juggling, the display of paintings about the martyrdom of Imam Hoseyn (*pardeh avikhtan*), beggars, dervishes, fire-eaters, jongleurs (*sini-gardan*), and puppet shows that were performed during Ramazan as well as the performance of stories of the Karbela tragedy during the months of Moharram and

---

[91] Soltani, *Joghrafiya*, vol. 1, p. 349.
[92] Pelly, Lewis. "Remarks on a recent Journey from Bushire to Shirauz," *Transactions of the Bombay Geographical Society* 17 (1865), p. 156, note. [pp. 141-74.]

Safar.[93] It comes therefore as no surprise that the performance of the passion play (*ta'ziyeh-khvani*) also was banned in the cities. The ban of this religious epic was not only because of its orgiastic character and display of customs that did not befit a modern state, but also because Reza Shah wanted to relegate religion and its leaders, the olama, to a less prominent position in society.

> The podium is covered with carpets and on those they put small tables for four people and chairs. It is categorically prohibited to have in coffee houses: puppet shows, poetic competitions, magic show, demonstrations of scenes of martyrdom, beggars and dervishes. Also, fire spitters are not allowed either, nor are people who rotate metallic disks or hoops at the end of a pole. In general, the people that are not allowed into coffee-houses are street artists, who were already evicted by the police from the city's squares. Anybody who has visited Persia knows the role of coffee-houses in Persian life. Coffeehouses are places to rest after a hard work-ing day, a place where political events are discussed, and lastly a place of entertainment where you can listen to storytellers, watch poetic competi-tions organized during Ramazan or watch puppet-theater or magicians. In Moharram and Safar you lived through some episode of the tragic Kar-bala events, which are shown here right in the middle of the smoky and crowded coffeehouse.

> Now all this has changed. A customer of a coffeehouse now does not feel cozy and at ease. Uncomfortable hard chairs have replaced benches cov-ered with carpets on which you could lie down. Square tables, bright burning lamps and very bad gramophones are now an indivisible part of the Persian coffeehouse of the new type.

> In truth, even if storytellers (*naqqal*) were not removed from coffee-houses by the last law they would not be able to do their performances there, though their target audience is the same. The performance usually lasted several evenings, sometimes one to two weeks. This was only pos-sible in the old coffeehouses, due to their comfortable interior that was conducive to long listening. However, street artists are being repressed in large towns, although they are still able to perform in the provinces. But you should note also that the interest in entertainment in the towns, where street life is more developed than in the provinces, is higher. With respect to collecting materials in the provinces it is much more difficult than in the cities.[94]

Storytelling therefore became limited in urban areas to the narration of the *Shah-nameh* only, because it promoted the idea of monarchy and thus was to Reza Shah's own interest. With the growing use of the gramophone, coffeehouse own-

---

[93] Menzel, *Meddah*, p. 34; Galunov, "Neskol'ko slov," p. 309.
[94] Galunov, "Neskol'ko slov," p. 309.

ers found it more convenient and cheaper to replace the storyteller.[95] Later with the advent of the radio and television the storyteller became obsolete. Although under pressure and finally disappearing in the urban areas, storytelling survived in the villages. Alberts reporting on his fieldwork in Davarabad (Khorasan) in 1961 observed the presence of several minstrels. These were men, who held a normal job (farming, shopkeeper), were able to play various musical instruments with skill and had "a rather impressive repertoire of slapstick, sleight-of-hand, storytelling, impersonations, jokes and amusing routines." They were invited for weddings and other social events and received a cash payment, tips, if they could get them, and a share of the money collection (*pul-andazi*). Although the minstrel held an occupation of low social esteem, once he was invited he enjoyed enormous social esteem and standing. He was given a place of honor, allowed to mingle with the guests, and was plied with tea, cigarettes and arak; his apprentice accompanied him with a drum.

> He may entertain almost continuously for hours, alternating serious declamations and remorseful ballads of unrequited love with comic songs and incidental patter bordering on the obscene. In the standard repertoire is the bit where the neckerchief is draped over the head to simulate a *chador*, and the nonsensical grumblings of a toothless village crone are imitated in a rasping falsetto. With the handkerchief establishing the role of a village maid, and the clarinet suggesting a passionate village swain, the dialogue of comic seduction is acted out. The host or principal *borzorgtar* present may suddenly find that he is being mimicked, usually with a decidedly unkind and penetrating burlesque on his speech, manner or some past *faux-pas*. Local minstrels are shrewd observers, and their incisive impersonations, greatly relished by *koochiktars* who may harbor similar sentiments, must be taken in good graces by the *bozorgtars*.[96]

The low social standing of the minstrelsy art may explain Galunov's call of warning in 1929 that even in the rural areas storytelling was to fade away.

> Because of the recent Persian government reforms, the strong influence of European culture that attaches little importance to the values of Persian culture, and because of the breakdown of the old way of life and other measures initiated by Reza Shah, which have as their objective to quickly introduce the European way of life into Iran, the urgent question arises of the need to collect folklore material in Iran which is doomed to extinction. This is a critical moment for Persia. The Persian intelligentsia consists of young people educated in Europe or in foreign schools in Iran. They support the government in all ways in its fight with the old way of life. The attitude of Persians toward the oral works of art has

---

[95] Shahri, *Tarikh*, vol. 5, p. 511, 519.
[96] Alberts, *Social Structure*, vol. 2, pp.1082-84.

hardly changed since the time when the late Zhukovski was collecting his materials in Iran, i.e., 40 years ago. This same attitude towards oral arts of expression persists and the interest shown in it by European collectors is met with open surprise.[97]

Story telling continued to be a way of life in Iran, although under the impact of growing literacy and the mass-media, in particular the cinema, television and other forms of electronic media the interest in storytelling decreased significantly during the second half of the twentieth century. The fact that narration (*naqqali*) as an art form has been re-introduced as part of Art Festivals in Iran only underscores this renewed interest (see chapter 6).

Figure 17: Storyteller in a hotel in Isfahan (1970)

---

[97] Galunov, "Neskol'ko slov," p. 307.

CHAPTER FOUR

ELEGY RECITATION OR *MARTHIYEH-KHVANI*

INTRODUCTION

A special kind of epic storyteller were those who told laudatory stories of the
prophet and his family, and of `Ali and the other Imams, as well as of other proph-
ets and holy men, as the case might be. This kind of storytelling started already two
decades after the death of the prophet Mohammad and took the form of elegy
(*marthiyeh*). Under the Ommayads, lamentations (*niyaha*) on account of the martyrdom of the Shi`ite Imams began and continued to be held.[1] *Marthiyah*s were also
recited in honor of non-religious persons.[2] In 963, the Shi`ite Buyid emir Mo`ezz
al-Dowleh ordered people in Baghdad to close all shops, dress in black and perform
public mourning ceremonies in commemoration of Imam Hoseyn during the first
ten days of Moharram. These ceremonies were accompanied by dirges. It probably
was begun under the influence of its celebration in Fatimid Egypt prior to that date.[3]
These measures also responded to a need felt by the Shi`ite community at large as is
clear from Jalal al-Din Rumi who recorded the `Ashura ceremonies held by the
Shi`ites at Aleppo in the mid-thirteenth century. They gathered at the Antiochia gate
and stayed there till the evening. During that period they chanted elegies about the
martyrs of Karbala, commemorated the injustice done by Yazid and Shimr, and
cried very hard and loud. The elegy (*nowheh*) that was sung was of the *tarji`-band*
kind where the mourners would repeat certain parts of the elegy. When a poet came
to find the reason for the lamentation the Shi`ites told him that "Love for the earring
(i.e. Hoseyn) is equal to the love for the ear (i.e. Mohammad). In the perception of a
true believer the mourning about this pure spirit is commemorated more than 100 of
Noah's deluges.[4]

In the Seljuq period, according to the *Ketab al-Naqz* of Sheikh `Abdol-Jalil Qaz-
vini Razi, a Shi`ite polemist, epic and religious drama was narrated in public
places, in particular in Tabaristan. The storytellers were called *manaqeb-khvanan*

---

[1] Mas`udi, *Prairies d'Or*, text and translation by C. Barbier de Meynard and Paver de Courteille 9
vols. (Paris,1661-1917), vol. 6, p. 3; Abu Hanifa al-Dinawari, *Kitab al-Akhbar* ed. W. Guirgass
(Leiden, 1888), p. 340f.
[2] Buergel, J. Christoph. *Die Hofkorrespondanz `Adud ad-Daulas* (Wiesbaden, 1965) pp. 105-06;
see in general Hanaway, W.L. "Marthiya," *Encyclopedia of Islam*[2].
[3] Busse, Heribert. *Chalif und Grosskönig; die Buyiden im Iraq (945-1055)* (Beirut, 1969), pp. 422,
427; Maqrizi, Ahmad b. `Ali. *Kitab al-Khitat al-Maqriziyah* 3 vols. (1959), vol. 1, p. 630f.
[4] Müller, Hildegard. *Studien zum persischen Passionsspiel* (Freiburg i. Breisgau, 1966), p. 96.

or *manaqebiyan* (singers of virtues, praiseworthy actions or *manaqeb*) and they
recited *qasideh*s (songs) in the streets and the bazaars to the praise (*maddah*) of
`Ali, the Imams in general, and propagated the Shi`ite faith. They sometimes also
sang about secular heroes. By word-of-mouth, people knew where a *manaqeb-
khvan* would perform, some of whose names are known such as Abu Taleb Shi`i
Manaqebi whose tongue was taken out at the command of Malekshah's daughter.
Sunnites were not pleased with the praise singers (*manaqeb-khvan*s). One of them
wrote that songs "should not contain obscenity, nor any insult to the pious, like
the poems of the Rafidis [i.e. Shi`ites] sing about the Companions."[5] There were
also Sunnite performers who were called *faza'el-khvanan* or *faza'eli*, who praised
the laudatory deeds (*faza'el*) of Abu Bakr, `Omar, and other persons whom the
Shi`ites considered to be the enemies of Imam `Ali and his family. According to
the Shi`ite source above mentioned (*Ketab al-Naqz*), these Sunni singers of vir-
tues performed in inns and other dens of iniquity, of course. To overcome their
handicap (i.e. being Sunnis and lauding Sunni caliphs), the Sunnite narrators told
stories from the *Shahnameh* exalting the prowess of its heroes to show that in
comparison `Ali's deeds paled. According to `Abdol-Jalil, the praise songs
(*manaqeb*) were written by the best poets, while those of the *faza'el* were but
folk-poetry of inferior quality. There does not seem to have been a follow-up to
this rivalry in narration, at least it has not been reported.[6]

Narration of epic and religious drama by elegists (*maddah*s) about the prophet's
family (*ahl-e beyt*), the Karbela tragedy, and in particular the recitation of the *Abu
Moslem-Nameh* was thriving. There also was a genre of tales that were spun about
the historical events of the early days of Islam, but not about the Karbala events,
which were known as the *Mokhtar-nameh* and became popular as of the fifteenth
century, if not earlier.[7] The narrators also drew upon so-called *maqtal-nameh*,
which were related to the old Arab genre of *Maqatel*. Not much is known about
them, but according to Mahjub they seem to have been written by Sunni poets, not
Shi'ites![8] This is not surprising because many Sunnites also held Imam `Ali and
his sons in veneration. *Manaqeb-khvani* faded away in the sixteenth century and
was replaced by *rowzeh-khvani*, of which the elegy as performed at Aleppo and
the *maqatel* texts were the forerunners. Although *manaqeb-khvani* still occurred,
it was relegated as a sideshow to other forms of entertainment. Nevertheless, the

---

[5] Meisami, *The Sea of Virtues*, p. 171.
[6] Qazvini Razi, Sheikh `Abdol-Jalil. *Ketab al-Naqz ma`ruf beh Ba`z Mathalib al-Navasib fi Naqz
ba`z Faza'ah al-Ravafiz* (Tehran, 1358/1980), pp. 64-68.
[7] Ja`fariyan, "Qesseh-khvani," vol. 2, p. 876; Monzavi, *Fehrest*, vol. 6, p. 3533-34 (lists two six-
teenth century manuscripts).
[8] Calmard, Jean. "Les Rituels Shiites et le Pouvoir. L'imposition du shiisme safavide: eulogies et
maledictions canoniques," in Jean Calmard ed. *Etudes Safavides* (Pars-Tehran, 1993), p. 133;
Safa, *Tarikh-e Adabbiyat*, vol. 2, pp. 192-94.

practice persisted, for even in the twentieth century during entertainments there was still the recitation of the *manaqeb-e* Abu'l-Fazl or of Imam `Ali and others.[9]

Religious epic storytelling received an enormous boost with the establishment of Shi`ism as the state religion of Iran in 1501. At that time, most of the population of Iran was not Shi`ite, although there was general veneration for the Shi`ite Imams. However, the Shi`ite message needed to be out there to win souls as a necessary complement to the *tabbara`iyan*, the professional cursers of Abu Bakr, `Omar, `Othman and A'isheh, all characters who had allegedly stood maliciously in the way of what Shi`ites considered to be `Ali's rightful inheritance of the mantle of the prophet. Shi`ism therefore needed more than the threat of death, high taxation, or official harassment to attract new believers, for most of Iran's population were not Shi`ites at that time. What Shi`ism needed was a ritual built on existing beliefs that would be attractive and had the potential to mobilize the masses, for Sunnis still had the numbers in the early 1500s. Although economic and physical threat also played a role, popular Shi`ite propagandists found their hook in the general veneration for the Imams that became the mother lode that Shi`ite promoters delved into and exploited.

Shi`ite devotion, after it had become the state religion of Iran, became centered on the days of the deaths, or murders (*qatl*) rather, of its Imams and members of the *Ahl-e Beyt*, for nobody was against commemorating that, in fact, everybody was in favor of it. In fact, even leading Sunni opponents of the Safavid regime composed works in the praise of the Imams. It is of some interest that the focus of this intense religious devotion is on death rather than on life, and the archetype model of the Adonis-Tammuz and the Siyavosh cult comes to mind. These also were religious rites focused on the death of the hero that thrived in the same cultural area until the year 1000. Of course, no direct relationship exists, but it would seem that there was a cultural pre-disposition to this type of ritual in Iranian religious experience and tradition. Whatever the truth of the matter, the following are the most important religious dates that became fixed over time. The first ten days of Moharram culminating in the frenzy of 10th day, the day of Imam Hoseyn's death (*`Ashureh*), followed by the 40th day commemoration of this event on Safar 20, are the most important and mournful days for modern Shi'ites. Also intense are Safar 27, 28, 29 commemorating the killing of Imam Reza, Imam Hasan and the natural death of the prophet Mohammad. As a result Moharram and Safar are the months of mourning par excellence. No festivities are allowed, dancers and singers cannot perform, and even the *naqqarehchi*s, who every day announced the rise and setting of the sun by playing their musical instruments, remained silent. Soldiers wore their rifles turned upside down, while sayyeds went out in black. Further important is Ramazan 21, which is the killing date of Imam `Ali, as well as

---

[9] Bayza'i, *Namayesh*, pp. 65, 67.

the three preceding days, which are the days of *ahya* or anguish, denoting the time during which `Ali suffered from his wounds before he died. Fatemeh died on 13 Jomadi I and Imam Musa on 25 Rajab and both events are also commemorated. The only religious day commemorating a death (9 Rabi` I) that is a day of rejoicing is that of `Omar, because he was an enemy of Imam `Ali, about which more later. Since death in Iranian culture had been the subject of various forms of elegy, it does not come as a surprise that lamentations and threnodies were the vehicle to experience these commemorations. There are three basic ingredients for these mourning ceremonies, in particular those for Imam Hoseyn: (i) lamentations; (ii) processions; and (iii) passion plays (*ta`ziyeh-khvani*). This was not the case for the other commemorations, where usually only *rowzeh-khvan*s were held, although in the case of the other death days increasingly passion plays were staged as well. In this chapter I only discuss the lamentations, which took various forms. The other two ingredients are the subject of the next chapter.

ROWZEH-KHVANI

Besides *marthiyeh* (pl. *marathi*) or threnodies, there was much literature of the sufferings of the Imams both in verse and prose, as discussed above. In the early Safavid period this led to recitations or public lamentations of these tragic events called *rowzeh-khvani*s, popularly called just *rowzeh*. They probably were called thus because the first recitations were from one of the earliest of this type, *Rowzat al-Shohada* (The Garden of the Martyrs) by Hoseyn Va`ez Kashefi. He probably was not even a Shi`ite, but a Sunnite, who venerated the Imams as well. Despite its Arabic title his work was written in Persian in 908/1502-03 in Eastern Iran, at the time when Shi`ism was being imposed as the state religion of Western Iran.[10] The book was an instant success and Hoseyn Nedayi Nishaburi almost immediately versified it and this poetic outburst was presented by its author to Shah Esma`il I.[11] Another important contributor to the genre was Mohtasham Kashani (d. 1588) who composed so-called *haftband* or poems of seven-verse strophes. Shah Tahmasp I richly rewarded him for this *rowzeh-khvani* and many poets followed his example.[12] There also were still *manaqeb-khvan*s and one of them (he also was a storyteller) wrote a book about Imam `Ali's virtues in the name of Shah Tahmasp I.[13] Recitations from similar works such as the popular nineteenth century books of *marthiyeh*s and Karbala stories, the "Deluge of Weeping" (*Tufan al-Buka'*) of Mohammad Ebrahim b. Mohammad Baqer Haravi Qazvini Jowhari (d. 1253/1837-8), and

[10] On this work and its author see the entry "Kashefi", *Encyclopedia of Islam*[2] and Ja`fariyan, Rasul. "Molla Hoseyn Va`ez Kashefi va Ketab va Rowzat al-Shohada," in Rasul Ja`fariyan, *Maqalat-e Tarikhi* 5 vols. (Qom, 1376/1987), vol. 1, pp. 168-210. See also the special issue of *Iranian Studies* 36/4 (2003) that deals with other works and aspects of Kashefi.

[11] Monzavi, *Fehrest*, vol. 4, p. 2931.

[12] Browne, E.G. *A Literary History of Persia* 4 vols. (Cambridge, 1959), vol. 4, pp. 172-75.

[13] Ja`fariyan, "Qesseh-khvani," vol. 2, p. 858.

Mohammad Hoseyn b. `Abdollah Shahrabi Arjastani's *Tariq al-Boka'*, the "Myster-
ies of Martyrdom" (*Asrar al-Shehadat*), and the "Book of Regrets" (*Ketab-e Lohuf*)
of Sayyed b. Ta'us were also used by *rowzeh-khvan*s. Except for the first one, these
seem to have been written especially for storytellers (*naqqal*s) and *rowzeh-khvan*s.
According to Browne, many other, anonymous texts were also used, as was improvisation. "The marthiyas in rowzeh-khani sometimes involve considerable oral
improvisation on well-known Karbala themes, and thus do not necessarily follow a
prescribed literary form. Mostly poets are unknown, but there are also signed texts,
although no particulars are usually known about them."[14] Today, despite the fact
that the elegy of Hoseyn's martyrdom is still called *rowzeh-khvani*, the original text
has been almost abandoned, because each *rowzeh-khvan* (i.e., the person who does
the recitation), in true form of the tradition of Iranian artistry of story telling, creates
his own story.[15] Although the subject of *rowzeh-khvani* is the life of Imams it is but
the recitation of a set of invented stories and therefore is forbidden (*haram*), according to the leading olama of the seventeenth and the nineteenth century. At any rate,
religion being man-made, man won out and was allowed to keep his *rowzeh-
khvani*.[16]

Formal *rowzeh-khvani* sessions were financed by rich notables, statesmen, merchants etc., while there also were informal ones that were started by dervishes
wherever they wanted to. It would seem that over time the frequency of *rowzeh-
khvani* grew. Originally, it was customary to recite or chant a chapter from 'The
Garden of the Martyrs' in public each day during the first ten days of the month of
Moharram. Gradually, it was staged during the whole month of Moharram and the
following month of Safar, eventually to be performed all year round. By the nineteenth century, especially during the two holy months of Moharram and Safar
there were *rowzeh-khvani* every day. Rich families would organize such a session
at least once a week. Preferably one or more skilled and well-known professional
rhapsodists or *rowzeh-khvan* would be hired, food and drinks would be prepared
for the audience, and the show was ready to go.[17] There is not much data on the
cost of such lamentations, but Basir al-Molk paid a *rowzeh-khvan* with his group
of flagellants 2,000 *dinar*s; they were just passing by to collect money, however.[18]
The kind of payment sometimes gave rise to amusement and exasperation on part
of the patron. E`temad al-Saltaneh related that a *rowzeh-khvan* that he had hired
wanted another binocular like last year and he commented: "he thinks it is a pension
or something."[19]

---

[14] Browne, *Literary History*, vol. 4, p. 194.
[15] See also Browne, *Literary History*, vol. 4, p. 181.
[16] Ja`fariyan, "Qesseh-khvani," vol. 2, p. 877.
[17] Aubin, *La Perse*, pp. 161-63.
[18] Basir al-Molk, *Ruznameh*, p. 56
[19] E`temad al-Saltaneh, *Ruznameh*, p. 1158.

Rouzakhānī, reading   Rousekhānī. Vorlesung über den Tod der Märtyrer   Raouzékhani, lecture
of the martyrdom of Saints   de la passion des martyrs
                                          روضه‌خوانی

Figure 18: *Rowzeh-khvani* in the open air (early 20th century)

There was no official announcement of the event, for the only sign was that a black banner would be hung above the door of the houses or buildings where such a lamentation would take place. It could be even right in a passage of the bazaar. "A great many readings are given. Part of a bazaar is carpeted and lighted up with lamps and candles, the audience sits on the ground, or on the front of the shops, while a mulla reads or recites from the Qur'an or Traditions."[20] There were no invitations either, all comers were welcome and free-of-charge. Its occurrence spread by word-of-mouth, of course, because there was free food and drinks, and often also a smoke for everybody. The poor could not live by devotion alone, therefore also went there to find material sustenance, for some of the *rowzeh-khvan*s were held on a splendid scale. "I counted over a hundred trays of food," wrote Browne.[21] This culinary garnish to the recitations

---

[20] Rice, *Persian Women*, p. 232-33.

[21] Browne, E.G. *A Year Amongst the Persians* (London: A. & C. Black, 1970), p. 602; "Free tea and smokes are often provided as savabs, or meritorious acts, by the faithful." Rice, Clara. *Persian Women and Their Ways* (London: Seeley, Service & Co, 1923), p. 233; 'Eyn al-Saltaneh, *Ruznameh*, vol. 2, p. 1116 records what was served at a play he attended.

was so important, for it allowed the patrons to show off their wealth, that a contemporary Qajar poet satirized "the ostentation of the host and the greed of the guests."[22] The rhapsodist did not come alone; he usually had a troupe with him, including boy-singers and entertainers. Although the lamentation was a deeply felt religious experience for the audience, at the same time it also was a kind of entertainment. People also came there to eat, drink, smoke a pipe, talk to friends, in short to have some fun. This seems to have been well understood by everybody concerned. Basir ol-Molk noted in his Diary that, "in the beginning of the evening there were *rowzeh-khvani* and prayers; at the end of the evening there were numerous dancers and musicians."[23] Usually, these events took place in the morning or afternoon, but in the evening during Ramazan, Moharram and Safar.[24] `Eyn al-Saltaneh, for example wrote, "Four hours till sunset the *rowzeh-khvani* started. There were eight *rowzeh-khvan*s from Tajrish and the other villages of Shemiran, and two elegists (*maddah*s). There were many people despite that it was the first day, but not many men. Because of the trees in the garden we did not need a tent; we only draw up some *tajir*s or canvass screens and a *zanburi* in front of one room [for the upper-class women]; one porch for HH. It was short and one hour to sunset it was over."[25]

Another contemporary observer gave a detailed description of the entire *rowzeh-khvani* performance.

> Rowzeh. Once the series of nouhas is completed a man rises and approaches the pedestal. He looks like a mollah, it is a mercia-khan [sic; marthiyeh-khvan], i.e. a teller of the passion of Ali and his children. While he mounts the pedestal, he stops at each step and he utters a prayer, while a group of young boys chanted a song, which ordinarily is very pleasing and moving. Having arrived on top of the pedestal, the mercia-khan amuses the public with some humoristic anecdotes about one caliph or the other of the bani-Omaya. They are totally taken apart and slandered in these anecdotes; they are either stupid, lack tact, or have such big bellies that these attached to the tail of the horse and the poor caliphs are thus taken to the mosques to render justice of a suspect nature. These enormities are really believed even by those who know history well; it I about ridiculing an enemy ad to take vengeance by targeted invented stories to show that this valueless enemy was only victorious by chance.

> After having amused thus the spectators he begins to bewail the fate of these heroes. He practically repeats word by word what the two singers

[22] Browne, *Literary History*, vol. 4, pp. 181-82.
[23] Basir al-Molk, *Ruznameh*, p. 275.
[24] Aubin, *La Perse*, pp. 161-63.
[25] `Eyn al-Saltaneh, *Ruznameh*, vol. 1, p. 298 (2 Safar 1308—17/9/1890).

have said, with this difference that he does so in prose and supports his claims by testimonies of learned and well-known men. The mercia-khan always has big tomes of the history of Ali and his children around him, and at each citation he indicates the page, the edition and year of the work. The spectators who have something better to do that to read histories thus believe him at his word. Comparing the zero morals and physic of the winners with the great morality and splendid physique of the losers the spectator passes from gaiety to sadness.[26]

The *rowzeh-khvan*s were the narrators of the passion stories and thus were essentially engaged in a specialized form of religious storytelling. They focused on the events of Karbala and thus were the natural successor of *manaqeb-khvans*. The *rowzeh-khvan* usually was not a learned person. He was basically a storyteller who specialized in religious epics, and knew a few texts by heart. Most of them were low-ranked mollas, and their number in the towns was large. Given the frequency of *rowzeh-khvani* throughout the year it was a well-paid occupation and the best ones became rich men. Dervishes performed that role in the rural areas, and to a lesser extent also in urban ones.[27]

The best of these speakers realize as much as 200 tomauns in the ten days of Mohurrum, lecturing at three or four places daily. This is a large sum for Persia, but it is hardly earned, for the great exertion that they are obliged to make cause them soon to lose their voices, and, I should think, must affect their lungs. The chief performer was unable to attend from hoarseness, and his place was taken by a speaker, who, to judge from his discourse, had not found it a profitable avocation: for his lecture, like an Irish sermon, was interlarded with much personal anecdote, and he occasionally forgot the sorrows of Hossein in his own. 'The eyes,' he commenced, 'which do not weep for Hossein, may they become sightless!-blessed are the tears shed for a martyr, they will cause the face of the believer to shine hereafter.!' The waters of the heart thus poured forth, he assured his hearers, would form large pearls, which the angel Gabriel would put into their hands as passports to Paradise; and he went on to say, 'It is now thirty years that I have been shouting the saint's praise in Meshed, and I am now in danger of wanting bread.' The only, to me, interesting man who spoke was an Arab, apparently not a paid performer, who, making his way through the crowd, ascended the steps, and struck at once into a vigorous

---

[26] Ahmad Bey, "La Société persane: le Théâtre et ses Fêtes," *La Nouvelle Revue* 14/77 (1892), pp. 531-32. [524-38]; Stuart, Lt. Colonel. *Journal of Residence in Northern Persia* (London: Richard Bentley, 1854), p. 293 ("We found a young Moollah in the pulpit, relating the history of Hoosein with perfect *sang froid*; he was soon followed by a Seyud, who continued the subject with great vehemence: women began to wail, and the men in the pit to beat their breasts, whilst the Seyud, ever and anon, urged them to remember the sufferings of the holy Imaum, and strike harder.")

[27] `Eyn al-Saltaneh, *Ruznameh*, vol. 1, pp. 298 (best ever *rowzeh-khvan*s to-day), 595, 597; E`temad al-Saltaneh, *Ruznameh*, pp. 872, 1108 (also *rowzeh-khvan*s of the 2nd and 3rd rank).

strain of nine feet [sic; ?], to which all returned a chorus of the same measure, beating their breasts in accompaniment.[28]

There were good ones and bad ones. Some of the *rowzeh-khvan*s were very good,
most were run-off-the-mill performers. According to `Eyn al-Saltaneh, Naqib al-
Sadat was one of bad *rowzeh-khvan*s. In July 1895 he noted in his Diary:

> He made a spectacle; for 50 years he has been a *rowzeh-khvan*, but he
> does not know even four Traditions. Today he said a good thing: "The
> pure one, PBOH, said: "do not sit in a *rowzeh-khvani* assembly." Then he
> held out his hand and said: "Ladies and gentlemen the Imam said: *amr*,
> *amr*." The people who were seated in the room laughed. After 60 years,
> he [still] cannot distinguish between good (*amr*) and bad (*nahi*). I could
> not remain seated because of the laughing and stood up and left.[29]

E`temad al-Saltaneh had a similar experience. He related how at a party where he
had been invited one *rowzeh-khvan* recited an elegy. When he was finished everybody thought it was over and wanted to leave, but then another *rowzeh-khvan*
started to recite, and then another and then a fourth. This was clearly too much,
and E`temad al-Saltaneh dryly remarked: "I fled."[30] But there also were perform-
ances that were beter appreciated. `Eyn al-Saltaneh related how in 1893, the Turk-
ish merchants and artisans in Tajrish and in Kamraniyeh had organized elaborate
rowzeh-khvani in the mosque of Sheikh `Abdol-Hoseyn for the last 3 years. He
commented: "In truth they had put a good assembly together." Isfahani and Kashani merchants had done something similar in other mosques.[31] At private gatherings it often happened that the organizer invited friends and acquaintances and
their families.[32]

There also was rivalry between the *rowzeh-khvan*s. E`temad al-Saltaneh records,
for example, that there was a row between two *rowzeh-khvan*s (Molla Musa and
Sayyed Musa), which made that the recitation lasted much longer than normal.[33]
What made a good *rowzeh-khvan* is not very clear, but one gets the impression
that he was able to tell a good story and kept the audience spell-bound. According
to Beyza'i, they needed to have a good voice and understand music, for they had
to make the tragic events come to life and be understandable and gripping for the

---

[28] Conolly, Arthur. *Journey to the North of India.* 2 vols. (London: Richard Bentley, 1834), pp.
278-79; see also Fraser, J.B. *A Winter's Journey*, vol. 2, p. 145; Wills, C. J. *In the Land of the Lion
and the Sun* (London: Ward, Lock & Bowden, 1893), p. 281.

[29] `Eyn al-Saltaneh, *Ruznameh*, vol. 1, p. 598 (21 Moharram 1313/July 14, 1895).

[30] E`temad al-Saltaneh, *Ruznameh*, p. 639.

[31] `Eyn al-Saltaneh, *Ruznameh*, vol. 1, pp. 538-39 (2 Moharram 1311—16/7/1893); see also p. 594.

[32] E`temad al-Saltaneh, *Ruznameh*, p. 589.

[33] E`temad al-Saltaneh, *Ruznameh*, p. 145 [4 moharram 1299]

common people.[34] Part of this was also the manner in which he behaved. `Eyn al-Saltaneh said of Sheikh Zeyn al-`Abedin the *rowzeh-khvan*, whom he considered to be a performer, that, he "is really a sight; he weeps and he laughs."[35]

Although it sometimes seemed that there were lamentations throughout the year this was not entirely the case. The frequency and number of lamentations depended on the time of the year; people lived by a solar calendar, but religious activities followed the Moslem lunar year. This meant that lamentations never were held in the same season of the solar year, and clearly winter and bad weather had their impact. `Eyn al-Saltaneh observed, for example, "this year [1316/1898] there are more *rowzeh-khvani* than ever because of the mild weather; they are everywhere; in each lane there are at least four to five tents, [as well as] in the passageways, cisterns, mosques, and whatever."[36]

Normally, the entire recitation was divided between a rhapsodist (*dhaker*) and a preacher (*va'ez*). It is the latter's task to guide the people, and of the former to tell the story of the tragedy, for the preachers were no storytellers. There were also female *rowzeh-khvan*s, at least from the Qajar period.[37] In the seventeenth century, Du Mans described the *va'ez* as a simple preacher. He may have confused him with a *rowzeh-khvan*, although that is unlikely given his long stay in Iran and his great familiarity with its society. He described the preacher as sitting on a chair preaching the tenets of Moslem law, interspaced with stories about their saints, to make some money. For at the end of his performance the preacher in person would go around with an open hand to collect whatever his audience wanted to give him.[38] However, Bafqi, a contemporary of Du Mans, provides a different appreciation of the standing of a preacher (*va'ez*), stating that he indeed had to know the stories about the prophets, imams, and saints, but also that he had to know exegesis (*tafsir*) and the Traditions (*hadith*), and had to be a wise and learned man.[39] Thus, it was a matter of partisan emphasis and characterization. This is also clear from the fact that in the nineteenth century the *rowzeh-khvan* was not confused with the preacher (*va'ez*), who occupied a much higher rank in social and religious prestige. They were olama, who had studied the Koran, the Traditions (*hadith*s), and history and were well-schooled orators. Actually, it did not matter much if you were a good speaker or not when reciting the stories of the

---

[34] Bayza'i, *Namayesh*, p. 73. For names of (well-known) *rowzeh-khvan*s see E`temad al-Saltaneh, *Ruznameh*, pp. 225, 363; `Eyn al-Saltaneh, *Ruznameh*, vol. 1, p. 597.

[35] `Eyn al-Saltaneh, *Ruznameh*, vol. 1, p. 595.

[36] `Eyn al-Saltaneh, *Ruznameh*, vol. 2, p. 1251; see also Ibid, `Eyn al-Saltaneh, *Ruznameh*, vol. 2, p. 1251 ("This year *rowzeh-khvani*s are more numerous than usual; in one street there were 7; in the mosque the Turks had good *rowzeh-khvani*."). Harvest or planting time also was a major obstacle to hold mourning ceremonies when these two activities coincided.

[37] Nasrabadi, *Tadhkereh*, pp. 371, 389; Bayza'i, *Namayesh*, p. 73.

[38] Du Mans, *Estat*, p. 214.

[39] Bafqi, *Jame`-ye Mofidi*, vol. 3, p. 382; see also Aubin, *La Perse*, p. 162.

Imams: the audience did not insist on much oratory skills to be moved and cried easily and spontaneously. Spreading the word had been so effective that "the most ignorant women and illiterate peasants" knew all the details of the life and sufferings of the Imams.[40]

The preachers did not limit themselves to the stories about the sufferings of the Emams, but spoke of religion, morality, and sometimes, and increasingly so after 1906, about politics. Their number is small and they were only found in the large towns. In Tehran, for example, there were only six preachers (*va`ezin*) of some renown. Each of them was affiliated with a mosque where he preached, generally after the afternoon (`asr*) prayer, but every day during Ramazan. Sometimes, a preacher would come to the house of one of the rich and wealthy of the town to preach for 10-15 *tuman*s. After having spoken the homily (*khotbeh*), the preacher would confirm that God was one, Mohammad his last prophet, and that the members of prophet's family were the best among humanity. Then he would recite a verse from the Koran in Arabic, which he would translate into Persian and provide some explanation as to its meaning. The preacher would then select a story from among the many relating to the martyrdom of one of the Emams, as appropriate. Usually, the stories concerned `Ali and his sons Hasan and Hoseyn. The preacher, as discussed above, had ample choice from the abundant martyrology literature.[41]

In addition to *rowzeh-khvani*, which focused of the martyrdom of the Imams at Karbala, the narration of religious epics such as *Romuz-e Hamzeh* and *Hoseyn-e Kord* came into being. Also very important became *hamleh-khvani*, which was the telling of parts of episodes from the *Hamleh-ye Heydari* by Mirza Mohammad Rafi` Badhal (d. 1124). He had migrated to India and at his death the work was unfinished but Mirza Abu Taleb Mir Fendereski completed it. The work deals with the life of the prophet Mohammad, his nephew `Ali, and their vicissitudes till the assassination of `Ali. Storytellers were specialized in one of these stories and therefore there were *hamleh-khvan*s, *rowzeh-khvan*s, etc., but they all served the same purpose, the spread of Shi'ism and the filling of their purse.[42]

Another form of religious elegy is the contest in rhetoric (*sokhanvari*), which is related to *manaqeb-khvani* and *faza'el-khvani*, which had gone out of fashion once Shi'ism became the official religion of Iran. This custom of a poetry contest in rhetoric is peculiar to the so-called `Ajam, a group affiliated with the *Khaksar* dervish order. The `Ajam recruited most of its membership from among the lower classes. According to legend this order ideally drew its members from the 17 professions of the members who originally had founded the order and hence these were known as the holy guilds (*asnaf-e moqaddaseh*) in their parlance. These holy guilds played an

---

[40] Browne, *Literary History*, vol. 4, p. 194.
[41] Aubin, *La Perse*, pp. 163-64.
[42] Bayza'i, *Namayesh*, pp. 71, 79.

important role in the symbolism of the dervish order that practiced *sokhanvari*. The
`Ajam were a very numerous group, whose members were found all over Iran singing
the praises of `Ali and the Imams. Around 1900 there membership was estimated at
10,000 persons. Whenever a dervish sat down in a coffeehouse or *takiyeh* and he
wanted to begin a contest in rhetoric he put down his animal skin (*sardam*) that every
dervish wore and sat down to await a contestant. He would also hang signs each
symbolizing one of the 17 holy guilds on the wall next to his animal skin. When the
other dervish arrived he would through a ritual greeting ceremony after which he also
would sit down. The public was seated around them. The dervish who had been chal-
lenged would start the contest by asking a question in verse with a particular meter
that he was allowed to choose. The challenger had to reply in verse with the same
meter. Often *bahr-e tavil* and versified repeat verses (*rajaz*) were used. The purpose
was to oust the other from the field or in their lingo to "undress" him. For if one of
the contestants was unable to reply he would have to hand over one of his dervish
patches (*vasleh*). The contest would continue until one of the two dervishes had no
more patches. These contests took place in particular during Ramazan in the evenings, and after `Ashura throughout the months of Moharram and Safar in some *taki-
yeh*s. The contests could last from morning till evening. The poetic contest took place
in many towns and was very popular with the public.[43] *Sokhanvari* was peculiar to
the `Ajam dervishes; they had seven ranks, amongst which *naqib* who was the chief
of the storytellers (*naqqal*s) and the chief storyteller (*naqqal-bashi*) of the royal court.
Dervishes needed his permission to tell stories and paid him an annual fee.[44] The
same model was also followed by the so-called `asheq, a class of wandering poet-
minstrels, who like the `Ajam dervishes sang and recited at public gatherings. They
came into being amongst the Anatolian and Azerbaijani Turks, from the late fifteenth
or early sixteenth century. Their repertoire included religious and erotic songs, elegies
and heroic narratives. At first they followed the syllabic prosody of the popular poets,
but later were subjected to Iranian influence, both directly and through the Iranian-
influenced Turkish Sufi poets. Köprülü has argued that they represent a social element distinct from the Turkish popular poets, the court poets, and the *madraseh* or
convent-educated religious poets, and are the successors of the earlier Turkish bards
known as *ozan*.[45] Beyza'i has provided a description of a contest between two minstrels (`asheqs) that took place at Saveh where they were called *beseleshmaq*.[46]

---

[43] Afshari, Mehran. "Ferqeh-ye `Ajam va Sokhanvari," *Hasti* 3/1 (1995), pp. 142-152; Mahjub,
Mohammad. Ja`far. "Sokhanvari," *Sokhan* 6 (1333/1954), pp. 530-35; vol. 7, pp. 631-37, and vol.
8, pp. 779-86; Meier, Fritz and Gramlich, Richard. "Drei moderne Texte zum Persischen Wettreden" *ZDMG* 23 (1961), pp. 289-327; Bayza'i, *Namayesh*, p. 75, n. 1.
[44] Bayza'i, *Namayesh*, p. 77.
[45] Lewis, Bernard "`Ashiq," *Encyclopedia of Islam*².
[46] Bayza'i, *Namayesh*, p. 78. The best description, be it in a book of fiction, of these poetic contests is that by Kurban Said. *Ali and Nino* translated from the German by Jenia Graman (New
York, 1971), pp 34-37. On Kurban Said, the pseudonym for Essad Bey or Lev Nussimbaum see Tom Reis.
The Orientalist (New York, 2005).

Dervishes were not only engaged in *sokhanvari*, but also engaged in *rowzeh-khvani*.[47] This was normal, because they had been *marthiyeh-khvan*s and story-tellers in general, before even the imposition of Shi'ism on Iran. The role of dervishes in the propagation of religious or any other form of drama was there-fore very pronounced. They were often the few 'holy men' that people in remote villagers saw, who sustained their beliefs and above all their hope. Dervishes had a hue of sanctity because they seemed not only to have utterly devoted their life to God, but also because they appeared to have been tinged with the divine. They handled snakes that bit them without dying from their bite as the credulous villagers usually did. Also, dervishes "display the white mark of the prophet's hand on their shoulders, with proof of sanctity and divine favour brings grist to their mill. The miracle is worked by pasting on the shoulder a piece of paper cut in the shape of a hand, which is removed when the surrounding skin has been well darkened by exposure to the sun."[48] Dervishes played a very particular role in storytelling, as they seemed to have been the first to use pictures to sustain their story line.

PARDEH-DARI OR PICTURE NARRATION

Picture narration was but a specialized form of religious dramatic narration as well as of epic narration, for although initially it would seem that the pictures used referred to religious themes, at least as of the sixteenth century there is also evidence of the use of pictures to narrate epic stories. A *pardeh-dar* or *shamayel-gardan* was a storyteller who used a painted screen with figures, mainly dealing with religious subjects, as a prop. He would select an appropriate place, usually in a corner and somewhere quiet, and hang his rolled screen on the wall. Subsequent scenes on the screen were mostly combined on one canvas covered by a curtain, which was gradually uncovered following the progress of his story. He would modulate his voice to bring tension etc. He took money. It was the most folksy and popular way to tell stories.[49]

In 1539, the Venetian envoy, Michele Membré observed in Tabriz that,

> "The Sophians paint figures, such as the figure of 'Ali, they take hold of
> their ear and bow their head, which is a kind of reverence. In their
> squares there are many Persian mountebanks sitting on carpets on the
> ground; and they have certain long cards with figures; and the said mounte-

---

[47] Such as Kaka Siyah with his hat (*taj*) and dervish clothes in Mashhad. E'tesam al-Molk, *Safarnameh-ye Mirza Khanlar Khan E'tesam al-Molk*. ed. Manuchehr Mahmudi (Tehran, 1351/1972), p. 102.

[48] Hale, F. *From Persian Uplands* (New York: E.P.Dutton, n.d.), p. 50.

[49] Beyza'i, *Namayesh*, p. 74. Picture-narration was also known as *surat-khvani*, according to An-andraj.

banks hold a little stick and point to one figure after another, and preach and tell stories over each figure. So everybody gives them some money. There are also others with books in their hands, reading of the battles of `Ali and the combats of the Princes of old, and of Shah Isma`il; and give money to hear. Others, called *tabbara'is*, are to curse the Ottomans and sing songs of how the Shah is to go to Constantinople and place his brother Sam Mirza there as King, and many other ceremonies; and all give them money."[50]

Some eighty-five years later, in 1624, the Russian merchant Kotov reported that of the main square of Isfahan, "the *Abdals* tell stories about how their 'damned' [=saints] lived and affirm their faith. ... And those *Abdals* go about the *maidan* and streets and the bazaars and tell stories about the lives of their 'damned' [=saints], how they lived and died."[51] In 1639, according to Olearius, wandering dervishes (*abdal*), who were dressed in coarse woolens or simply animal skins and who had a snakeskin as a kind of belt, spread Shi`ism.[52] Around 1694, Sanson reported: "Derviches, or Abdals; they lead a poor and austere Life; they preach the Alcoran in the corners of Streets, Coffee Houses, publick Ways, and, in short, where ever they can find Auditors. They talk with a great deal of Zeal, and some of 'em have a little Eloquence. They know nothing but the Fables, with which they amuse the Vulgar. They are no more esteem'd of by Men of Wit, than the Charlatans are in France."[53] According to Zarrinkub, itinerant storytellers referred to as sufis, i.e. dervishes from Ardabil (*sufiyan-e Ardabil*) till the end of the Safavid period narrated stories about Mohammad b. Hanafiyyeh and Abu Moslem to draw parallels between the nature of Abu Moslem's and the early Safavid's objectives and to propagate and teach their ideas.[54]

---

[50] Membré, Michele. *Relazione*, ed. G.C. Scarcia (Rome, 1969). English translation by A.H. Morton as *Mission to the Lord Sophy of Persia (1539-1542)* (London: SOAS, 1993), p. 52.

[51] Kemp, *Russian Travellers*, pp. 20, 25. Kotov wrote the 'damned,' because from a Russian Orthodox point of view that is what they are. For Moslems these same dead persons were saints.

[52] Olearius, *Vermehrte newe Beschreibung*, pp. 684-85; Anonymous. *A Chronicle of the Carmelites in Persia and the Papal Mission of the Seventeenth and Eighteenth Centuries*, 2 vols. (London, 1939), vol. 1, p. 156.

[53] Sanson, N. *The Present State of Persia* (London, 1695), p. 153-54. See also Du Mans, *Estat*, pp. 216-17 who distinguishes between *qalandar*s and dervishes, although both of them were engaged in telling religious stories.

[54] Zarrinkub, *Donbaleh*, pp. 228-29; Ja`fariyan, Rasul. *Din va Siyasat dar Dowreh-ye Safavi* (Qom, 1370/1991), p. 235.

HOLY MEN WHO ENTERTAIN AS WELL AS PRAY.

Figure 19: Dervishes with portable painted screens with scenes from the life of the Imams

Dervishes were not the only ones who made use of pictures as a prop for their story. Della Valle relates how during Moharram, sayyeds, performing as *rowzeh-khvan*, did the same with regards to the Karbala events. "From time to time he shows some painted figures illustrating what he is recounting; and, in brief, in every way he tries as much as he can to move the audience to tears."[55] Dervishes and other story tellers continued to be active in a similar manner throughout the Qajar period. About 1810, on the road to Rey, for example, Price saw a number of entertainers. "Among the latter was a man exhibiting some plates, with their names and explanations in French and Italian; the fellow intreated me to tell him the meaning of them: I told him two or three, but finding the Persians flocking round in great numbers, I was glad to get away."[56] The American missionary Bassett in the mid-1880s described how a dervish was telling stories about the prophets and imams to a village audience. "The likenesses of these revered persons painted upon a large canvass were suspended on the wall of the village."[57] This popular practice of the propagation of the faith was not limited to out of the way villages, but was also performed close to the shrine of Imam Reza in Mashhad, one of the holiest shrines of the Shi'ite faith. As the following description of some of the activities taking place in the shrine's cemetery shows it was only one of the many enterprises that vied for the attention and the money of the believers.

> On dead walls not far off some traders in religion had fixed up large canvas
> paintings, fifteen feet square, representing various scenes in the massacre of

[55] Della Valle, Pietro. *Les Fameux Voyages* 4 vols. (Paris: Gervais Clouzier, 1664), vol. 2, p. 180.

[56] Price, William. *Journal of the British Embassy to Persia.* 2 vols. in one (London: Thomas Thorpe, 1832), vol. 1, p. 34.

[57] Basset, James. *Persia, the Land of the Imams* (New York: Charles Scribner's Sons, 1886), p. 204.

Hasan and Hussein, and some combats of Rustam with the White Demon, that everlasting subject of Persian art. Whenever a crowd collected, and many of them were women, some of whom descended from their red horse litters, the two exhibitors commenced a kind of recitative chant, descriptive of the event represented in their painting, occasionally bursting forth into song of a very monotonous character. Around, old moullahs were seated among the tombs, reading the Koran in a loud voice with a view of extracting charity from the hadjis; and deformed beggars almost in a state of nudity whined and howled at the passers-by.[58]

In Qazvin, only dervishes did *pardeh-dari*. They appropriately lived in Dervish Street (*Kucheh-ye Dervish*) in the Ab-Anbar-e Sardar quarter. They performed at the tomb of `Ali b. Shadhen near the cemetery south of town.[59] Till the end the Qajar dynasty and beyond, dervishes continued to propagate religious fervor among the credulous population, while the population itself used all kinds of items to give expression to their belief and, above all, their hope of salvation from their daily misery.[60] They usually traveled and performed in couples. One would narrate the story, while the other would react from time to time to boost the attention of the spectators. Or the one would hold the banner with the images, while the other would beat his chest while declaiming religious chants (*qasideh*s or *mathnavi*s) about the world's vanity. The one holding the images explained their meaning. The images often showed fantastic animals, sinners in hell, and epic Iranian heroes; all were painted in bright colors and primitively drawn. The images were bound together so that they could be opened like a book, or in the fashion of an accordion, and sometimes they were just rolled up. They acted the story in a very dramatic manner and stopped at important developments in it to get contributions of copper coins from their audience.[61] Picture narrators were still found in Iran until recent times. I saw one myself in a village in 1966 and he was probably one of last practicing the art. He was not a dervish, but just a man trying to make money.

Picture narrators, like other storytellers, were made obsolete by modern technology, the increase in the literacy rate and reading habits. The radio, cinema, and television had a stronger attraction than the painted screen that was always the

---

[58] O'Donovan, Edmond. *The Merv Oasis*. 2 vols. (London: Smith, Elder & Co, 1882), vol. 1, p. 490. For a 1927 picture of a traveling theater group with religious pictures as their props, see Norden, Hermann. *Under Persian Skies* (Philadelphia: McCrea Smith, n.d.), p. 206.

[59] Varjavand, *Simay*, vol. 2, p. 895.

[60] See Kellermann, *Auf Persiens Karawanenstrassen* (Berlin: S. Fischer, 1928), p. 80. For a picture see Norden, *Under Persian Skies*, p. 206 (story tellers of the Imams.) American missionaries used the same medium and hung pictures of bible scenes on the wall, "told the stories, and taught the lessons of them." Jewett, Mary. *My Life in Persia* (Cedar Rapids, 1909), p. 120. British missionaries used the 'magic lantern' to project pictures of slides.

[61] Rezvani, *Le théatre*, p. 121; Wegener, Walther. *Syrien, Irak, Iran* (Leipzig, 1943), p. 83. For a picture see Shahri, *Tarikh*, vol. 6, p. 39.

same (although the story was duly embellished) and only came occasionally. The modern forms of entertainment are available on demand. But before the electronic age replaced storytelling there were new mechanical Western inventions that vied for people's attention. Galunov described a picture machine that he saw in use at Isfahan in the 1920s, which was called the *shahr-e ferang* (the European town; probably because the pictures were of a European city). It was a metal case inside which a roll (*tumar*) was rotated to show pictures one by one through an opening at the front of the case. This phenomenon was followed by the peep show, which was either the same or an improved version of the same machine.[62]

CHILDREN AT A PEEP SHOW
Operator is wearing the Pahlavi cap which has
recently been discarded.

Figure 20: Children watching a picture machine or *shahr-e ferang* (1938)

---

[62] Galunov, R. A. "Narodniy Teatr Irana," *Sovietskaia Etnografiya* 4-5 (1936), p. 67 ff. For a picture of what is probably the same machine see Morton, Rosalie Slaughter. *A Doctor's Holiday in Iran* (New York, 1940), p. 129 (photo of kids at a peep show).

CHAPTER FIVE

RELIGIOUS EPIC DRAMA

INTRODUCTION

Religious epic drama is limited to the Shi`ite denomination of Islam, and like threnodies (*rowzeh-khvani*), concerns the martyrdom of Imam Hoseyn, his family and his companions. This type of drama is known as *shabih-khvani* or *ta`ziyeh-khvani*.[1] The form and content of the drama may have been modeled after the pre-Islamic Siyavosh epic drama. After all, many pre-Islamic customs and beliefs still persist till this day in Iran and the transformation of the pre-Islamic elegiac tradition therefore may have been transformed easily into a Moslem one. A case in point is the Moharram observance such as it is performed in Yazd. Percy Sykes wrote that the *Meydan-e Chakhmaq* in Yazd

> is entered by the second of the very lofty gateways referred to above, and in it stands an octagonal tile-covered pillar some nine feet high, which is known as a *kalak*. This puzzled me for some time, as the word literally means a clay bow for holding hot charcoal. All the Parsi shrines include a pillar of this sort, and it would appear that the Mohammedans of Yezd and Kashan have adopted it from the members of the older religion. During the month of Moharram lamps and, if necessary, fires are lighted upon it, and it is the centre for the breast-beating ceremonies.[2]

This was not the only pre-Islamic custom that was still celebrated in the nineteenth century. Morier reported around 1812 that,

> An *Eyd* or festival peculiar to Demawend took place on the 31st August. It is remarkable from being unconnected with Mahomedanism. Its ceremonies are designed to commemorate the death of *Zohak*, the celebrated Iranian tyrant, and consist of a general rejoicing, in which all the inhabitants of the town and villages of Demawend join, gathering together in the fields on horses, mules and other beasts, and rising about on the full

---

[1] Krymskij, A. *Pers'kii Teatr* (Kiev, 1925) stated that the term *ta`ziyeh* referred to the entire range of mourning ceremonies, whereas for the religious drama the terms *ta`ziyeh-shabih* or *ta`ziyeh-gardani* were used. In Ardabil, but also elsewhere, the passion play was called *shabiyeh-khvani*. Safar, *Ardabil*, vol. 3, pp. 255.

[2] Sykes, Percy M. *Ten Thousand Miles in Persia or Eight Years in Iran* (New York: Charles Scribner's Sons, 1902), p. 422.

gallop, with loud shouts. At night they light fires on the tops of their houses, and make illuminations in all parts of town.[3]

There are other historical connections with folk traditions, such as the installation of a mock king at the time of the New Year festival, which was and probably still is practiced in parts of Iran, as discussed in chapter one.[4] Whether historically linked to the Siyavosh Passion or not, a fact is that the Shi`ite passion literature has been inspired by and has borrowed from many of the literary devices that have been used to evoke the suffering of Siyavosh in Iranian epic literature.[5] This is quite understandable given the fact, as discussed above, that the "Death of Siyavosh" and the "Death of Sohrab" were the most popular episodes of the *Shahnameh* and their narration always drew large crowds.[6]

*Ta`ziyeh-khvani* or the performance of the Shi`ite passion play grew out of public mourning ceremonies, which transformed themselves into processions with floats on which actors represented or performed legendary scenes from the Tragedy that later merged into the enactment of the story in a more recognizable dramatic form. The accepted wisdom is that *ta`ziyeh-khvani* started at the end of the eighteenth century. I have no major problem with that conclusion, because there is solid evidence for such a position. It is further rightly argued that the passion play drama evolved throughout the nineteenth century. This implies that the year 1786, when there is the first evidence that a passion play was performed on a stage, was not the beginning but just one stage in the evolution of the *ta`ziyeh-khvani* ritual. For the passion play could not have originated *ex nihilo* at that time and therefore logic dictates that this type of theater must have started much earlier. The Tragedy of Hoseyn as experienced and performed in 1700 was, of course, different from the way it was played in 1800 as it was different in 1900 from the performance in 1800, but the basic elements were common to the performance at all three periods. Apart from logic, what arguments, or better, what evidence is there for such a point of view?

The following elements coalesced to produce the passion play. By the end of the seventeenth century after almost 200 years of having been exposed to Shi`ite indoctrination that had transformed a predominantly Sunni country into one that was mostly Shi`ite every Shi`ite Iranian knew the stories of the Karbala martyrdom very well. The dervishes with their story-screens (*pardeh*) told the stories of the Imams throughout the year. The *rowzeh-khvan*s did the same and regularly, in particular

---

[3] Morier, James. *A Second Journey through Persia, Armenia, and Asia Minor ... between the years 1810 and 1816* (London: Longman, Hurst, Rees, Orme, and Brown, 1818), p. 357.
[4] Qazwini, "Mir-e Nowruzi," pp. 13-16; Başgöz, "Marasem," pp. 130-41; Anjavi Shirazi, *Baziha-ye Namayeshi*; Ibid., *Jashnehha va Adab*.
[5] Meskub, Shahrokh. *Sug-e Siyavosh: dar marg va rastakhiz* (Tehran: Khvarezmi, 1350/1971); Hasuri, `Ali. *Siyavoshan* (Tehran: Cheshmeh, 1378/1999) both have argued that the stories of the *ta`ziyeh-khvani* cycle are but a transposition of the ancient Siyavosh rituals.
[6] Shahri, *Tarikh*, vol. 5, pp. 517-18.

during the months of Moharram, Safar, and Ramazan, and they did so in *takiyeh*s, complete with tiered circular seating arrangements, while food and drinks were served to the participants in the mourning ceremonies.[7] The *rowzeh-khvan*s also made use of painted scenes to make their points. Most important was the annual dramatic enactment of the martyrdom of the Imams during Moharram. This enactment assumed two forms. The first one was that of entertainers who performed in mime the grief believers felt on account of the Imams. They did so in public places and for money. The second one was the neighborhood associations that each year put together an increasingly more elaborate series of tableaux-vivants (*shamayel*), each of which was the representation of a well-known scene that were the substance of the later passion plays. The mourning processions of the seventeenth century were quite elaborate and consisted of a number of "floats" with representations or depictions of Imam Hoseyn and his family, the caliph Yazid and other villains. The various floats each represented a distinct episode of the Karbala drama. The elaborate nature of each float, their number and decoration, all indicate financial support if not from rich individuals, at least from the community.

Figure 21: Moharram procession with floats and banners (Darband, 1740s)

I do not describe the development of the Moharram procession or the entire mourning ritual over time, because that would require a separate study. I only focus on the floats within that procession. These floats constituted part of the building blocks of the later passion play. A trumpeter usually opened the `Ashureh

---

[7] Chardin, *Voyages*, vol. 9, p. 64.

procession, and led horses followed. Next came triangular banner (*beyraq*) preceding a music band. The next component of the procession was a man carrying a water vessel on his head to remind spectators of the thirst suffered by the Karbala martyrs. Boys accompanied the men; they were dressed as Arab Bedouins and carried pumpkin bottles and offered people a drink saying: "drink in memory of the Karbala martyrs" (*benush beh yad-e shahid-e Karbala*). After the water carrier came men carrying long poles (*kotol*) or standards with black banners with a hand sticking out on top.

Figure 22: Children from the episode of Qasem's Marriage
(Moharram procession at Shusha, 1869)

The main part of the procession then followed; a series of floats of varying nature and order that represent different episodes of the Karbala drama. The men were clad in white, were mailed and blood covered, while arrows were sticking in their clothes. Some missed an arm; others had an ax sticking out of their head. Further, headless corpses were shown. A child was lying on the bier dressed in a bloody and arrow pierced shirt. Above the head of the child within the neck of the up- turned head a freshly slaughtered sheep in such a manner that only the bloody cut neck was visible. The space in between was filled with cotton and arrows. Be- cause the feet of the child stuck out of the shirt the spectators got the impression that they saw a real beheaded corpse. Also, human heads made out of wax or cardboard were carried on lances. Hoseyn's head was carried on a golden casket, according to legend it was in this manner that it was presented to Yazid. On the corpse of Hoseyn a young boy lay dressed as a panther, for, according to Shi`ite legend, a panther had protected the corpses of the martyrs from abuse. Then fol- lowed a caravan driver carrying a bloody finger with a gold ring, for allegedly one of Yazid's soldiers had cut off Hoseyn's ring-bearing finger. Another man carried a small room on his head, symbolizing Qasem's nuptial room. A newly born had an arrow sticking out of its throat, symbolizing the death of `Ali Akbar, who died when Hoseyn begged for some water for his son. A horseman carried two boys who represented the sons of Moslem b. `Aqils, a cousin of Hoseyn, who had been sent ahead to Kufa and had been martyred there. The procession was closed with the banners (`alam) of neighborhood groups and guilds followed by flagellants.[8]

All of these elements also were found in the passion play as is clear from its de- scription in what follows. It was also clear to de Bruyn who, after his description of the Moharram procession, commented: "every part of this procession refers to some circumstance or other of the death of *Hussein* and his seventy two friends slain with him, and canonized for martyrs by the *Persian*." He also remarked upon the use of faked body parts, such as heads, which were made of wax, "and indeed it must be acknowledged the Persians are very artful in these sorts of representations."[9] De Bruyn further observed the use of simulacra in a country where officially the por- trayal of living being was banned. "The murder of this saint is represented by per- sons in arms, and by his image which is very large and hollow, and put into motion by a person inclosed within it, and whose legs are plainly to be seen. Those con- cerned in this mummery and who carry this image about, receives a reward from the spectators, who give them certain small pieces of silver of very little value' tho' indeed there are some who are more generous to them."[10] The use of "counterfeit figures" is also mentioned in a Persian text written in 1700 or thereabouts. "On day 10, after the recitation from the *Rowzat al-Shohada*, the processions of the various city quarters of Isfahan, the Tabrizis, Qazvinis, Yazdis, Hindu elephant keepers,

---

[8] The above is a summary of a composite description by Massé, *Croyances*, vol. 1, pp. 126-28.

[9] Le Bruyn, Cornelius. *Travels into Moscovy, Persia and part of the East-Indies*, 2 vols. (London, 1737), vol. 1, pp. 216-17. On the *nakhl*s, which de Bruyn describes in some detail and which he referred to as "machines or resting-places." Ibid., *Travels*, p. 218.

[10] Le Bruyn, *Travels*, vol. 1, p. 215. See also Gemelli-Careri, *Giro*, vol. 2, p. 175.

nakhlaha, and the adorned likenesses of the persons of the martyrs (*ashbah-e ashbakh-e shohada*) came to the Ala Qapi."[11]

Della Valle wrote in 1618 that *rowzeh-khvan*s during their narration of the martyrdom of the Imams showed several painted figures to reinforce their message.[12] Olearius in 1637 observed that a *rowzeh-khvan*, as in the nineteenth century, was introduced by a choir of elegists, before he started to read from or told the story of `Ali's life and murder from a *maqtal-nameh*. He also played the public that responded on cue with their cries of woe and lamentation. After the narration had finished the procession with the various 'floats' made their appearance.[13] In 1704, de Bruyn also noted that *rowzeh-khvan*s "hold some written papers in their hands, upon which they cast their eyes, pronouncing the elegy, and reciting the actions and wonders of the saint."[14] Chardin remarked that after the narration on `Ashura, "they sang a chant to laud Hoseyn and family. It was sung by two groups, each singing as loud as possible."[15] Della Valle, observed that pipers, drums and singers performed around the bier of `Ali, just as musicians and singers would play a supporting role in the passion play 200 years later.[16]

Della Valle, and Chardin, described, *inter alia*, how some men went around naked, except for their private parts, had painted themselves black or red from head to foot. Black to denote the misery felt over Hoseyn's death and red to denote blood and the violent death that had been inflicted on Hoseyn. "All of them together go singing in a dirge in his praise about the way he died, and beating with castanets of bone or wood, which they hold in their hands to create a mournful sound, while gesticulating and moving their bodies to suggest great melancholy. They also perform in front of everyone in the middle of a circle, like mountebanks or like teams of tumblers doing their trucks on the public square; and in this guise they make money, which the bystanders give to them as alms."[17] What is interesting about these proceedings is that they were not *rowzeh-khvan*s nor were they part of the tableaux-vivants. They were professional entertainers, who adapted themselves and their arts to the seasons and to whatever their audience wanted to see and hear. What is of further interest is that the performers through their coloring aimed to help the spectators to identify the persons they were portraying. As is

---

[11] Nasiri, Mohammad Ebrahim b. Zeyn al-`Abedin, *Dastur-e Shahriyan*. ed. Mohammad Nader Nasiri Moqaddam (Tehran, 1373/1995), p. 33.

[12] Della Valle, *Voyages*, vol. 2, p. 180.

[13] Olearius, *Vermehrte Newe Beschreibung*, p. 435 (Machtelnamae); Chardin, *Voyages*, vol. 9, p. 53f.

[14] Le Bruyn, *Travels*, vol. 1, p. 215.

[15] Chardin, *Voyages*, vol. 9, p. 63.

[16] Della Valle, *Voyages*, vol. 2, p. 115; Le Bruyn, *Travels*, vol. 1, p. 216.

[17] Della Valle, *Voyages*, vol. 2, p. 179; Le Bruyn, *Travels*, vol. 1, p. 215; Chardin, *Voyages*, vol. 9, pp. 50-51.

discussed in what follows in the later passion play similar symbolism was and is used.

**Figure 23: Marriage chamber of Qasem in the Moharram procession
in Shusha (Caucasus) in 1869**

All these elements (*takiyeh*; actors; poets; music; depiction and representation of episodes of the martyrdom stories in the [a] body of literature, [b] paintings, and [c] tableaux-vivants) together produced the passion play (*ta`ziyeh-khvani*). It was not a conscious development, but a gradual evolution that coalesced around 1700 and thereafter grew into the passion play over the next decades. Some of the *row-zeh-khvan*s used painted figures to narrate certain episodes of the martyrdom of the Imams, which were slowly transformed into the scenes of the passion play. Poets writing scripts for the passion play drew heavily upon that imagery as well as on classical Persian literature to give it form. Lerch in the 1730s already implied that there was dramatic acting.[18] This was no fluke. In 1772 Gmelin observed that certain parts of the history of the martyrs were read, sometimes also sung, to represent Hoseyn's death really vividly. He also recorded that the singers accompanying the tableaux-vivants or in the *takiyeh*s sang songs that had been specially written or had been adapted for that occasion. Meanwhile, specialized

---

[18] Lerch, Johann Jacob. *Lebens- und Reise-Geschichte von ihm selbst beschrieben* (Halle: Curtts Witwe, 1791), pp. 392-93.

singers sang a song appropriate to this or the other circumstance.[19] This suggests that (i) there existed organized performances of the passion plays in dedicated spaces (*takiyeh*s); (ii) poet wrote songs or prose for these performances, and (iii) a stage director made sure that the texts chanted were relevant to the occasion, implying both casting and directing. These facts indicate that literate dramatic hands were at work to enhance the poetic value of the singers' message.

From Niebuhr's description of the `Ashura ceremony on the island of Khark in 1764 it is clear that the passion play was being staged earlier than the accepted date of 1786. Niebuhr observed that during the first nine days of Moharram there were daily processions and other ceremonies on Khark. The `Ashura festival was performed on the main square. Those representing Yazid's army under Shemr were on one side of the square. When Hoseyn and his companions arrived Shemr and his troops attacked them. There was real acting. "From the faces and their entire posture one saw signs that they had been driven to the greatest despair and were determined, in view of their near death, to sell their lives dearly." One of the actors, playing the role of Qasem, was toppled from his horse several times. "When he wanted to mount his horse again his daughters begged him not to return to fight; they wept so sincerely as if their father really was going to expose himself to the greatest danger." The actor who played `Abbas held his arms close to his body and the sleeves of his overcoat hung empty from his shoulders, signifying that he had lost both arms when trying to get water from a well. After fierce fighting, Hoseyn's party was overcome and the survivors were taken prisoner. The children were given a wooden contraption around their neck and were taken to Yazid's general. "Some of them answered the victor very defiantly. Then orders were given to execute them." Yazid was also present on the square and was seated on a European chair with a stone hammer in his hand. When the survivors of Hoseyn's family were taken to him an ambassador of the Byzantine emperor appeared at the same time. The ambassador was dressed in European clothes, without socks, and a gold-braided hat. Three times he interceded with Yazid to grant the life to `Ali b. Hoseyn (Zeyn al-`Abedin) and after the third time he was executed. There was music during the performance as well as breast-beating prior to and during its performance.[20]

What the above shows is that there were a number of elements that already existed before 1786 that also were essential elements in passion plays in the nineteenth century, to wit: (i) professional entertainers performing the tragedy of Hoseyn and his companions for money; (ii) *rowzeh-khvan*s reading their elegy from a written text; (iii) texts especially written to be sung or recited during the Moharram ceremonies; (iv) music played and groups of singers chanted to accompany the *rowzeh-khvani*

---

[19] Gmelin, S.G. *Reise durch Russland*, 4 vols. (St. Petersburg, 1774), vol. 3, pp. 316-17.
[20] Niebuhr, Carsten. *Reisebeschreibung nach Arabien und andern umliegende Ländern* (Zürich, 1992), pp. 575-78.

and the floats; and finally, (v) tableaux vivant displaying single episodes of a full-fledged passion play. Some of them even going so far as to actually perform "the burial" of the corpses of the martyrs, or in the case of Khark actually playing of episodes of the Karbala drama. In short, they were engaged in ta'izyeh-khvani, i.e. they performed the passion play. Monchi-zadeh has argued that the elements that make ta'ziyeh-khvani dramatic theater rather than something else are the following: (1) the takiyeh, or the gathering point for the performance of the play; (2) the characters: children of the Imams, caravans, family of the prophets, etc.; (3) music; (4) singing and choirs; and above all (5) the paintings that the rowzeh-khvan showed to illustrate the story he told and that later would serve as a scene for the passion play.[21] Although it would seem that I have forgotten the takiyehs, for otherwise Monchi-zadeh and I are in agreement, this is not the case because this element is discussed in detail in what follows. What the above also implies is that the passion play (ta'ziyeh-khvani) as it has developed on Iran is entirely homegrown. Like Mohammad Mahjub, I have not seen any hard or circumstantial evidence for European, Russian, or Indian influence on this dramatic typically Iranian art form.[22]

THEATER (TAKIYEH) TO STAGE THE PASSION PLAY

Mourning rituals and passion plays were held in a so-called takiyeh.[23] What is a takiyeh exactly, i.e. how did it actually look like? Chodzko reported: "In the nomad camps and villages the shows are put up in tekkehs [sic], or porticos specially built for that purpose. In towns public places, caravanserais, courtyards of mosques and palaces serve as the stage. Because the presentation is always in the open air, and because the lunar month Moharram is not always in the same solar month, enormous pieces of canvas protect, if need be, actors and public from the intemperate weather. This is really necessary during the hot summer. The galleries and windows also covered are reserved for the nobility and invites, amongst which often diplomats."[24] This means that a takiyeh is: (i) often a performance site in the open air; (ii) a kind of portico; and (iii) a building solely dedicated to the performance of the religious drama. It also meant that there were both temporary and permanent takiyehs.

---

[21] Monchi-zadeh, Davoud. Ta'ziya. Das Persische Passionsspiel (Stockholm, 1967), p. 16.

[22] Mahjub, Muhammad Ja'far. "The Effect of European Theatre and the Influence of its Theatrical Methods Upon Ta'ziyeh," in Peter J. Chelkowski, Ta'ziyeh: Ritual and Drama in Iran (New York, 1979), pp. 137-53.

[23] According to Massé, Croyances, vol. 1, p. 123, n. 3, "strictu sensu, the tekiye, with a central stage, serves [to perform] the religious drama (ta'ziyeh). The enclosures for the recitation (rowze), with pulpit, but without stage, are called hosainiye." Originally, the term referred to a monks' convent.

[24] Chodzko, Théatre Persan, pp. xxii-iii; Calmard, Jean. "Le mécénat des representations de ta'zie. I," Le Monde Iranien et l'Islam 2 (1974), p. 94.

Figure 24: Open-air *takiyeh* in Tabas (1907)

There is general agreement among the contemporary reporters that "Places [to perform the passion play] are prepared in every city, town, and village."[25] In villages, passion play theater was often performed in a construction, "often used at other times as a market-place, where, for four weeks of the year, daily performances are given." By the turn of the twentieth century almost every major village had one of those constructions, which also were used as a sleeping place for travelers.[26] In many villages, the passion play was staged in the open air, such as at the fort of the village of Eyvan-e Keyf.[27] In tribal areas the mourning ceremonies took place entirely in the open air.[28] There seems have been also a kind of ambulatory performance of the passion play along the Tehran-Mashhad road, an important highway for pilgrims going to Mashhad.

---

[25] Fraser, *A Winter's Journey*, vol. 2, p. 145.

[26] Wishard, John G. *Twenty Years in Persia. A Narrative of Life under the Last Three Shahs* (New York: Fleming H. Revell, 1908), p. 157; Fraser, J.B. *A Winter's Journey from Constantinople to Teheran*, 2 vols. in one (London, 1838 [New York: Arno, 1973]), vol. 2, p. 146; Eastwick, *Journal*, vol. 2, p. 141 (Aradun) ; Wills, *In the Land*, p. 283; Browne, E.G. *A Year Amongst the Persians* (London: A. & C. Black, 1970), pp. 84 (village of Kirishkin), 273 (the village of Zangavar (near Persepolis) had a *takiyeh* in which Browne slept)

[27] Eastwick, Edward B. *Journal of a Diplomate's Three Years' Residence in Persia*. 2 vols. (London, 1864 [Tehran: Imp. Org. f. Soc. Services, 1976]), vol. 2, p. 136.

[28] Sykes, Ella. *Through Persia on a Side-Saddle* (London: MacQueen, 1901), pp. 144. In the village of Taregurap (Gilan) the annual passion play was performed next to its mineral spring. Melgunof, Gregorii Valerianovich. *Das südliche Ufer des Kaspischen Meeres oder die Nordprovinzen Persiens* translated by J. Th. Zenker (Leipzig, 1868), p. 251.

A scene in the religious drama founded on the massacre of the Imams Hassan and Hussein was about to be acted. ... [it] is exceedingly long, the proper representation of the piece requiring a daily performance of a couple of hours for weeks at a time. As the pilgrims march they are treated to one act at each halting-place throughout the journey." [Description of the play, including of a British soldier's scarlet uniform with dark blue facings] "There was a good deal of monotonous chanting and declamatory singing, coupled with a stage compact between the man in armour and the other in the red coat, a good deal of going to and fro of the white horse and its rider, and, after an hour or so, the acting wound up by a collection of money from the onlookers.[29]

As far as the urban areas are concerned, "In every mahal [sic; *mahalleh* or quarter] of the town, [there are] one or more large buildings, called takiehs."[30]

The builder of a *takiyeh* sometimes also built a public fountain (*saqqa-khaneh*) next to it in memory of the parched martyrs. The patron also might build a tomb (*maqbareh*) there for his burial.[31] Irrespective of the location, the simplest form of the *takiyeh* was in the open air, to accommodate not only the large number of people that attended, but also the large number of performing men and animals and their props. People therefore usually erected large canvas tents in several parts of the town, some days before the beginning of Moharram.[32] Usually the locations were the open squares in the town, but invariably next to some large building so as to allow the mounting of a canvas awning over the scene of the play and/or spectators. "Rude theatres covered with awnings called 'tazeers,' [sic; *tajir*] are erected in all the open parts of the city, for the representation of the martyrdom of Hoosein."[33] These tents were placed at 8-10 meters high, tightly spread and fastened to trees or windows all around to protect the actors and public from intemperate weather.[34] These tents were luxuriously embellished with costly fabrics, shawls, lent by devotees. Also hanging were animal skins to which mail-coats, shields, sabers, and all kinds of arms were attached.[35] Passion plays were also performed in a mosque, a

[29] O'Donovan, *Merv Oasis*, vol. 1, p. 406.

[30] Holmes, W.R. *Sketches on the Shores of the Caspian, Descriptive and Pictorial.* (London: Richard Bentley, 1845), p. 296; Fowler, George. *Three Years in Persia* 2 vols. (London: Colburn, 1841), p. 122; Melgunof, *Das südliche Ufer*, pp. 39, 140, 232, 235, 279; O'Donovan, *The Merv Oasis*, vol. 1, pp. 405-06.

[31] Rabino, H.L. *Mazandaran and Astarabad* (London: Luzac, 1928), p. 40.

[32] Price, *Journal*, p. 29; Fowler, *Three Years*, p. 122.

[33] Stuart, *Journal*, pp. 292-93; Wilbraham, Richard. *Travels in the Transcaucasian Provinces of Russia* (London: John Murray, 1839), pp. 420-21; Mounsey, Augustus H. *A Journey through the Caucasus and the Interior of Persia* (London: Smith, Elder & Co, 1872), p. 311; Safa al-Saltaneh, *Safarnameh*, p. 71.

[34] Thalasso, *Le Théatre Persan*, p. 882.

[35] Flandin, E. and Coste, P. *Voyage en Perse ... 1840-41* (Paris, 1851), vol. 1, pp. 250-55. As to the meaning of the skins see the description of the *sardam* by Mahjub, Mohammad Ja`far. "Sok-

caravanserai, or in front of a private person's house, which was usually the case with the town's notables.[36] They were also held in the garden of the governor's palace, or in the "court of the dewan-khana ... covered with canvas."[37] Sometimes passion plays were also staged at *emamzadeh*s.[38]

But even when there were tents or a building these often were not large enough to accommodate everybody, in which case the entire show was moved out of the city or village. Rice, a member of the 1810 Ouseley embassy, saw a play in a village in Isfahan. "During the early days of the month the performances took place in a compound, but on the tenth there was gathering of at least five thousand people." ... "The performance was to take place out in the desert."[39] O'Donovan experienced a similar situation in 1880 in Khorasan. For the last day of the play, "the market-place in which the previous scenes had been enacted was entirely inadequate to contain the concourse of spectators. Every shop in the town was closed, and men, women, and children flocked to a wide space entirely without the town walls, where the necessary reparations had been made."[40] At Mohammadabad, "The market-place outside, flanked by the caravanserai, constituted the theatre. Some three thousand spectators were present."[41] In Golpeygan the entire population attended in the governor's courtyard, 5,000 to 6,000 people. The stage was in the middle; it only had a wooden stage on which the choir that at intervals between the scene would recite verses in honor of `Ali.[42] Rice saw play in a village in Isfahan around 1920. "During the early days of the month the performances took place

---

hanvari," *Sokhan* 9 (1337/1958), p. 631. The sequence was longer than 10 days. Flandin, *Voyage*, vol. 1, p. 253.

[36] Ahmad Bey, "Le Théatre," p. 529; Ussher, John. *Journey from London to Persepolis* (London: Hurst & Blackett, 1865), p. 618; `Eyn al-Saltaneh, *Ruznameh*, vol. 1, pp. 538-39 (mosque); Ibid., vol. 1, p. 467 (house); Aubin, *La Perse*, p. 170.

[37] Wills, *In the land*, p. 297 ("Zill-es-Sultan's garden in Shiraz"); Wilson, S.G. *Persian Life and Customs* (New York: Fleming. H. Revell, 1895), pp. 62-63 (Tabriz); Sykes, *Through Persia*, p. 274 (Ahvaz). On Moharram 10, Naser al-Din Shah received the neighborhood groups (*dasteh*s) and actors (*ta`ziyeh-khvan*s) at Government House (*divan-khaneh*), after which the passion play would take place there in his presence. *Ruznameh-ye Ettefaqiyeh-ye Vaqaye`* 4 vols. (Tehran: Ketabkhaneh- Melli, 1373-74/1994-95) no. 91, 14 Moharram 1269/28 October 1852.

[38] `Eyn al-Saltaneh, *Ruznameh*, vol. 1, p. 223 (Emamzadeh-ye Qasem); Homayuni, Sadeq. *Ta`ziyeh dar Iran* (Shiraz, 1368/1989), p. 128 (at Vanak).

[39] Rice, *Persian Women*, p. 236; Hommaire de Hell, X. *Voyage en Turquie et en Perse*. 2 vols. (Paris: P. Bertrand, 1856), vol. 2, p. 11 (in the bazaar "theaters in the open air."); Ahmad Bey, "Le Théatre," p. 529.

[40] O'Donovan, *Merv Oasis*, vol. 2, p. 51

[41] O'Donovan, *Merv Oasis*, vol. 2, p. 41. In Khorramabad in November 1849 the performance of the passion play took place in the tent (*sarapardeh*) of the governor outside the town. Afshar, Hasan `Ali Khan. *Safarnameh-ye Lorestan va Khuzestan* ed. Hamid-Reza Dalvand (Tehran,1382/2003), pp. 82-84.

[42] Texier, C. *Description de l'Armenie, la Perse et la Mesopotamie* (Paris, 1852), part 2, pp. 102-03; Browne, E.G. *A Year*, p. 615 (In Barforush the passion play was in progress in the main street).

in a compound, but on the tenth there was gathering of at least five thousand people." … "The performance was to take place out in the desert."[43]

Figure 25: *Takiyeh* **(building plus awning) in Shamakhi (1637). Note the** *rowzeh-khvan*
(right), the floats and the banners (`alam) of the Moharram procession

From the preceding it is clear that a *ta`ziyeh* was seldom performed in a specially built building, but more often than not in an open space in front or next to an existing building or in the courtyard of such a building (mosque, house, villa, caravanserai). This was the situation during the hey-day of the passion plays. How much different was the situation during the period when the passion play drama allegedly was not yet performed?

---

[43] Rice, *Persian Women*, p. 236.

In 1624, when in Isfahan, in the Chahar Bagh quarter, the Russian merchant Kotov described two mosques one of which Shah `Abbas I visited.

> Also in the same mosque their idol, the image of a man, is painted on a
> board, and there in the mosque lie poles with flags, [which], like our
> church banners, are not used for anything except to be carried on festi-
> vals with the ikons, and among them [the Persians] these poles are car-
> ried on their festivals and in front of the dead. And these poles are vine
> rods, long and thin, about 10 *sazhen* in length, and when they lift them
> the poles bend; and tied to the tops of them long, narrow streamers about
> 5 *sazhen* long hang half way down the poles and on the top of the poles
> there are iron things like scissors or like a stork's beak and on other poles
> there are wicker crosses and spikes (?).[44]

One could argue, of course, that Kotov just referred to a mosque as storage space
for the implements of the Moharram procession, while acceding the point that it
shows that there was a separate dedicated space for the Moharram events. However, as is clear from the description by Della Valle and de Bruyn, for example,
rowzeh-khvani took place in mosques and public places, "which they purposely
adorn with many lights and with funeral displays" and "are full of seats and
benches." The public places, "especially in cross-ways and the other more frequented parts, which they enclose with tapestry and spread with carpets," while
adorning its walls piece of armor and arms.[45] Moreover, Olearius in February
1637 mentioned that the `Ashureh ceremony in Shamakhi took place outside the
city walls in "a building constructed to that end."[46] One might submit that it was
not much of a building, as shown by Olearius's drawing, and opine that it only
served to seat the governor, his guests and other spectators for whom there was
room. However, these descriptions nicely fit those of *takiyeh*s described in the
nineteenth century. Furthermore, Dr. Lerch reported, referring to the situation in
the 1730s in the Caucasus, that the Moharram ritual was partly performed in the
mosque, which is what you would expect, for in the nineteenth century mosques
also still served as *takiyeh*, as discussed above. The existence of *takiyeh*s is also
attested from the second half of the eighteenth century. Gmelin reports that in
1770 in Resht there was such a special dedicated space to stage the mourning
ceremonies in Resht in each of the seven town quarters. "Each one has its special
place of assembly, which represents a large gallery, more or less decorated at the
expense of the quarter and covered with gold pieces, velvet, textiles, metal pieces,
guns, helmets, &c."[47] Gmelin in fact literally writes that "the houses, in which the

---

[44] Kemp, *Russian Travellers*, pp. 24-25.

[45] Della Valle, *Voyages*, vol. 2, p. 180; Le Bruyn, *Travels*, vol. 1, p. 215.

[46] Olearius, *Vermehrte Newe Beschreibung*, p. 435 (for the picture see p. 436).

[47] Gmelin, *Reise*, vol. 3, p. 316; Anonymous, *Histoire des Decouvertes faites par divers savans
voyageurs* 6 vols. (Lausanne: Heubach, 1784), vol. 2, p. 368.

meetings of the Hussein festival take place, are called tekia," of which there were nine in Resht, two in Amol, nineteen in Barforush in 1772.[48] A dervish *takiyeh* in Astarabad (built in 1201/1786) was clearly used for the mourning ceremonies given the inscription's frequent reference to the martyred Imams and the events of Karbala.[49] Furthermore, Varjavand mentions that the Dowlat, Javanshir and Af-sharha *takiyeh*s in Qazvin all date from Safavid period. They may, of course, have been originally dervish convents, just like the one in Astarabad, but it is quite likely that Moharram mourning ceremonies were held there.[50]

THE MONTHS OF MOURNING

During the death (*qatl*) commemoration days, but in particular during the month of Moharram, the entire country was in mourning. During the month of Moharram the minarets were "covered with precious flags with gold or silver hems, of white color as they were of the Bani Hashem, `Ali's family with the ornament of the lion and the sun."[51] Mosques were hung with black, while their insides were lined with black for this occasion.[52] Other public buildings and houses, "in every city, town, and village, [were] hung with dark clothes or shawls, and furnished forth with other emblems of mourning."[53] The entire Moslem population, from the shah to the poorest person (men, women and children) put on black or dark-blue during this month, the symbol of mourning. "During the whole of this season of the Mohareem, it is deemed a time of mourning; the business and ceremonies of the court are suspended; and his Majesty appears in black."[54] Small girls let stream hair ringlets from their ears as they did when a brother of father had died; men and women had a serious mien.[55] "During these two months most people dress in black, many old garments being dyed and worn out during this season of mourning."[56]

There were no weddings or festivities during these months.[57] "During this season, wine-drinkers abstain from such an infraction of their holy laws, and those at other

[48] Gmelin, *Reise*, vol. 3, pp. 229, 411, 464.

[49] Massé, Henri. "Epigraphy. B. Persian Inscriptions," Pope, Arthur and Ackerman, Phyllis, *A Survey of Persian Art* (Oxford, 1939), vol. 2, p. 1797-98.

[50] Varjavand, *Simay*, vol. 2, p. 889; Mehrabadi, Abu'l-Qasem Rafi`i. *Athar-e Melli-ye Esfahan* (Tehran, 1352/1973), pp. 91-92, 97-98, 138, 163, 182 etc. For historical *takiyeh*s see, for example, Mostafavi, Sayyed Mohammad Taqi. *Athar-e Tarikihi-ye Tehran* 2 vols. ed. Mir Hashem Mohaddeth (Tehran, 1361/1982), vol. 1, pp. 386-90.

[51] Ahmad Bey, "Le Théatre," p. 529.

[52] Francklin, William. *Observations made on a tour from Bengal to Persia in the years 1786-7* (London 1790 [Tehran: Imp. Org. f. Soc. Services, 1976]), p. 246; Fowler, *Three Years*, p. 122.

[53] Fraser, J.B. *A Winter's Journey*, 2, 145; Wilson, *Persian Life*, p. 190.

[54] Fowler, *Three Years*, p. 126.

[55] Ahmad Bey, "Le Théatre," pp. 529-30

[56] Rice, *Persian Women*, p. 232; Ahmad Bey, "Le Théatre," p. 529; Wilson, *Persian Life*, p. 190; Wishard, *Twenty Years*, p. 156.

[57] Rice, *Persian Women*, p. 232.

times little scrupulous will not eat with such as are considered unclean by strict Sheahs."[58] Very important for the majority of the people, this month was also one when the government and its agents stopped maltreating the people, and met with notables to talk about the people's problems.[59] At many places lamentations were held, which was indicated by a black flag over the door of the house where they were held as a sign of invitation to join 'daily readings,' a sort of cottage prayer-meeting, being held for the public. "At these meetings, the priest reads from the Koran, recites poems touching upon the life and character of the martyrs, and follows these with an exhortation that generally meets with a response on the part of the audience, of tears and amens."[60] As the people flocked to the lamentations and religious plays the shops were half shut, while on the 10th day of the month (`Ashurah) every shop in the town would be closed.[61]

TAKIYEH BUILDINGS

There were, of course, also permanent *takiyeh*s dedicated to the performance of *rowzeh-khvani* and passion plays only. Allegedly, such a *takiyeh* was built in 1799-80 by Fath `Ali Shah. It was known as *takiyeh-ye Nowruz Khan* and situated in the bazaar of Tehran.[62] Tancoigne in 1808 reported, however, that the passion play that year was performed "on a theatre erected opposite the king's kiosk in the court of the Gulestan Palace."[63] This would indicate that even if this royal *takiyeh* existed at that time that the shah did not make use of it. This is also clear from the fact that a few years later Fath `Ali Shah attended the annual passion play at the same location.

> The Shah invited the Embassy to this annual ceremony, and ordered a tent to be pitched over some buildings adjoining the palace for the use of Sir Gore and his suite, and sat himself in an apartment contiguous. A pure tajeer (walls of tents) was fixed nearly opposite to the palace, and inside were several men buried up to the chin, to represent the heads of the martyrs. The populace were ranged along the tops of the houses and in the square in every direction; but in front of the palace, in order to give room, two semicircles were formed, one within the other, the people sitting on their heels according to Oriental custom. The Shah made his appearance a little before noon: he sat upon the throne that was placed near

---

[58] Holmes, *Sketches*, p. 296.

[59] Ahmad Bey, "Le Théatre," p. 535.

[60] Wishard, *Twenty Years*, p. 156; Wilson, *Persian Life*, pp. 190-91.

[61] O'Donovan, *Merv Oasis*, vol. 2, p. 51; Hale, F. *From Persian Uplands* (New York: E.P.Dutton, n.d.), p. 38; Wishard, *Twenty Years*, p. 158.

[62] Mamnoun, P. *Ta`zija, Schi'itisch-Persisches Passionsspiel* (Vienna, 1967), p. 43, n. 1 citing the *Divan-e Ash`ar-e Fat `Ali Khan Saba*, p. 684; Beyza'i, *Namayesh*, p. 123; Aubin, *La Perse*, p. 160 describes the public fountain attached to this *takiyeh*.

[63] Tancoigne, J. M. *A Narrative of a Journey into Persia* (London: William Wright, 1820), p. 198.

the window; no person entered the apartment but when he gave his commands his Farosh bashee came several times to receive his orders.[64]

In addition to the many large temporary *takiyeh*s created each year by the wealthy, Hajji Aghasi, the Prime Minister (1838-48) "constructed an immense building, holding several thousand persons, for these representations. It fulfilled all the purposes of a theatre, though after a design somewhat novel. The stage, instead of being at the bottom of the building, was formed of a large elevated platform in the middle of the pit, if I may so call it, perfectly open on every side, and revealing, to the entire destruction of all exercise of the imagination, the mysteries which ought to pass behind the curtain. Two tiers of boxes surround the platform.[65] It was either known as *takiyeh Hajj Mirza Aghasi* or *takiyeh-ye `Abbasabad*.[66]

Royal Theater (Takiyeh-ye Dowlat)

The first *takiyeh-ye dowlat* (different from the later one in the *Meydan-e Arg*) was two-storied with richly accoutered loges with shawls, crystal lusters, etc. The shah often came every day to watch the performance.[67] The *takiyeh-ye dowlat* was lit up with 5,000 lights and did not have its peer in other countries, or so the government newspaper claimed. Thanks to the *kalantar* (mayor) and *kadkhoda*s (quarter chiefs), the rowdies (*luti*s) and other bad elements did not cause any fights and trouble.[68] The next large government *takiyeh* built was one in Niyavaran in 1273/1856-57, next to the royal palace, which still exists.[69]

---

[64] Price, *Journal*, p. 29.

[65] Sheil, Lady. *Glimpses of Life and Manners in Persia* (London, 1856 [New York: Arno, 1973]), pp. 126-27.

[66] Dhoka, Yahya. *Tarikhcheh-ye Sakhtemanha-ye Arg-e Saltanati-ye Tehran* (Tehran, 1349/1970), p. 284. For a detailed description and drawings of this *takiyeh* see Calmard, "Le mécénat I," pp. 106-118.

[67] *Ruznameh-ye Ettefaqiyeh* no. 141 (9 Moharram 1270/12 December 1853); Ibid., no. 191 (12 Moharram 1271/5 October 1854). Sasan Khan Malek, *Siyasatgaran-e dowreh-ye Qajar*. 2 vols. (Tehran, 1338/1959) vol. 1, p. 13 describes the old *takiyeh*, which was situated where now is the Palace of Justice. According to Calmard, it does not appear on any map of Tehran after 1858. Calmard, Jean. "Le mécénat des representations de ta`ziye. II," *Le Monde Iranien et l'Islam* 4 (1976-77), p. 155, n. 84.

[68] *Ruznameh-ye Ettefaqiyeh* no. 142 (16 Moharram 1270/19 October 1853).

[69] Algar, Hamid. *Religion and State in Iran 1785-1906* (Berkeley, 1969), p. 158, n. 37, who is wrong as to the construction or extension of *takiyeh*s by Naser al-Din Shah as pointed out by Calmard, "Le mécénat" II, p. 159, n. 91. For a description see *Ruznameh-ye Ettefaqiyeh* nr. 293 (Moharram 1273). There is also news about the *takiyeh* in *Ruznameh-ye Ettefaqiyeh* nrs. 342, 343, 344 (Aug-Sept 1857) and Ibid., nr. 394 (9 Moharram 1275/19 August 1858).

THE TAKIÉH, OR ROYAL THEATRE.

Figure 26: The *Takiyeh-ye Dowlat* or Royal Theater (ca. 1900)

After his first voyage to Europe in 1873, Naser al-Din Shah, after having attended a concert in Albert Hall in London, gave orders to Dust ‘Ali Khan Mo‘ayyer al-Mamalek to build him a theater similar in design next to the Golestan palace within the Citadel (*Arg*). It was to be the biggest and most important *takiyeh* in Tehran. It was built on a site on old ruined bathhouse and part of a prison. Because the previous *takiyeh*s had all been too small to accommodate the audience it was from the very beginning seen to that it would be a big theater. The building was known as *takiyeh-ye homayuni*, or *dowlat*, or *dowlati*.[70]

The shah sent one of his staff, probably an engineer, to Europe on a special mission to study for the preparations of new royal theater.[71] The newspaper *Sharaf* reported in 1887 that construction took four to five years and at great expense. At that time 300,000 *tuman*s had already been spent and the building was not finished yet.[72] Although the final product did not resemble the Albert Hall very much the circular, four-storey building was a marvel of Qajar technical ability.

---

[70] *Sharaf* nr. 53 (Dhu’l-Hijjah 1304/August 1887); E‘temad al-Saltaneh, *Ruznameh*, p. 591.

[71] Amin, Ahmad. “Iran dar sal-e 1311 AH,” translated by Gharavi, Mohammad. *Barrasiha-ye Tarikhi* 9/4 (1353/1974), pp. 90.

[72] *Sharaf* nr. 53 (Dhu’l-Hijjah 1304/August 1887).

The entire building was made of stone, bricks, gypsum and cement. The walls were about 24.4 m high and 15 m thick and ground level, and the width of the circle about 60 meters square. The inside was entirely covered with tiles. The building's capacity was about 3,000 persons. A three-tiered circle of seats surrounded the stage; each tier had rooms. Only two tiers had arched loges; the highest tier of loges was exclusively for the royal harem and the lower one for the princes, ministers and dignitaries. Four arcs spanned the walls, and each arc was half the circle, and was made of wood and iron. It would be able to support a roof made of wood, planks and glass, but it is not ready yet. Although it had no roof canvas was used to cover the building using the wooden and iron poles and the brick supports (*posht-e bandi*) Because Mozaffar al-Din Shah was afraid that the roof would fall in he sent M. Baton [?] to France to get iron pillars that were installed so that there was no need for the brick supports. The building was embellished with 5,000 lamps that were lighted when there was a performance. There also was one big luster in the middle of the stage, which dropped at one occasion. The entry was via a vaulted hall; in the center was the brick stage (*saku*) of about 1 meter high, which was called *takht*. The novelty was that prior to the show the stage was hidden behind curtains. On its four sides there were steps. There were stone pillars at all four sides of the stage with wooden poles in the form of the bottom of lanterns on top of which were gas lights, which were later changed into electric lamps. There also was a large pulpit (*menbar*) with 20 steps for the *rowzeh-khvan*. There also were access routes for the actors, elephants, musicians, camels, carriages, and horses to get in and out. There also was a pulpit, not a normal wooden one, but in this case one of marble. The *taqnama* or foyer was at the side of the center. During Moharram the open theater was covered with a canvas cover to protect the audience against the sun and rain. Around it also a few large buildings had been constructed so that a travelers approaching Tehran would see the building from a distanced of 30 km. The upkeep of the building was partly assured by the 'rent' paid by the elite for the loges that they occupied, representing an annual amount of 16,250 *qeran*s (488 pounds).[73]

---

[73] Curzon, G.N. *Persia and the Persian Question* 2 vols. (London, 1892), vol. 1, pp. 327-28, vol. 2, pp. 406-13, 481; Dhoka, *Tarikhcheh*, p. 283ff; Forugh, Mehdi. "Takiyeh-ye Dowlat," *Honar va Mardom* 29 (1343/1964), pp. 7-10; E'temad al-Saltaneh, *Ketab al-Athar va'l-Ma'ather* (Tehran, 1306/1884), p. 85; Ibid., *Ruznameh*, p. 364, 440 (the royal box); Aubin, *La Perse*, p. 169; E'temad al-Saltaneh, *Ruznameh*, p.. p. 413; Serena, C. *Hommes et Choses en Perse* (Paris: G. Charpentier, 1883), pp. 174-74; Laessø, Agnate. *Fra Persien* (Copenhagen, 1881), pp. 214-21; Basset, *Persia*, pp. 382-86; Benjamin, *Persia*, pp. 406-09; Ponafine, Pierre. *Life in the Moslem East* (London, 1911), p. 347; Binder, Henry. *Au Kurdistan* (Paris: Quantin, 1887), pp. 406-16; Shoemaker, Michael Myers. *The Heart of the Orient* (New York: G.P. Putnam's Sons, 1904), p. 182 (excellent photo of the interior of government theater in Tehran); Mo'ayyer al-Mamalek, Dust 'Ali. *Yad-dashtha'i az Zendegani-ye Khosusi-ye Naser al-Din Shah* (Tehran, 1351/1972), p. 97f

After 1880, the walls were covered with faience tiles. Prior to that time they had been not even been whitewashed, and just displayed mud and brick walls. The exterior was covered with faience tiles and glass-mirror pieces (*a'ineh-kari*) in the *muqarnas* porticos. Arnold reported that: "The front of this building is a good specimen of modern Persian architecture, which in England we should recognize as the Rosherville or Cremorne style-the gewgaw, pretentious, vulgar, and ephemeral style, erected in those places of amusement, only to be seen at night, and to last for a season. The façade is shaped like a small transept of the Crystal Palace, and covered with florid, coarse decorations in plaster, with beadings of bits of looking-glass, bright blue, red, yellow, and green being plentifully laid upon the plaster wherever there is opportunity."[74] The management of the building was the royal steward's (*nazer*) responsibility.[75]

MUSAFFER-ED-DIN'S BURIAL-PLACE IN THE THEATRE OF THE ROYAL PALACE

Figure 27: *Takiyeh-ye Dowlat* and the burial place of Mozaffar al-Din Shah (1907)

Although quite a feat for the Qajar engineers, they were unable to cover the building with a roof. Therefore, canvas awnings, just like in the more simple *takiyeh*s, were applied over the framework of the wooden arches reinforced by iron braces. Naser al-Din Shah did not like it one bit and it was only after members of the diplomatic community had made it clear to him that what he wanted was not possible with the available materials to the Iranian engineers. After his assassination he

---

[74] Arnold, A. *Through Persia by Caravan* (New York: Harper & Brothers, 1877), p. 164.
[75] Aubin, *La Perse*, p. 169.

was put there in state, and then was temporarily buried there.[76] After the death of Naser al-Din Shah religious passion play was not performed anymore in the *taki-yeh-ye dowlat*, while around 1907 it was not considered safe anymore to be used for theatrical performances.[77] Official patronage fell off, while also some of the leading olama were hostile to the very idea of the performance of religious tragedy. After the fall of Mohammad 'Ali Shah (1910) no more use was made of the *takiyeh-ye dowlat*; the performances of the passion play fell into disuse and so did the royal theater. It was demolished in 1948.[78]

A show rivaling that of the shah was staged by his favorite mignon, 'Aziz al-Soltan. According to E'temad al-Saltaneh, writing on October 15, 1886, "nowadays the shah's harem is [the scene of] Malijak's passion play. They have pitched a tent. The singers are children. The flagellants are the children of the stable hands who guide the led horses. Old men and the shah's wives are sitting unveiled. Of course, the expense for this child's pl;ay is 1,000 *tumans*."[79] This very much upset him and he noted with some acerbity on April 4, 1893 that, "to-day, 'Aziz al-Soltan's annual *ta'ziyeh-khvani* at the eunuch's building at the door of the harem has begun."[80] 'Eyn al-Saltaneh, Naser al-Din Shah's nephew noted the same event. On March 14, 1895 he wrote in his Diary:

> In the evening 'Aziz al-Soltan had a show in the courtyard of the eunuchs. It was very well decorated and accoutered. He had made the same set-up as in the government's *takiyeh*. HM and the [royal] harem were also there. Two, three years ago this show was performed right in the middle of the harem. Outsiders, men and women, were not allowed. All harem inmates were nicely dressed up and sat on chairs and sofas, and the performers had to be old men or children. However, old meant 40 years and child meant 18-19 years. Both sides enjoyed the show. Now this arrangement fell apart and it has to be in the eunuchs' court and the harem inmates have to watch from behind trellis (*zanburi*). They talk and joke with the men and women of the show. The above I have been told by members of my family who attended these shows. 'Aziz al-Soltan is continuously in the harem and does what he likes.[81]

One year later 'Eyn al-Saltaneh recorded that "The passion play of Aziz al-Soltan has still not ended; from the 10th till now he still has shows at the harem's gate and

---

[76] Sykes, *Through Persia*, p. 346; Wishard, *Twenty Years*, p. 157. It also served as a kind of zoo for the shah's menagerie of chained animals.
[77] De Lorey, Eustace & Sladen, Douglas. *Queer Things About Persia* (Philadelphia-London: J.B. Lippincot Co, 1907), p. 282.
[78] Dhoka, *Tarikhcheh*, pp. 127-28; Homayuni, *Ta'ziyeh*, p. 128.
[79] E'temad al-Saltaneh, *Ruznameh*, p. 522 (16 Moharram 1304/October 15, 1886).
[80] E'temad al-Saltaneh, *Ruznameh*, p. 989 (17 Ramazan 1310/April 4, 1893).
[81] 'Eyn al-Saltaneh, *Ruznameh*, vol. 1, p. 711 (17 Ramazan, 1312/14/3/1895)

very well done up. It is better than that of the Imperial theater. At royal orders all these items are there; and each evening they perform a passion play. But most of the time it is closer to farce than to Tragedy drama."[82]

LAY-OUT AND EMBELLISHMENT OF THE *TAKIYEH*

Whether in the open air, under an awning or tent, or inside a building, dedicated for that purpose or not, the lay-out of the *takiyeh* was the same and simple. There was a stage, a kind of elevated platform with two or more ramps; a couple of feet high, in the center of a large circle or parallelogram surrounded by rows of seats. The stage was either open to all sides or had one or more walled off or fenced off sides. There was neither coulisse nor décor, but there was decoration. Thus the spectators surrounded the actors on all sides, which created a special dynamic between them. Whether in a mosque, a public space, a caravanserai, or a garden of house, tiers of seats were erected; usually a double rowed range of superimposed seats was set up in the form of a circle. These two rows of banks that encircled the stage represented the balcony and galleries. Sometimes special recesses had been made, opening towards the stage, of the same size and form as the royal box in foreign theaters, according to Fowler. Often these boxes were just plain rooms of a house. The boxes or large rooms opening towards the stage were reserved for the invited of the better class, religious and government officials, courtiers, the bourgeoisie and the merchants. If the play were performed in front of a house, then the terraces and balconies (*shah-neshin*) of the neighboring houses, which were all decorated with precious stuffs for the occasion, would be transformed in loges. Its owners offered these to important strangers, to diplomats, and the town's notables. The cobbled courtyard and hard soil of the gardens were for the common people. It was literary the parterre. Here they sat *à la persane*.[83] The carpets on the side are for seniors, men or women; to the invalids and to the hosts. The latter are Christians or people from other towns.[84]

Irrespective of what kind of *takiyeh* it was, the men, on the right, were separated from the women, who sat on the left. Those who had been invited, as stated above, received the better seats, the balcony seats so to speak. Here also men and women were separated; the latter were all closely veiled. On the higher tiers the women of middle class families were seated, and below them, in spaces behind a

---

[82] `Eyn al-Saltaneh, *Ruznameh*, vol. 1, p. 908 (22 Ramazan 1313/March 7, 1896).
[83] Anonymous, "Die Passionsspiele der schiitischen Mohammedaner," *Globus. Illustrierte Zeitschrift für Länder- und Völkerkunde*, vol. XVI/23 (1870), p. 535; Thalasso, *Le Théatre Persan*, p. 882; Stuart, *Journal*, p. 293; Wills, *In the land*, p. 280.
[84] Ahmad Bey, "Le Théâtre," pp. 533-34.

trellis screen (*pardeh-ye zanburi*),[85] sat the high-ranking ladies, facing the crowds of women at parterre level. At ground level, separated from the men and wedged together as closely as possible, the common women sat in spaces roped off to accommodate them. They sat where they wanted, on a carpet, or a small stool that they bring with them. The general public, seated on their knees, occupied the rest of the parterre.[86]

The center of the *takiyeh* was the stage or *saku*. It was

> A platform, some thirty yards square, ... formed by placing together a number of takhts, or wooden platforms. These were planked over, and a level stage made by placing on them big doors and planks. The whole was carpeted with thick felts, and at one corner was placed a pulpit, draped in black. This pulpit, like all Oriental ones, is merely a flight or wooden steps, some eight feet high, leading to a platform some two feet square, on which squats the preacher or reader, as the case may be. The stage is placed some twenty feet from the principal front of the prince's palace, the rooms of which thus form private boxes.[87]

A slope to the left and right facilitated the entry and departure of caravans, led and pack animals.[88] Often the play was performed in the garden or courtyard of a house. In that case, "The stage is erected over the tank; stands are put up on every available spot; the walls, trees, roofs, all help to afford accommodation for the thousands of spectators, of both sexes."[89] The actual stage was much larger than the *saku*, which was just the central stage. Around it there was a sand-covered space where other theatrical asides would take place, and even battles would take place there.

A third area was the so-called *taqnama* or foyer, where during the show, the artists rested exposed to the views of the spectators. It was linked to the stage (*saku*) via a small straight passage through the public, right between the women's and men's section.[90]

---

[85] E`temad al-Saltaneh, *Ruznameh*, p. 1157; Stuart, *Journal*, p. 292-93. According to Rice, *Persian Women*, p. 234, "the window I had to look through had two white curtains and then a black one stretched across it."
[86] Chodzko, *Théâtre Persan*, p. xxiii; Stuart, *Journal*, p. 292-93; Ussher, *A Journey*, p. 619; O'Donovan, *Merv Oasis*, vol. 2, p. 51; Wilbraham, *Travels*, p. 422; Wills, *In the land*, p. 281. See also Calmard, "Le mécénat" I, p. 95.
[87] Wills, *In the land*, pp. 279-80.
[88] Thalasso, *Le Théâtre Persan*, p. 882.
[89] Rice, *Persian Women*, p. 234; Wishard, *Twenty Years*, p. 158 (beautiful picture of a play on a platform over a pond).
[90] Thalasso, *Le Théâtre Persan*, p. 882; Wilbraham, *Travels*, p. 422; Rice, *Mary Bird*, p. 34-35.

The passion play theater had very little theater decoration, which given the fact that it was mostly held in the open air and the circular arrangement of the stage was what one would expect. With the construction of dedicated theaters with walls, patrons felt the need to decorate one or more of these walls. It even happened with open air performances under a tent that patrons sometimes had a scaffold constructed behind one part of the stage and had it decorated as well. Around 1880, Dr. Wills was a spectator of the passion play that Zell al-Soltan, the new governor of Shiraz had organized in the garden of his palace.

> Behind the stage is raised a huge scaffolding, covered with red cloth, and hung with Cashmere shawls. On this are arranged all the glass and crockery that the prince possess, and all he can borrow by hook or by crook, all his mirrors, lamps, and chandeliers, and the whole are set off by rows of brass candle-lamps hired from the bazaar, the general effect being that of a very miscellaneous broker's shop. Considerable care is, however, devoted to this display, and its grandeur, or the reverse, is one of the subjects of town talk for a week.[91]

Although Wills did not care much for the display his compatriot Mounsey found such displays "tastefully ornamented with carpets, shawls, vases of flowers, mirrors and candelabra."[92] According to Chodzko, this display was a show of vanity, because it allowed the patrons to vaunt their wealth, to show what carpets, shawls, curtains, dresses, jewelry, glasses, pictures, etc. they owned. They were further also decorated with tinsel, festoons of artificial flowers, evergreens, and printed calicoes Moreover, if they did not have enough for their display they would borrow from friends; anything to make an impression. The most beautiful decors of our theaters cost 10 times less. In 1833, Abu'l-Hasan Khan had displayed two *korur*s or three million francs in shawls and jewelry.[93]

NUMBER OF *TAKIYEH*S

The previous section may have created the perception that the number of *takiyeh*s was very large. Contemporary travelers had the same impression. No wonder that Melgunof reported that, "the numerous takiyeh (holy buildings) on almost every street in which people gather to listen to the narrative of the tragic fate of ʿAli's

---

[91] Wills, *In the land*, pp. 280-81.

[92] Mounsey, *A Journey*, p. 312.

[93] Chodzko, *Le Théatre Persan*, p. xxi; Stuart, *Journey*, p. 296; Holmes, *Sketches*, p. 296; Rice, *Persian Women*, p. 234; Wilson, *Persian Life*, p. 63; Wilbraham, *Travels*, p. 422. Abu'l-Hasan Khan had also porcelain, glasswork etc. on display. Calmard, "Le mécénat" I, p. 100. Some *takiyeh*s had one or more walls covered with tiles on which scenes from the martyrdom of the Imam had been painted. See Peterson, Samuel R. "The Taʿziyeh and Related Arts," in Chelkowski, Peter ed. *Taʿziyeh: Ritual and Drama in Iran* (New York, 1979), pp. 64-87 (Kermanshah); Homayuni, *Taʿziyeh*, pp. 116-17, 122, 409 and appendix with color picturesn (Shiraz).

sons." In Shahrud, he reported, there were four, only one less than the separate numbers of mosques, baths, and caravanserais, and in Resht 36, which had 22 mosques and 36 *madrasehs*.[94] The number of *takiyeh*s was mostly determined by the number of quarters of a town or a large village, because usually neighborhood wards organized the Moharram events. For example, the census of 1880 showed that there were eight *takiyeh*s in Qazvin, which had eight quarters. Golriz wrote that in 1919 only the Mohammad Khan Beg, Mirza Gholagh and Taq-e Bohlul *takiyeh*s still existed; the others had become ruined and private property.[95] In Astarabad towards the end of the nineteenth century there were nine *takiyeh*s.[96] Berezin stated there were 58 *takiyeh*s in Tehran in 1842-43, but not at the same time, because there were not enough actors, who therefore moved from one location to the other. There also was a *takiyeh* installed at the Russian and the British embassy.[97] Naser al-Din Shah, some weeks prior to the execution of Amir Kabir in 1851, went personally to the new bazaar in Tehran and ordered government officials to commemorate (*ta`ziyeh-dari*) the Emams' martyrdom in the *takiyeh*s.[98] One year later, 105 passion play and 150 *rowzeh-khvani* performances were held in Tehran until the 5th Moharram and as many were expected to be held up to the 10th of Moharram.[99] As a result, there were in total 54 *takiyeh*s in Tehran, which explains why Aubin some 55 years later observed that in Tehran each quarter had a *takiyeh*.[100]

Table 1: Number of inhabitants, *takiyeh*s, mosques and shrines per city quarter in Tehran (1268/1852)

Quarter	Inhabitants	# *Takiyeh*s	# Mosques	# *Emamzadeh*s
Ark	3,014	3	3	-
`Udlajan	36,485	12	34	-
Bazar	26,674	17	29	3
Sangalaj	29,673	12	21	-
Chalmeydan	34,547	10	20	2
Total	133,393	54	107	5

In some towns there was only one *takiyeh*. `Eyn al-Saltaneh reported that the passion play in Hamadan was performed in Government House, "because there is no other place in the town for *ta`ziyeh-khvani*."[101] There also were towns where there was no passion play at all. "In some parts of Persia, for instance in Yazd, instead of the

[94] Melgunof, *Das südliche Ufer*, p. 39, 130, 242; Rabino, H. L. "Les provinces Caspiennes de la Perse: La Guilan," *Revue du Monde Musulmane* 29 (1915-16), pp. 72, 86-88 mentions the same number of *takiyeh*s.
[95] Eyn al-Saltaneh, *Ruznameh*, p. 230 (August 6, 1889).
[96] Dhabihi, Masih ed. *Astarabadnameh*, (Tehran, 1348/1969), p. 24.
[97] Calmard, "Le mécénat" I, p. 95.
[98] *Ruznameh-ye Ettefaqiyeh* 38 (27 Dhu'l-Hejjeh 1267/23 October 1851).
[99] *Ruznameh-ye Ettefaqiyeh* 90 (7 Moharram 1269/21 October 1852).
[100] Haqani, Musa. "Moharram az negah-e tarikh va tasvir," *Tarikh-e Mo`aser-e Iran* 6/21-22 (1381/2002), p. 508. See also Calmard, "Le mécénat I," p. 94 quoting Berezin; Aubin, *La Perse*, p. 170.
[101] `Eyn al-Saltaneh, *Ruznameh*, vol. 1, p. 385.

Tazieh, a great erection hung with daggers and looking-glasses, and called the 'Nakl,' is carried through the city. It is supposed to be moved by Fatimah, but many people seem to be needed to help her."[102] There was, however, performance of the passion play in the environs of Yazd as well as in the towns of Yazd province such as Meybod, Ardakan, Taft, Mehrjerd, and Mehriz.[103]

The large number of *takiyeh*s is an indication of the enormous popularity that the mourning ceremonies and in particular the passion plays enjoyed. The number of spectators to a single performance was large and some performances were attended by up to 6,000 persons. This was only the case, of course, where there was only one passion play performance in a town or village and usually only on the day of the killing (*Ruz-e Qatl*), when Hoseyn was martyred.

Figure 28: Passion play performance on the main square of Tehran (January 25, 1812)

FINANCING *TA`ZIYEH-KHVANI* IS A PIOUS ACT

The preparation for the mourning ritual, the making and construction or repairing of parts of the floats, the acquisition of dresses and other props, the training

---

[102] Rice, *Persian Women*, p. 237.
[103] Shari`ati, "Sargarmiha," vol. 1, p. 511.

of the actor-singers to know and sing their role well, the securing of the financing and/or in-kind contributions (food, drinks, animals), and the selection of the right location for the performance implies long preparation times and community involvement. Also, those not actively involved in the preparation looked forward to the day the "mourning cycle" would begin. Not only for its religious experience, but also because it promised fun, drama, spectacle, excitement, in short entertainment. This is also clear from the fact that literally everybody was involved. For example, there was "the boy's playing 'procession.' Grasping one another's girdles, they form lines, waving sticks in the air, one blowing a trumpet, another beating a drum, and all shouting, 'Shah Hussein! Hasan, Hussein!' This is a childish imitation of the more serious acts of the men."[104]

Financing a passion play performance, including that of erecting a *takiyeh*, was considered a pious and above all a meritorious act. For the organizer would receive spiritual points for the saving of his soul. The scenes of the drama that he financed "are the bricks that he has made down-here to build his celestial palace up-there." This meant that he gained indulgencies or *thavab*s, and at the same time he edified the public. According to Chodzko, the Iranians called it a *bakhsh-e khalq*, i.e. a gift to the people for their edification and amusement. Pious considerations often were intermingled with less pious ones, of course. Rich men thus tried to increase their religious and political influence.[105] The financing of a passion play performance could be very high. Eyn al-Saltaneh, wrote on August 6, 1889 that Sa`d al-Saltaneh had built a new *takiyeh* in Qazvin. He had a tent come from Tehran that weighed 8 *kharvar*. The total cost was 800 *tumans*.[106]

Calmard, who has made a study of the patronage of passion plays, concluded, amongst other things, Naser al-Din Shah was not known as patron of *taziyeh-khvani* nor for that matter were his father and great grand-father.[107] Under Fath `Ali Shah, in 1809, the five last episodes of the Karbala cycle were enacted in the great court of the shah's palace. "The viziers pay the expences of the first day, and the city of Teheran, which is divided into four districts, pays those of the remaining four."[108] Although initially Naser al-Din Shah was no great patron of the passion play this changed after a decade or so into his reign. De Gobineau reported that Naser al-Din Shah and several ministers supported passion play performances.[109] Thereafter, royal support for the passion play became structural. By

---

[104] Wilson, *Persian Life*, p. 191.

[105] Chodzko, *Theatre Persan*, pp. XX-XXI.

[106] `Eyn al-Saltaneh, *Ruznameh*, p. 230 (August 6, 1889). For a description of such a large tent, which took one week to set up see Wills, *In the land*, pp. 279-80.

[107] Calmard, "Le mécénat" II, p. 160.

[108] Tancoigne, *A Narrative*, p. 198; see also Morier, *A Second Journey*, p. 177.

[109] De Gobineau, *Les religions*, vol. 2, pp. 129-32; Watson, *A History of Persia* (London, 1866), p. 21; Calmard, "Le mécénat" II, p. 135.

1907, "The representation of the tragedies cost the Royal Treasury an annual sum of 30,000 tomans. On 7 Moharrem, in the evening, it is usual that the shah visits successively all the loges; the titled persons acknowledge the honor by gifts of money, shawls and carpets. In this way on average 10,000 tomans is collected and are used to reduce the cost."[110] This was not always a pleasant occasion, if we may believe E'temad al-Saltaneh, who wrote on August 13, 1891, "On the 7th attended *ta'ziyeh*; it cost the shah 1,500 tomans, but it was an insult and also makes a mockery of the state."[111] According to Amanat, the purpose of Naser al-Din Shah's patronage of the passion play, apart from his own attachment to popular religion, was that it offered an alternative to the legalistic Shi'ite tradition over which the state had no control, as the olama had no control over the passion play. It allowed the shah to affirm and acknowledge his attachment to Shi'ism without the intermediacy of the olama. It was a conscious effort to demonstrate the link between king and people.[112]

The shah (in Tehran) and the (prince) governor in the provincial capitals financed the most beautiful and impressive show, of course. The other performances in the same town would be mostly at a much less lavish scale. For example, Berezine noted that the *takiyeh* Mirza Abu'l-Hasan Khan was one of the best in Tehran.[113] In Tabriz, in the 1890s, prince Mozaffar al-Din Mirza had built a large *takiyeh*. He offered the loges to the city's notables, with the charge to decorate them. Each notable wanted his loge to be better than that of his neighbor; they spent more than 2,000 *tuman*s for these decorations. They further put easy chairs and divans in the middle, while on a table a samovar had been placed to offer tea to the visitors during intermissions.[114] In Shiraz, "Almost all of the wealthy did some public act or other in the Mohurrim, the month of mourning. ... The tazzia, or dramatic representation, was given by the Zill-es-Sultan, the Governor, in the garden of his palace, on a very large scale indeed, and in a smaller way by the Muschir and the Kawam and others."[115] The shah or the prince-governor was often only the main financier, and would receive assistance from his adherents. In Tabriz, for example, "After the 'Tazia' each nobleman sends a present of a shawls, sweetmeats, and gold coins to the prince, as a contribution to the celebration."[116] This followed a visit of the prince-apparent with his suite on 8 Moharram to all those invited who co-financed theater the cost and upkeep of his theater (*takiyeh*) with presents and

---

[110] Aubin, *La Perse*, p. 174.

[111] E'temad al-Saltaneh, *Ruznameh*, p. 873; see also 'Eyn al-Saltaneh, *Ruznameh*, vol. 2, p. 1886.

[112] Amanat, Abbas. *Pivot of the Universe* (Berkeley, 1997), pp. 434-35.

[113] Calmard, "Le mécénat" I, p. 99. Also good were those of Nabi Khan (former vizier of Fath 'Ali Shah), Rajab 'Ali, a rich *kadkhoda*. Calmard, "Le mécénat" I, p. 100. Mirza Aqa Khan continued to finance the staging of *ta'ziyeh-khvani*. *Ruznameh-ye Ettefaqiyeh* nr. 193, (10 Moharram 1273/10 September 1856); Calmard, "Le mécénat" II, p. 160-62.

[114] Thalasso, *Le Théatre Persan*, p. 882.

[115] Wills, *In the land*, p. 279.

[116] Wilson, *Persian Life*, p. 63.

money proportional to their wealth and rank of the loge allotted to them.[117] One of these cost items were the cost of the hiring of actors.[118] This was different from the "numerous bands of well-drilled supernumeraries who combat on stage [and] are eager volunteers.[119]

It even happened that a grateful poet, or one who expected the shah to be even more grateful, wrote in the text of the play a few lines thanking the shah for his support. In the play named "Fath `Ali Shah" there are a number of lines, Imam Hoseyn says to the shah:

Of your family many will help me	and will organize mourning ceremonies for me
In particular the peerless Naser al-Din Shah	who with great care arranged for my death commemoration[120]

Figure 29: Performance of a passion play in a village (1930s)

Although it cost money to stage a performance it were not only the rich who organized the staging of a passion play drama. Holmes reported in the mid-1840s, referring to the situation in the Caspian provinces, "In every mahal of the town, one or more large buildings, called takiehs, had been prepared at the expense of the inhabitants, or by some rich individual, as an act of devotion, for the various performances of the season, and were open to all classes without payment of any

---

[117] Thalasso, *Le Théatre Persan*, p. 882.
[118] Holmes, *Sketches*, p. 302.
[119] Wills, *In the land*, p. 283.
[120] Mamnoun, *Ta`zija*, p. 35.

kind."[121] To ensure that passion play performances could also take place in the future rich individuals bequeathed funds as *vaqf* (foundation) for this specific purpose. This had become quite a common practice in the nineteenth century.[122] Aubin reported in 1907 that, "in Tehran each quarter has a takiyeh maintained by a foundation or contributions by the inhabitants; the most beautiful ones in the royal takiyeh." This also held for the free distribution of food.[123] People gladly came for the food, sherbet and the water pipe. The *takiyeh*s were lighted in the evening with lampions and alcohol lamps.[124] The same situation existed in other towns. In Ardabil, for example, each quarter or sub-quarter (*khula*) had its own passion play (*shabiyeh*) troupe.[125] In large villages there also were passion play performances such as in Shurin and Sangestan in the Hamadan area with the help of military musicians from a nearby regiment.[126]

A striking example of how part of the cost were co-financed by the public is given by O'Donovan, relating his experience in Mohammadabad in Khorasan in 1880.

> Before this final act of the drama commenced, a scene was enacted which forcibly recalled to my mind what I had seen at home. The conductor of the theatrical representations, clothed in a long chintz gown, got up on a kind of table and addressed the assembled multitude, reminding them of the blessed Imams and of himself and his company likewise. The Khan had paid the actors the sum of twenty krans (francs) per diem during the ten days of the performances, but the audience were expected to contribute something also. The Khan set the example, bidding five krans. This was announced by a man who acted as collector, and who shouted, 'The Khan gives five krans.' Then the man on the table invoked the blessing of Allah, Mahomet, Ali, and the Imams, on the Khan. Some one else bid ten krans, whereupon followed a volley of benedictions. Then some unlucky wight of a priest, who looked poor enough, bid one kran. 'May the Lord bless him!' exclaimed the speaker. It was only when the bids or votes rose to five krans that Ma-

[121] Holmes, *Sketches*, p. 296. "Sometimes, the entire town, or quarters, or the rich finance its staging." Ahmad Bey, "Le Théatre," p. 529.

[122] Werner, Christopher, *An Iranian Town in Transition* (Wiesbaden: Harrassowitz, 2000), pp. 140, 287.

[123] Aubin, *La Perse*, 165 (free food and drinks; the rice plates went around), 170; Rice, *Persian Women*, p. 234 (endowment); Arbab, Mohammad Taqi Beg. "Ketabcheh-ye Tafsil-e Halat va Nofus va Amlak-e Dar al-Iman-e Qom," ed. Hoseyn Modarresi Tabataba'i, in *Farhang-e Iran-Zamin* 22 (2536/1977), pp. 178, 180 (Villages or parts thereof were endowed for the financing of the passion plays.).

[124] Calmard, "Le mécénat" I, p. 99. Food and other goodies were only available where the play was supported by a rich patron. Otherwise only water was being offered. Hamadani, Hajji `Abdollah Khan Qaraguzlu Amir-e Nezam. *Majmu`eh-ye Athar* ed. `Enayatollah Majidi (Tehran, 1383/2003), pp. 43-44.

[125] Safar, *Ardabil*, vol. 3, pp. 256; Soltani, *Joghrafiya-ye Tarikhi*, pp. 208-10.

[126] `Eyn al-Saltaneh, *Ruznameh*, vol. 1, p. 385.

homet and the Imams were requested to contribute their share of benediction. Sometimes two, or three krans were bid; and the blessing was
nicely apportioned, in quantity and unction, to the sum given. A portly
man, with a long robe and a merry face, who was one of the Khan's
chief servants, received the money, handed it to the treasurer, and pro-
claimed aloud the sum given and the name of the giver. After each
benediction from the stage manager, his entire company, as well as the
audience, cried 'Ya Ali,' by way of confirming the prayer.[127]

In the large village of Maiamid (Khorasan), in 1881, a passion play was performed (probably by professional actors), and after an hour or so, "the acting
wound up by a collection of money from the onlookers."[128]

The bitter-sweet pill of having to contribute to another man's display was sweet-
ened by that fact "that it is considered a meritorious action to contribute furniture
for their decoration and costumes for the actors: indeed a refusal to do so exposes
its author to vituperation and persecution. The Shah and most of his grandees
have their own private tekkyehs, which are fitted up with considerable splendour;
but, though application is frequently made to Europeans for the dresses of the foreign ambassadors, who play an important part in them by interceding with Yezyd
for the lives of Hossein's family."[129] Also, the contribution might be one of lend-
ing properties only rather than having to send money or expensive presents. Wilson reported that "tiers of seats [in the *takiyeh*] are erected, the sections are
adorned with carpets, curtains, and lamps by the officials and wealthy men."[130]
Even the British legation, "as the Squire of Golhek village had to contribute to the
outlay of feasts in the village such as ta'ziyeh."[131] The absence of a rich financier
was immediately noticeable. In 1848, Hommaire de Hell observed that, "Although
it is Moharram, the absence of the prince governor has resulted in the stifling of the
large representations, that usually take place in public, and those that are being held
now only at some mosques and bazaars."[132]

This is not a surprise, because staging dramatic performances of this kind was expensive. The tent for the *takiyeh*, if there was one, was expensive. Although in
villages and in some city quarters the actors performed free of charge, this was not
the case in most urban performances. For the best performers were professionals
who insisted on being paid. In Tabriz, for example, "The Vali Ahd defrays the expenses of the actors, amounting to fifteen hundred tomans."[133] A good singer earned

---

[127] O'Donovan, *Merv Oasis*, vol. 2, pp. 52-53.
[128] O'Donovan, *Merv Oasis*, vol. 1, p. 406.
[129] Mounsey, *A Journey*, pp. 311-12.
[130] Wilson, *Persian Life*, p. 63.
[131] Eastwick, *Journal*, vol. 1, p. 242.
[132] Hommaire de Hell, *Voyage*, vol. 2, p. 54.
[133] Wilson, *Persian Life*, p. 63; Conolly, *Journey*, vol. 1, 269.

more than all the other members of the troupe. De Gobineau mentioned as an example the case of a 14-year old boy, whose voice was so beautiful that he was treated as a star. As a result, he was able to earn 250 to 300 *tuman*s during the first ten days of Moharram, which was a lot of money around 1860.[134] Chodzko's characterization of the entire phenomenon, "What is really medieval that nobody is interested in profit; the actors, the directors, the poets, and even the merchants of the refreshments, nobody thinks about money," is therefore a bit off-the-mark.[135] He is right that when he writes that the public had gratis access as were the refreshments, and this is also confirmed by other contemporary observers. The financiers, wrote Connolly, "provide refreshments for all who choose to come, always ice-water, and sometimes sherbets."[136] But they had to pay for this and all other services that were offered to the public.

NATURE OF THE TEXT OF THE PASSION PLAY

Over time the passion play performance became more elaborate and dramatic. The performance of 1700 was not the same as in 1800, nor was that of 1800 the same as in 1900. Skilled and highly literate authors wrote the texts for the drama. They enlivened the sequence of the drama by borrowing from classical poets as well as from contemporary sermons and lamentations. The text was in verse usually, poetic in style, composed in long meter (*bahr-e ta'vil*) and verse. According to de Gobineau, the text was written in the vernacular so as to facilitate people's understanding what was being said. But among modern scholars there is a difference of opinion whether the texts were really written in the vernacular or in more literary style.[137]

Although the text of most of the plays has been written in Persian there are also plays that were written in Arabic, Azeri and Chagatay Turkish.[138] There are no

---

[134] De Gobineau, *Les réligions*, vol. 2, pp. 119-120 (they also had all the trappings and behavior of an idol down to groupies, clothes, and staff).

[135] Chodzko, *Théatre Persan*, p. XX; see also "Everybody who participates in ta`ziyeh does that free of charge; text writers do not even write their name under the play." Thalasso, *Le Théatre Persan*, p. 881

[136] Conolly, *Journey*, vol. 1, 269; Anonymous, "Die Passionsspiele," p. 535 (During intermission also free refreshments).

[137] De Gobineau, *Les réligions*, vol. 2, p. 145. As to the problem of the language and the literary style of the passion play see for example, Ellwell-Sutton, L.P. "The Literary Sourcs of the Ta`ziyeh," in Chelkowski, *Ta`ziyeh*, pp. 167-81, Hanaway, William L. "Stereotyped Imagery in the Ta`ziyeh," in Chelkowski, *Ta`ziyeh*, pp. 182-92 and Genet, *Le Martyre d'Ali Akbar—Drame Persan* (Liege-Paris, Droz, 1947), p. 16.

[138] `Anasari, Jaber. "Mo`arrefi-ye barkhi az noskh-e tarafeh-ye shabih-khvani," *Ganjineh-ye Asnad* 5/3-4 (1374/1985), pp. 7-11 (introduces a number of *mokalemeh*s or texts of passion plays in Azeri; it also has facsimiles of some of the pages and illustrations); O'Donovan, *Merv Oasis*, vol. 2, p. 43; Kovalenko, Anatoly. *Le Martyre de Husayn dans la poésie populaire d'Iraq* (Thesis University of Geneva, 1979).

known authors of the texts and likely there are many, who modified existing texts. Good dramatic parts of one text were also put in another one. The language was that of the people, without any decoration and often artless in form, so that the common man could understand the piece. They were often uneven of style and faulty in terms of rhythm and rhyme. But the public loved it, and, "it has an electrifying impact on them, far more than in Oberammergau. Everybody, high and low, is affected by the play. It is national in character, because each harm, each hurt, each death is felt by the nation at large as being their own."[139] Conolly opined that, "The parts are written by the cleverest doctors; it is not, therefore, to be wondered at, that" [people are attracted to it][140] But leading Iranian literati did not think much of it and considered it an importation from Europe.[141] The reason for the disdain of these literati is that passion play texts are not necessarily works of literary art that were meant to be read. They first and foremost were scripts to be performed. Each role was written down on a piece if paper small enough so that the actor could keep it in the palm of his hand as an aide-mémoire. Europeans like Rice had a similar opinion. "There is no plot; it has no distinctive character; it is full of repetition; it is most intolerably long, and tedious and dreary. It certainly cannot be judged by any of our literary standards, but attraction it certainly has."[142]

Depending on the circumstances and the episode a passion play lasted 2-4 hours. The plays were all of the same length, although not divided into acts or scenes. They were usually shortened when the director had to cut out the battle and dying scenes, which were best performed when the play was done in the open. Inside buildings this was not really feasible and then often pieces from other plays were inserted to make up for such cuts. This also explains why in some of the surviving passion play texts there are changes and rewrites as compared with the texts of other similar episodes.

The mode in which the actor had to recite or chant his lines was brought into harmony with the role. The villains were usually dressed in chain mail, the martyrs in normal Arab dresses. Although initially probably all actors chanted a similar mode this changed over time. For later the "good guys" were not only dressed differently from the 'bad guys' but they sang their lines using classical Iranian musical modes, whereas the often gaudily clad "bad guys" only recited their lines, sometimes making their voice unpleasant to better portray the nature of the character. By the end of the nineteenth century this distinction had become so well developed that at that time each major role was characterized by the use of a distinct mode, which also might change per episode. This on the one hand indicates that there was standardization, while on the other hand it shows the will and ability to

---

[139] Anonymous, "Die Passionsspiele," p. 535.
[140] Conolly, *Journey*, vol. 1, p. 268.
[141] Malek al-Sho`ara Bahar, *Sabk Shenasi*, vol. 3, 400; see also Kasravi, *Shi`agari*.
[142] Rice, *Persian Women*, pp. 233-34; Sheil, *Glimpses*, p. 129.

match voice or musical expression to dramatic requirement. Theatrical conventions included, for example, circling the stage several times to simulate a long journey; not moving in a straight line, thus indicating distance between two points; use of visible and invisible devices, such as a tub of water with some green stalks representing the river Euphrates and a pot of plants representing a grove of palms.

Initially the repertory was simple. Many of those were brought together by Hoseyn `Ali Khan, a palace eunuch and director of the passion plays at the royal court during Naser al-Din Shah and were later bought by Chodzko in the mid-nineteenth century and numbered 33 plays in all.[143] In 1900, Thalasso wrote, "there are about 50 passion plays that make up the drama."[144] However, there was a continuous stream of new adaptations and/or new plays due to improvements made or to reflect local preferences, so that when Cerulli collected these texts around 1950 he was able to gather more than 1055 manuscript texts of passion plays.

Court patronage set the standard for style, literary and dramatic form for ta`ziyeh production, at least in the major large towns. This was mainly due to the fact that it employed a large number of professional actors and stage directors, whose vocal and declamatory skills people elsewhere wanted to emulate. Not only the acting skills were imitated but also the dressing-up and the staging of passion play productions. The court director for passion plays, as was noted above, also had a large collection of scripts of passion plays. The fact also that many the scripts of many passion plays were printed had an impact on the development of the literary style and content of new scripts and adaptation of old scripts. At least 80 scripts has been published by 1843.[145]

Algar intimates that Mirza Taqi wanted to do away with the passion play, and that he was supported in this by the religious authorities.[146] However, that does not accord with actual practice. There were no orders banning its performance. In November 1850, for example, Querry attended a ta`ziyeh-khvani at the Ala Qapi at the governor's invitation.[147] It was more likely, therefore that Amir Kabir opposed ta`ziyeh-dari, i.e. the flagellants. This is clear from the fact that he took steps to improve the quality of the passion play. According to the Tadhkereh-ye

---

[143] Chodzko, Théatre Persan, p. xxxv. For the list of 33 passion plays known to Chodzko and the rendition of their plots see Ibid., Théatre Persan, pp. xxxii-xv, 1-217 (originally in Journal indépendente 1844; for the German text of Chodzo, see "Das persische Theater," Das Ausland (August 1844), nr. 226, pp. 901-11; nr. 229, 913-15; nr. 230, pp. 917-19; nr. 231, pp. 921-23; nr. 232, pp. 925-28; partly also in "Le Théatre En Perse," Revue de l'Orient 6/1845, pp. 119-25.

[144] Thalasso, Le Théâtre Persan, p. 885; Pelly, L. The Miracle Play of Hasan and Husain (London, 1879) counted 52 episodes.

[145] Calmard, "Le mécénat" I, p. 98.

[146] Algar, Religion, p. 135

[147] Querry, "Rouz-e Qatl," Revue de l'Orient III (1856), p. 371-80.

Ganj-e Shayegan, Amir Kabir asked the poet Mirza Nasrollah Shehab Isfahani to write 12 passion plays.

> At the beginning of this government ... when the prime ministry of the kingdom and the command of the army was bestowed upon the late Mirza Taqi Khan, Amir-e Nezam [Amir Kabir], who was one of the capable men of the epoch and one of the prodigies of the period. ... Since most of the poetry that was spoken by those playing the members of the Holy Family in the ta`ziyeh performances and the assemblies depicting the mourning and calamity of the Fifth Person of the Family of the Robe [Imam Hoseyn] is poor, inappropriate, nonsensical, and erroneous, Mirza Taqi Khan commissioned him, saying, 'Elegantly prepare twelve texts about those events in a style both pleasing to the aristocracy and comprehensible to the commons. ...' He wrote the firebrand of verses so movingly ... that if the heart of the auditor was as hard as the stone of Moses, listening to them would have had the effect upon it of the rod of Moses.[148]

This probably was the first time that en effort was made to improve and conventionalize the text of the passion play. The results of this possibly first effort to do so were clear some 25 years later when, in 1882, Ahmad Bey remarked that "in Tehran they already have started to impose fixed rules on the theater and to purge popular elements. The danger is that it will lose its heroic and spontaneous character."[149] The experimentation that artists were engaged in is clear from the variety in texts of the same drama and the varied indications for chanting. It was also at that time that non-Karbala dramas were written and enacted, but staged in a purely *ta`ziyeh* mode. These non-Karbala plays were based on themes such as the story of Yusef, Soleyman and the Queen of Bilqis (Sheba), Musa and the Pharaoh, and other religious stories. They were not only produced during Moharram and Safar, the months of mourning, but also in the evenings of Ramazan and whenever there was a demand for it.

SEQUENCING OF PASSION PLAY EPISODES

Moharram was the holy month of mourning and because the martyrdom is said to have taken place of the tenth day, the whole performance of the Karbala cycle plays originally lasted 10 days, but depending on time and location the time period could be longer. "These performances are called tazieh, or mourning, and continue generally ten days-in some places still more; and where the people are very holy, or would be thought so, as at Koom and Mushed, they are kept up for forty days."[150] Over time, the Karbala cycle lasted longer than 10 days in most towns, usually to

---

[148] Adamiyyat, Fereydun. *Amir Kabir va Iran* (Tehran, 1348/1969), p. 322.
[149] Ahmad Bey, "Le Théatre," p. 535.
[150] Fraser, *A Winter's Journey*, vol. 2, p. 146.

perform episodes showing the fate of Hoseyn's womenfolk, who were taken as prisoners to Damascus to the evil Yazid.[151]

The events leading up to the climax of martyrdom are divided into a multitude of separate episodes. There was no fixed sequence of plays, the only episode that was fixed, was that of martyrdom of Hoseyn of the 10th of Moharram (*`Ashurah*), "as on that day the Imam's murder is represented."[152] On the other days a variety of annually changing episodes were performed. According to Wills, "the most popular being the wedding of Kasim, from the great mount of spectacle, the death of Houssein, the death of Ali Akbar, and the Dar."[153]

Usually, the plays on the other days dealt with the martyrdom of members of Hoseyn's family and his companions. Each of these episodes prepares the spectator for the final day; the lead actor battles the enemy and is martyred; the other remaining protagonists deliver religious observations on their fate. In the large cities such as Tehran, where according to Mostowfi, between 200 to 300 performances might take place during Moharram, the number of attendants was usually between 300 and 400 persons.[154] Therefore, 30 or more different plays might be performed during that ten-day period. In Ardabil, in the large Hoseyniyyeh of Hajj Mirza Mohsen Mojtahed they played some 40 different episodes during these days.[155] According to de Gobineau, it was rare that a theatrical troupe did not stage an episode of the passion play at least seven to eight times per day! "At the end of the sacred ten-day period the actors are literally exhausted."[156]

`Eyn al-Saltaneh reported that in 1884, the repertory was as follows:

> Day 1: Fatemah-Zahra;
> Day 2: Fatemah Saghra;
> Day 3: [left blank];
> Day 4: Moslem;
> Day 5: `Abbas;
> Day 6: `Ali Akbar;
> Day 7: Qasem;
> Day 8: Yusef and mother Vahab;
> Day 9: Syrian bazaar;
> Day 10: Sayyed al-Shohada, i.e. Lord of Martyrs (Hoseyn).

---

[151] Wills, *In the land*, p. 283.
[152] Usher, *A Journey*, p. 619.
[153] Wills, *In the land*, p. 283.
[154] Mostowfi, *Sharh*, vol. 1, p. 289; de Gobineau, *Les religions*, vol. 2, p. 131.
[155] Safar, *Ardabil*, vol. 3, pp. 44, 256-57 (names of well-known actors). The Tehran police reports logged 35 different passion plays in the years 1885-87. Reza'i and Adhari, *Gozareshha*, Index.
[156] De Gobineau, *Les réligions*, vol. 2, p. 120.

He further reported that during that period, on the eve of day five they staged the marriage of Fatima at another location, and on the eve of day six the Qanbar episode; and on eve of day seven Dorrah al-Sadaf.[157] The purpose of the performance of the various episodes during the first nine days of Moharram is to slowly build up the growing emotional ground-swell that comes to a climax on the tenth day when the final battle takes place ending in Hoseyn's death.

In case of the *Takiyeh-ye Dowlat* there was even a kind of program (see Figure 30) as to which episodes of the passion play would be played during the time that the theater was open, i.e. Moharram and Safar. The first of such programs dates from December 1880. It not only listed which play would be performed on what day it also listed the main actor for each play, which suggests that actors had acquired a reputation and that spectators were particularly drawn to attend when such actors performed. The three programs discussed (1298/December 1880; 1299/November 1881; and 1303/November 1883) also show that each year the program of the episodes played was changed, so as to make attendance more attractive to the audience. Unfortunately, nothing is known how these programs were distributed and what its targeted market was. Presumably, the management of the *Takiyeh-ye Dowlat* wrote and distributed the programs.[158] Although Naser al-Din Shah liked the passion play very much and did not miss even one,[159] it also happened that there were no performances in the *Takiyeh-ye Dowlat*. `Eyn al-Saltaneh noted in February 1893 that, "It is for two years now that there was no performance of the passion play. This month HM has decreed it will be played again. It started as of to-day; it was a good show."[160]

[157] `Eyn al-Saltaneh, *Ruznameh*, vol. 1, p. 52 (3 Moharram 1302/23 October, 1884). In Khorammabad in November 1849 the sequence was as follows: (1) ?; (2) *Vorud-e Karbala*; (3) *Vafat-e Sakineh*; (4) *Teflan-e Moslem*; (5) *Pesaran-e Zeynab*; (6) *Bazar-e Sham va Ferangi*; (7) *Shahadat-e Hazrat-e `Abbas*; (8) *Shahadat-e `Ali Akbar*; (9) `*Arusi-ye Qasem*; and (10) *Shahadat-e Shahid-e Shohada*. Afshar, *Safarnameh-ye Lorestan*, p. 84-85; for another program in Tehran see Aubin, *La Perse*, pp. 171-72.
[158] `Anasari, "Asnad va Madarek" pp. 7-10 (with facsimiles of three of these programs).
[159] Feuvrier, J.B.: *Trois ans à la Cour de Perse*. (Paris: F. Juven, 1900), pp. 296.
[160] `Eyn al-Saltaneh, *Ruznameh*, vol. 1, p. 513 (25 Rajab, 1310/12 February, 1893).

Figure 30: Programs for the perfomance of episodes of the passion play in the Takiyeh-ye Dowleh (years 1298/December 1880 and 1299/November 1881)

STAGE DIRECTORS

In Tehran in 1907, the stage director and executive producer of the royal theater was Mo`in al-Boka', who at that time had already organized performances for 37 years. He had succeeded his father in that function. He was an old man with a white beard dressed in a long coat with a cashmere shawl belt in which he had stuck many rolls containing the various plays. Each year during the month of Ramazan he recruited his actors for that year from among the best singers and musicians in Tehran or the provinces. Most of these actors played some kind of popular theater during the remainder of the year. He signed up 200 of actors (*ta`ziyeh-khvan*s) and their 10 sub-chiefs for a period of four months. During the remaining months prior to Moharram they would rehearse the pieces and roles that they would play during the months of Moharram and Safar. The entire troupe would only remain together for the performances for the shah after which they would be broken up in as many troupes as there were sub-chiefs and would play in the various city quarters of Tehran under the overall guidance of Mo`in al-Boka. There might be as many as 50 sub-troupes playing each 10 days.[161] Sometimes, the shah himself would hire actors. E`temad al-Saltaneh noted that Naser al-Din Shah met a group of actors (ta`ziyeh-khvans) from Taleqan; he told them to come with him to Kalardasht and then to Shahrestanak where arrangements were made for the show.[162]

The situation was, of course, different in small towns and villages. In 1837, at Tehran, the schoolmaster of the quarter (mahalleh) was the stage director and prompter.[163] In Soltanabad in 1935, "the village barber was also a director of the sacred play."[164] These are examples of what was one of the strengths of the passion play, viz. that it was really a popular art form that was borne and lived by the people concerned. They were the actors, stage managers, rehearsers, prompters, etc., etc. and they also took care of the clothing, implements, and other props. In Qazvin, for example, all the implements and props of the local city quarters' passion play troupes and the neighborhood groups (dastehs) were stored in 1935 in the Madraseh-ye Sardar and in mosques.[165] The situation was different, however, when the organizers wanted to hire people from outside. The entrepreneur had to pay for the travel and stay of the poet, rowzeh-khvans, and actors as well as all the clothing and other theatrical material.[166] He did so, of course, with the money of the sponsor of the play.

ACTORS

All of the actors, even for the women's parts, were males, adults and children.[167] According to Berezine, the female roles, played by men were badly acted.[168] There were, however, exceptions. In the beginning of the Qajar period, a well-known performer of women's roles, a certain Hajji Molla Hoseyn, played so well that each year he left his farm in Saveh to play at the royal takiyeh during the months of Moharram and Safar. Two well-known actors of female roles of the late Qajar period were Hajji

---

[161] Aubin, La Perse, pp. 170-71; RMM 4/1908, p. 486; E`temad al-Saltaneh, Ketab, p. 240; Varjavand, Simay, vol. 2, p. 1120 (Mo`in al-Boka, the director or ta`ziyeh-ara); De Gobineau, Les réligions, vol. 2, p. 118. The director, or as Chodzko calls him, the chief entrepreneur. Chodzko, Théatre Persan, p. 174
[162] E`temad al-Saltaneh, Ruznameh, p. 872 (2 Moharram 1309/August 8, 1891).
[163] Wilbraham, Travels, p. 422.
[164] Fullerton, Alice. To Persia for Flowers (Oxford: OUP, 1938), p. 123.
[165] Varjavand, Simay, vol. 2, p. 1119 (in an aside he asks: where are they now?)
[166] Chodzko, Le Théatre Persan, p. xxii.
[167] Rice, Persian Women, p. 234; Stuart, Journal, p. 296 ("The female parts are of course acted by boys, which is a sad drawback"); Wilbraham, Travels, p. 422 ("The female characters who figured upon the stage were personated by boys"); Thalasso, Le Théatre Persan, p. 884.
[168] Calmard, "Mécénat" I, p. 98 quoting Berezine.

Molla Hoseyn and Qoli Jahan Shahi; they were especially hired to play the role of Zeynat.[169]

Figure 31: Actor Mirza Gholam Hoseyn dressed as `Abbas brother of Imam Hoseyn (1886)

Traditionally actors (*moqalled*) were selected based on their physical characteristics and voice for particular roles. This is understandable; a thin, sickly looking man with a reedy voice was not deemed appropriate play Hoseyn, or a very pleasant and attractive fellow with a marvelous voice would not play Shemr or Yazid. In fact, those playing the villains such as Shem needed to have a hoarse, rude, disagreeable voice.[170]

> Some by the nature of their role have to satirize government's abuse, or the prevailing vices; always the actors chosen to be the enemy of Hoseyn commit these abuses or defend the government abuse, which suffices for the public to hate them. The preferred roles all play highly moral qualities such as resignation, loyalty, trust, bravery, frankness, etc. This month is

---

[169] Beyza'i, Namayesh, p. 152.

[170] De Gobineau, *Les religions*, vol. 2, p. 122. Those having a melodious voice played the good guys. Calmard, "Mécénat" I, p. 98 quoting Berezine.

also one when the government and its agents stop maltreating the people, and to meet with highly placed persons and talk about their problem.[171]

Also, because women were not allowed to perform, actors had to be found with high voices had to act the female roles, which meant that preferably young boys, whose voices had not changed yet, were chosen. This was not always possible, of course, and thus some bearded 'women' also were found on the stage, but as they were veiled it did not matter. Ahmad Bey summed up the requirement for the selection of passion play actors.

> The actors are recruited from everywhere. It does not matter, they may be a grocer, a cobbler, a merchant, a sayyed, all may become an actor or *shabihkar* [sic], which gives social prestige. The only requirement is to have a good and agreeable voice and sufficient instruction in Arabic and Persian. The public esteem and a relatively rather high compensation attract each year a large number of aspirants every year for the momentary job. Some months prior to the show those who already have shown their ability choose from among the young aspirant some candidates. While continuing their normal daily job these experienced men trained their young favorites to develop their voice and talents, and chose, at the same time, those dramatic works that are most appropriate for the ability of their wards.[172]

This is also confirmed by other contemporary sources. Connolly, referring to the situation in Mashhad wrote that "The performers on these occasions are men selected for their powers of elocution,"[173] while Wills reported that "small boys, chosen for their clear and sympathetic voices, from among the singers of the town, sustain the little parts of the granddaughters and grandsons of the prophet,[174] while corpses were often played by children.[175] This despite the fact that "the wives are veiled, and these characters are played by bearded men, as are angels and prophets, who are also veiled by glittering handkerchiefs. ... Yezeed, the infidel king, and Shemr, the actual slayer of the saint, are clad in gay attire, booted and helmeted, and, with shirts of chain-mail, rant as do the heroes of a Surrey melodrama; but the language is effective, the action rapid and the speeches, though often long, accompanied by vigorous pantomime."[176] To ensure

[171] Ahmad Bey, "Le Théatre," pp. 534-35.
[172] Ahmad Bey, "Le Théatre," p. 530.
[173] Conolly, *Journey*, vol. 1, p. 268. According to Berezine, those having a melodious voice play the good guys. The female roles, played by men, were badly acted. Calmard, "Le mécénat" I, p. 98 quoting Berezin. People indeed took note when actors had a good voice. `Eyn al-Saltaneh, *Ruznameh*, vol. 2, p. 1372 noted, for example, that a boy singer from Qazvin had excellent voice; "he was first a *ta`ziyeh-khvan*, but now has joined the musicians." Furthermore, Ibid., *Ruznameh*, vol. 1, p. 467 ("There are many good singers in Nehavand").
[174] Wills, *In the land*, pp. 281-82.
[175] Anonymous, "Die Passionsspiele," p. 355.
[176] Wills, *In the land*, p. 281.

that there was sufficient new and young talent to fit the requirements of the cast young boys were selected by a *morshed* to learn the craft.[177] There were, however, more requirements for the selection and accoutrement of the actors for the right role. According to Sadr al-Ashraf,

> the person playing Imam Hoseyn had to be a perfect man (*mard-e kamel*) with an average beard, nice face, good-voiced, and his clothes and appearance had to be luminous and his voice and gestures had to suggest strength of spirit, courage, and bravery so that the injustice done to him be obvious. His brother `Abbas, also courageous, had to be a man of 20-30 years, very strong, handsome, well-limbed, sweet-voiced, chain-mailed on a strong horse and his bravery and courage compared with his older brother should be obvious, while a dried water skin should be on his back. `Ali Akbar had to be about 18 years, good looking, with a nice voice and he had to be grief-stricken and be able to project the ill-luck that befell his family.[178]

Given those requirements care was taken to ensure that the best actors/singers were selected. It is not a surprise to learn that, "The principal parts are taken year after year by the same actors."[179] This was only the logical consequence of the fact that the actors usually specialized in a role, given the generally accepted requirements for character actors. "They trained (*mashq*) their roles under a director in the mosques or *hoseyniyyeh*s. For each actor there were special characteristic clothes that were kept in the neighborhood mosques."[180] It would seem that some of the best "actors come from villages near Kasvin, whose inhabitants have for generations made the acting of the passion-play a profession."[181] These were actors who performed in Tabriz, but also many of those performing in Tehran hailed from that area. The Taleqan region (Qazvin) was also well-known for its tradition of supplying passion play actors. One of the famous passion play actors in Qazvin was Nazem al-Boka'.[182] The existence of professional actors in Qazvin is also recorded in the local census where in the one quarter for which data have been published there was one professional, *ta'ziyeh-khvan*.[183] Wills remarked that the actors that he saw perform in Shiraz at the governor's palace "are mostly well up in their *rôles*; many of those sustaining the principal characters have come from Ispahan, where the tradition of the tazzia is handed down from father to son; and

[177] Varjavand, *Simay*, vol. 2, p. 1131.

[178] Sadr, Mohsen, *Khaterat-e Sadr al-Ashraf* (Tehran, 1364/1985), pp. 44-45.

[179] Rice, *Persian Women*, p. 234; Stuart, *Journal*, p. 296 ("The female parts are of course acted by boys, which is a sad drawback"); Wilbraham, *Travels*, p. 422 ("The female characters who figured upon the stage were personated by boys").

[180] Safar, *Ardabil*, vol. 3, pp. 255; De Gobineau, *Les religions*, vol. 2, p. 118.

[181] Wilson, *Persian Life*, p. 63.

[182] Varjavand, *Simay*, vol. 2, p. 1117; `Eyn al-Saltaneh, *Ruznameh*, vol. 1, p. 513.

[183] Sadvandian, Cyrus. "The Inhabitants of Meydan-Gusfand", *The Journal of the Middle East Studies Society at Columbia University* 1 (1987), p. 50.

year by year they have played the mournful tragedy, making it a business as well as a religious act. They are fed, dressed, and paid by the Governor."[184] It may be for this reason that Thalasso stated, although mistakenly, that the amateur actors formed a kind of corporation.[185]

During the hey-day of the performance of passion plays (1870-1896) there was competition between patrons who put on the best show and this was not just limited to the richness of the show's embellishment. Zell al-Soltan, for example, also wanted to compete with the quality of the actors/chanters in Tehran and therefore gave instructions to find him boys with good voices in the villages around Isfahan, and then to take them to Isfahan where they were to be taught by musical teachers the art of chanting and be as good as those of Tehran. After Zell al-Soltan's powers were curtailed in 1888, he lost interest in the entire matter and allowed all the singers to return to their homes.[186]

Figure 32: Cast of passion play actors; note the veils over the faces of the actors playing the Imams

COSTUMES

The choice of costumes of the actors was not an accidental affair. "Everything was done to make the scene as real as possible."[187] First and foremost actors were

---

[184] Wills, *In the land*, p. 283.
[185] Thalasso, *Le Théatre Persan*, p. 884.
[186] Homayuni, *Ta`ziyeh*, pp. 115, 120.
[187] Sheil, *Glimpses*, p. 128.

dressed in what people believed to be Arab dresses. "The actors are dressed in the supposed Arab costumes and armour of the seventh century; they have no scenery, and for all music there is little but the fateful blare of the trumpet and the beat of drums."[188] Ja`far Shahri, the historian of old Tehran par excellence, defined an actor of the passion play as someone who was dressed in a Arab dress.[189] Hoseyn's enemies invariably were dressed in chain armor, if the organizers could afford it.[190] People had certain stereotype ideas how an Arab, a villain, a European, etc. looked like and stage directors, therefore, had cater to that symbolism. The costumes may not have been historically authentic, but they looked like what people believed they had been. "Out in this far-off quarter the people have but little notion of what a Frankish Ambassador looks like. In this instance he wore ordinary Persian garb, qualified by a crimson sash across his left shoulder. ... My hats, scarves, and umbrella were freely borrowed for the sacred play, so that the merciful *ferengis* should look more *vraisembable*."[191] Like the décor and stage props actors' dresses were therefore chosen with the intent to send a message; these are the good guys (dressed shabbily as Arabs) and those are the bad guys (dressed splendidly). Together with the nature of their voices (beautiful, pleasing versus shrill and grating) the costumes sent subliminal messages to the audience, so that even without knowing the plot it would know the lay-of-the-land and who's-who. The caliph Yazid, for example, was "made to look as fierce and inhuman as possible."[192] It usually was well-done and even Europeans unfamiliar with story knew immediately who were the Sunnis and who the Shi`ites.[193] "The family of Hussein is represented by men in women's dress; and as the performances proceed to the dismal fate of the Iman on the plains of Kerbeleh, they utter dreadful shrieks and groans, and fill the air with their lamentations."[194] According to Beyza'i, actors playing women's roles wore a long black shirt, which was sometimes decorated with flowers. A piece of black fabric covered the head, arms and hands. Another piece of fabric covered the face, so that only the eyes would be visible. The women belonging to Yazid's side wore the same clothes, but in red.[195]

Some of the actors were dressed up in splendid manner at no cost to the organizer. "The enemies of the Imaum were all clothed in chain-armour, one suit of which was very valuable. It now belonged to Suleiman Khan; but had formerly been worn by a brother of Aga Mohamed Khan, Jaffer Kooly Khan, who was so treacherously murdered by that monarch."[196] `Eyn al-Saltaneh reported that the women of the royal

[188] Hale, *From Persian Uplands*, p. 38.
[189] Shahri, *Tarikh*, vol. 5, p. 521.
[190] Stuart, *Journey*, p. 294.
[191] Fullerton, *To Persia*, p. 76.
[192] Mounsey, *A Journey*, p. 313.
[193] O'Donovan, *Merv Oasis*, vol. 2, p. 43.
[194] Fowler, *Three Years*, p. 124.
[195] Beyza'i, Namayesh, p. 153.
[196] Holmes, *Sketches*, p. 311.

harem "had prepared six jewel-studded dresses in the royal harem for the water carriers of Yazid. The following women [names listed] had each dressed up a man; it
was quite a spectacle, a total of 100,000 *tuman*s of jewels and pearls was on display.
The shah had sent a photographer to take a picture."[197]

Figure 33: Cast of passion play actors some of whom have animal masks (Soleyman episode)

But not every actor, or *ta`ziyeh* play, was so well endowed. In the simple rustic
presentations there were no rich patrons and people had to make do. In April 1892
`Eyn al-Saltaneh wrote, "The singers were good but had no props; one of the boys
sang beautifully. There are many good singers in Nehavand."[198] In March 1899 he
commented, "a ta`ziyeh-khvan troupe was performing under my verandah, not bad;
they only had one shield, two helmets and one sword. Shemr nowadays has only a
dagger, and the imam-khvan is seated on the stool (*korsi*)."[199] Not much had
changed when in 1935 in the village of Soltanabad, the botanist Fullerton attended a
rustic passion play performance. "The play was evidently in strict convention; the
actors sang or said their parts in sing-song voices. In such a poor village, only a few
scarves and hats were added to their daily dress to alter their character."[200] She further reported that, "Ali [one of the headmen] explained that he was acting the part
of Hussein in the religious play, which seemed to go on for months, and proceeded
to change before us all. His wife unlocked the chest and took out a better black suit,
which he put on, trousers and all, without any false shame."[201]

[197] `Eyn al-Saltaneh, *Ruznameh*, vol. 1, pp. 513-14.
[198] `Eyn al-Saltaneh, *Ruznameh*, vol. 1, p. 467 (25 Ramazan, 1309/April 22, 1892).
[199] `Eyn al-Saltaneh, *Ruznameh*, vol. 2, p. 1415 (9 Dhu'l-Qa`deh 1316/March 21, 1899).
[200] Fullerton, *To Persia*, p. 76.
[201] Fullerton, *To Persia*, p. 116.

Because stage directors wanted the scene to be as much 'authentic' as possible they would ask any European who would be in the neighborhood for the loan of pieces of clothing and other items that were European, such as chairs. Sir John Malcolm had given "an entire suit of red regimental cocks' feather cap and all."[202] As pointed out above, the costume did not have to be historically correct, but it should be recognizable to the audience as European, which often meant something outlandish. When Conolly saw this episode of the passion play in Mashhad in 1831, he observed that "The actor, who personated the Elchee, wore a velvet foraging cap, upon long ringlets which fell down his back and the sides of his face; one coloured handkerchief was tied round his neck, and another on his arm, and the rest of his apparel was Persian. The ambassador 'muttering some gibberish which passed for a European language."[203] Europeans were often baffled by the lack of historical sense. In 1835, "this 'Eelchee' of the seventh century: cocked hats are in particular request, and at one 'tazeer' His Excellency is this year to appear in the uniform of His Majesty's 4th Light Dragoons."[204] To make it even more evident that the actor was playing the role of a European in some renderings of the play, "The Eelchee was accompanied by his wife, who had a European bonnet on, with the curtain hanging over the forehead and the front of her neck."[205] To make it even more realistic, "when the three foreign ambassadors were introduced they entered in great state, dressed as far as possible in the costume of European diplomats, and preceded by led horses, richly caparisoned. Unluckily, it had been impossible to find cocked hats for the whole party, and the senior and spokes-man of the three was obliged himself with what is commonly called a chimney-pot."[206] To be as 'authentic' as possible stage directors went even father in creating the right symbol of a European by not only selecting the 'right ' costumes and paraphernalia (wife, led horses), but even making an effort to have the "ambassador" speak like a European. Browne reported that when he was at the village of Kirishkin people told him that was a pity he had were not there earlier, because "you might have even taught us some words of your language to put in the mouths of the actors who personated them. As it was, not knowing anything of the tongue of the Firangis, we had to make the actors who represented them talk Turkish, which seemed to us the nearest approach possible to Firangi speech."[207] Europeans were not always pleased with the stage-setting of the passion play. Browne, for example, commented, "the effect was spoiled in some measure by the introduction of a number of the Shah's carriages, with postilions

[202] Conolly, *Journey*, vol. 1, pp. 282; Wilbraham, *Travels*, pp. 421-22; Sheil, *Glimpses*, p. 126.
[203] Conolly, *Journey*, vol. 1, pp. 282-83.
[204] Stuart, *Journey*, pp. 295-96 (They borrowed a tricorn from French embassy); Flandin, *Voyage*, vol. 1, p. 251.
[205] Sheil, *Glimpses*, p. 130.
[206] Mounsey, *A Journey*, pp. 313-14.
[207] Browne, *A Year*, pp. 84-85.

barbarously dressed in half-European uniform, in the middle of the piece. This ab-surd piece of ostentation seemed to me typical of Kajar taste."[208]

Mise-en-Scene

According to de Gobineau, the French chargé d'affaires and later ambassador in Iran (1856-58; 1862-63), who took a great interest in the Shi`ite passion play, "The attraction of other forms of traditional Persian art fades totally when com-pared with the passion play performances with which nothing may rival. It is a fury of the entire nation; men, women, children have the same rapture under this rapport, and a show makes the entire city run."[209] Indeed, the passion play was the orgiastic experience par excellence. It was literally an enactment of Imam Hoseyn's tragedy. It was like a time machine; you could be there, view and ex-perience the events leading up to Imam Hoseyn's martyrdom.

> The stage then represents Karbala, then the palace of the caliphs at Damas-cus, then a church, etc. but there is no indication, because there is no décor, only the imagination. The roles and events were therefore important; the actors were not. The actors were only enacting the feelings and expecta-tions of the public. Unlike improvisatory comedy (*taqlid*), which was spontaneous and improvisation, passion play was unlike that. Everybody knew what was going to happen and people were waiting for that to let their feelings go. From the beginning of the play the public was told where the scene of the play was. The actors who played their role did not leave, but only stepped aside, and most of them had their roll in the hand, which they often read from. Thus, there was no illusion. No attention was paid to the reliability of the historicity of the costumes. Pomp in dress and arms was the main object. As to acting, how to behave, gesture, mimic, etc. every actor did as he liked. But it was this naturalness that attracts.[210]

Above all, the actors were believers. That belief made them assume the persona of their character. The main purpose of their acting was to communicate to the public the emotion that filled them. That emotion was raw and real and the actors often shed real tears. The tears of the spectators served as applause. Idolized by the pub-lic, the high clergy, strongly disapproved of this popular orgiastic outburst, which in their view made a spectacle of the Imams' lives.[211]

---

[208] Browne, *A Year*, p. 604.
[209] De Gobineau, *Trois Ans*, vol. 2, p. 217.
[210] Anonymous, "Die Passionsspiele," p. 355
[211] De Gobineau, *Les religions*, vol. 2, pp. 112-13.

Start of the Performance: rowzeh-khvani

Given the fact that there were a limited number of theatrical troupes they had to play at least seven times per day in different city quarters. Performances therefore started as early as five o'clock in the morning, according de Gobineau.[212] However, the passion plays financed by the rich started at a more comfortable time during the day. "At noon every seat is taken, all being ready, the band plays a march, a gun is discharged, and the governor takes his seat."[213] After the patron of the play, or his delegate, had taken his seat the performance could begin. Then the *rowzeh-khvan* started, while the play lasted from two to four hours, which in the afternoon meant from 15.00 to 19.00,[214] unless it was Moharram 10. In that case the *rowzeh-khvani* would start one hour before sunset.[215] "By way of prelude to the piece, a band of music traversed the stage, playing a most dismal air."[216] The first to appear was the *rowzeh-khvan*, usually more than one, followed by the actors and a dozen *pish-khvan*s (boy singers). The first *rowzeh-khvan* mounted on a stool or chair to the left of the stage. The actors meanwhile gathered at the *taqnama* or foyer and the *pish-khvan*s sat down on the carpets, below the stage.[217] Sometimes, the prelude was a bit different reflecting local preferences. In Tehran, according to Stuart, "Three orators then entered, bearing a standard and accompanied by the *professional beaters* of the Imaun Jooma Mosque, with their breasts bared."[218]

Then the show began. A man rose and cried three times: Ya `Ali! or a dervish with long hair stood up from among the public, showed his axe and declaimed at loud voice with an Arabic accent some ode in the honor of `Ali and his children.[219] The crowd became quiet and all took their place. The show began with "an amateur chant by boys and old men, than which nothing more discordant could well be imagined. Next, boys mounted the lower steps of the membra [sic; *menbar*], or pulpit, to recite verses composed for the occasion."[220] Above them there would be a white flag with the inscription: Ya `Ali, Ya Hoseyn. They had a paper with the text in their hand while chanting. Each refrain was taken up by a choir of young boys of 10-15 years, who were placed at the foot of the pedestal. The verses referred to were so-called *nowheh*s. "It is the simple poetical form about any subject of Hoseyn's tragic life. It is sung in unison by two boys of 18-20 years old …

---

[212] De Gobineau, *Les réligions*, vol. 2, p. 120.

[213] Wills, *In the land*, p. 81.

[214] Aubin, *La Perse*, p. 170 ("That recitation lasts three to four hours each time."); De Gobineau, *Trois Ans*, vol. 2, p. 217. According to Wills, *In the land*, p. 283 "Each act lasts from two to four hours." He added, however, that "there are no actual acts."

[215] Thalasso, *Le Théatre Persan*, p. 882.

[216] Mounsey, *A Journey*, p. 312.

[217] Chodzko, *Théatre Persan*, p. xxvi; Thalasso, *Le Théatre Persan*, p. 882.

[218] Stuart, *Journey*, pp. 293.

[219] Ahmad Bey, "Le Théatre," pp. 530, 534.

[220] Conolly, *Journey*, vol. 1, p. 278; Calmard, "Le mécénat" I, p. 96.

They have hardly begun to sing some couplets when the public starts to weep."[221]
The lamentations (*nowhehs*) chanted by the boys "are a genre of strophic poems
in classical metres which often have unconventional rhyme-schemes and arrangements of lines and refrains within the stanza. The number and placement of
stresses in each line are important in nawhas, those for breast-beating having a
more rapid rhythm than those for chain-flagellation."[222] This lasted 20 minutes,
during which time the actors dressed.[223]

After these introductory acts and chants, it was the *rowzeh-khvan*'s turn. He had to
prepare the public for the sad events to come through sermons, and legends recited in prose or chanted in verse, of which the contents often has nothing to do
with that which follows.[224]

> Once the series of nouhas is completed a man rises and approaches the
> pedestal. He looks like a mollah, it is a mercia-khan [sic; *marthiyeh-
> khvan*], i.e. a teller of the passion of Ali and his children. While he
> mounts the pedestal, he stops at each step and he utters a prayer, while a
> group of young boys begin to chant which ordinarily is very pleasing and
> moving. Having arrived on top of the pedestal, the mercia-khan amuses
> the public with some humoristic anecdotes about one caliph or the other
> of the Beni-Omaya [the caliphs of the Ommayad clan]. They are totally
> taken apart and slandered in these anecdotes; they are either stupid, lack
> tact, or have such big bellies that these attached to the tail of the horse
> and the poor caliphs are thus taken to the mosques to render justice of a
> suspect nature. These enormities are really believed even by those who
> know history well; it is about ridiculing an enemy and to take vengeance
> by targeted invented stories to show that this valueless enemy was only
> victorious by chance.

> After having thus amused the spectators he begins to bewail the fate of
> these heroes. He practically repeats word by word what the two singers
> have said, with this difference that he does so in prose and supports his
> claims by testimonies of learned and well-known men. The mercia-khan
> [sic] always has big tomes of the history of Ali and his children around
> him, and at each citation he indicates the page, the edition and year of the
> work. The spectators who have something better to do that to read histo-
> ries thus believe him at his word. Comparing the zero morals and physi-
> cal qualities of the victorious enemy with the moral grandeur and

---

[221] Ahmad Bey, "Le Théatre," p. 530.
[222] Hanaway, "Marthiya," *Encyclopeadia of Islam²*.
[223] Ahmad Bey, "Le Théatre," p. 534.
[224] Chodzko, *Le Théâtre Persan*, p. xxvii.

splendid physique of his defeated heroes he passes brusquely from gaiety to melancholy and sadness.[225]

Often there was more than one *rowzeh-khvan* as discussed in the previous chapter, because they were not always able to maintain their voice. Therefore, a second or even a third would perform and continue the story where his predecessor had left off. The *rowzeh-khvan* spoke and recited with perfect *sang froid* and vehemence the facts of the Imam's death in a loud and clear voice. People wailed at the right moment: 'Woe for Hoseyn' and the men beat their breasts.[226] He added comments of his own, and much action, in a singing tone of voice. "In fact, it is a sort of recitative, in which, as he comes to the affecting parts, he works himself and his auditors up."[227]

> With a grave voice, the rowzeh-khvan prepares the spectators for the tragic events that they are going to see and says: "Oh my brothers! Oh my sisters! Offer your heart in sacrifice, be sad and cry dearly about the calamities that recall the memory of that sad month of Moharram, so that nobody among you forget that the constant and persistent thinking of the misfortune of the august family of the Prophet (may God be with him and his descendents) transforms itself in a golden key to which accede to the doors of Paradise. Do not forget that one day, saintly Fatima, that pearl of chastity, while combing the hairs of her child Hoseyn, saw in the teeth of the comb a hair that by mischance had been taken from her beloved child and she could not stop herself from crying. That is past. The holy books guarantee the authenticity of this fact. O believers! Oh my brothers, listen well to my words and that nothing may distract you. This appears insignificant to you, a single hair! Fatimah when seeing this taken from the holy hair lets her tears flow. Alas. Alas. Tear your clothes, beat your breasts, 'bestir' your hearts, bite your hands until blood flows, bow your fronts to the ground while you tear out your hair. I do not have the strength anymore. My voice fails me! A single hair caught in the teeth of the comb! I let you judge the enormity of her pain when from high-up in paradise where she was at the time of Hoseyn's death, Fatima the saint saw the head of her well-beloved roll in the desert! The pain is going to kill me; the pain kills me! The poet acts upon his words and rends his clothes, beats his naked breast, tears his hairs, bites his hands, cries the names of the two martyrs: Hasan! Hoseyn! His exaltation rouses the public, and finds an echo in the tears of the people, the men beat their breasts; the women rend their veils, and thousands of mouths cry now the sainted names of the Imams.[228]

The orators occasionally paused to smoke their kaleeoons [sic; *qalyan* or water pipe], an occupation freely indulged in by the mournful crowd. A

---

[225] Ahmad Bey, "Le Théatre," p. 532.

[226] Stuart, *Journey*, p. 293; Aubin, *La Perse*, p. 165.

[227] Fraser, *A Winter's Journey*, vol. 2, p. 145.

[228] Chodzko, *Théatre Persan*, pp. xxvii-xxxi; Thalasso, *Le Théatre Persan*, pp. 882-83.

x

x

x

pigeon, with pink feet and wings, was introduced, who, by the mouth of one of the performers, told the sister of Hosein, that he had flown from Kerbela to Mecca, sprinkled with the blood of the martyr, to brig her the direful news of his death: she answered this amiable and active pigeon through the same channel. The lamentations of the ladies now increased, and our friend, the Moollah, thought it decent to put his handkerchief to his eyes. The beaters were sixty in number, many of their breasts were discoloured and bleeding from self-inflicted blows; but I detected several shirkers, who tapped themselves with extreme discretion. When they had retired, the great show commenced.[229]

The Tragedy

Once the *rowzeh-khvan* was finished the military band played a funeral march, and then the actors left the tents and entered onto the stage.[230] This consisted of a raised, sometimes brick, platform in the center raised some feet from the ground, without any contrivances for scenic effect, only covered with a black cloth. There was seldom a curtain and never any scenery, as discussed above.[231] The public is part of the scene and experiences the course of events as a participant rather than as a spectator. There is no problem either with the need to adjust to the changing scenes from Damascus, Mecca and the Euphrates River. The latter was usually represented small copper basin, filled with water, placed in the middle of the stage.[232]

Depending on the professionalism of the actors they either knew their text by heart, or they when they needed prompting consulted the text, or in many cases they just read it from a scroll. "The dialogue was carried on in recitative, each actor holding in his hand a long scroll of paper containing his part, while the schoolmaster of the 'Mahalla' hurried from the one to the other, prompting or changing the scroll."[233] The text of the play was written on long rolls of paper, which each actor held in the palm of his hand, and from which they frequently read their parts.[234] According to Wills, it was a small scroll with only the actor's role, and from which he "calmly reads it when memory fails him."[235] The difference in quality of the actors was not only noticeable in how far they knew their

[229] Stuart, *Journey*, pp. 293-94.
[230] Ahmad Bey, "Le Théatre," p. 534; Thalaso, *Le Théatre Persan*, p. 883.
[231] Wilbraham, *Travels*, p. 422, Ussher, *A Journey*, p. 618; Conolly, *Journey*, vol. 1, p. 268; Thalasso, *Le Théatre Persan*, p. 883; Rice, *Persian Women*, p. 234; Wills, *In the land*, p. 283.
[232] Thalasso, *Le Théatre Persan*, pp. 883-84.
[233] Wilbraham, *Travels*, p. 422.
[234] Stuart, *Journal*, p. 296; E`temad al-Saltaneh, *Ruznameh*, p. 533; Ahmad Bey, "Le Théatre," p. 530; Conolly, *Journey*, vol. 1, p. 268; Ussher, *A Journey*, p. 618; Fraser, *A Winter's Journey*, vol. 2, p. 146; Mounsey, *A Journey*, p. 315.
[235] Wills, *In the land*, p. 283. According to Price, *Journal*, vol. 1, p. 29, the color of the paper was blue.

text,[236] but also how they played. According to Rice, "some of the actors bawl, others cannot be heard."[237] This also explains why the stage-director/prompter (*ostad*) was constantly on the stage in the middle of the scene with a piece of paper where the roles of all actors are written, directing the actors, assigning them to their proper place; he "never quitted the stage, and gave us frequent explanation of what appeared to him ambiguous in the acting or declamation."[238]

Figure 34: Open-air performance of the passion play (1861)

Stage directors aimed for drama and emotion; he brought that about by adapting the script, by the right choice of actors and costumes, and the appropriate and unexpected choice of props. This was necessary, because there was not much action; the play was mostly focused on situation and atmosphere.[239] Some Europeans opined that "The performances taken as a whole are very crude," while others had a more favorable opinion.[240] Irrespective of the episode that was performed the acting was the same. The actors spent most of their time singing their part. Some would dance on occasion as well as act out certain scenes in pantomime. As in a silent movie, certain gestures, movements or implements spoke for themselves. For example, "Hoosein's sister hung a winding-sheet (a very ragged napkin) round his neck; his relations fell at his feet exhausted by their grief, and he threw

---

[236] Some knew their text by heart, while others had to read it from the scrolled text. Afshar, *Safarnameh-ye Lorestan*, p. 83 (in Khorramabad most actors knew their role by heart).

[237] Rice, *Persian Women*, p. 234.

[238] Mounsey, *A Journey*, p. 315; Chodzko, *Théatre Persan*, p. 174; Calmard, "Le mécénat" I, p. 98; Fowler, *Three Years*, p. 122; Ahmad Bey, "Le Théatre," p. 533; Rice, *Persian Women*, p. 234.

[239] Anonymous, "Die Passionsspiele," p. 355.

[240] Rice, *Persian Women*, p. 234.

a black covering over the afflicted circle."[241] This refers to a white cloth that
Hoseyn's sister put on him to indicate to the knowledgeable public that he would
soon be killed and become a martyr, a symbolic gesture that was not lost on the
spectators. Similarly, many among the flagellants wore a white short symbolizing
a shroud and their willingness to become Hoseyn's sacrifice.

Likewise, the following contemporary description of part of a play does not require much explanation to anyone. Hoseyn "repeatedly embraced his sister, wife,
niece, sister-in-law, and children; and snatching up two little nephews, whose father had just been killed, he knelt with them in his arms and implored for them the
protection of the Father of the orphan." It was quite normal that such acts of fa-
milial love or that between man and wife were enacted. In Mohammadabad there
was a scene showing

> the manner in which a wife shows her respect and affection for her hus-
> band. The pseudo-female with the jack-boots turned out to be the wife of
> the man who was being beaten. Previous to his being tied to the whip-
> ping-post, she came forward and prostrated herself before him, her fore-
> head touching the ground. The she walked around him, kissing the back
> of his shoulders as she passed, again prostrating herself on coming to the
> front. There were some other examples of marital etiquette during the
> play, and in all of them it seemed to be the proper thing for the lady to
> make the entire circuit of her husband before coming to a halt before
> him.[242]

To ensure that despite the symbolism of the costumes some spectators might not
recognize the lead roles, whenever Hoseyn would lay down to sleep "little cher-
ubs with black crape veils sang and capered around him." Also, the antagonists
would all behave rudely, threateningly and abusive *vis à vis* Hoseyn and his companions. Heroic behavior was also acted in a manner that could not be misunder-
stood and was aimed to raise emotions and pity. Hoseyn "soon returned
staggering, faint, and bristling like a porcupine with the arrows by which he had
been struck, and threw himself on the body of his sick son. His sister and relations
came and wept over him, after which he rose and prayed." Similarly, the behavior
of the antagonist, the enemy, is also clear from his acting and is also done in such
away to arouse passion. "The murderer then entered, and drawing a long knife,
whetted it on his thigh, walked round and round the Imaun, whom he held by the
head, and occasionally amused himself by making false thrusts at his throat.
Hoosein's youngest child, whose part was particularly well acted, threw himself

---

[241] Stuart, *Journey*, p. 294.
[242] O'Donovan, *Merv Oasis*, vol. 2, p. 44.

with a Korân into his father's arms, and interposed to save him. After a great deal of pantomime, the boy was killed."[243]

Stage directors, as I have pointed out above, wanted to recreate reality as much as possible, or at least a semblance thereof. When this was not possible they invented all kinds of methods to fake it or make the action so suggestive that the public understood without further explanation what was happening. For example, to indicate that an actor has to travel much he walks or rides a number of times around the stage. He can emphasize fatigue and thirst by dragging his feet, stumbling, and by other moves and gestures. At other times, the stage directions were very realistic. In Mohammadabad (Khorasan) the play was performed outside the walls and near the caravanserai. The enemy at long last and with overwhelming numbers had captured Hoseyn's champion. They dragged him "by the heels a good fifty yards, to the gate of the caravanserai. On this occasion his coat of chain mail must have stood himself and his garments in goods stead, the ground being in no wise like a skating rink, but, on the contrary, strewn with stones and broken earthenware." The antagonists took the vanquished champion inside and on top of the building where the hero after much pantomime had his throat slit. His convulsing and struggling limbs were shown, his head being out of sight. Then the man was withdrawn and

> a lay figure was thrust forward, exhibiting the severed bleeding neck. This was immediately lowered to the ground by ropes, and dragged back to the centre of the ground-still struggling and kicking. Within the headless lay figure was a little boy, who gave the requisite movement to the limbs. The figure, still twitching in a most horrid manner, was hung up on the centre of the cord extending between the two poles fixed in the ground; and the climax of the entertainment, the disemboweling of the body, commenced. In the breast and stomach of the figure had been stowed away the lungs, heart and stomach of a freshly killed sheep. The executioner, with his dagger, cut the figure open, and the still bleeding viscera were dragged out one by one with expressions of savage glee, and flung into the midst of the space.[244]

The public was not upset with incongruities such as talking actors after their death. For example, "Then followed the tragedy of the murder of Allee Acber, Hossein's eldest son, who at the *finale* entered with a sword struck into the brain of a false head, and living long enough to recite some pathetic verses, died after the approved fashion of stage heroes."[245] The same held for stage hands entering the stage during a performance to make the scene more realistic by adding the necessary finishing touches to actorswho had died. "Three boys, the martyr's sons, were laid out in grave-clothes. A ferrash approached them, and proceeded

---

[243] Stuart, *Journey*, p. 295.
[244] O'Donovan, *Merv Oasis*, vol. 2, pp. 46-47.
[245] Conolly, *Journey*, vol. 1, pp. 279-80.

with great *sang-froid*, but amidst loud cries of 'Wai, wai!' (woe, woe!), and violent expressions of grief on the part of the audience, to stick pegs, in the form of arrows, into the pretended corpses, and to sprinkle them with pomegranate juice, so as to produce the effect of blood."[246]

As in the floats effigies were also used in the enacting of the passion play, and nobody was upset by such ungodly or disrespectful (according to the olama) portrayal of not just human beings, but Imams.

> The scene if the Imaum's leave-taking with the disconsolate members of his family, was really affecting and well-acted." He could hardly keep himself from laughing "when an infant son of the Imaum was presented to him, to receive a last adieu,-the infant son being a wooden representation of a little man, with a great head, garnished with a most luxuriant pair of zulphs,* [Note in the original: *Long lock which the Persians wear behind the ears.] but minus the nose, which had been knocked off by previous ill usage. The whole length of the figure was about two feet and a half, and terminated in an excessively short pair of legs, very wide apart, both arms sticking out stiff at right angles from the body. Hossein has already mounted his horse, and, taking this ludicrous thing, is in the act of kissing it, when one of his enemies rides up, and stabs it in his arms. This produced such a burst of grief, that it was immediately acted over again.[247]

The use of effigies was a dramatic method to rouse the passion of the spectators, for it allowed, for example, the killing of a character several times. It was quite normal to do so when the 'dirty deed' received a good response from the public. It was like the "encores" after a concert. Eastwick reported of the killing of Zachariah, "the sawing of the neck was then repeated for the sixth time, and the prophet was carried out, after which a pasteboard head, with a face of ghastly whiteness, and without any hair, was brought in and exhibited to the spectators, who sobbed aloud as they looked at it."[248] Of course, the actors who had to play dead could not always lie still, but the public did not mind, and "accords unlimited credit to the good will of the actors and who easily imagine that the hacked straw with which they are covered is desert sand.[249]

Stage directors wanted to be as dramatic as possible and make the stories of Hoseyn's martyrdom as realistic as possible. If human beings could not do certain things effigies were made use of. It does therefore not come as a surprise that animals also had a role to play in the performance of the Passion. The use of

---

[246] Mounsey, *A Journey*, p. 315.
[247] Holmes, *Sketches*, pp. 310-11.
[248] Eastwick, *Journal*, vol. 2, pp. 141-42.
[249] Thalasso, *Le Théatre Persan*, pp. 883-84.

horses was a must, if only for the enactment of battles, or for some other events. Even the horses needed to have realistic roles so that they were regularly seen pierced with arrows after a battle.[250] Already in the seventeenth century pigeons had been used as messengers of Hoseyn's martyrdom. "A pigeon, with pink feet and wings, was introduced, who, by the mouth of one of the performers, told the sister of Hosein, that he had flown from Kerbela to Mecca, sprinkled with the blood of the martyr, to brig her the direful news of his death: she answered this amiable and active pigeon through the same channel."[251] But animals also had another role to play, in particular the lion, which itself was another name by which `Ali was known.

> The next act represents the Imam and all his devoted followers slain, and their bodies left on the plain, denied the rites of burial by the ferocious Shamer. The corpses all lie about the platform, those of some of the murderers being among them, the latter with small bits of meat on their breasts. A tame lion is led in through the crowd. He smells first the body of one of the Imam's children, and, as there is no meat on his chest, turns away from it, or in other words refuses to touch the holy corpse of the child of the Imam. He is next led to that of one of the party of Shamer, from which he immediately tears the flesh which had been laid on it, and devours it amidst the loud applause of the spectators. The bodies are thus visited one by one, those of the companions of Hosein being respected by the animal, each rejection being greeted by the sobbing and wailing of the women, while loud expressions of satisfaction welcomed the destruction of the remains of his enemies.[252]

In a variation on the same theme "A lion was then led in, and made to lie down peaceably by the side of the murdered boys, in order to show that even wild beasts have better hearts than the Sunnies, and can commiserate the fate of the descendants of Ali."[253] Even when the lion or whatever animal was used looked ridiculous to a European it did not fail to have its aimed for effect. O'Donovan observed: "With regard to the appearance of a lion, the stage manager seemed to be even still more astray. ... I had been noticing an odd-looking object creeping about the centre of the arena on all-fours. It looked like an ape with a long white shirt on, who had fallen foul of a pot of red paint and smeared his garments with it. This object kept gathering up dust and throwing it on its head, in Oriental token of grief."[254]

---

[250] Francklin, *Observations*, p. 252.

[251] Stuart, *Journey*, pp. 293-94; Francklin, *Observations*, p. 250; Le Bruyn, *Travels*, vol. 1, pp. 215-16.

[252] Ussher, *Journey*, pp. 619-20. See also Hommaire de Hell, *Voyage* vol. 2, p. 55-56.

[253] Mounsey, *A Journey*, p. 315.

[254] O'Donovan, Merv Oasis, vol. 2, p. 52.

The actors did not stay all the time on the stage. As soon as their role was over, even intermittently, they stepped down from the stage and sat or stood at the adjacent *taq-nama*, until it is their turn to perform. Then they got up, passed the small passage through the spectators and went to the *saku*, let those leaving pass and presented themselves to the public. Europeans were often amazed at this. Rice, for example, remarked that "Actors killed in one way or another get up and shuffle off!"[255] But others pointed out that the public was only interested in those performing on the *saku*; the others in the *taqnama* did not exist for them, until it was their turn.[256] At the end of each performance "the actors leave the stage; and a long procession of horses, camels and litters and biers, on which are carried the kotol (dummies) of the dead saints, enters with much noise, music, shouting, and drumming; followed and preceded by the volunteer mourners and breast-beaters [details; noise making band][257] The real end, of course, was that on day 10 of Moharram (`Ashurah*), when "The whole performance concluded with the supposed burning of Kerbela, which was represented by setting fire to a few old tents, when the multitude quietly departed to their respective homes."[258]

Although the passion-play was all about the suffering of the Imams, the shah saw to it that proper respect was also paid to him on that occasion. In 1852, the official newspaper reported that "Mahmud Khan, the *kalantar* of Tehran would supervise the heads of the city quarters (*kadkhoda*s) and see to it that the passion-play performances were held everywhere and that nowhere there would be opposition. In each *majles* there should be prayers said for the august person of HM."[259] It had become customary during the second half of the nineteenth century to praise the glory of the shah at the end of the introductory act to the passion play. "And now a curious chant in honour of the king is sung by a band of youths; after this the priests leave the stage, and the professional exponents of the drama make their appearance."[260] This practice acquired considerable political significance after the assassination of Naser al-Din Shah on May 1, 1896. The then Prime Minister, Amin al-Soltan, with a view to calm the public's fear because of the regicide gave the performers instructions to portray the good deeds of the martyred king as Naser al-Din Shah soon was called by the public.[261]

---

[255] Rice, *Persian Women*, p. 234; Ussher, *A Journey*, pp. 618-19.
[256] Thalasso, *Le Théatre Persan*, pp. 884-85.
[257] Wills, *In the land*, p. 283.
[258] Holmes, *Sketches*, p. 311.
[259] *Ruznameh-ye Ettefaqiyeh* nr. 90 (7 Moharram 1269/21 October 1852).
[260] Wills, *In the land*, p. 281; Afshar, *Safarnameh-ye Lorestan*, pp. 83-84. Prayers were also given for the shah. *Ruznameh-ye Ettefaqiyeh* no. 141 (9 Moharram 1270/12 December 1853); Ibid., no. 142 (16 Moharram 1270/19 October 1853).
[261] Amanat, *Pivot of the Universe*, p. 441.

Consequences for Actors

In each scene there are sympathetic and antipathetic actors, and the public expressed their discontent by loud cries after each victory. Sometimes the exasperation is so great that they take them out of the scene and take their papers and arms.[262] Emotions sometimes ran so high that the actors who played the role of Yazid, Shemr (the murderer of Hoseyn), Yazid's soldiers, and other antagonists had to suffer the, sometimes serious, consequences. One source reported that when Hoseyn had been 'killed' on stage the aroused public wanted to attack Yazid's soldiers and pelted them with stones.[263] "When the singing was over, several horsemen, dressed in armour, entered; they were accoutered with swords and shields, and commenced a sham fight: the populace at this instant began to shower a volley of stones upon them, in memory of Ali's being stoned to death.[264] In addition to stones attacks on the actors also occurred. "When the death blow is given by the executioner, the lamentations of the people increase; they fall upon the enemy almost with personal violence, so much so, that it is difficult to procure people to perform this part of the tragedy. They then attempt to represent the dead bodies of the martyrs."[265] Wills reported, "The cruel Shemr, generally very vigorously represented, is at times roughly handled by the mob."[266] In one case, according to Ussher, the shah's mother had been present and the actors "had exerted themselves to the utmost. Highly excited by the cruel and relentless behaviour of Shamer, at the conclusion of the scene she had him summoned before her, when she ordered the unhappy actor, whose only fault was his too faithful representation on his part, to be soundly bastinadoed in her presence!"[267] These were the normal risks of being an actor, but sometimes allegedly worse happened. Fowler reported that in the mid-1830s, "It has been stated, that the executioner, in his extreme zeal to please the King, did on one occasion actually cut of the head of the man who performed Hussein [sic!; must be Shemr]." He had to pay a fine of 100 *tumans*.[268] This was apparently not an exception, for O'Donovan reported in 1880,

> Instances have been known in which, on the last day of the theatrical representations, when Hussein comes to grief, the executioner has perished at the hands of the frenzy-stricken spectators. Here at Muhammadabad, during my visit, a mild outbreak of this kind occurred. When the massacre of the two children of Hussein was being acted, an Akhal Tekke Turcoman rushed

[262] Ahmad Bey, "Le Théatre," p. 533. OR 534

[263] Anonymous, "Die Passionsspiele," p. 359.

[264] Price, *Journal*, p. 29.

[265] Fowler, *Three Years*, vol. 2, pp. 124-25.

[266] Wills, *In the land*, p. 284.

[267] Ussher, *Journey*, p. 620.

[268] Fowler, *Three Years*, vol. 2, p.125, note. For a similar mistake where Yazid is being depicted as the innocent party see Eichwald, Eduard. *Reise auf dem Caspischen Meere und in den Caucasus Unternommen in den Jahren 1825-1826*. 2 vols. (Stuttgart und Tübingen: J.G. Cotta, 1834), pp. 172-73 (description of the performance of a passion play in 1826 in Baku).

from among the spectators, sabre in hand, to rescue the infants, and had to be withheld and disarmed by half-a-dozen ferashes. From this it may be judged what a powerful influence the Mussulman 'mystery plays' exercise on the impressionable minds of an impulsive and unlettered people.[269]

The actors concerned probably accepted this kind of treatment with either equanimity (after all one would go to Paradise if killed) or trepidation (one was not ready for Paradise yet). This latter held, for example, for those who had been forced to participate in the play. Price, a member of the Ouseley embassy in 1810, reported: "The horsemen represent the troop of Yezid, who attacked and slaughtered the Imams Hasan and Hosein. It fell to the lot of some Russian prisoners to perform this part, and several of them got severely wounded by the stones thrown at them."[270] The choice of the Russians rather than being fortuitous must have been on purpose for exactly this natural effect. On the other hand, from de Gobineau's description of the performance of the passion play, it is clear that some of the actors were as much emoted as the spectators. He noted that the actors also cried and "I have seen the one playing the role of Yazid, who was so upset with himself, threatening the Imams in that atrocious manner, that while he was doing so he was weeping and could hardly speak."[271] But then again it may have been a protective measure to avoid being attacked by an aroused spectator, for he was one of the good guys, after all. It also happened that the actor playing the role of Shemr did not show up.[272]

Even though people believed that participating in a passion play was meritorious, still there were fewer volunteers to play the part of the villains than of the good guys. An amusing story about this is as follows:

> In Darband (Caucasia] no one wanted to appear in the role of Shemr. After a great deal of searching, the producers of the ta`ziyeh finally found a Russian laborer who knew a few words of Persian and was ready, for a sum, to play the role of the killer of Imam Hussein.
>
> The ta`ziyeh director, considering the Russian laborer's circumstances, shortened Shemr's part as far as was possible. In reality he was only to wear Shemr's costume and stand behind a wooden tub representing the Euphrates River, not allowing anyone to approach it. As the time of his performance approached, the laborer put on Shemr's costume and, taking a whip in hand, stood by the tub. The children and companions of Imam Hussein one by one tried approach the water while the laborer assiduously kept them away. Unfortunately the person playing the role of

---

[269] O'Donovan, *Merv Oasis*, vol. 2, p. 49.

[270] Price, *Journal*, p. 29; Ouseley, W. *Travels in various countries of the East: more particularly Persia*, 3 vols. (London, 1819-23), vol. 3, p. 169.

[271] De Gobineau, *Trois Ans*, vol. 2, p. 218.

[272] Morier, *Second Journey*, p. 175f.

Imam Hussein was an old and respected elder. When he neared the water, the ta`ziyeh director saw, to his astonishment, that the laborer never even tried to prevent him from reaching the water according to the demands of his role; instead he called out to him to drink without any fear or anxiety. The ta`ziyeh director shouted at the Russian not to let the old man get to the water, but the laborer humbly replied, "Let him drink; he's an old man!"

This incident was not the occasion for consternation or astonishment among the audience and it did not cause laughter; on the contrary it was a strong stimulus to even greater and more intense weeping and tears. The sobbing spectators said, "See! How mean and evil Shemr was! He showed mercy neither to the children nor to Imam Hussein who was the grandson of the Prophet. He killed them, but when the Russian fellow who is outside the faith saw the old actor with a white beard he showed him mercy and permitted him to quench this thirst!"[273]

A less risky role to be played was that of the European ambassador. However, sometimes the actor concerned wanted to avail himself of the presence of European spectators to seek compensation for this strange act. O'Donovan relates that when he left the passion play show, a figure tapped him on the shoulder and said, " 'Sahib, I am the Frankish Ambassador.' He evidently considered that the Frank present ought to compensate him in some measure for the ordeal he had undergone in adopting, even for so short a time, a character so uncanny."[274]

The Tragic Interspersed with Comedy

As I have pointed out already in Chapter One it was quite normal to change from the tragic to the comic element as has been attested by a tenth century author. The same phenomenon was observed in the nineteenth century. Dervishes not only were engaged in tragic story telling, but also in lighter and even comical drama. O'Donovan noted that right after the end of the passion play performance a lighter note was struck. This seems to have been a rather general occurrence and not necessarily limited to dervishes.

When the [passion play] actors had departed, several dervishes divided the attention of the crowd. Some gave religious instructions; others narrated funny stories to any who would listen to and pay them; others, again, played juggling tricks, and vended small articles, such as plated earrings, combs, and medical nostrums. The Persian dervish is a jack-of-all-trades. He acts as priest, mountebank at a fair, story-teller, pedlar, or doctor, as occasion may require. At bottom he is generally a sharp fellow,

---

[273] Rezvani, *Le Théatre*, pp. 68-69.
[274] O'Donovan, *Merv Oasis*, vol. 2, p. 53.

living comfortably by his wits, despite the external squalor which some
of the confraternity affect.[275]

Percy Sykes described how at Rahbur (Kerman), a Moharram mourning ceremony was held among a group of nomads. "At last it ended, and as a relief to the
feelings the whole thing was turned into a comedy, thus recalling the plays in
Ladakh, where the same course is pursued."[276] His sister Ella Sykes described a
similar event in the Sardu region in Kerman province, also at the beginning of the
twentieth century. There had been an intense session of the singing of mourning
songs by a group of nomads and immediately after it was over, "one of their number turned the whole thing into ridicule, and the crowd roared with laughter at the
parody on the sufferings of the martyrs, whose fate they just had been lamenting
with religious zeal. This episode reminded us of the Miracle Plays in the Middle
Ages, when the spectators would weep one moment as the mysteries of their Faith
were presented to them, and at the next would break into peals of merriment as the
Devil, playing part of a buffoon, was brought upon the stage."[277] But the same phenomenon was also observed in an urban context such as in Berjand in 1915. "Tragedy, of course, is relieved by lighter entertainments, and occasionally the comic
element is introduced as it was by us in the Middle Ages."[278] It also happened in Tehran itself. E'temad al-Saltaneh noted in his Diary on September 13, 1888: "last
night there was in the *takiyeh* [the performance of] the Passion of Salomon. The ambassadors of Great Britain, Italy and their staff were also there. When it had ended
the famous comedian Esma'il Bazzaz came into the *takiyeh* with about 200 actors
and musicians with white false beards and dressed up in various clothes from
Europe, Turkey and Iran and performed their vile [*qabih*] acts. It was done in such a
way that that the *ta'ziyeh* session was worse than the comedy show."[279] In some instances the tragic was not even ended by the comic, but it was turned into a farce, at
least according to E'temad al-Saltaneh, who was not amused by apparently funny
display he saw on November 26, 1881.

> It became clear that last night they had staged the Tragedy (*ta'ziyeh*) of
> the Marriage of Fatima in the *takiyeh*. They had made this Tragedy quite
> despicable, but last night it as even viler. The chanters wailed like dogs.
> Their impudence has grown such that the laughter of the women of the
> harem came down from the loge to the stage of the *takiyeh*. People who
> were there told that it was funnier than a comedy theater in Europe. This

[275] O'Donovan, *Merv Oasis*, vol. 1, p. 407.
[276] Sykes, *Ten Thousand Miles*, p. 209.
[277] Sykes, *Through Persia*, p. 142. See, for example, Brander Matthews, "The Medieval Drama," in
The Development of the Drama. (New York: Charles Scribner's Sons, 1912), pp. 107-146; Ibid.,
"Medieval Church Plays," *The Drama: Its History, Literature and Influence on Civilization*, vol.
7. ed. Alfred Bates. (London: Historical Publishing Company, 1906), pp. 2-3, 6-10.
[278] Hale, *From Persian Uplands*, p. 38.
[279] E'temad al-Saltaneh, *Ruznameh*, p. 676 (7 Moharram 1306/September 13, 1888).

neither befits the station of royalty nor does this behavior befits the mourning cycle of the Lord of Martyrdom (*sayyed al-shohada*).[280]

It may be, as suggested by Sykes, that the despair and the orgiastic experience became too much for the spectators and that they needed to lighten up their spirits so as not to become overwhelmed by this intense experience. This is also clear from what Ella Sykes related about the pressure to weep and mourn. "Yet a spirit of levity occasionally creeps in even at these gatherings; for a Persian told the writer that he was thankful for his handkerchief when a very stout man among the audience wept so loudly in a high falsetto voice, with such an absurd resemblance to that of a woman, that it was difficult for him to refrain from bursts of unseemly laughter."[281] It was not only after the passion play performance people that laughed or showed a less serious mean, but also during the play. Fowler reported in the 1830s that, "The women were particularly noisy in their grief; and I thought that, in many instances, it was not feigned. When, however, the angel brought down the infant again, the rejoicings were equally boisterous. The whole was a singing pantomime, if I may so-and much singing! The ceremonies having lasted some hours, they were adjourned to the following day.[282]

Wills described the performance of a passion play put up in the garden of the young prince-governor of Shiraz, Zell al-Soltan.

> In the lower room, also veiled, and facing the crowds of women, sit the prince's ladies. Above their apartment, at a large open window, is the prince himself, and during the waits, and sometimes even during the most pathetic parts, the young fellow amuses himself in ogling the ladies, the better-looking of whom seize these opportunities of raising their veils and casting coquettish glances in his direction. I have even known him, when very young, to have a basin of frogs handy, and he would toss the animals out among the thickest throng of the tightly-packed women, and shriek with laughter at the cries and confusion produced.[283]

The prince's attitude and youthful behavior may be better understood when we take into account Moshtaq Kazemi's remark that in his youth "*ta'ziyeh* was fun, because there was no cinema."[284]

---

[280] E`temad al-Saltaneh, *Ruznameh*, p. 145 (4 Moharram 1299/November 26, 1881).

[281] Sykes, Ella. *Persia and its People* (London: MacMillan, 1910), pp. 155.

[282] Fowler, *Three Years*, p. 123. O'Donovan, *Merv Oasis*, vol. 2, p. 43 also describes bouts of merriment during the performance.

[283] Wills, *In the land*, pp. 280.

[284] Kazemi, Moshtaq. *Ruzgarva Andisheh* 3 vols. (Tehran, 1350/1971), p. 10.

WATER CARRIERS

Because the spectators sat there for hours they needed refreshments. To that end water-carriers (*saqqa*) went among them with iced water, bidding them drink and be thankful, remembering the thirst of the blessed martyr in the desert. Or, as a meritorious act it happened that parents of children with a weak health, had made a vow (*nadhr*) when they were still young that, if, e.g., the boy reached a particular age, they would make him a water carrier in honor of Emam Hoseyn, during one or more *ta'ziyeh* seasons. These minor water carriers were therefore called *nadhri*, devoti, ex-voto. These children, some of whom carried small goatskins filled with sherbets, with a cup held in the hand that was always filled, which they offered to passers-by. Others carried small flags with the inscription: "Ya `Ali, Ya Hoseyn." Boys from elite families were luxuriously dressed with floating curls on their shoulders and with a *shab-kolah* of splendid cashmere with pearls and precious stones when they gave the public ice water to drink and often sherbets. According to Berezin, an ostrich feather protruded from their water bottles. All these refreshments were at the expense of the patron who financed the staging of the passion play. After the water carriers came the renters of pipes, sellers of *mohr*, or seals made of the sand of the desert of Karbala perfumed with musk, on which the believers put their forehead when praying; then sellers of baklava, but above all *nakhudchi* or sellers of roasted peas, melons seeds, pear seeds, millet seeds. The spectators ate much of those. It married the pleasant with the useful, because it was believed that millet helps weeping. Women ate them constantly, because they believed it refreshed their breath, whitened the teeth, reinforced the gums, and stopped them from talking too much. During the performance, the elite guests were silently served coffee; the obligatory drink for sad occasions or smoked the water pipe, as well as drank tea.[285] Wilbraham reported that "at either end [of the theater] stood a platform, rising in successive tiers, and loaded with huge bowls of every variety of sherbet."[286]

KEEPING THE HOUSE IN ORDER

The 'house' was always completely filled, and usually there were several thousand persons present. This even held for minor locations such as Daragez (Khorasan) in 1880, where O'Donovan estimated that more than 3,000 persons assisted to the play. Similarly, at Hamadan, where `Eyn al-Saltaneh estimated that on Moharram 7 some 3,500 women and 600-700 men were present.[287] Sometimes there were so many spectators that a building collapsed on which people were standing, which

[285] Chodzko, *Théatre Persan*, pp. xxiii-xxv, Calmard, "Le mécénat" I, p. 96 quoting Berezin; Ahmad Bey, "Le Théatre," p. 533; Conolly, *Journey*, vol. 1, p. 269; Mounsey, *A Journey*, p. 312; Wills, *In the land*, p. 284; Globus nr. 23, vol. 16 (1870) 535; Thalasso, *Le Théatre Persan*, p. 882.
[286] Wilbraham, *Travels*, p. 422
[287] O'Donovan, *Merv Oasis*, vol. 2, p. 41; `Eyn al-Saltaneh, *Ruznameh*, vol. 1, p. 385.

seems to have been a regular occurrence, according to Flandin.[288] In the *Takiyeh-ye Dowlat* the policing of the crowd was the responsibility of the *farrash-bashi*.[289] A few minutes before the show started soldiers of the irregular Kurdish cavalry and *farrash*es, who have to keep order, entered. At their entry the voices lessened, the noise abated and a deathly silence descended on the crowd.[290] The *farrash*es had first assisted in putting the stage in order, including the sweeping and sprinkling of the soil. They had large sticks, an attentive eye, and with their hands in the air made room where needed. They often had to intervene in the parterre women's section, because the women often fought with one another. According to Lady Sheil, "fights broke out between these women, using their iron heel of their sleepers and tearing off one's veil."[291] The *farrash*es were equal opportunity discriminators and when needed used their stick on both men and women. They further made sure that that the stage (*saku*) was allowed considerable space in the middle of the parterre, which had been swept and sprinkled beforehand. The *farrash*es also ensured that the actors could enter and leave the stage to go to the foyer without hindrance.[292] In the 1830s, and probably prior to that date too, when the passion play was held in the great court of Fath 'Ali Shah's palace at Tehran, "the 'shah zadehs,' or princes, sometimes attend barefooted, and superintend the ceremonies, dealing about their sticks to keep order amongst the multitude."[293]

PASSION PLAY FOR AND BY WOMEN

The passion play was enormously popular; people showed up in droves, in majority women. It was great fun, deeply moving and it provided freedom to move about without male interference. According to some, it also was an occasion for trysts.[294] Wilbraham was struck by the fact that "the women hurried from one theatre to another, to weep over the melancholy fate of the sons of 'The Lion of God.'"[295] Not excluding the day of Moharram 10, the audience of either a *row-zeh-khvani* or a *ta`ziyeh-khvani* play were women. Women came especially from the outskirts of town to assist to the plays. Rice reported that in Isfahan, women had come to the dispensary from the village, and were told to wait another day, which they did not mind, because they had come to town "for some of the Muharram weeping services."[296] `Eyn al-Saltaneh wrote: On day 7, I counted 3,500

---

[288] Flandin, *Voyage*, vol. 1, p. 252-53. Ahmad Bey, "Le Théatre," p. 533 (the roofs of the houses, the branches of the trees are filled with women with covered faces).

[289] Aubin, *La Perse*, p. 169.

[290] Thalasso, *Le Théatre Persan*, p. 881-82.

[291] Sheil, *Glimpses*, p. 128.

[292] Chodzko, *Théatre Persan*, pp. xxv-xxvi; Conolly, *Journey*, vol. 1, p. 268; O'Donovan, *Merv Oasis*, vol. 2, p. 41.

[293] Fowler, *Three Years*, vol. 2, p. 124; Morier, *Second Journey*, p. 179f.

[294] De Gobineau, *Trois Ans*, vol. 2, p. 219.

[295] Wilbraham, *Travels*, p. 421.

[296] Rice, *Mary Bird*, p. 139.

women and 600-700 men present. Many groups came on day 10. Three hours before sunset it started.[297] In March 1895, he remarked, "I do not know how many women Tehran has. But all these mosques, bazaars and houses are full of women. Some of them go each day two or three times. Most of the spectators were women; in fact the entire *ta`ziyeh* performance is a spectacle for women.[298] Later he wrote, "On day 10 [of Moharram] they all came out; truly it is the women's parade. For each man there were eight women."[299]

There were also *takiyeh*s put up inside the harems of the very rich where they only invited friends, and where the actors were women. Calmard states that these female passion plays were performed for the first time in the house of Qamar al-Saltaneh, daughter of Fath `Ali Shah. They were performed during the afternoons of the first six days of Moharram. They were done in the open air, garden, or salon. The actors were or old female *rowzeh-khvan*s or female storytellers or entertainers.[300] Qamar al-Saltaneh organized the staging of the passion-play at her house to an exclusively female audience in the first ten days of Moharram each year. After the usual *rowzeh-khvani*, the episodes of the passion play were performed in the evenings. The actors were an all-female cast; the leading roles were played by female *rowzeh-khvan*s such as Molla Nabat, Molla Fatima and Molla Maryam. Unlike male actors, the women recited their parts from memory, because most women were illiterate. They were trained on purpose for these roles in the following manner. Mo'in al-Boka', the director/producer of the royal passion plays trained literate eunuchs to learn the various roles by heart, including the musical scores. These trained eunuchs then would scour the harems in Tehran for suitable female *rowzeh-khvan*s, whom they taught the lines of their designated role. The eunuchs would accompany the performance by playing the musical instruments, while it also happened that blind male actors performed on stage. During the reign of Fath `Ali Shah there also were all-female musical groups that performed in the royal harem. Qamar al-Saltaneh directed the staging of the plays inside her own quarters and like the male directors appeared on stage and gave directions with a walking stick. On occasion she even would slap one of the female actors to make them cry as required by their role.[301] The female actors played unveiled, unlike the male ones who played female roles. When playing male roles the actresses dressed up as men, applied make-up, beards and moustaches. They also carried swords and when required were on horse-back on stage. A particular breed of horse, the *tatu*,

[297] `Eyn al-Saltaneh, *Ruznameh*, vol. 1, p. 385.

[298] `Eyn al-Saltaneh, *Ruznameh*, vol. 1, p. 908 (25 Ramazan, 1313/March 22, 1895); Eastwick, *Journal*, vol. 2, p. 141.

[299] `Eyn al-Saltaneh, *Ruznameh*, vol. 2, p. 1255 (11 Moharrem, 1316/July 4, 1895).

[300] Calmard, "Le mécénat" I, p. 95; Beyza'i, *Namayesh*, p. 160.

[301] Mo`in al-Dowleh. *Khaterat* ed. Sirus Sa`dvandiyan (Tehran: Zarrin, 1380/2001), p. 105.

was bred for the occasion and eunuchs held their bridle walked and guided them during the performance.[302]

The selection of the scenes of the all-female cast passion-play was often one where women played a major role, clearly to please the female audience. Mu'nis al-Dowleh records that the staging of *Shahr-banu* or "The wedding of a Qoreyshi daughter" was one of the most popular female plays. Women came from distant towns and villages to participate in it when it was staged in Tehran. In this play, the Qoreyshi women prepare a wedding for an ugly bride. They decide to invite Fatima the prophet's daughter. Fatima decides that she has neither the time nor the clothes to go to a wedding. Then the angel Gabriel (played by a tall beautiful woman with wings) appears singing to the houris that they need to clothe and prepare Fatima for the wedding. Next twelve houris arrive at Fatima's house with gifts and treasure. Overwhelmed by this divine intervention Fatima decides to attend the wedding. When the beautiful Fatima arrives the ugly bride faints and falls to the ground. The Qoreysh women then beg Fatima to pray for the bride. She does, and the bride immediately comes to. The pagan Qoreysh women then all convert to Islam.[303] From this description it is clear that this play belonged to the lighter plays that were performed in the month following the months of mourning.

SPECTATOR BEHAVIOR DURING THE PERFORMANCE OF THE PASSION PLAY

The impact of the passion play was a powerful one. Wilbraham, who saw performances in 1837, remarked, "The dresses were poor and mean, and the whole outward show was little calculated to impress the mind, yet the effect produced upon the audience was powerful. Not only did the women sob convulsively and beat their breasts, but I could see large tears chasing each other down the weatherbeaten face of many a hardy muleteer."[304] There was so much weeping, a very meritorious act, that certain people went around to collect those tears in bottles to be used as a medicine.[305] It was not only believing Shi'ites who were effected by the drama. Lt. Col. Stuart admitted, "I could have scarcely restrained my own tears, had I not turned and seen the wry faces made by old Meerza Aly Nuckee, the 'Maimoon,' who sat blubbering behind me. Our Gholâms and servants, men with long black beards, wept like children.[306] Another British officer wrote that even foreigners were touched by the emotions.[307] Not to forget women, Lady Sheil noted that the weeping was very contagious. "I too felt myself forced, would I or

[302] Mo'in al-Dowleh. *Khaterat*, p. 98.
[303] Mo'in al-Dowleh. *Khaterat*, p. 104.
[304] Wilbraham, *Travels*, p. 422-23; Aubin, *La Perse*, p. 172; de Gobineau, *Trois Ans*, vol. 2, p. 217.
[305] Sykes, *Persia and its People* p. 155. In general see Floor, Willem. *Public Health in Qajar Iran* (Washington DC, 2004), p. 94.
[306] Stuart, *Journal*, p. 294.
[307] Hale, *From Persian Uplands*, p. 38.

not, to join my tears to those of the Persian women round me, which appeared to give considerable satisfaction to them." … "the parts are acted with great spirit and judgment."[308] Not crying was not an option apparently, for it showed that the person concerned was an unbeliever. "The priests say that such a one will be consigned to hell at his death, while every tear shed in remembrance of Husein washes away many sins."[309]

FOREIGN SPECTATORS

Normally there was no objection against the attendance of foreigners (non-Moslems) to the performance of the passion plays. In fact, if that had been the case there would not be so much material available on this type of drama. Most, if not all, European travelers had seen at least one performance of the passion play. In Tehran,

> the foreign ministers receive a formal invitation to attend the Tazeeya, as these performances are called, of the Prime Minister, to refuse which would be resented as highly discourteous. I too was included in the invitation. On reaching the building, I was conducted to a very comfortable *loge*, with an antechamber, or kefshken, 'slipper-casting' room, where one leaves the outer shoes. He front of the box was carefully covered over with a thick felt carpet, pierced with small holes, which, while they allowed us to see all that passed, completely excluded us from the view of the audience. The Shah's box was at the top, facing the performers; on his right were the boxes of his mother, who has no other title than Mader a Shah, the king's mother, and his wives; then that of the prime minister's wife, then mine, and next the Russian minister's wife. The fatigues of the day were relieved by constant supplies of tea and coffee, with pipes incessantly for those who liked them.[310]

Likewise, Europeans who were in Iran in a private capacity also received invitations from whomever among their acquaintances or associates organized the performance of a passion play. There were, however, exceptions to this rule. These exceptions were partly due to respect for the guests (not willing to hurt their feelings) or to political consideration (there was cold in the air). For example, in 1809, the French embassy was not invited for the episode of the European ambassador. "The king wishing to spare the legation from witnessing the assassination of a Greek ambassador, who Yezid caused to be put to death, for having interceded with him for the pardon of Hussein's brother. The Persians … produce this ambassador in the modern European dress."[311] During the British-Iranian conflict

---

[308] Sheil, *Glimpses*, p. 129.
[309] Sykes, *Persia and its People*, pp. 155.
[310] Sheil, *Glimpses*, p. 127.
[311] Tancoigne, *A Narrative*, p. 200.

in 1856, the British Minister, Murray, protested to Prime Minister that the Legations had not been invited. The Prime Minister promised to invite him the next year.[312] Referring to the situation in 1871, Mounsey maintained that, "Christians are now as absolutely excluded from these performances, as they are from all the mosques and the baths used by Mussulmans." Other contemporary European travelers do not mention such a blanket exclusion of Christians. Moreover, Mounsey himself attended a performance of a passion play having been invited by a friend. "I was, therefore, obliged to content myself with witnessing two of the ten acts into which the drama is divided-one for each of the ten days of mourning-in an inferior bour-geois tekkyeh, the proprietor of which happened to be a personal friend of mine."[313] In fact, the more normal Iranian attitude, as reported by Holmes, was that "The people had no scruples in our witnessing their representations, but, on the contrary, seemed rather pleased."[314] It would seem that participation by European diplomats during the climax of Moharram, the `Ashura, tended to be exclusionary. In an undated note from Moshir al-Dowleh to Naser al-Din Shah he asks whether the Russians can attend again the `Ashura performance as he had allowed unofficially last year. If affirmative, he suggested assigning a separate loge (*taq-nama*) for them. The shah answered in the affirmative, but stipulated that they only could attend in the evening and not during the day and that there should be a grille (*zan-buri*) in front of their loge.[315]

BEHAVIOR OF SPECTATORS AFTER THE PERFORMANCE OF THE PASSION PLAY

Keeping order in the streets during the month of Moharram, in particular on the 10th, was an additional problem, if not a head-ache, for the authorities. After the performance of the passion play was over, "Sets of morris-dancers them came in, clapping pieces of wood together, and we were lastly entertained by some Bun-gushes (men of a Sheah tribe south-west of Caubul), who beat themselves with chains."[316] The problem was that each town and large village was often divided into two groups (Heydari and Ne`mati) that had an antagonistic relationship with one an-other. Although the origins of this division are not known it probably dates back to pre-Islamic times.[317]

---

[312] Amanat, *Pivot of the Universe*, p. 263; Calmard, "Le mécénat" II, p. 158. The latter (Calmard, "Le mécénat" II, p. 160, n. 95) disagrees with Algar, *Religion*, p. 158 that prior to the refusal to invite the English Minister Murray the court was in the habit of inviting accredited diplomats.

[313] Mounsey, *Journey*, p. 312.

[314] Holmes, *Sketches*, p. 302.

[315] `Anasori, "Asnad va Madarek," pp. 9-10.

[316] Conolly, *Journal*, vol. 1, p. 281; Le Bruyn, *Travels*, vol. 1, p. 215.

[317] Varjavand, *Simay*, vol. 2, p. 1129-30; Aubin, *La Perse*, p. 167. In general see Perry, John. "To-ward a Theory of Iranian Urban Moieties: The Haydariyyah and Ni`matiyyah Revisited," *Iranian Studies* 32 (1999), pp. 51-70.

Figure 35: A group (*dasteh*) of flagellants (ca. 1900)

The groups called *dasteh* consisted of flagellants (*sineh-zan*), who beat themselves with many-tailed whips, while chanting lamentations (*nowheh*s) in rhythmic
cadence. There also were those who had two sticks of wood or stones in their
hands that they beat against one another, hence they were called *sang-zan-e Kashan*. Then followed the chain beaters (*zanjir-zan*). Their shirt was open at the
back; marching in two columns and hearing the beat of the beckon they rhythmi-
cally beat their back with the chain alternating the shoulder. The most bloody display was that of the *tigh-zan*, who beat themselves with sabers. They also
marched in two columns, one holding the swords in the right the other in the left
hand. They beat themselves on their shaved head till blood was flowing profusely.
To prevent too much excess some people walked between the columns and try to
soften the blows by stopping it with a stick. These men often participated because
of a vow made. Massé observed that was only those seventeenth century contemporary travelers who described the situation in the Caucasus and Azerbaijan who mentioned the blooding of the flagellants in the Moharram procession. Elsewhere in Iran
they did not report the same phenomenon.[318] He therefore raised the question
whether this custom had not been introduced from that area to the rest of Iran. Wilson, an American missionary who knew Iran intimately, was of the same opinion, for
he wrote, "its origin is traced to the Karabaghlis of Transcaucasia, and thence it has
spread through Persia."[319]

---

[318] Massé, *Croyances*, vol. 1, pp. 135-36.
[319] Wilson, *Persian Life*, p. 196.

There always were some people among the flagellants who killed themselves.[320] "Every year some Persians are severely injured from the laceration which they inflict on themselves-death even in some cases ensues; while bloody fights constantly take place during the Mohurrem between the youths of different districts, to assert the superiority of their respective tazeers."[321] It was not only due to the fights with other groups or due to the self-inflicted wounds that some of the men died. For some of the deaths were due to the fact that, "Many people fall victims to pneumonia or exhaustion as a consequence of the share they have taken in the day's celebration."[322]

Figure 36: Members of a group (*dasteh*) of flagellants using swords (*tigheh-zan*) (Shushah-1869)

---

[320] Momtahen al-Dowleh, *Khaterat*. ed. Hoseynqoli Khan-Shaqaqi (Tehran: Amir Kabir, 1353/1974), p. 112.
[321] Stuart, *Journal*, p. 296.
[322] Rice, Clara. *Persian Women*, p. 235.

The government tried to curb the activities of the neighborhood groups, because the unruly elements (*luti*s) in the quarter that they represented usually saw the procession as an opportunity to make trouble. Already during the seventeenth century the authorities took steps to keep the groups from one another and they continued to do so in the centuries thereafter.[323] This was also necessary, because the number of these neighborhood groups could be quite substantial. For example, the flagellants in Shushtar were divided between the Heydari-Ne'mati affiliation. There were some 2,000 of them in December 1879. Nezam al-Saltaneh-Mafi, the governor of the town, therefore banned the breast-beating groups and the carrying of the *nakhl* on the evening of days nine and ten of Moharram, which traditionally were the most emotional days.[324] In July 1895, the breast beater groups were so numerous in Tehran that the governor sent out heralds to announce that women were not allowed to go out of their homes on day nine."[325]

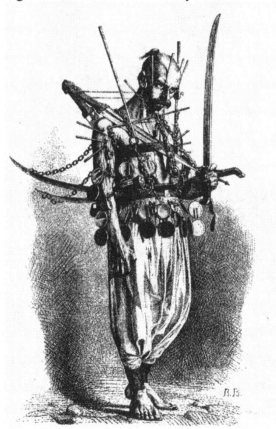

Figure 37: Flagellant at Shusha (1869)

---

[323] Le Bruyn, *Travels*, vol. 1, p. 216; Rice, *Persian Women*, p. 236.
[324] Nezam al-Saltaneh-Mafi, Hoseyn Qoli Khan. *Khaterat va Asnad*. 2 vols. eds. Mansureh Ettehadiyeh (Nezam-Mafi) and Hamid Ram-Pisheh (Tehran, 1361/1982), vol. 1, p. 74.
[325] 'Eyn al-Saltaneh, *Ruznameh*, vol. 2, p. 1255 (11 Moharram, 1313/July 4, 1895).

The *luti*s were occasionally also used for political purposes by both the secular and religious authorities. For example, the Heydari and Ne`matollahi factions fought one another in Qazvin in 1594 "by royal decree." The same happened in 1617 in Isfahan.[326] This also happened in 1835 at the height of the conflict between Iran and Great Britain about Herat. On that occasion Mohammad Shah (r. 1834-48)

> "has endeavoured to turn to account the excited and bigoted feelings against the Soanis, which this season always awakens. This morning the officers of the garrison were desired to accompany Kuhurman Meerza to the principle mosque, where Hajee Ibrahim preached religious war against the hostile sect: the number of Sheeahs enslaved by the Afghâns and Turkomans was mentioned, and all true Persians were exhorted to march, without pay, but certain of eternal reward, against the enemies of their religion and country. 'Never,' said the Hajee,' has Persia had such an army or such a king, since the days of the Sefis'-and I believe he is right! A book has been opened to inscribe the names of volunteers."[327]

The *dasteh*s when making their rounds through their town, in whatever forms the procession were constituted, usually went to the chief of police (in Tehran at the *Sabz-e Meydan*) to demand the release of a prisoner. If the wrong one was released or it took too long rioting might follow. In 1907 the *dasteh*s also paid a visit to British embassy to thank the British government for its support of the Constitutional Revolution.[328] In 1922 Reza Khan for political purposes supported and even participated in the Moharram processions. His Cossack brigade also was part of the mourning groups and at the end of the procession a group of them went to City Hall and released more than 300 prisoners. The same phenomenon occurred in 1924 and the Cossacks released more than 800 prisoners from the city's jail.[329] This did not happen anymore once Reza Khan had become Reza Shah one year later. Apparently even in Tehran the demand for prisoner release was not a regular item. In Tehran of the 1830s, "the procession is closed by the moolahs, bearing torches of yellow wax; the chief or 'Sheik ul Islam' stops a moment under the King's window, and implores a blessing on the 'Zil Allah,' or 'Shadow of God.' The crowd then disperse, and the court is broken up, which must be observed in deference to the religious prejudices of the Shiahs."[330] This demand for the release of a prisoner was not only the custom at Tehran, for Wilson reported that "one company [of flagellants went to the Vali Ahd [crown prince] and procured the release

---

[326] Monajjem, *Ruznameh-ye `Abbasi*, p. 131; Della Valle, *Les Fameux Voyages*, vol. 2, p. 181.
[327] Stuart, *Journal*, pp. 296-97.
[328] Aubin, *La Perse*, p. 168.
[329] Qaddusi, Hasan A`zam. *Khaterat-e Man* 2 vols. (Tehran, 1349/1970), vol. 2, p. 52; `Eyn al-Saltaneh, *Ruznameh*, vol. 8, p. 226.
[330] Fowler, *Three Years*, vol. 2, p. 127.

of several prisoners."[331] A Russian observer, Perlin, reported the same custom of demanding the release of a prisoner for Kermanshah fifteen years later. He added an interesting piece of information, viz. that on his release the prisoner had to suffer the wounding of his head.[332] In Resht, this custom of the prisoner release apparently did not exist, for Holmes reported in the 1840s that, "a group of half-naked man bleeding from self-inflicted gashes. The Khan said barikallah, and everybody went home. ... Later we were told that the Khan, his sons and chief attendants had mingled with the mob, and, bareheaded and unshod, were beating their breasts and using the chains with as much vigour as any one."[333]

THE OPPOSITION AGAINST THE PASSION PLAY

The uncontrolled passion that often ran amok during the passage of the groups of flagellants through the city quarters did not please everybody. Rather than controlling the outburst of passion they wanted to ban it altogether. Fowler wrote in 1835, "The great Nadir Shah attempted to extinguish these fêtes."[334] Indeed, in 1738 he had banned all *ta`ziyeh* activities. When asked why he had done so Nader Shah replied: "Your are wounding yourself because of two Arabs who have done nothing for Iran; what will you do when I, who has done so much for Iran, die. Will you kill yourselves? It is to protect you that I have banned these activities."[335] Nader Shah's attitude was shared by the orthodox olama. Various contemporary nineteenth century travelers mention that religious disapproval, while pointing out that that people did it anyway.[336] "In cities such as Meshed, where the priests set their faces against theatrical representations, the populace attends *ruzakhana* (sic), or recitals of the tragic tale, which are given by the *mullas* in different houses."[337] The olama regularly asked the government to ban these shows, because they were not orthodox. The government, however, was incapable of doing so. Also it wanted to curry favor with the public and recalled the attempt to ban the presentation of "The Marriage of Qasem," which led to serious riots.[338]

---

[331] Wilson, *Persian Life*, p. 195; Adams, Isaac. *Persia by a Persian* (n.p., 1900), p. 419.

[332] Perlin, L "Ozherk zapadnoi Persii (pis'mo iz Kermanshaxa)," *Novyi Vostok* III (1923), 443-45; Ponafidine, Pierre. *Life in the Moslem East* (New York, 1911), p. 345.

[333] Holmes, *Sketches*, p. 309; Adams, *Persia*, p. 420.

[334] Fowler, *Three Years*, p. 121.

[335] Floor, Willem *Hokumat-e Nader Shah* (Tehran: Tus, 1367/1988), translated by Abu'l-Qasem Serri, p. 61.

[336] Wills, *In the Land*, p. 283; Flandin, *Voyage*, vol. 1, pp. 254-55. See also Wills, C. J. *Persia As It Is* (London, 1886), pp. 204-216; Wilson, *Persian Life*, p. 195.

[337] Sykes, *Persia and its People*, pp. 155.

[338] Ahmad Bey, "Le Théatre," p. 531.

There were also people who mocked the mourning ceremonies, although they were careful to act outwardly differently.[339] Then there were those, usually government officials, who considered the processions of the neighborhood groups with its usual violence to be barbaric and also unruly. E'temad al-Saltaneh, Naser al-Din Shah's Minister of Information, also had a low opinion of the breast beaters.[340] In May 1895, the breast-beating (sineh-zani) groups were told not to go from one quarter to another unless under police supervision.[341] In 1916, the governor in Hamadan forbade all ta'ziyeh related pageants.[342] According to one government official, it was very difficult to enforce a ban on the Moharram flagellation, and only a strong governor was able to do so.[343] This was a sign of things to come, because in 1932, Reza Shah banned all Moharram processions, including the flagellations, in the urban areas. He in particular opposed blade beating, the rarest and the most brutal of the three named practices, because it not only caused the most harm to the body, but also violated religious law that considered blood impure (najes). Henceforth, Moharram processions only were staged in rural areas.[344] The flagellants were banned, not only for 'modernizing' reasons, but also because of its relations with Turkey the government did not want to have ceremonies that were anti-Sunni.[345] Reza Shah thus acted in accordance with the will of the leading olama of his period, who wanted to curb, if not ban, these practices altogether. They argued for this suppression of the flagellations on the grounds that chest-beating, chain-beating and blade beating caused injury to the body and thus violated the religious no-injury principle (la zarara wa la zirara fi'l-Islam).[346]

---

[339] Ouseley, *Travels*, vol. 3, p. 163; see also Browne, *Literary History*, vol. 4, pp. 182-85 for a parody of the ostentation of the host and the greed of the guests attending a passion play.

[340] E'temad al-Saltaneh, *Ruznameh*, p. 364

[341] 'Eyn al-Saltaneh, *Ruznameh*, vol. 2, p. 1252 (5 Moharram 1316/May 23, 1898).

[342] Dwight, H.D. *Persian Miniatures* (New York: Doubleday, Page & Company, 1917), pp. 130-39, 150.

[343] Sadr, *Khaterat*, pp. 44-46.

[344] Merritt-Hawkes, O. A. *Persia—Romance & Reality* (London: Nicholson & Watson, 1935), p. 134. In 1935, Reza Shah banned the performance of ta'ziyeh and the flagellants dastehs. Filmer, Henry. *The Pageant of Persia* (New York, 1936), p. 372; Emanuel, W.V. *The Wild Asses, a Journey through Persia* (London, 1939), p. 262. There were, of course, also Iranians who believed that the British were behind this policy. See, e.g., Qaddusi, *Khaterat*, vol. 2, p. 16.

[345] Homayuni, *Ta'ziyeh*, p. 128.

[346] For the controversy among Shi'ites about the Moharram practices see Ende, Werner. "The Flagellations of Muharram and the Shi'ite 'Ulama," *Der Islam* 55/1 (1978), pp. 19-36. Mahmoud Ayoub's theological treatise "Redemptive suffering In Islam" (1978) expounds on the theological and historical aspects of Shi'a devotional rituals.

**Figure 38: Moharram procession in Sari (Mazandaran) in 1932 on the Sabz-e Meydan.
Note the floats and banners.**

Galunov already had remarked in 1929, that "because of the fight with the clergy
and the tendency to possibly limit the size of the processions ta`ziyeh is doomed to
a slow death."[347] However, neither the leading olama nor the Pahlavi regime succeeded in stamping out the practice. This was partly due to the fact the believers
strongly clung to this orgiastic traditional practice, while the clergy was divided on
the issue (the lower ranks were in favor, because they made a good living of it).
Whereas the government was able almost to eliminate the practice in the urban areas, it continued to be practiced, although on a reduced level, in the rural areas. In
1932, the Moharram ceremonies still were performed in, for example, Mazandaran.
Heinrich observed that every evening there was chanting, music, flagellation, and
the passage of the procession via the market place passed the podium on which the
local notables were seated. The military kept the route open for the procession,
which carried floats with allegorical representations such as a decapitated corpse,
the prison of the martyrs, etc. The entire happening was accompanied by serious

---

[347] Galunov, "Neskol'ko slov," p. 311.

weeping.[348] The olama continued to oppose the more violent and bloody aspects of the Moharram ceremonies, among them the late Ayatollah Borujerdi who was the single, uncontested source of emulation (*marja` al-taqlid*) of the Shi`a at that time. He once (around 1950) tried to close his doors to a band of chain beaters that traditionally passed through his courtyards on `Ashura. The band forced its way in, arguing that in exchange for a year of following the *marja`*, they were entitled to a day of obedience by the *marja`*.[349]

NON-KARBALA BUT RELATED PASSION PLAYS

In addition to *ta`ziyeh-shabih*, plays that are exclusively focused on the martyrdom (events and persons) at Karbala, there were other scripts. Whereas the scripts of the Karbala cycle portray the real event or *vaqe`eh*, the other categories of plays depict the vicissitudes of Shi'ite martyrs before or after the Karbala events as well as of religious figures that are not even related to the Karbala events. They were categorized either as being prior-to-the-event (*pish-vaqe`eh*) or as an allusion-to-the-event (*gusheh*). *Vaqe`eh* is the real thing, i.e. it is exclusively about the Karbala Tragedy. *Pish-vaqe`eh* are those plays that deal with religious figures and the Karbala events, but in an indirect way. *Gusheh* are comical plays and are stand-alone and have no relation to the Karbala event. These plays deal with both religious and non-religious characters. They are plays that move towards non-religious drama. They are so-called *shabih-e mazhak*, i.e. plays that are comical and satirical in nature and focused on enemies of the Imams.[350]

These kinds of plays probably came into being because directors introduced preludes to the performance of the passion plays, which later were extended and made more elaborate to be performed as plays in their own right, during the evenings in Ramazan. These included plays such as Amir Timur, Nacre, Joseph, the Marriage of the daughter of the Qoreysh, which had nothing to do with the mourning ceremonies.[351] The fact that the main characters of some of these new plays were saints or prophets (such as Zakharia) for whom prior to the performance of a passion play elegies had been sung may have assisted this development.[352] As a result, so-called comical plays (*ta`ziyeh-ye mazhak*) were developed in the second half of the nineteenth century. Due to their popularity they were performed throughout the year, except for the months of Moharram and Safar initially. However, already around 1885, this scruple had already disappeared. For according to Wishard, "After the tenth day [of Moharram], the play takes on a lighter character,

---

[348] Heinrich, Gerd. *Auf Panthersuche durch Persien* (Berlin: Reimer/Vohsen, 1933), pp. 93-100 (with pictures on pp. 98-100).

[349] Communication by Ahmad Sadri (2004).

[350] Malekpur, *Adabiyyat*, vol. 1, pp. 242-63.

[351] De Gobineau, *Les réligions*, vol. 2, pp. 195ff.

[352] Chardin, *Voyages*, vol. 9, p. 69; Francklin, *Observations*, p. 191.

and often drifts into comedy."[353] However, there was still much weeping in the month of Safar, as reported by `Eyn al-Saltaneh, for example, in case of of the performance of "Hend va Kharabeh."[354]

The *ta`ziyeh-ye Ebn Moljam*, concerning the killer of Imam `Ali, is an example of religious drama that is basically a farcical satire, which ridicules and abuses the enemies of Imam Hoseyn and his family.[355] E`temad al-Saltaneh saw a number of these comical plays that he considered to be strange. One of which was played for Naser al-Din Shah in Aziz al-Soltan's *takiyeh*, of which he unfortunately did not note the name. It was a play in "which St. Mary dies and St. Jesus weeps for her. This is contrary to our Traditions, or histories and the traditions of the Europeans and the entire world, who have it that Mary died a few years after Jesus." Furthermore, there was a performance of a play about the three caliphs that was presented in the most insulting way. For example, Abu Bakr had a dog's skin around his head, and they committed all kinds of despicable things to him.[356] Indeed Christians sometimes thought that the playwright took too much liberty with their belief, although Lady Sheil took it with some measure of amusement. "Our Saviour was made to appear in garments denoting poverty, though certainly not with any intention of indignity. Two women sat at his side, who, in answer to my inquiry, I was told were his wives."[357] E`temad al-Saltaneh further wrote in September 1887, "I had not been to the *takiyeh* for three years; they arranged a seat for me; it was the scene of Bilqis [Queen of Sheba] and Salomon that ends with the death of Qasem. Salomon's bride was all decked out got onto an elephant, when it had to kneel it shied away. The bride got up and it left, which gave rise to laughter (*khandeh dar gereft*). I was not pleased with this."[358] `Eyn al-Saltaneh attended the same comical *ta`ziyeh* play in February 1893, and reported: "They played Salomon, Bilqis [queen of Sheba] and Qasem. They had made strange figures of djinns, *div*s and *dad*s [beasts of prey]. They had desirable women in this play, and of all days the number of spectators was highest to-day. Bilqis was seated on a platform on an elephant; to-day the troupe of Mo`in al-Boka` sang."[359] The British attaché Eastwick, when he was in the village of Aradun, he saw a passion play that had little to do with Ali's sons. "It was by Jauhari, and was called Zechariah, and the subject was the life and martyrdom of a prophet so named. The actors chaunted their parts from MSS., and the audience, chiefly women, wept incessantly."[360]

---

[353] Wishard, *Twenty Years*, p. 157.

[354] `Eyn al-Saltaneh, *Ruznameh*, vol. 1, p. 244.

[355] Rezvani, *Le théatre*, p. 106; Massé, *Croyances*, vol. 1, p. 140.

[356] E`temad al-Saltaneh, *Ruznameh*, p. 991 (29 Ramazan 1310/April 16, 1893).

[357] Sheil, *Glimpses*, p. 130.

[358] E`temad al-Saltaneh, *Ruznameh*, p. 588 (7 Moharram 1305/September 25, 1887).

[359] `Eyn al-Saltaneh, *Ruznameh*, vol. 1, p. 514 (28 Rajab, 1310/February 15, 1893).

[360] Eastwick vol. 2, p. 141.

Figure 39: Scene from the episode of the European ambassador (19th century woodcut)

The Episode of the European Ambassador

There is even a passion play in which a Christian ambassador comes to support the right of the Shi`ite Imam to the caliphate.[361] "According to Sheeah tradition, a Feringee Ambassador expostulated with the murderers of Hoosein, and fell victim to their rage, but not until he had embraced the faith of Islam."[362] This European ambassador had allegedly been sent by King John.[363] The *Dar*, as it usually referred to, "is more than usually comic, and relates to the supposed conversion and immediate martyrdom of a Christian ambassador. … There are other irregular interludes, Adam and Eve, Cain and Abel etc. Some of the scenes are very comic; as that between Yezeed the tyrant and his physician.[364] Lady Sheil further reported that the European ambassador by the late 1840s had become the English ambassador. "There is always great anxiety that the costume of his Excellency should be European and military, and, above all, a cocked hat and feather are highly prized. At Serab, some years ago, a

---

[361] Chodzko, *Théatre Persan*, p. xiii.

[362] Stuart, *Journal*, p. 295.

[363] De Gobineau, *Trois Ans*, vol. 2, p. 218.

[364] Wills, *In the land*, pp. 283-84; Afshar, *Safarnameh-ye Lorestan*, p. 83.

deputation once waited on my husband to borrow his coat and cap for the Elchee
Fering, now generally called with immense contempt of chronology, Elchee Inglees.
At Tehran our horses and chairs too, are in constant requisition during the month of
Moharrem, at the private performances in the city-the former to appear in the pag-
eant, the latter to accommodate the European visitors."[365]

The female counterpart of the play about the European ambassador is that of the
Christian Woman or the *Majles-e Zan-e Nasrani*. It is one of the few passion-
plays with a female lead character. De Gobineau saw it performed in Tehran and
noted that it was written only two years or so before he saw it. He further observed that the playwright or director had introduced an innovation. For instead of
the usual open stage this time the stage was curtained off. As soon as the band
struck announcing the arrival of the actors the curtain was quickly lifted. The
spectators saw the deserted plains of Karbala after the battle. The only things in
sight were abandoned weapons signifying the end of the battle and coffins with
the corpses of Imam Hoseyn and his followers. Lit candles above a few of the coffins indicated the holiness of the corpses within. Then a caravan arrived with its
camp followers. Next a European woman entered on horse-back with her servant.
According to de Gobineau, the clothes of the Christian woman showed that the
stage director had studied European lithographs and maybe the dresses of European women in Tehran and that he had not done a bad job. Also, the young boy
playing the woman was very beautiful. He wore a green satin fanning skirt, a
shawl cross-wise over his breast like French peasant women, a broad-brimmed
straw hat, a necklace of pearls and emeralds, and tall black boots. Not knowing
where she had arrived, the Christian woman dismounted and instructed the chief
farrash to pitch camp. But when and wherever a peg is struck in the ground,
blood gushed forth as if from a fountain. Everyone in her party became greatly
disturbed. Finally, the Christian woman mounted her horse and with her servant
went to the *taqnama* where she laid down to sleep. While asleep she has a dream.
Christ enters the stage and tells the Christian woman about the battle of Karbala.
Meanwhile an Arab Bedouin enters the stage; he had benefited from Imam's
Hoseyn munificence prior to the events. He had come there looking for booty. The
actor who played this Arab thief knew his role by heart and performed the thief's
innate evil character very well, de Gobineau wrote. Unaware of Imam Hoseyn's
fate, he opened his coffin. The Arab does not notice the candles or the doves that
encircle the holy corpse. Looking for weapons and valuables he then attacks the
corpse. He is first frightened and then angered by the voice of the martyred Imam
who speaks to him. After dismembering the Imam's corpse, the Arab thief leaves
the stage. Then all the prophets prior to Mohammad and the Fourteen Immaculate
Ones enter with veiled faces. They hurry to the Imam's corpse. At the end of the

---

[365] Sheil, *Glimpses*, p. 126.

performance the Christian woman, of course, converts to Shi`a Islam having already been prepared to do so by the prophet Jesus.[366]

The `Omar-Koshan Festivity and Play

The most famous of the *gusheh* class of plays is the play of `Omar's Death (*ta`ziyeh-ye `Omar-koshan*). Since the beginning of the establishment of the Safavid state and of Shi'ism as its state religion the cursing of the first three caliphs (Abu Bakr, Uthman and `Omar) and A'isheh was formalized by the state through the offices of so-called *tabbari`yan* or professional cursers[367] In addition, there was a special day to commemorate the killing of `Omar, which took place on 9 Rabi` al-Avval. This festival, also called `*Eyd-e Baba Shoja` al-Din* as well as `*Eyd-e khandeh* (Festival of Laughter),[368] usually lasted three days, although any delay up the seventeenth was acceptable. This festival invariably included among its ceremonies the burning of `Omar in effigy. More elaborate and interesting was the performance of a play about the killing of `Omar. This play had, of course, a different purpose than those that commemorated the martyrdom of Hoseyn and his family. The `Omar play was both ridicule and parody in nature as well as edifying, because it showed that evil behavior was punished, while it also served to arouse the devotional and righteous passion of the believers. Although `Omar had been murdered during the last ten days of the lunar year (Dhu'l-Hejja), the date had been moved forward to the ninth day of the third month to provide relief after the two months of mourning. According to Mostowfi, after two months (Moharram and Safar) of mourning people needed to have some fun. Therefore, they did away with their mourning clothes and put on colorful ones, in accordance with their age and status. Two-months' old beards were shaven and hennaed, while the women hennaed their toe and fingernails.[369]

However, before proceeding any further it is necessary to determine which `Omar was actually symbolically killed. The various people who reported about this festivity for the most part wrote that the effigy was that of the second caliph `Omar,

---

[366] De Gobineau, *Les réligions*, vol. 2, pp. 201-07.

[367] The practice had already existed and been put in practice prior to that time, of course. However, when this happened it was because of the initiative by a Shi'ite religious leader (and sometimes even Sunni olama), which was tolerated by the local governor. Safa, *Tarikh-e Adabiyat*, vol. 2, p. 195; see also Vasefi, vol. 2, p. 224f. On the historical problems of the timing of the introduction of the *tabbari`yan* and their historical antecedents see Jean Calmard, "Les rituals shiites et le pouvoir. L'imposition du shiisme safavide: eulogies et maledictions canoniques," in Jean Calmard ed. *Etudes Safavides* (Paris/Tehran, 1993), pp. 109-50.

[368] Afshar, *Safarnameh-ye Lorestan*, p. 109; Mostowfi, *Sharh*, vol. 1, pp. 320, 326 (it was also known as the Festival of Zahra, because `Omar allegedly had mistreated her more than anyone else). According to E`temad al-Saltaneh, *Ruznameh*, p. 597 (10 Rabi` I 1305/ November 26, 1887) "in the parlance of the common people it is `*Eyd-e `Omar-koshan* [today]."

[369] Mostowfi, *Sharh*, vol. 1, pp. 320, 326; Shahri, Ja`far. *Tehran-e Qadim*. 5 vols. (Tehran: Mo`in, 1377/1999), vol. 2, p. 369.

while some of those who practiced it thought it was a minor official involved in the battle of Karbala. Originally the Omayyad general `Omar b. Sa`d, who had been sent to stop Hoseyn and his party, was meant. Later, this general was confused with the second caliph `Omar ibn Khattab, who was killed by an Iranian slave Abu Lu'lu Firuz a.k.a Shoja` al-Din, whose good deed was commemorated with this festival. It was therefore also known as `Eyd-e Baba Shoja` al-Din.[370]

In 1539, the Venetian envoy, Michele Membré observed in Tabriz that when Shah Tahmasp I left the harem to go the place of audience that two men preceded him, each with a steel drum, who cried out, "praising God and cursing `Umar, `Uthman and Abu Bakr, and says, 'Sad hazar la`nat bar `Umar, `Uthman, Abu Bakr', and goes behind crying out until the King comes to sit. Then they fall silent. And when he wishes to return to his chamber they cry out in the same manner until he enter the chamber."[371] Chardin relates that Persian archers practicing their skill said before ending practice, "the last one is right in Omar's heart."[372] Thevenot reported that on 19 September [1665, or 9 Rabi` I, 1076] people in Iran celebrated the event of Omar Koschodgiazade (i.e. Shoja` al-Din the killer of `Omar), a famous miller.[373] Du Mans also mentions the cursing of `Omar, because of his usurpation of `Ali's rights and his scandalous behavior towards Fatimeh, `Ali's wife and daughter of the prophet. `Omar is furthermore accused of being the offspring of an incestuous relationship, of being a sodomite, and worse. He also tells the story of Chegea-Eldin the miller (i.e. Shoja` al-Din the killer of `Omar), `Ali's friend, as does Olearius.[374] Bedik reports that the Shi'ites cursed the first three caliphs.[375] Morier reported that people in Iran chose to depart on the day of `Omar's death, because it was a lucky day.[376] Ferrier also mentions the cursing of `Omar as did Sheil, who also relates that the brick-layers did so in their regular working chant.

Khishtee bideh mara janum	Give me a brick then, my life
Laanet ilahee ber Oma-a-r	And the curses of God light on Omar
Yekee deeger bideh bimun azeezum	Give me another, now, my darling
Inshallah kheir neh beneed Oma-a-ar	Please God, Omar will not have any luck

---

[370] Afshar, *Safarnameh-ye Lorestan*, p. 109.

[371] Membré, *Mission*, p. 20, see also p. 52.

[372] Chardin, *Voyages*, vol. 3, p. 349, vol. 9, pp. 34-36, 52 (cursing of `Omar).

[373] Thevenot, vol. 2, p. 110.

[374] Du Mans, *Estat*, p. 50-53; Olearius, *Vermehrte newe Beschreibung*, pp. 497-98 (Schutza Adin).

[375] Bedik, Petro. *Cehil Sutun seu explicatio utriusque celeberrisimi, ac pretiosissimi theatri quadriginta columnarum in Perside Orientis* (Vienna, 1678), p. 92 (la`nat bar Yazid, bar `Omar, `Uthman, AbuBakr. In reaction to this curse bystanders would respond with: hazar, hazar bar).

[376] Morier, *Journey*, pp. 249, 62 (for a quaint belief that a lion would not attack a Shi`a if he would shout Ya `Ali, but would attack if he inadvertently would say Ya `Omar)

She further related that, "the women distinguish themselves by their devotion on this anniversary, though their mode of evincing their piety is both inconvenient and whimsical. Perched on the flat roof of their houses overlooking their street, and armed with a large pot of water, they lie in wait for the passers by, and the heedless passenger is souses with water, while a triumphant scream proclaims "Omar, laanehoo Allah (Omar, God curse him)."[377] Bishop relates that the Bakhtiyaris, who were rather lax in the observance of their religious duties, nevertheless were believed "to compel any one entering their country to swear eternal hatred to Omar [, which] is not absolutely correct," she added.[378]

The annual burning of the effigy of the caliph `Omar was another example of the representation of living beings used in a religious context. The use of effigies in religious processions and *tableaux vivant* was already practiced since at least the early seventeenth century. The Russian merchant Kotov recounts that when he was in Isfahan in 1624, he saw the annual Moharram procession. "In front of those same coffins they lead the effigy of a man made of skin and stuffed with straw, with bow and quiver and arrows made of pine (?) slivers seated upon an ass, and on his head a helmet with five fingers; they support him from the sides, so that he may not fall, and they curse him and spit upon him."[379] Della Valle relates that on the eve of `Ashura they burnt the effigies of `Omar and some other leading figures of the opposing sect (i.e. the Sunnis) and that they curse and excommunicate them publicly on the meydan in Isfahan.[380] According to Bedik, it was the caliph Yazid who was burnt in effigy.[381] To increase the confusion, Struys reported that in Shamakhi in 1671 a straw puppet was taken around town on a donkey and at the end of the tour it was set fire to. But in this case it was allegedly Shemr, the killer of Hoseyn, who was burnt in effigy.[382] In 1694, Gemelli-Careri observed that on a Wednesday a straw manikin was led around all the city quarters just like a criminal, which manikin was sometimes called Omar, sometimes Abumurgian, his companion. Then they still their rage by killing the donkey and by burning the manikin in effigy.[383] De Bruyn relates that in the corner of what clearly was a *takiyeh* where a *rowzeh-khvani* was held, "they had placed a great figure indifferently well counterfeited, and stuffed with straw, to represent the

---

[377] Sheil, *Glimpses*, p. 139-40.
[378] Bird, Isabella (Mrs. Bishop). *Journeys in Persia and Kurdistan*, 2 vols. (London, 1891 [London, 1988]), vol. 2, p. 101.
[379] Kemp, *Russian Travellers*, p. 32; Strauszens, J. J. *Reisen durch Griechenland, Moscau, Tartarey, Ostindien, und andere Theile der Welt* (Amsterdam 1678), p. 151; Le Bruyn, *Travels*, vol. 1, p. 215 (a kind of Golem); Salmon, Th. Van Goch M. *Hedendaagsche Historie of Tegenwoordige Staat van Alle Volkeren. IV. Deel Behelzende den tegenwoordige Staat van Persia, Arabia, en het Asiatisch Tartaryen* (Amsterdam: Isaak Tririon, 1732), p. 341
[380] Della Valle, *Voyages*, vol. 2, p. 182.
[381] Bedik, *Cehil Sutun*, p. 90.
[382] Strauszens, *Reisen*, p. 151.
[383] Gemelli-Careri, *Giro*, vol. 2, p. 171.

murderer of Hussein, called Omar, whom they burnt at night in several parts of the city."[384] The cursing of `Omar was continued in the eighteenth century and was in particular strong during Moharram.[385]

In 1802, Waring observed in Shiraz the celebration of Omar's death. "They erected a large platform, on which they fixed an image, disfigured and deformed as possible. Addressing themselves to the image, they began to revile it for having supplanted Ali, the lawful successor of Moohummud; at length, having exhausted all their expressions of abuse, they suddenly attacked the image with stones and sticks, until they had shattered it into pieces. The inside was hollow, and full of sweetmeats, which were greedily devoured by the mob who attended the cere-mony."[386] The same sweet after taste of the killing of Omar was also recorded by Binning, also in Shiraz, but 50 years later.

> On thirteenth of January, the festival of Omar' assassination (*eidi omar kooshan*) took place. On this day, it is the practice of Sheeahs to make large images, something like our Guys on the fifth of November, of sticks and paper or any fragile materials, the insides of which are filled with bonbons. These effigies, intended to represent the obnoxious Kha-lieefa, are paraded about the town, and then torn and hacked to pieces, while there is a general scramble for the sweetmeats they contain. The prince made a great public feast for all his dependants, the harmony of which was enlivened by the humane spectacle of sundry bullfights, be-sides feats of jugglers and ropedancers, with fireworks at night. Some Persians suppose that any sins they may commit on this day-suicide, I believe, excepted-are not counted against them hereafter; and accord-ingly they have license to take their full swing of iniquity.[387]

The staged version of `Omar's villainy could be simple as well as elaborate and it all depended on the time, the place, the funds, and the artistry of the actors. In Mashhad, in the early 1830s, Burnes saw an Omar killing, an effigy on the gibbet. "We had a real exhibition of a man suspended from a beam laid across the street, and that, too, in a blaze of light. How the contrivance was made I did not dis-cover; for he had a rope round his neck, and kicked and acted to reality. As the crowed gazed."[388] `Eyn al-Saltaneh described a somewhat more succinct version.

---

[384] Le Bruyn, *Travels*, vol. 1, p. 215.

[385] Anonymous, *Histoire des Decouvertes*, vol. 2, p. 370.

[386] Waring, Edward Scott. *A Tour to Sheeraz*. (London 1807 [New York, 1973]), pp. 42-43. This text was also translated into French in Dubeux, Louis. *La Perse* (Paris: Firmin Didot Frères, 1841), p. 395 and by Jourdain, Am. *La Perse ou Tableau de l'histoire, du gouvernement, etc.* 5 vols. (Paris: Ferra & Imbert, 1814), vol. 4, pp. 73-74.

[387] Binning, *A Journal*, vol. 1, pp. 428-29. See also Donaldson, Bess Allen. *The Wild Rue* (London, 1938), pp. 117, 125.

[388] Burnes, Alexander. *Travels into Bokhara*. 3 vols. (New Delhi: Asia Educational Services, 1992 [London, 1834]), vol. 3, pp. 85-86.

He noted in his Diary, "In the morning of 8 Rabi` I, 1308 [October 22, 1890], in the Madraseh-ye Dar al-Shafa there was a *bazi-ye `Omar*. There were two *row-zeh-khvan*s, one a carpenter, the other a felt maker. They recited; it was good. They said many meaningless and foolish words."[389]

Usually, the Festival was celebrated with fireworks and the burning of effigies. The latter were made either by families themselves (in particular by children helped by their elders) or bought ready-made from the arsenal. Fireworks were for sale all over the towns. The festival was an occasion for people to get together, eat and drink and be merry. The wealthier families hired musicians and actors, while in Mostowfi's family the male servants had their own separate party. The musicians also recited self-composed verses in praise of the effigy before these were set fire to.[390]

Dr. Wills attended the most elaborate staged version. He had been invited to a *ta`ziyeh* of `Omar in Shiraz, to be followed by dinner and to be concluded by an *`Omar-koshan*, the killing of `Omar. He reached the house at five in the afternoon. All the buffoons had been collected in well-sprinkled courtyard.

> Over the hauz or tank which is seen in every decent house in Persia stood a platform, some four feet high." [a Jewish band was playing] "Before each group of buffoons, or Jews, was a bottle of spirits, and a brass drinking-cup." [...] "A luti (professional buffoon) attired as a burlesque of a moollah, or priest, ascends the stage. He solemnly curses Omar; he takes off the particular habits of the Mahommedan priest amid shouts of laughter: he tells his beads; he preaches a comic sermon. The music strikes up again, and the procession of actors makes its circuit around the crowded courtyard, Omar himself leading a dog, the type of defilement. And such a dog: one of the street pariah, which, unused to the leash, howls dismally and tries to bite! Then come his followers, all riding on asses. Then, angels and demons; last of all the Sheitan, or 'Old Nick' himself: a gruesome devil with horns, nude to the waist, painted in black spots, and yellow face, and white round eyes and mouth. The climax is to be the descent of Omar and the Sheitan to regions below. All ascend the platform. Omar makes a speech; he dines; at the suggestion of the devil he gets very drunk; the fun grows fast and furious. Omar dances; his attendants, angels, demons, buffoons, all dance." [391]

[389] `Eyn al-Saltaneh, *Ruznameh*, vol. 1, p. 311.
[390] Mostowfi, *Sharh*, vol. 1, p. 326.
[391] Wills, *Persia As It Is*, pp. 217-22.

The `Omar cycle is a comical drama that allows the Shi'ites to express their ha-
tred for the Sunnis by ridiculing `Omar and Abu Bakr, which they consider as
usurpaters. `Omar is the most despised person, even more so than Judas to the
Christians. No vilification is strong enough to characterize him. Anything is allowed to dishonor him. Certain carpet makers insert his name in the carpet's pat-
tern so that true believers may walk over him. The leather makers scratch his
name on the soles of shoes that they make, and the real fanatics went even so far
as to have his name tatoed on the underside of their feet.

The set of the scene of the *ta`ziyeh-ye `Omar* is much like that of the normal religious drama. In the center of a mosque's courtyard a platform is erected on which
a *luti* or clown takes place. He is dressed in the clothes of a mollah, but a la burlesque. His antics arouses the laughter of the spectators, because he ridicules the
particularities of the behavior of a Sunni mollah. He recites his prayers and deliv-
ers a comic-heroic sermon accompanied the most suggestive grimaces. After this
the music plays up and a procession is formed that circles around the mosque that
is packed with people. The caliph Omar has of course the main role; he holds a
dog, symbol of impurity, which bellows sadly. Because it is not accustomed to the
leash it tries to bite the attendees. The cavalcade continues with the companions
of Omar mounted on donkeys; then a procession of angels and demons led by Sa-
tan in person. The prince of darkness is represented by a man who is half-naked,
covered with large spots of paint, his face is yellow with white circles around his
mouth and eyes; his head has been embellished with horns that give him a fright-
ening aspect.

The apogee of the drama is Omar's descent into Hell. All of a sudden the actors
climb the platform that has been constructed over the water basin in the courtyard.
Omar gives a talk, then he eats and, at the suggestion of the devils, he gets drunk.
Then the scene gets more and more comical. Omar dances, his suite follows his
examples, the angels, demons and thee buffoons do their part. But at a given moment the planks suddenly give way and everybody fall into the basin to the great
joy of the attendees. The feast is concluded by the burning of Omar in effigy to
the applause of the attendees.[392] In Yazd, where there was no *ta`ziyeh* perform-
ance, there was "a night set apart for the burning of Omar, the usurping Khalif,
and the carrying of the effigy through the town is the occasion of extreme excitement,"[393] and the same was the case in Tehran, where fireworks added sparks and
glitter to the event. Minorsky saw the `*Omar-koshan* play performed in 1902 in

---

[392] D'Allemagne, H. *Du Khorasan au Pays de Bakhtyaris*, 4 vols. (Paris, 1911), vol. 1, 157-59 (this
seems to have been copied from Wills).

[393] Malcolm, Napier. *Five Years in a Persian Town* (London: John Murray, 1905), p. 135; Rice, W.A.
Mary Bird in Persia (London, 1916) p. 35.

Qazvin.[394] But by 1907 the celebration of this event was already less important than in previous times and was fading away.[395]

A Persian Guy Fawkes, outside Shiraz.

Figure 40: `Omar-koshan or a Persian Guy Fawkes photographed outside Shiraz (1909)

Bradley-Birt saw it still performed at Shiraz in that year and even produced a photograph of the event (figure 40). He wrote:

> Outside a little mosque a group of men and boys have gathered round a typically English Guy Fawkes, and it stand there against a long low wall for all the world like a fifth of November figure; and inquiry elicits the fact that it is made with much the same intent. It represents Omar, who slew Ali, the son-in-law of the Prophet, the bystanders inform one; and every year on the anniversary of the occurrence the Shiahs, who revere the latter as the Prophet's true successor, burn his murderer in effigy. It is an unexpected scene. The central figure, a thing of rags, is the same. The fun and the enjoyment of the boys is the same. The cheerisness and general good humour of the bystanders differs but little from the English counterpart. But there the similarity ends. The little mosque, the long low mud-wall, the figures and costumes of the actors in the scene, all are strange.[396]

---

[394] Krimsky, *Pers'kiy Teatr*, p. 77.
[395] Aubin, *La Perse*, pp. 161-62.
[396] Bradley-Birt, *Through Persia*, p. 114.

The `Omar-koshan festival still was celebrated in the Caucasus, where prior to World War I a puppet representing `Omar was stuffed with gunpowder and other inflammables. The puppet was set fire at the back and once the flames reached the head the head exploded with a loud bang. Much mocking, joking, and jeering accompanied this spectacle.[397] At Baku young boys would smear their face with flour or put on grotesque masks, clownish dresses, or animal skins and would go around the streets singing satirical songs about `Omar and performing comical dances. These antics were referred to as kos-kossa. The same term also was used to denote a kind of masked theater played at the occasion of the `Omar-koshan festival. It was played by amateurs using cardboard Russian-made masks, which Rezvani, who was one of the spectators found of no particular interest.[398] Bricteux relates that on the 26th Dhu'l-Hejjah people celebrated with joy the day of Omar's death, but out of respect for the Sunnites (or was it the police?) they did not burn his effigy anymore, thus indicating the decline of this custom's importance.[399] Shahri, Tehran's historiographer, when discussing the `Eyd-e `Omar, as he calls it, does so in footnote indicating that it had lost much of its attraction already some decades ago.[400] This may have been due to the fact that after 1910 the Qajar government formally banned the burning of `Omar'e effigy. Every year it sent public criers into the street to remind people of the ban, although they did not heed the ban. In fact, even the public crier made funny jokes about the ban in between his announcements. It was only when Reza Shah issued a ban on the burning of the effigy that the custom died out, at least in the towns. However, Donaldson, writing in 1938 but perhaps referring to an earlier period, still mentions the burning of `Omar in effigy as well as the cursing of `Omar, Othman, Abu Bakr, A'isha, Hafsa and Hinda. She mentions that, "On the ninth day of the month of Shavaal [sic], which is Umar's birthday, he is publicly burned in effigy and cursed. An old garment is stuffed with straw and grass, and explosives are inserted here and there throughout. When the image is set on fire there is much merriment and each explosion is accompanied by shrieks of delight."[401]

Massé provides a short description of the enactment of Omar's feast in an unnamed village. Apart from the text of the threnody that he has recorded, Massé noted that people would make a puppet, whose head was an old water pipe's jar; to its clothes firecrackers were attached and in its hand it had a rosary made of dung. Towards the end of the evening, after having finished singing `Omar's threnody, people would

---

[397] For ta`ziyeh-ye `Omar also see Smirnov, K. Persy, otcherk religii Persii (Tiflis, 1916), p. 109.

[398] Rezvani, Le théatre, pp. 106, 133.

[399] Bricteux, Pays, p. 67; Ponafidine, Life, p. 355

[400] Shahri, Ja`far. Tarikh-e ejtema`i -Tehran dar qarn-e sizdahom, 6 vols. (Tehran: Farhang-Rasa, 1368/1989), vol. 4, p. 268, n. 3.

[401] Donaldson, The Wild Rue, pp. 117-18, 125.

put two jars with gunpowder next to the puppet and set fire to it. When `Omar's head exploded people applauded and exulted.[402]

There also seems to have been the recitation of the *rowzeh-ye `Omar*, which apparently was done by women only, about which, unfortunately no further information is available.[403] According to Rezvani, only women inside their homes celebrated the *`Omar-koshan* festivity by the mid-twentieth century.[404] This was certainly the case in rural Iran. Alberts, who made a study of the village of Davarabad (Khorasan) noted that although it was a religious day of celebration the villagers had no precise notion about the reason for this celebration and in fact linked it to the life and death of Imam Hoseyn rather than to the Caliph `Omar. In fact, the `Omar that symbolically was killed by the villagers was, according to their belief, a minor figure among the forces that opposed Hoseyn, and it was he who set fire to Hoseyn's tents. A certain Mokhtar, a partisan of Imam Hoseyn then captured him and burned him alive. It is this event that the Davarabadis were celebrating. During that day people danced, made fun and music. An effigy of Omar, made of rags and stuffed with straw, was abused for a few hours as well as spat upon, splattered with yoghurt and dung, mostly by boys and men, while onlookers chanted the following ditty:

Omar! Omar! Omar-oo!	Omar! Omar! Omar-oo!
Omar! Omar! Sag pedar-oo!	Omar! Omar! You son of a dog!
Omar az hamum daresh konid!	Throw Omar out of the bathhouse!
Sikh-e hamum koonesh konid!	Ram the bathhouse furnace's poker up his anus![405]

After the crowed got tired and ran out of ideas of further abuse that it might inflict on the effigy, it was doused with kerosene, hitched to a rope, set afire and then dragged by a donkey through the village's streets. Participation in this celebration was meritorious to show one's contempt for the Sunnis while reaffirming one's commitment to Shi'ism.[406] A decade or so later, in the village of Talebabad (Veramin), the day only was celebrated by groups of women who usually also would invite a molla, and instead of a display of grief and crying, they would laugh and clap their hands, when the molla told funny stories and declaimed light poetry. The invitees got tea, not with sugar but with *dhorrat* (pop-corn) and instead of pieces of chocolate, cakes. Also many seeds (melon, sun-flower, etc.) were shelled, and when shelling they laughed and said bad things about `Omar. Before the feast began the person who had invited the other women showed a

---

[402] Massé, *Croyances*, vol. 1, pp. 167-69.

[403] Shari`ati, "Sargarmiha," vol. 1, p. 511.

[404] Rezvani, *Le théatre*, p. 106.

[405] The reference to the bathhouse, which Alberts was not able to explain (nor the villagers) may have to do with one variant of `Omar's threnody where he visits the bath. See for the relevant text Massé, *Croyances*, vol. 1, p. 169.

[406] Alberts, R. *Social Structure and Culture Change in an Iranian Village*. 2 vols. Unpublished dissertation (University of Wisconsin, 1963), vol. 2, pp. 899-901.

strangely shaped skeleton made from paper and fabric on which she had painted eyes and eyebrows. The cheeks had been rouged, and a tufted hat had been put on its head. It had a rosary made of sheep's dung in its hands, and usually firecrackers were hanging from its face. At the end of the festivity some kerosene was poured over the `Omar effigy and set fire, while the women clapped their hands and shouted excitedly. While it burnt the women and children made a circle around it, spat at the effigy, kicked at the embers and cursed it. In the past the occasion was celebrated in a much more elaborate manner, indicating that the social pressure to kill `Omar was low in less remote villages.[407]

Figure 41: Persian musicians (*tombak* or drum; *dayereh* or tambourine and *kamancheh* or string instrument)

---

[407] Safinezhad, Javad. *Talebabad* (Tehran, 2535/1976), pp. 437-38.

CHAPTER SIX

MODERN THEATER

THE EARLY BEGINNINGS

Western theater was not unknown to members of the Iranian elite in the early nineteenth century. Those who had been abroad had experienced it at first hand. On January 12, 1810, the Iranian ambassador Abu'l-Hasan Khan attended a performance of Shakespeare's *King Lear* in Covent Garden Theater. On June 29, 1810 he attended a theatrical performance at Sadler's Well, which included dancing, a pantomime, and a play.[1] On his return to Iran, Abu'l-Hasan Khan was Minister of Foreign Affairs for a long time (1824-34; 1840-46) and he also financed the performance of religious drama (*ta`ziyeh*) in Tehran. His experience as well as that of other Iranians who had been to Europe certainly helped to pave the way for theatrical developments later in the nineteenth century. The embassy led by Khosrow Mirza to Russia in 1829 also visited concert halls and theaters in St. Petersburg and his Travelogue contains a detailed description of theatrical performances in St. Petersburg and its theater arrangements.[2] Furthermore, European actors also occasionally performed in Iran itself. For example, on April 15, 1835, Italian actors performed in the public court of Malek Hoseyn Mirza's palace at Orumiyeh.[3] However, European theater was not the success that its patron had expected. Some forms of European theater Iranians did not appreciate at all. Perkins, the founder of American missionary activities at Orumiyeh, reported on April 11, 1835: "The Persians are not very fond of such [i.e., theatrical] entertainments. A German ventrilioquist was here, not long ago, and the people ascribed his performance to the direct agency of the devil and treated him with corresponding abhorrence."[4] Whereas educated Iranians were interested in and slowly adopted modern theater the latter was not true of Western music. A Tehran police report recorded that "On 4 Safar 1304 [November 2, 1886] there was a performance in the theater of the *Dar al-Fonun*, which was attended by several ministers, notables, ambassadors and other members of the corps diplomatique and their ladies. A group of European musicians gave a concert and a recital. It was not very interesting

---

[1] Abu'l-Hasan Khan, Mirza. *A Persian at the court of King George 1809-10. The Journal of Mirza Abul Hassan Khan*. Translated and edited by Margaret Morris Cloake (London: Barrie & Jenkins, 1988), pp. 92, 278. Abu'l-Hasan Khan also attended many opera performances in London.
[2] Abu'l-Hasan Khan, *A Persian at the court*, pp. 278-82
[3] Perkins, J. *A Residence of Eight Years in Persia* (Andover, 1843), p. 208.
[4] Perkins, *A Residence*, p. 208.

(*tamasha'i*) for the Iranians, such that when the second piece of music and recital started most of them left."[5]

When in 1851, the Prime Minister, Amir Kabir, saw to the construction of the *Dar al-Fonun* (Polytechnic School) he also gave orders to include an auditorium or theater hall in the northern segment of the building. It is not clear why it had been included for the space did not have a clear well-defined purpose. Amir Kabir had been abroad (Russia, Turkey) and thus may have been influenced by what he had seen in St. Petersburg. The theater hall in the Polytechnic was decorated in Western style and sat 300 persons. It was not much used due to hostility of the olama to the very idea of a theater. It was therefore soon used as a prayer-hall where the students made their daily prayers.[6] There also were students that went to Europe (mainly France) to study where they were exposed to Western life, including theater. The same happened to Naser al-Din Shah during his first European trip in 1873. After his return from Europe he wanted a theater hall to be built in Iran, as discussed in the previous chapter. Although it had to function as the royal theater for the performance of passion play, the first theatrical performance was that of a Western play.[7]

The first time that modern theater was performed in Tehran was in 1878 when a group of young Armenians, some of whom had studied in Europe where they had developed a liking for theater, established a theatrical group. Because there was no theater in Tehran at that time one of the theater-loving Armenians, put a house of his that had large rooms at the disposal of the group. After having transformed one room into a theater the group performed *Usta Petros* (Master Pedros) as its first play. The second play that they performed later was *Do Gorosneh* (Two Hungry Men). When some people in the Armenian community opposed these performances the owner of a tailor shop, Hovsep Tatevossian made a house available to the group. There the group staged a performance of *Shushanik*. After the membership of the group increased, it was able to stage more performances and in 1879 put on two tragedies. The members of the group not only performed in the plays but also took care of all other staging requirements. The proceeds of the sale of tickets were donated to the the Armenian Haigazian school. In 1880 the Armenian community built a school and next to it a theater with a stage. The theatrical group was managed by the principal of the school and in 1881 a Club of Theater Lovers (*Anjoman-e dustdaran-e te'yatr*) was created. Its purpose was the education of the youth, development of the art of theater, and assistance to the school. The reason for this financial support was that American missionaries had opened a school in the Armenian quarter where education, books and school uniform were gratis. One of the founders of the Theater Club,

---

[5] Sheikh-Reza'i, and Azari, *Gozareshha*, pp. 244-45.

[6] Adamiyat, Fereydun. *Amir Kabir* (Tehran: Khvarezmi, 1348/1969), p. 367. On the *Dar al-Fonun* see Ekhtiar, Maryam Dorreh. *The Dar al-Funun: Educational Reform and Cultural Development in Qajar Iran* (unpublished thesis, New York University 1994).

[7] Curzon, *Persia*, vol. 2, p. 481.

and for some time its president, was Harutiun Mardirosian. He was also its first director and decorator and during 25 years he continued to stage plays. The "Club" was helped by a number of Armenians who translated famous European plays. One of their most prolific translators was Hovhannes Khan Masehian Mosa`ed al-Saltaneh who translated plays by Molière and Shakespeare into Armenian and Persian, which later were also used by non-Armenian theatrical groups. Other well-known translators that worked for the Club were Avetis Karabegian and Hovhannes Tomasian. Some of the plays staged in 1886 were 'Narses the Great' (*Narses Kabir*) and the comedy "Anjir Khaju". There were also separate performances for Armenian women. All plays were preceded and/or closed with music, sometimes of the military kind. The Armenian theatrical group not only performed in Armenian, but also in Persian (for the non-Armenian Iranians) and French. In the latter case the target audience was the expatriate European community.[8]

Probably under the influence of his European journey in 1873, which resulted *inter alia* in the construction of the Royal Theater (*Takiyeh-ye Dowlat*) Naser al-Din Shah ordered Mozayyen al-Dowleh, a teacher of French and painting at the *Dar al-Fonun*, to organize the performance of modern theater in Tehran for the court. Because the shah was wary of the olama's reaction to the performance of a modern European play he gave instructions to use the hall of the *Dar al-Fonun* for these theatrical performances for the time being rather than the Royal Theater. With the help of some foreign residents, Mozayyen al-Dowleh translated a number of French plays into Persian, amongst which "The Miser" of Molière, and put them on stage. To satisfy the shah's orders, Mozayyen al-Dowleh organized each year a number of performances, to which foreign residents also were invited. E`temad al-Saltaneh noted the opening of the theater (*te'ater* or *tamasha-khaneh*) as one of the accomplishments of Naser al-Din Shah, although he noted that this had not yet led to its widespread use.[9]

There was not only court sponsored modern theater in Tehran, for the Armenian community also continued with its theatrical activities. In the evening of February 21, 1887, a number of Iranian officials, most of them attached to foreign embassies as well as a number of Armenian merchants and craftsmen and other people attended a theatrical performance at the Armenian school. There had been even more visitors at the performance on February 20; at six o'clock after the beginning of the evening the spectators left.[10] Plays were also performed at private homes. For example, in the evening of April 9, 1887, many Europeans and their

[8] Hovayan, Andaranik. "Te'atr-e Armaniyan dar Tehran," *Faslnameh-ye Te'atr* 4-5 (1378/1999), pp. 185-90. Narses the Great was an Armenian Catholicos (353-373 CE).
[9] E`temad al-Saltaneh, *Ketab al-Athar*, p. 163. On the painting career of Mozayyen al-Dowleh, who also was *naqqash-bashi* or the royal painter for some time see Willem Floor, "Art (Naqqashi) and artists (Naqqashan) in Qajar Persia," *Muqarnas* 16 (1999), p. 146.
[10] Sheykh-Reza'i and Azari, *Gozareshha*, vol. 1, p. 368 (27 Jomadi I 1304/January 27, 1887).

ladies as well as some Iranians, amongst whom the Chief Painter (*naqqash-bashi*, i.e. Mozayyen al-Dowleh) came for a play at the house of Mr. Nat. [?] There was also music.[11] Men, of course, played all roles.

It is clear that the Armenians played an important pioneering role in promoting the spread of modern theater. `Eyn al-Saltaneh, a nephew of Naser al-Din Shah noted in his Diary,

> In the Armenian teachers training college (*mo`allem-khaneh*) artists per-formed shows on 21 Jomadi I [1305/February 4, 1888]. The price per seat was from two tomans to 3,000 [dinars]. I gave 4,000 and got a seat in the third row. The show started at 2 o'clock. There were four acts (*pardeh*). Each act lasted 30-60 minutes. They played very well. Last year, they also played in the state teachers' college (*mo`allem-khaneh-ye dowlati*), but only for three nights. Some time ago, in the same school they performed two nights in Armenian. To-night it was in Persian. The show was about a miser; it was very good. Because it was the very first time that I saw it, it comes good to my mind. Between each scene there was half an hour's intermission so that people could relax. It was also a hotel. Everyone could have food and tea. I returned at 8 o'clock. There also were musicians. It was a comedy; the behavior of the miser was very comical and funny. There were many European and Armenian women. Of the notables there were not that many. Tonight and tomorrow evening there will be another show. Tonight it will be in a European language, i.e. French, and tomorrow night in Armenian. To-night some of the notables, such as the ambassadors, [also came].[12]

The theater performances were continued in November 1888, when `Eyn al-Saltaneh noted:

> For some nights now there have been plays in the Armenian teachers training college [23 Rabi` I 1306/November 27, 1888]. In all there had been three performances, of which one entirely in Armenian. I took four seats at four *tuman*s. [...] Two plays were in Armenian, which I did not understand at all except for the sister's role. The other play was in Per-sian. It was a play by Duker [?]. It was very funny and amusing. There was also a European woman in it, [she was] not so good, but not bad ei-ther. Na`eb al-Saltaneh was also there, but there were not many specta-tors. I was there till six; to go there once is allright. *Naqqash-bashi* said that a few evenings later they would change the plays and it would then be in Persian. It was not bad.[13]

---

[11] Sheykh-Reza'i and Azari, *Gozareshha*, vol. 2, p. 431 (15 Rajab 1304/April 9, 1887).
[12] `Eyn al-Saltaneh, *Ruznameh*, vol. 1, p. 152 (29 Jomadi I 1305/February 12, 1888).
[13] `Eyn al-Saltaneh, *Ruznameh*, vol. 1, p. 182 (23 Rabi` I, 1306/November 27, 1888).

In 1889 the Armenian Theater Club was reinforced by the arrival of two Armenian actors from Tiflis, Mrs. Parantsem and Mr. Grigor Abrahamiants'. They performed in Tehran with local Armenian amateurs, and performed twice for the shah. The Armenian plays that were staged during their presence included: *Shusanik* or *Dokhtar-e Vartan*, the Miller's Daughter (*Dokhtar-e asiyaban*), the Enchanted Soltan (*Soltan sehr shodeh*), "Sacrifice for Sacrifice" (*Fedakari dar barabar fedakari*) and in Persian: "The doctor in spite of himself" (*tabib-e ejbari*), "The forced marriage" (*ezdevaj-e ejbari*), "The knaveries of Scapin" (*Khed`eh-ye Eskapon*), and "Two pigs" (*Du khuk*). The proceeds were for the Armenian School, whose principal was Mosa`ed al-Saltaneh at that time.[14]

For a time, modern theater performance became a fad among the elite. Naser al-Din Shah's favorite, `Aziz al-Soltan even built his own theater in 1889 and he staged a performance there on April 17, 1890. Everybody had to buy a ticket at a price of 4-6 *tuman*s per seat. The money he gave to `Ali Akbar Khan Mozayyen al-Dowleh, the royal painter (*naqqash-bashi*), who previously had staged theater performances for the shah. Mozayyen al-Dowleh also taught marching music to `Aziz al-Soltan's musicians. In all the actors did 3-4 plays and also performed gymnastics for the public. What is of further of interest is that Moslems now also started to act in the modern Western plays. `Eyn al-Saltaneh notes that, "It was funny. The show and rain did not let up. At 7.30 [p.m.] the show was over; it was really a good laugh. Hasan `Ali Akbar, who is one of our own actors (*moqalledan*), with his own troupe had become *acteurs* [sic; actor]. *Naqqash-bashi* had translated the piece. There were many people. There was no Armenian in the play; all were Moslems, and they did well. What was wrong was that it was too long and thus it ended late."[15] Naser al-Din Shah also continued to be interested in theatrical performances, including the modern western form. E`temad al-Saltaneh noted that, "Last night [March 15, 1889] the shah went to the theater (*tamasha-khaneh*). Esma`il Bazzaz performed the play "The forced colonel" (*sarhang-e majburi*)."[16]

None of these performances were real public ones. Apart from the high cost of the tickets, which excluded most people, the performances were aimed at a limited target group, which included the officials of the royal court and other members of the Iranian elite, as well as the leading members of the European and the Armenian community. Also, there do not seem to have been public announcements to

---

[14] Hovayan, "Te'atr-e Armaniyan dar Tehran," pp. 192-93. Shushanik was the Armenian martyr St. Hushanik, daughter of Vartan. See e.g. *The Passion of St. Shushanik*. Translated by Father Kriko Maksoudian (New York, 1999).

[15] `Eyn al-Saltaneh, *Ruznameh*, vol. 1, p. 271 (27 Sha`ban 1307/April 18, 1890). E`temad al-Saltaneh, *Ruznameh*, p. 794 (27 Sha`ban 1307/April 18, 1890), only noted, "`Aziz al-Soltan has invented (*ekhtera`*) [sic] a *tamasha-khaneh* and sells tickets to people. Each seat costs 5 *tuman*s."

[16] E`temad al-Saltaneh, *Ruznameh*, pp. 714, 783 (another performance).

inform the public about the plays, for this information was rather diffused by word-of-mouth and /or by direct invitation. After the shah lost interest in modern theater and censorship became stricter theatrical performances for the royal court even were discontinued after some time. This did not mean that Iranians lost interest in theater per se. Naser al-Din Shah was a great lover of traditional theater and attended many shows put on by Karim Shireh'i and Esma`il Bazzaz, the leading comedians of the late nineteenth and early twentieth century.[17] Many of these shows were staged in the theater of the *Dar al-Fonun* as well as at the mansions of the notables. Furthermore, some of the Iranian notables continued to visit the Armenian theater next to the Armenian school. For example, in June 1897, Moshir al-Dowleh and a number of Ministers and notables came to see one of the performances of Molière's "The knaveries of Scapin" and donated 2,500 *tuman*s for the school at the end of the play.[18] Also, those Iranians traveling abroad, whether in Europe or the Middle East, visited the local theaters,[19] while in Iran itself modern theatrical activities continued to be staged by private Armenians groups in Tehran, Tabriz, and Isfahan; about the last two later.

The Armenian community of Tehran continued with its performances of Armenian and translated European plays. Between the years 1881-1897 the main Armenian actors performing in Tehran were Harutiun Mardirosian, Simuluf Badrusian, Ghukas Ghukasian, Nerses Khan, and Hushang Papazian. They were the stalwarts of theater in Tehran. As of 1897, female roles were also played by women. In that year, Mrs. Babayan, the wife of Gabriel Babayan, the principal of the Armenian school, performed in Molière's "Scapin." From 1898 until 1901 the Club performed *Shushanik*, *Arshak-e dovvom*, *Nerses Kabir*, and *Khakpa-ye siyah*, which were all tragedies. Usually, a comedy, invariably one by Molière who was very popular, was played immediately after the performance of a tragedy. In 1902, two sisters from Tabriz, Vartitr and Haranush Faligian came to Tehran and created there the Tehran Women's Theater Group (*goruh-e te'yatr-e banovan-e*

---

[17] Although Naser al-Din Shah also visited theater and opera performances during his last visit to Great Britain in 1889 he and his suite do not seem to have been greatly interested in them. "The only thing which really amused them was an intinerant troupe of nigger minstrels, whose quaint antics were generously rewarded whenever they went through their entertainment in front of the hotel. Nigger minstrelsy, indeed, seemed to tickle the Persian taste. When some time before the Shah had paid a visit to Brighton, a troupe he had seen in the Aquarium had pleased him almost as much as the aerial flights and feats of the beautiful Geraldine, a clever athlete, whom the King of Kings would have liked to have taken back to Persia." Nevill, Ralph. *Unconventional Memories. Europe-Persia-Japan* (New York: George Doran, 1923), pp. 205, 210-11.

[18] Hovayan, "Te'atr-e Armaniyan dar Tehran," p. 196.

[19] Hamadani, *Majmu`eh-ye Athar*, pp. 238, 243 (Istanbul), 274-75 (Egypt); Pirzadeh, Mohammad `Ali. *Safarnameh-ye Hajji Pirzadeh*. ed. Hafez Farmanfarma'iyan 2 vols. (Tehran, 1342/1963), vol. 1, pp. 226-32 (opera in Paris), 244-47 (entertainers and comedy in Paris); vol. 2, pp. 57-61 (Vienna); Kuhestani-Nezhad, *Gozideh-ye Asnad*, vol. 1, part 1, pp. 100-01 (Mozaffar al-Din Shah attended a performance of a play in Baku in November 1900 on his return from his first European trip); *Tarbiyat*, vol. 2, p. 1666 (24 Shavval 1322/January 1, 1905).

Tehran). During 1902 and 1903 they staged a number of performances and they were also invited to play at Mozaffar al-Din Shah's court. Their performance was a great success and they were well rewarded. However, in 1903 the two sisters moved to Egypt. In 1905, the Armenian community constructed a school and auditorium in Hasanabad on a piece of land that been bought for the construction of church. As of that time the Armenian had two theaters. In 1906, the Club organized an anniversary performance for Harutiun Mardirosian, because he had been directing and acting 25 years by that time.[20]

There also were some modern theatrical activities outside the Armenian community. On December 12, 1900 in Borjnord (Khorasan) local reformers organized the performance of a "Moslem play" during three nights to benefit the construction of a new school in that town, which yielded 1,000 rubles. In 1905 the books *Teyatr-e `Arusi-ye Janab Mirza* and *Teyatr-e Zahhak*, which had been translated from Osmanli Turkish and was about the evil king Zahhak and the hero Fereydun were on sale in Tehran.[21] The reformers were in favor of theater because of its educational and moralizing value and made this point, for example, in the newspaper *Tarbiyat* in 1897.[22]

Translations and Iranian plays

Because this European form of theater was new to Iran, there were as yet no plays written by Iranian authors for this genre. Stage directors, therefore, had to use foreign plays as a vehicle for the introduction and dissemination of this type of dramatic art. Plays by Molière were the first to be translated, or rather to be adapted to an Iranian audience. For these translations often were not so much translations as adaptations of the original text. Browne noted that, "The characters are Persianized, and the text is in verse and follows the original very closely, though occasionally Persian idioms or proverbs are substituted for French."[23] For example, Mirza Hahib Esfahani, who had translated *The Misanthrope*, had taken so much

---

[20] Hovayan, "Te'atr-e Armaniyan dar Tehran," pp. 196-97. Arshak II (r. 350-368 CE) was a play about the Armenian king of the same name.

[21] Kuhestani-Nezhad, Mas`us. *Gozideh-ye Asnad-e Namayesh dar Iran* 2 vols. (Tehran, 1381/2002), vol. 1, part 1, pp. 99-100, 102 (In Tehran, since 1895, books on theater and literary subjects were printed and sold by the *Sharekat-e Danesh-e Mozaffari*); *Tarbiyat*, vol. 3, pp. 1875 (16 Jomadi I, 1322), 1972 (10 Sha`ban 1322).

[22] *Tarbiyat*, vol. 1, p. 111 (23 Moharram 1315), 379 (12 Dhu'l-Hejjeh 1315); vol. 2, p. 1312 (20 Ramazan 1321) regarding the large revenues of theaters due to the number of visitors of the International Exhibition in Paris, thus emphasizing that there also was a material benefit; 1610, note, 1612 note (24 Sha`ban 1323/October 24, 1905) about the moral value of theater.

[23] Browne, *Literary History*, vol. 4, pp. 459-62. Contrariwise, Hovannes Khan Masehiyan Mosa`ed al-Saltaneh only made literal translations without changing the names of persons or events. Hovayan, "Te'yatr-e Armaniyan dar Tehran," p. 189. See also Sanjabi, Maryam B. "*Mardum-Guriz*: an early Persian translation of Moliere's *Le Misanthrope*," *International Journal of Middle east Studies* 30 (1988), pp. 251-70.

liberty with the text (changing names and even the very characters) that it was more an Iranian than a translated French play in the end. At least three plays by Molière were initially translated, including "The Misanthrope" (*Gozaresh-e mardomgoraz*), which was published at Istanbul 1286/1869-70, further "The doctor in spite of himself" (*Tabib-e ejbari*) and "George Dandin or the confused husband" (*Gij*). Most Iranians who had been and/or studied abroad had been to France and thus French was the lingua franca for cultural matters.[24] According to E`temad al-Saltaneh, in 1887, there were 4,000 to 5,000 people in Tehran who knew French.[25] The preference for French plays was therefore more a function of the linguistic abilities of the translators rather than a conscious choice based on serious knowledge of or preference for certain European theatrical works. The problem was that there were no plays written by Iranian authors, as yet. The adapted translations were, strictly speaking, no homegrown product, but it was close.

Maybe of greater import for the development of Iranian drama were the works of Mirza Fath `Ali Akhundzadeh who between 1850 and 1856 wrote six comedies in Azeri Turkish (the language of Azerbaijan). He was the son of an Iranian immigrant and the official translator of the Russian governor of the Caucasus for 26 years. In Tiflis he had become acquainted with the Russian tradition of drama, which contained an influential strain of critical comedy. His plays were published in Tiflis in Russian translation in 1858, and the Turkish text in 1859. The plays of Akhundzadeh were translated into Persian by Mirza Ja`far Qarajehdaghi, who in his preface stressed their educational intent. The Persian translations were published first at Tehran in 1864, but the lithographed edition was almost as rare as the original manuscript, while it also was badly printed and thus difficult to read and full of mistakes. It contained the following six plays: (1) The Vizier of the Khan of Lenkoran (four acts); (2) The Thief-taking Bear (three acts); (3) The Miser (three acts); (4) The Court-Pleaders (three acts); (5) Monsieur Jourdan, the Botanist and Musta`ali Shah, the reputed Sorcerer (four acts); (6) Molla Ebrahim Khalili, the Alchemist (four acts), and the Story of Yusef Shah, which was in between the fourth and fifth plays, and is written partly in narrative and partly in drama form.[26]

A decade later they were edited as well as translated in Europe by several scholars. Foreign interest in Qarajehdaghi's translations was roused in particular by his use of colloquial Persian. Most Western editions are for that reason accompanied by vocabularies. In 1882, "The Vizier of the Khan of Lenkoran" was edited with a translation, notes, and vocabulary by W. Haggard and Guy le Strange, and in 1886 le Strange published a translation of "The Alchemist". Rogers published the text

---

[24] Ardakani, Hoseyn Mahbubi, *Tarikh-e Mo'assesat-e Tamaddon-e Jadid dar Iran* 3 vols. (Tehran: Daneshgah, 1368/1989), vol. 1, pp. 353-55.

[25] E`temad al-Saltaneh, *Ruznameh*, p. 597 (6 Rabi` I 1305/November 22, 1887)

[26] Browne, *Literary History*, vol. 4, pp. 462-63; Thalaso, *Le Théâtre Persan*, p. 877; Amjad, Hamid. *Teyatr-e Qarn-e Sizdahom* (Tehran, 1378/1999), pp. 27-98.

and English translation of "The Bear", "The Pleaders", and "The Sorcerer". In 1886, Barbier de Meynard and Stanislas Guyard published the Persian text of "The Alchemist", "The Vizier of the Khan of Lenkoran," and "The Pleaders", enriched with notes and a glossary, based on the Tehran edition. Two years later Alphonse Cilière published the French translation of "The Vizier of the Khan of Lenkoran" and "The Pleaders", with an introduction on Akhundzadeh's literary works. Edward Ross published an English translation of "The Story of Yusef Shah Sarraj (The Saddler)" in 1895. A French translation of the same story as well as the Azeri text with glossary by Lucien Bouvat was published in 1903.[27]

Despite the significant impact Akhundzadeh's plays had on both political thought and budding playwrights in Iran they had not been performed there.[28] The first performance of Akhundzadeh's plays took place not in Tiflis or Tehran, but in Paris where Mme Jane Dieulafoye organized a performance in her house in 1900. The play was the "Vizier of Lenkoran" in the translation of Cilière. Barbier de Meynard introduced the play with a talk about the literary qualities of Akhundazeh' works. Given the fact that the play contained strong criticism of the system of government prevailing in Iran it is understandable that its performance had not yet been possible in Iran. Moreover, by 1890, the shah had lost interest in Western theater and therefore no more modern theatrical performances had been produced for the royal court in Tehran.[29]

Other plays written by Iranian playwrights for modern theater were influenced by traditional Iranian theater (*taqlid*) in that they used drama as a medium to criticize social conditions and the spread of modern ideas. The anonymous *Baqqal-bazi dar hozur*, for example, contains criticism on the administrative reforms introduced by the reforming Prime Minister, Mirza Hoseyn Khan Sepahsalar (1871-73). Apart from the title itself, the contents itself also shows how drama of the

---

[27] Browne, *Literary History*, vol. 4, p. 462; see also Brands, H. W. *Azerbaidschanisches Volksleben und modernistische Tendenz in den Schauspielen Mirza Feth-`Ali Akhundzade's (1812-1878)* (The Hague-Wiesbaden 1958). G. Le Strange, "The Alchemist," *JRAS* 1886, pp. 103-126; Akhund-Zadeh, Fath Ali. *Persian Plays. Three Persian Plays*, with a literal English translation and vocabulary by A. Rogers. London and Calcutta, 1890; Ross, Edward. C. "The Story of Yusuf Shah Sarraj (The Saddler)," *JRAS* (1895), pp. 537-69; Bouvat, Lucien. "Histoire de Yousouf Chah," *Journal Asiatique* (1903), pp. 393-489. For a modern text edition see Akhundzadeh, Mirza Fath `Ali. *Tamthilat: shesh namayeshnameh va yek dastan; tarjomeh-ye Mohammad Ja`far Qarajehdaghi* ed. `Ali Reza Heydari (Tehran: Khvarezmi, 1349/1970). For an early Indian printing see Hoseyn `Ali, Sayyed. *Chamanestan-e Farsi* (Cawnpore, n.d.). This is an anthology of Persian prose and poetry for school use. It contains amongst other things a translation of Akhundzadeh's play *Sargodhasht-e Monsieur Jourdain, hakim-e nabatat wa Musta'li Shah mashhur beh Jadugar*.
[28] Adamiyyat, Fereydun. *Andishehha-ye Mirza Fath `Ali Akhundzadeh* (Tehran, 1349/1970).
[29] Thalasso, "Le Théatre Persan," p. 878 (with pictures of the actors in Persian dress). For an appreciation of its contents and style see Javadi, Hasan. *Satire in Persian Literature* (Cranbury, 1988), pp. 257-58.

traditional *baqqal-bazi* type was used in this manner. Iranian playwrights would continue to do so even in the twentieth century.[30]

THE CONSTITUTIONAL REVOLUTION OF 1906:
A BOOST FOR MODERN THEATER

A new boost to modern theater was given with the advent of the constitutional revolution in 1906. In its wake many plays were published and played by newly formed theatrical troupes. In fact, the power of theater had grabbed the imagination of many deputies such that the draft law for the newly established municipalities had as one of its aims to create theaters. The law was not adopted, however.[31] Its proposal was a symptom of the force and intensity of the modernist forces and their interest in the cultural and educational values of theater. It was strongly believed that theater was one of the vehicles to diffuse the reformist and constitutional ideas among the population at large. The failed counter-revolution, the political club or *anjoman*s, and the arrival of theatrical groups from the Caucasus would reinforce these interests. The reformists wanted to express their desire for political freedom and their other ideals via theater.[32]

Three plays initially ascribed to Mirza Malkom Khan, one of the reformists' leaders, were published in 1326/1908 in serialized form in the Tabriz newspaper *Ettehad* (Tabriz), are of interest in this connection. In the same year a bi-weekly newspaper in Tehran called *Te'yatr* (Theater) printed "scenes cast in dramatic form referring to the conditions of administration under the [Qajar] Autocracy."[33] However, after the discovery of a letter by Akhundzadeh preserved in the Akhundov Archive at Baku scholars have concluded that the likely author of these three plays was the recipient of this letter. He was Mirza Aqa Tabrizi, an Iranian secretary at the French embassy in Tehran. The plays must have been written already about 1870.[34] The plays are a satire of the social ills and political conditions prevailing in Qajar Iran, especially the oppression exerted by local governors and their corruption. However, as Akhundzadeh pointed out in his letter to Mirza Aqa Tabrizi, "the plays

[30] Javadi, *Satire*, p. 256 gives a short description of the play and discusses its authorship. See also Aryanpur, Yahya. *Az Saba ta Nima*, 2 vols. (Tehran, 1357/1978), vol. 1, p. 326; Kushan, Naser. *Tarikh-e Te'atr dar Esfahan* (Isfahan, 1379/2000), pp. 41-43. For the text of this play see Ibid., pp. 44-75 and *Faslnameh-ye Te'atr* 11-12 (1369/1990).
[31] Malekpur, *Adabiyat*, vol. 2, pp. 15, 27.
[32] Nasr, Sayyed `Ali Khan. "Honar-e Te'atr va Namayeshnameh-nevisi dar Iran," *Rahnameh-ye Ketab* 4/4 (1340/1961), p. 310-13; Kuhestani-Nezhad, *Gozideh-ye Asnad*, vol. 1, part 1, pp. twelve, 24, 46, 63.
[33] Browne, *Literary History*, vol. 4, pp. 462-63; Ibid., *The press and poetry of modern Persia* (Cambridge, 1914), pp. 34, 66; a complete edition based on a ms. then owned by Fr. von Rosen appeared at Berlin (Kaviyani Press, 1340/1921-22).
[34] Javadi, *Satire*, pp. 259; Amjad, *Teyatr*, pp. 99-178.

are more for reading than for performing on the stage."[35] The plays strongly reflect the tradition of comic theater (*taqlid*). There is no unity of time and place; virtually every character uses a different type of language (e.g. an Armenian speaks a kind of Persian that is stereotype for this ethnic group), and the plays read very much like film scripts. Bricteux who translated three of Tabrizi's plays into French commented that they were not "real comedies in the proper sense of the term, but rather farces (the *Schwanke* as Rosen calls it), or, if we want to use a less civil word, sketches or scenes with dialogues: innumerable changes of the scenes make it impossible to stage the plays, whereas they will go wondrously well on the screen."[36] Mirza Aqa Tabrizi's plays although they had not been and were not performed did not fail to have an impact on aspiring authors, about which later. For the Constitutional Revolution not only led to a wave of new Iranian plays, but also to the performance of plays in the large towns, in particular in Tehran.

Tehran

The first play performed in Tehran after the occurrence of the Constitutional Revolution was in Zahir al-Dowleh's hall (*talar-khaneh*), behind the *Anjoman-e Okhuvat* building in November 1907. He had written the play himself. All the members of the *Anjoman-e Okhuvat* were there; they also had sold tickets to outsiders, i.e. mostly politicians, government officials and foreign diplomats. The play was a pantomime and was accompanied by music. An actor, a Mohammad 'Ali Shah look-alike, was seated on the throne and next to him the corpse of the State of Iran had been laid out in state. A servant entered, he motioned and indicated to the shah that the British ambassador was there. The latter entered and seeing that the shah paid no attention to him took the corpse's (i.e. the nation's) hat and left; then the servant entered and announced that the Russian ambassador wanted to see the shah. The latter paid no attention while the Russian diplomat took Iran's jewels. This continued with other foreign diplomats wanting to see the shah and subsequently plundering the corpse of Iran. Finally, well-meaning friends and nationalists try to draw the shah's attention to the state of the corpse (Iran). They erected the corpse in front of the shah and put its hands in that of the shah. At that moment another group of foreign and Iranian plunderers arrive to take advantage of the corpse, but this time the shah and the corpse (the nation) hold hands and are thus united and are able to kick them out. This play depicting the importance of unity between shah and nation was so popular that it played for three consecutive evenings and had a profound influence on people's thoughts.[37]

---

[35] Javadi, *Satire*, pp. 259-61. The plays were published together with two others as Mirza Aqa Tabrizi, *Chahar Te'atr* (Tehran 2536/1977). The first three plays have been translated into French by A. Bricteux, *Les comédies de Malkom Khan* (Liege, 1933) and into Italian by G. Scarcia, *Tre commedie* (Rome, 1967).

[36] Javadi, *Satire*, p. 259.

[37] Safa'i, Ebrahim. *Rahbaran-e Mashruteh* 2 vols. (Tehran: Javidan, 13344/1965), vol. 2, pp. 151-53; Osku'i, *Pazuheshi*, p. 97 mentions another three-act pantomime.

The *Anjoman-e Okhuvat* was established in 1899-1900. The club met in Zahir al-Dowleh's house and gave concerts for philanthropic purposes. Political activities were not allowed, but with the beginning of the revolution its songs (*tasnif*s), for example, acquired reformist overtones. Together with the music concerts plays were performed, and these usually contained criticism of social and political conditions. Pantomime was one of the main vehicles of expression.[38] The *Anjoman-e Okhuvat* was affiliated with the *Hezb-e Demokrat* and its political enemies even set fire to the club's theater. It shows that the *Okhuvat* club flouted its own ban on political activities and that political parties actively used theater as a channel to propagate their message. According to announcements in the *Iran-e Now* newspaper, the plays dealt with issues during the period of absolutism rule. These plays were probably written by Zahir al-Dowleh himself, as is intimated by an announcement in the *Ra`d* newspaper. Of his plays only one is known, "The Evildoers or the Nightmare of Despotism" (*Gonahkaran ya Kabus-e Estebdad*). On December 30, 1909 a manifestation was held at Zahir al-Dowleh's house to celebrate the capture of the arsonists of the *Chaharsuq-e Khandaq* and this event was theatrically depicted by a performance. The attendants were patrons of education and dignitaries of Tehran.[39]

The *Anjoman-e Okhuvat* was not the only group that was active in staging performances of plays. At that time an unknown group performed two comedies in Tehran in Azeri Turkish by Ghanizadeh Qafqazi.[40] Also, on November 17, 1910 the *Hey'at-e Kheyriyeh-ye Vataniyeh* staged a play from the Osmanli Turkish author Nameq Kamal. It had been translated into Persian by Malekzadeh-ye Tabrizi.[41]

A very important development was the creation of the *Sharekat-e `Elmiyeh-ye Farhang* in 1327/1909 by graduates of the Political School in Tehran. Its purpose was educational and philanthropic like other similar clubs. Because of the connotation that the word *anjoman* (political club) had acquired they changed the name to company (*sharekat*). The members established new schools and in general wanted reforms. Its executive committee consisted of Mohammad `Ali Forughi, Soleyman Mirza Eskanderi, `Abdollah Mostowfi and some others. Those active in supportive theatrical activities (prompting, directing, etc.) included `Ali Akbar Khan Davar, Reza Maleki, Mirza Mohammad `Ali Khan Maleki, and Mahmud

[38] Bamdad,Mehdi. *Tarikh-e Rejal-e Iran qorun-e 12-13-14*. 6 vols. (Tehran, 1347/1968), vol. 2, pp. 368-69; Osku'i, *Pazuheshi*, pp. 94-98.

[39] Malekpur, *Adabiyat*, vol. 2, pp. 33-35; Kuhestani-Nezhad, *Gozideh-ye Asnad*, vol. 1, part 1, pp. 103-04. See also Hoseyni, Mohammad. "Enhedam va gharat-e Anjman-e Okhuvvat," *Tarikh-e Mo'aser-e Iran* 6/24 (1381/2003), pp. 79-113.

[40] Kuhestani-Nezhad, *Gozideh-ye Asnad*, vol. 1, part 1, p. 105 (*Akhsham sabri kheyr olar* and *Dursun `Ali baleli*).

[41] Malekpur, *Adabiyat*, vol. 2, p. 50 (*Vatan ya Silisiteriya*).

Bahrami. Mostowfi, Forughi and Bahrami even wrote a play and translated others. The Company had a short life for it was dissolved in 1329/1911.[42] `Abdollah Mostowfi, one of its active members, wrote:

> A group of the alumni of the School of Political Sciences and some others had founded the *Farhang* Company, with motives of promoting educational and cultural activities. Since the undesirable results of the political clubs of the early period of democracy were clear to everyone, it was decided to avoid calling the organization a 'club'; hence the reason for it being called a company. All that was necessary for anyone to join was two member sponsors and a secret vote. I was invited to join by friends and became a member of the board of directors. Mohammad Forughi was the president and Soleyman Mirza Eskanderi was one of the members. The meetings were held on Friday mornings in one of the classrooms of the Military Academy next to the *Dar al-Fonun*. During the week, the members met in the home of one of the board members. Plays were translated and produced as money-making projects for publications, etc.
>
> One of the regulations of this organization was not to discuss politics. One's political affiliation was to be left outside before entering the premises. This rule was enforced religiously by the board. [Davar also joined] … The first time that Dr. Valiollah Khan Nasr came to see one of the plays, it was one of my works about the old and new military system. It took place in the large auditorium of the Mas`udiyeh. The play was a success and by demand of the Ministry of War and some of the officers it was performed for a second time. Mirza Mohammad `Ali Khan Maleki played the part of the old head of the provincial army, Mahmud Bahrami was the recruiter and Mahmud Duladi was the young modern assistant. They played their parts so well that I praised them from my promotor's box. I left the script with the company. Later Mr. Nasr tried to locate it with the intention of a new production. It had been lost. `Ali Akbar Davar played the part of the public defender. On one occasion, when the play was based on the system of justice, he did not even need to change his clothes. He played his part as he was. Everyone contributed according to his talent. Forughi translated a few plays as well, and Mr. Fahimi was also of great help.[43]

---

[42] Malekpur, *Adabiyat*, vol. 2, p. 37; Osku'i, *Pazuheshi*, pp. 99-100. For a statement on *Farhang*'s objectives see Kuhestani-Nezhad, *Gozideh-ye Asnad*, part 1, pp. 5-7 and for its theatrical activities (plays and mimes) see Ibid., pp. 3-4, 7-8.

[43] Mostowfi, *Sharh*, vol. 2, pp. 315-16. On the resentment against *anjoman*s see De Lorey, Eustace & Sladen, Douglas. *The Moon of the Fourteenth Night: Being the Private Life of an Unmarried Diplomat in Persia during the Revolution* (London: Hurst & Blacket, 1910), pp. 243-44. On the performance of `Abdollah Mostowfi's play "Nezam-e qadim va jadid" in April 1911 see Kuhestani-Nezhad, *Gozideh-ye Asnad*, vol. 1, part 1, p. 10.

Soon after *Farhang*'s demise, Sayyed ʿAbdol-Karim Mohaqqeq al-Dowleh created the Teʾatr-e Melli (also referred to as the *Sharekat-e Namayesh va Konfer-
ans*) with some others in October 1911. Its members included ʿAli Nasr, Mahmud
Bahrami, Mohammad ʿAli Khan Maleki and ʿEnayatollah Sheybani, some of
whom were former *Farhang* members. Malekpur called it the first independent
theater group in Iran, because its sole objective was to stage plays. Its repertoire
included critical comedy, family and historical tragedies, translations (of Molière
and Beaumarchais) and original Iranian plays (by Fekri Ershad Moʾayyad-al-
Mamalek and Akhundzadeh). At first the group had no separate venue, but later it
rented a room above the *Farus* printing shop in Lalehzar Street, where it performed a few times each month. This room had a seating capacity of not more
than 50 seats. Teʾatr-e Melli was the most active theatrical group of its day and
the first one that sold tickets for its performances. The group existed till 1916-17,
for with the death of its founder in that year it fell apart. He had been its driving
force, the jack-of-all-trades who directed, managed, translated, and wrote plays.
The members did not get any payment for their work, and also contributed to phi-
lanthropical works.[44] Pavlovich recorded that Nader Mirza, an official of the Ministry of Foreign Affairs had translated Gogol's comical drama 'The Inspector-
General,' which the Teʾatr-e Melli performed on May 13, 1911. This was not the
first time that this comedy had been performed in Tehran. The first performance
had been on May 31, 1910 in the Atabeg Park by the *Sharekat-e Namayesh-e
Iraniyan*.[45]

In September 1914 the *Sharekat-e Namayesh- ʿAli-ye Ershad*, affiliated with the
weekly *Ershad* and the *Anjoman-e Okhovat*, announced that just like in the preceding year it would stage performances of a play to finance a new printing-
machine. It also staged a performance for the benefit of the Sepehr school. The
name of the play was "New and Old Governors" (*Hokkam-e qadim, hokkam-e
jadid*) in three acts by Fekri Ershad Moʾayyad-al-Mamalek. As the name of the
play suggests its theme was a juxtaposition of governors of the old absolutist regime and the governors of the new constitutionalist regime, showing how bad the
former were. The *Ershad* Company probably had organized the annual performance of plays since about 1913, and it continued to do so till September 1917,
when it is mentioned for the last time. The *Ershad* Company at first staged its

[44] Malekpur, *Adabiyat*, vol. 2, p. 40; Oskuʾi, *Pazuheshi*, pp. 101-03; Fekri, Gholam ʿAli "Tarikhcheh-
ye si va panj saleh-ye teʾatr dar Iran," part I. *Salnameh-ye Pars* (Tehran, 1325/1946), p. 147; Kuhestani-Nezhad, *Gozideh-ye Asnad*, vol. 1, part 1, pp. 24-42.

[45] Pavlovich, M. *Enqelab-e Mashrutuyat-e Iran* translated by M. Hushyar (Tehran, 1330/1951), p.
55; Kuhestani-Nezhad, *Gozideh-ye Asnad*, vol. 1, part 1, pp. 13-14 (the price of a ticket was 3 *tuman*s), 15, 23-42, 44-49; Oskuʾi, *Pazuheshi*, p. 102. For a list of plays performed by *Teʾyatr-e Melli*
see Malekpur, *Adabiyat*, vol. 2, pp. 42-43 and Kuhestani-Nezhad, *Gozideh-ye Asnad*, vol. 1, part
1, pp. 42-43.

plays in the old site of the Te'atr-e Melli (i.e. above the Farus printing shop), but as of about 1915 in the Grand Hotel.[46]

In January 1915 the *Goruh-e Namayeshi-ye Azad* organized the performance of a play called "Obsessed with gambling" (*Malikhuliya-ye qomar-bazi*) by Afrasiyab Khan Azad and performed by a number of Iranian students. They were part of a group that referred to itself as *Hey'at-e Javanan-e Azadikhah-e Iran* and wanted to promote the freedom and development of Iran. The group further performed one evening in February 1915 a moral play "How long are we going not to know ourselves?" (*Ta beh ki khodra nashanesim*), followed by a comedy "Two travel stages in Iran" (*Du manzel-e mosaferat dar Iran*) all by Azad, which were also played by young students. At another occasion, in May 1915, the group played "One noble family" (*Yek Khanevadeh-ye A`yan*). Its performance was preceded by an orchestra playing music and followed by a historical discussion. On another evening in the same month it played "Every one who has no power gets clobbered" (*Harkeh zur nadarad kotak mikhorad*); all plays were by Azad. The group continued to perform other plays in the months thereafter, and also started a new cycle of plays in 1916, when its activities are mentioned for the last time on March 30, 1916 with the announcement of the performance of Akhundzadeh's play *Mons. Zhourdan Tabib—Mast `Ali Shah-e Jadugar*.[47] Afrasiyab Khan Azad continued to write plays after his *Azad* group had stopped performing. In 1923 his "Naked King" (*Shah-e `oryan*) was performed.[48] In May 1916 the *Hey'at-e Khurshid* was founded and to herald this auspicious event it organized the performance of a play. There is no mention of this group thereafter.[49]

In February 1917 a new Comedy Company of Iran (*Sharekat-e Komedi-ye Iran*) appeared on the theatrical scene of Tehran. As so many other similar groups its purpose was to use its net benefits for good works. It therefore asked permission to stage plays and also asked for the allocation of police agents to keep orders during performance nights. It was one of the companies that gave regular performances and was led by Sayyid `Ali Khan Nasr, who had returned from studies in France. He and his colleagues (Bayegan, Namdar, Zahir al-Dini, Bahrami, Maleki and Sheybani) had chosen comedy as his main repertory, because that was what most people liked. On April 15, 1917 the Comedy Company performed its first play named. In November 1917, it staged the performance of four plays for women to benefit the victims of the drought and famine in Tehran.

---

[46] Kuhestani-Nezhad, *Gozideh-ye Asnad*, vol. 1, part 1, pp. 66-76. On Mo'ayyad al-Mamalek and his works see Amjad, *Teyatr*, pp. 181-262.

[47] Kuhestani-Nezhad, *Gozideh-ye Asnad*, vol. 1, part 1, pp. 77-82; Malekpur, *Adabiyat*, vol. 2, p. 50-53 (they were also known as *Komiteh-ye Javanan-e Iran*).

[48] Kuhestani-Nezhad, *Gozideh-ye Asnad*, vol. 1, part 2, p. 9; Malekpur, *Adabiyat*, vol. 2, p. 53 (other plays were Divanegan-e `aqel; `Aqelan-e divannama, Ehsasat-e javanan-e Irani; Tabeki-ye khodra neshenasim); Osku'i, *Pazuheshi*, pp. 113-14 (with a list of his works).

[49] Kuhestani-Nezhad, *Gozideh-ye Asnad*, vol. 1, part 1, p. 83.

The plays were performed in the afternoons rather than in the evenings as was usual, but also in the Grand Hotel. In the months thereafter the Comedy Company continue to stage plays at the Grand Hotel, one of which was for the benefit of the families of gendarmerie agents killed-in-action. On January 15, 1918 it staged the performance a play "All you do, do it to yourself" (*Harcheh koni beh khud koni*) with the participation of a foreign actress, who performed the song and dance that were part of the play. The Comedy Company is further mentioned in April 4, 1919 when Messrs. Bahrami, Maleki and Mohammad `Ali played the lead roles in "I want to sleep" (*Mikhvaham bekhvabam*) for which new music and songs had been written.[50]

The main problem of the Comedy Company was not lack of interest, because ticket sales went well. The problem was that the Company was too small and depended too much on the willingness of one individual to shoulder most if not all of the responsibilities. The troupe's members were all government officials, who only could devote part of their time to the company in the evenings. This meant that when `Ali Nasr who was the driving force of the group left the theatrical activity also came to an end. The Komedi-ye Iran performed in the Grand Hotel (Lalehzar Street) owned by Mr. Baqerof, which, at that time, was the only theater in Tehran. The rent was 100 *tuman*s per evening and Baqerof also demanded free tickets for himself and his family. The price of a theater ticket was 3 to 15 *qeran*s, which made paying the rent an almost impossible task, for there was no financial help from others. According to Nasr's account, he had to write the play, to play the lead role as well as to be the make-up man. Because he was a government official he occasionally had to leave Tehran on official missions, which meant that the theater did not operate until his return.[51] In November 1921 the Comedy Company announced that after a few months of having been idle it would resume its activities with the help of Armenians, both men and women. Its first play was a novelty, an American comical play named "My Baby." It had been translated by `Ali Nasr under the title *Kuchulu, Muchulu*. `Ali Nasr wrote many plays for his own group, which were also performed by others. These included "Ferdowsi", "Aqa Mirza", and "We are freeloaders" (*Ma moft-khvarim va tofili*).[52] Concretely, the Armenian assistance to the Comedy Company consisted in the acting of Armenian women in the comedy "My baby" (*kuchulu, muchulu*).[53] Furthermore, as part of its new make-up, the Company moved its office to that of the *Sharekat-e Aramaneh* on February 18, 1921. It seems likely that the Company may also have benefited from

[50] Kuhestani-Nezhad, *Gozideh-ye Asnad*, vol. 1, part 1, pp. 84-89; Fekri, "Tarikhcheh I," pp. 147-49 and a photo of the troupe's leading members (Ibid., p. 148). On the famine see Floor, Willem. "The creation of the food administration in Iran," *Iranian Studies*, vol. 16 (1983), pp. 199-227. There is also the sensational and erroneous account by Majd, Mohammad Gholi. *The Great Famine and Genocide in Persia, 1917-1919* (Lanham: University Press of America, 2003).
[51] Nasr, Sayyed `Ali Khan. "Honar-e Te'atr va Namayeshnameh-nevisi dar Iran," *Rahnameh-ye Ketab* 4/4 (1340/1961), pp. 310-11.
[52] Kuhestani-Nezhad, *Gozideh-ye Asnad*, vol. 1, part 2, pp. 167-69.
[53] Kuhestani-Nezhad, *Gozideh-ye Asnad*, vol. 1, part 2, p. 191.

other material assistance from the Armenian community. On January 26, 1921 the Comedy Company announced that every Friday evening it would perform a play. Those that would buy a subscription would receive a 10% discount. The first play of the Company's new program was "The Mazandarani Barber" (*Dallak-e Mazanda-rani*), which had been made more attractive because song, dance and music also were part of the program. The Comedy Company further staged performances by Europeans such as in 1921 when Mr. Ruba, of the [Russian] imperial ballet, Mrs. Aqabayef, and other European actresses played a comedy, danced Salome's Seven Veils' dance, performed a Russian opera, and gave a concert of Iranian music in the Grand Hotel.[54] The Comedy Company also performed plays such as "The Workers" (*Kargaran*) and "Eagle of Governors" (*'Oqab al-Hokama*) with music by the Abakarian brothers. There also were performances of Molière's "The Miser" to benefit the *Zanbil* newspaper and the National Library.[55]

The drama section of *Iran-e Javan* (1921), an organization of progressive intellectuals, who had studied in Europe, also put on plays such as *Ja'far Khan az ferang Amadeh* by Hasan Moqaddam (who also led the group), *Mahpar* by Siyasi and *Dokhtar-e Qarn-e Bistom* by Nafisi. Mr. and Mrs. Taraban [?], Mr and Mrs. Hayak [?], Ms. Loretta, Messrs. Behruz, Fekri and others.[56] After the discontinuance of *Kelub-e Muzikal* and of Komedi-ye Iran due the absence in Europe of 'Ali Nasr in 1925, Mahmud Zahir al-Dini, who was the most renowned comedian of his time and had started his theatrical career with Nasr's Komedi-ye Iran, founded the *Sharekat-e Komedi-ye Akhavan* that performed Molière's play "George Dandin" several times in early March 1925.[57] Also unrelated with the Comedy Company was the *Komedi-ye Parsan* that staged in May 1923 a play called "Dawn of Freedom—Reactionary of the State" (*Shafaq-e Azadi, Erteja' al-Molk*), which was about the contemporary political situation and intrigues. The lead role was played by Simu Simunian.[58] Other groups, such as the *Majma'-ye Adabi-ye Aramaneh* and the *Majma'-ye Javanan* (of the American School), also staged comedies, which were very popular. These plays usually were enlivened by a concert during the intermission.[59]

---

[54] Kuhestani-Nezhad, *Gozideh-ye Asnad*, vol. 1, part 2, pp. 190-91.

[55] Kuhestani-Nezhad, *Gozideh-ye Asnad*, vol. 1, part 2, pp. 190, 192-94.

[56] Fekri, "Tarikhcheh I," p. 149.

[57] Osku'i, *Pazuheshi*, p. 141-43 (Zahir al-Dini died in 1935); Fekri, "Tarikhcheh I," p. 149; Kuhestani-Nezhad, *Gozideh-ye Asnad*, vol. 1, part 2, p. 188.

[58] Kuhestani-Nezhad, *Gozideh-ye Asnad*, vol. 1, part 2, pp. 200-01 (for the benefit of the newspaper *Siyasat*).

[59] Kuhestani-Nezhad, *Gozideh-ye Asnad*, vol. 1, part 2, pp. 204-08 (with a discussion of the comedy *Maktabkhaneh*). The comedy "The Living Dead" (*Amavat-e zendeh*) was performed in Hasanabad school on December 21, 1919. Ibid., vol. 1, part 2, pp. 229-30.

Non-Moslem Theatrical Groups

Non-Moslems dominated the scene in Iranian theater, also after the 1906 Revolution. The most important group was that of the Armenians. They eagerly had embraced Western culture and as the first in Iran saw theater as an educational tool to improve themselves just like Moslems reformers also would do, but later. The Armenians in Iran included both those who were subjects of the shah and there were those who were subjects of foreign nations such as the Russian and the Ottoman empires.

As discussed above, Iranian Armenians already had started performing modern plays in 1878 in Tehran and continued their theatrical activities in the following years. After 1906, Armenians like Moslems had high hopes and they also used theater to promote socio-economic and cultural development among the population. Armenian groups such as the *Sharekat-e Te'atr-e Aramaneh*, for example, performed its plays in the Armenian School in Hasanabad, either in Armenian or Persian, although occasionally plays in Azeri and French also were staged there.[60] They performed Molière's "The Imaginary Invalid" in Persian, and more than 250 people showed up. Thereafter, a second play was performed, "Three Braves" (*Seh Shoja`*), which had been translated into Armenian. Also in 1328/1910, "Nader Shah Afshar" was performed. The women's club associated with the Social Democratic Hanchakiyan party staged performances such as "Disaster or the Bloody Path" (*Faje`eh ya Rah-e Khuni*) by Grigor Yeghikian in 1911 in the Mas`udiyeh together with a comedy "In the Lawyer's Court" (*Dar Mahkameh-ye Vakil*) translated by Haratiun Galustian. It was performed in Armenian, but there was a Persian translation available for the attendees.[61]

The year 1910 coincided with 30th anniversary of the activities of the Armenian playwright Aleksandr Musian Shirvanzadeh. On May 7, 1911 the Armenian community of Tehran organized a major festivity in his honor in Hasanabad and at this event one of his plays was performed. The Club of Theater Amateurs had come a long way since its creation in 1881. As of 1906 the Club of Theater Amateurs even had two locations where they performed, i.e. in Hasanabad and in the Qazvin Gate quarter. It had always been under management of the principal of the Armenian School, but in 1912 the general assembly of the Club decided to become independent of the school.[62]

It was also from the non-Moslem segment of society that female actors originated, for due to strong religious objections the appearance of Moslem women on the

---

[60] Kuhestani-Nezhad, *Gozideh-ye Asnad*, vol. 1, part 1, p. 22.
[61] Malekpur, *Adabiyat*, vol. 2, p. 48 (his wife Asturik Yeghikian was a pioneering actress and opera singer in Iran); Kuhestani-Nezhad, *Gozideh-ye Asnad*, vol. 1, part 1, p. 110.
[62] Hovayan, "Te'atr-e Armaniyan dar Tehran," p. 200.

stage was still not possible. Whereas Moslem women were excluded Armenian women not only visited the theater but also performed in plays as of 1897. The Organization of Armenian Actors and Actresses, for example, gave a performance in the "Museum" for Ahmad Shah and the crown prince in 1913. The performance was in Armenian. Aleksandr Abeliyan, the first Iranian professional actor, led the troupe.[63] There was also a performance of a play in the spring of 1910 at the Ata-bak Park and 500 women, including some Europeans, attended. The purpose was to raise funds for the women's movement, and 400 tumans were raised for a school for female orphans, a women's clinic, and adult education classes.[64] In 1916, the general assembly of the Welfare Club of Armenian Women of Tehran (Anjoman-e kheyriyyeh-ye zanan-e Armani-ye Tehran) decided to establish a kindergarten. Because they had no money they staged a number of plays. They asked Hovhannes Tomasian, a leading performer, to help them. He staged the Azeri musical "The by the yard cloth seller" (Arshin Mal Alan) using members of the Women's Club as actors. First, the musical was played at Hasanabad, but later the Qajar court asked that the performance take place inside the royal harem. To make sure that the women who played male roles (with beards, moustaches, etc.) were really women the court eunuchs frisked the actors. The operetta was performed several times for the royal harem. Later it also was performed at the Grand Hotel for the womenfolk of the nobles and notables of Tehran. Finally, performances took place for the womenfolk of less august Tehrani families. The women who played the major roles were: Arusiak Petrosian (as Soltan Beg), Shushanik Barseghian (Soleyman), Takuhi Sahakian (servant), Arusiak Golnadarian (`Askar), Maryam Negogosian (Neli), Katrin Sarkisian (Khaleh) Lusig Khachaturian (Golchehreh) and Knarig Abovian (Asya).[65]

Although the Welfare Club of Armenian Women of Tehran was dissolved in 1916 the acting women of the Club established a theatical group and staged plays. The Armenian theater in Tehran was reinforced in 1916 when Gaspar Eypakian became the principal of the Armenian School. A short while thereafter he was joined by his brother Armenak. Both of them were actors and helped stage many plays. Gaspar even became mayor of Tehran in 1920, but after a short while he left for Egypt. His brother returned to Russia.[66]

The broad appeal of the Armenian community's theatrical activities also is clear from the fact that it often staged a varied theatrical program in its performances, often in more than one language. For example, in February 1921, the Anjoman-e Adabi va Sana`i-ye Tehran launched its first theater performance with a program consisting of "An Oriental Tragedy" in four acts in French, followed by an Iranian

---

[63] Malekpur, Adabiyat, vol. 2, p. 49 [Ra`d].
[64] A Play by the Anjuman of Ladies of Iran, Iran-e Now April 25, 1910, nr. 187, p. 3.
[65] Hovayan, "Te'atr-e Armaniyan dar Tehran," pp. 200-01.
[66] Hovayan, "Te'atr-e Armaniyan dar Tehran," p. 202.

music concert, then a European music concert, followed by the play "The Striking Smiths" in French, then a recitation of Sa`di's poems, thereafter Salome's dance, and the evening program was concluded by "How to Speak English" a one act comedy in French. The predominance of French that evening probably was due to the fact that many members of the diplomatic community attended the performance at the Armenian School.[67]

Other religious/ethnic groups also occasionally organized the performance of one or more plays to support the educational needs of their community. The Zoroastrians founded their own Iranian Theatrical Company (*Sharekat-e Namayesh-e Iraniyan*). Its first performance was of Gogol's Inspector-General on May 11, 1910 in Atabeg Park. The driving force of this group was Da'i, the Zoroastrian School head, who was generally known as Homayun the Translator. He also wrote plays.[68] In June 1924 the Association of Progressive Zoroastrians (*Hey'at-e Taraqqi-khvahan-e Zartushti*) staged the play "Ferdowsi" in the Grand Hotel to benefit its reading room.[69] The Central Zionist Club of Iran (*Anjoman-e Markazi-ye Sahiyunist-e Iran*) also organized the performance of a play in April 1919 to benefit Jewish education. The play was a comedy, "Excorcising Jinns" (*Tashkhir-e Ajenneh*) and the performance took place in the Alliance Israélite.[70] The American School also staged plays to support its operation such as in December 1921 when it performed "Ferdowsi" a play about the life and work of the great poet by Sayyed `Ali Nasr.[71]

Groups of Foreign Actors

Foreign theatrical groups had even greater influence on the theatrical performances of Iranian artists. There were Armenian and Moslem foreign groups that performed in Iran, and even some European artists. In the fall of 1913 an Armenian group from the Caucasus, under Mr. Iliman, came to Iran and staged some performances in Armenian in the Armenian Hasanabad School in Tehran. The same group also performed in other unnamed Iranian towns, undoubtedly including Tabriz. The group also performed for Ahmad Shah on November 28, 1913.[72] Another of the foreign groups that operated for some time in Iran was that of Ruhollah `Arabeski, a Moslem artist from Baku, who in June 1910 staged the performance of two plays "The Unfortunate Youth" and "Who is Guilty?" (*Moqasser kist?*) in the Armenian Hasanabad School in Tehran. Both plays were advertised as moral Moslem theater. He also performed two plays by

---

[67] Kuhestani-Nezhad, *Gozideh-ye Asnad*, vol. 1, part 2, p. 173.

[68] Malekpur, *Adabiyat*, vol. 2, p. 53.

[69] Kuhestani-Nezhad, *Gozideh-ye Asnad*, vol. 1, part 2, p. 210.

[70] Kuhestani-Nezhad, *Gozideh-ye Asnad*, vol. 1, part 1, p. 152. For other Jewish plays see Ibid., vol. 1, part 2, pp. 230-31.

[71] Kuhestani-Nezhad, *Gozideh-ye Asnad*, vol. 1, part 2, pp. 174-75.

[72] Kuhestani-Nezhad, *Gozideh-ye Asnad*, vol. 1, part 1, pp. 50-51.

`Abdol-Rahim Haqqverdiyof as well as one comedy by Soltan Majid Ghani-zadeh Qafqazi for the youthful Ahmad Shah. All these performances were given in Azeri.[73] `Arabeski and his group then left for Gilan where they performed a play in Enzeli, which earned more than 386 *qeran*s for the Education Club (*Anjoman-e Ma`aref*).[74] This is last we hear about this group.

The next foreign group was that of `Othman Beg Bektashzadeh from Turkey. In June 1914 he was advertised as a famous Turkish Moslem actor, who was accompanied by two actresses from the theater in Istanbul. This group, which performed in Osmanli Turkish, stayed for a few months in Tehran and performed "The Unfortunate Youth" (*Zavaleli chujuq*), "The Son-in-law who had eaten flowers" (*Aldamanash adakheli*) and "National disaster" (*Faje`eh-ye Melli*), a tragedy in three acts, all by the Osmanli Turkish writer Nameq Kamal (1840-88). Malek Sasani wrote a favorable long description and review about one of the performances in the newspaper *Barq*.[75] In June 1915, `Othman Beg had moved to Gilan where he wanted to perform. However, by that time World War I had broken out and the Russian authorities who to all intents-and-purposes controlled northern Iran did not allow him to do so. He had to return to Tehran and from there, presumably, went to the Ottoman Empire in about June 1916 the last time there is a report on the group's activities. But before leaving, `Othman Beg performed a number of plays in the Te'atr-e Melli in Lalehzar Street. One of the plays was `Ebrat-e `Alam* by Tolstoy and the other "They Do not Understand and You Cannot Make Them" (*Nah qayez nah qanderir*) by the well-known Baku actor Uvofski[?].[76]

The outbreak of World War I had, of course, a dampening effect on the willingness and ability of foreign troupes to come to and perform in Iran. Nevertheless, a group of Caucasian actors and actresses came to Resht in December 1917 to stage performances. Because drought raged in Gilan at that time the net proceeds of the performances were allocated for the drought victims.[77] In January 1918 "The Robbers" by Schiller was performed by a group of European actors. Nothing more is known about this event, not even in which language it was performed.[78] In January 1919, under the patronage of Lady Sykes, the wife of the British Minister in Tehran, Leo Norris and his group gave a theatrical performance to benefit soldiers and sailors who had suffered eye injuries during the Great War.[79] In Tehran, in the summer of 1919 a play and an operetta were staged by Ahmad Beg Qamarlinski, who did the

---

[73] Kuhestani-Nezhad, *Gozideh-ye Asnad*, vol. 1, part 1, p. 16-18.

[74] Kuhestani-Nezhad, *Gozideh-ye Asnad*, vol. 1, part 1, p. 107-08.

[75] Kuhestani-Nezhad, *Gozideh-ye Asnad*, vol. 1, part 1, pp. 52-57 (with a description of the story).

[76] Kuhestani-Nezhad, *Gozideh-ye Asnad*, vol. 1, part 1, pp. 57-62, 62-63 (with a review of one the performances, which was considered to have been well acted and moving); Malekpur, *Adabiyat*, vol. 2, pp. 43f.

[77] Kuhestani-Nezhad, *Gozideh-ye Asnad*, vol. 1, part 1, p. 134.

[78] Kuhestani-Nezhad, *Gozideh-ye Asnad*, vol. 1, part 1, p. 134.

[79] Kuhestani-Nezhad, *Gozideh-ye Asnad*, vol. 1, part 1, p. 148.

same in Mashhad.[80] Another foreign group was that of Gholam Reza Sharifzadeh, who started its performances after the coup d'etat of February 1921. He staged historical plays such as "Kaveh the Smith" and "Leyla and Majnun."[81] In 1921, the *Hey'at-e Javanan* performed the play "Appearances and Influence of Love" (*Tazahorat va nofudh-e `eshq*) by Morteza Qoli Khan Farjam. The play was directed by the Russian-Armenian Christopol Ma'ar, who had been living in Tehran for some time. There also was an orchestra with new songs and tunes to enliven the audience's amusement.[82] In October 1925 a theatrical group in the new Republic of Azerbaijan asked for permission to come to Iran. This group was led by actress Leyla Khanom. For that reason the police department refused a visa, because all of a sudden it was considered improper and against religious law for a female to perform a concert in public, unless it was for a female public.[83]

Theater was an expression of committed people. They were not only committed to theater, in fact for some theater was a means to an end, above all the development of Iran and the uplifting of its people, morally, socially, politically and economically. For this reason most theatrical performances benefited a social worthy activity such as a school, equipment for a school, a hospital, orphans, destitute people, reading rooms, library, newspapers or even political parties. It is also for this reason that often the announcements for performances stressed that the play concerned was a moral one meant to bring home a message aimed to uplift people morally, to teach a lesson, to present a political message, or to show a model to follow. The *Sharekat-e Kafeh-ye Laleh-Zar* was founded in 1912 to promote educational and other socially worthwhile objectives that it wanted achieve by staging plays.[84] There were other groups in Tehran that organized the performance of plays, invariably to benefit an educational purpose, orphans, a newspaper, a hospital, or some other public good.[85] Some had more limited objectives. For example, in December 1909, the *Sharekat-e Kheyriyyeh-ye Khvatin-e Irani* organized a performance to benefit the creation of a school for women. However, it ceased to exist due to opposition to the participation of women in acting on stage with men.[86] Sponsors of plays also organized plays within the context of so-called garden-parties.[87]

There also were groups that used theater to promote political objectives, which were not incompatible with the general social objectives that most theatrical

---

[80] Kuhestani-Nezhad, *Gozideh-ye Asnad*, vol. 1, part 1, p. 158.

[81] Kuhestani-Nezhad, *Gozideh-ye Asnad*, vol. 1, part 2, p. 247-49.

[82] Kuhestani-Nezhad, *Gozideh-ye Asnad*, vol. 1, part 2, pp. 213-14.

[83] Kuhestani-Nezhad, *Gozideh-ye Asnad*, vol. 1, part 2, p. 300-04.

[84] Kuhestani-Nezhad, *Gozideh-ye Asnad*, vol. 1, part 1, pp. 111-12,

[85] Kuhestani-Nezhad, *Gozideh-ye Asnad*, vol. 1, part 1, pp. 117; part 2, p. 196

[86] Kuhestani-Nezhad, *Gozideh-ye Asnad*, vol. 1, part 1, p. 107; Malekpur, *Adabiyat*, vol. 2, p. 55.

[87] Kuhestani-Nezhad, *Gozideh-ye Asnad*, vol. 1, part 1, pp. 19, 78f, 95, 99, 117, 119-24, 131-33, 135, 139-40, 147-49 (benefit plays), 137-39, 142, 155 (cost-benefit results of some benefit plays), 109-110, 146, 157. (garden-party).

groups pursued. The *Komisiyun-e Te'atr-e Adabi-ye Ferqeh-ye Demokrat* was, as indicated by its name, affiliated with the Democratic Party. In April 1918 it organized the performance of a play for the benefit of those affected by the famine. The play "The wedding that became a mourning or victims of tyranny" (`arusi-ye mobaddel beh `azza ya qorbaniha-ye zolm), written by Mirza Monazzam al-Molk, was touted as being based on actual historical events and aimed to bring home to the audience the horrors of famine.[88] The Trade Union also had its own theatrical group, which performed all kinds of plays, which they had translated into Persian. The leader of the group was Rezaqoli `Abdollahzadeh (Seyfi), a printer by profession, and member of the Central Committee of the Communist Party of Iran.[89] The government after 1921 also used theater as an instrument to mobilize popular support. After the coup d'etat in 1921, the new government paid for a free-of-charge cinema and theater performance of "Nader Shah Afshar".[90] To laud the role of Reza Khan Pahlavi, and the young national Iranian army, the *Goruh-e Aryan* staged a play about Napoleon's army in Warsaw, a play that glorified a soldier's sacrifice for the nation. There also was an orchestra to conclude the show with national songs.[91] In 1924, after the imposition of central government rule over Khuzestan there were general festivities in Tehran as well as a party for dignitaries during which a play was performed about a girl who was so enamoured with the deeds and progress of the Iranian army that, because she could not marry the army, she forced her fiancée to enlist. A few days later the same play was performed again; there was no fee.[92] By 1925, it was not unusual to start the evening with a song and talk in honor of Reza Khan, the Prime Minister.[93]

Operettas and Musicals

Usually the performance of a play was preceded by some vocal or instrumental musical event and/or closed by such an activity. This combination of drama and music was, of course, standard fare for traditional Iranian theater, as I have discussed in chapter three. Therefore, it is not surprising that both Iranian and European music (e.g. piano pieces) also found their way into the modern theatrical program.[94] This

---

[88] Kuhestani-Nezhad, *Gozideh-ye Asnad*, vol. 1, part 1, pp. 95-96.
[89] *Haqiqat* nr. 55 (April 5, 1922 and advertisement for the play "Kaveh the Smith" (*Kaveh Ahangar*); Ibid., nr. 63 (April 20, 1922 the play "Nader Shah Afshar", and Ibid., nr. 69. (April 30, 1922 a comedy). See also Kuhestani-Nezhad, *Gozideh-ye Asnad*, vol. 1, part 2, pp. 283, 288.
[90] Kuhestani-Nezhad, *Gozideh-ye Asnad*, vol. 1, part 2, pp. 246-47.
[91] Kuhestani-Nezhad, *Gozideh-ye Asnad*, vol. 1, part 2, p. 202-03.
[92] Kuhestani-Nezhad, *Gozideh-ye Asnad*, vol. 1, part 2, pp. 292-95 (with description of the story of the play).
[93] Kuhestani-Nezhad, *Gozideh-ye Asnad*, vol. 1, part 2, p. 300. It was quite normal to treat the shah's portrait as a *locum tenens* for the shah himself as is clear from many examples from similar events involving portraits of Qajar shahs. Floor, Willem. *Wall Paintings and other Mural Decorative Arts in Qajar Iran* (Costa Mesa: Mazda, 2005).
[94] Kuhestani-Nezhad, *Gozideh-ye Asnad*, vol. 1, part 1, pp. 3-5, 9, 13-14ff.

appreciation for musical accompaniment also may have given rise to the demand for what usually was called opera and more often operetta in the contemporary documents. The term often refers to musical comedies that involved acting, dancing, singing, and music making. There also was the performance of the occasional European opera such as *Carmen* in Russian in November 1923 in the Grand Hotel. Mrs. Aqabeyof, the soprano, received many bravos from a mixed Iranian-European audience.[95]

On May 2, 1917 the operetta, *Arshin Mal Alan*, was performed in Tehran three times by a group of actors and actresses led by Mr. Abovian, who had come from Tiflis. The operetta was performed in the Grand Hotel in Turkish with music specially composed for it. This was followed by a second operetta called *Adam and Eve* on June 11, 1917. Before the group left Iran at the end of 1917, it once again performed *Arshin Mal Alan*; one performance was done in Armenian. The group returned six months later, in early June 1918. It once again performed *Arshin Mal Alan*. In the following months the group staged several operettas: "If slanted it's OK as long as it is sweet" (*Kaj olsun, Shirin olsun*); "The foreign lover"; "Asli and Keram"; "Arshin Mal Alan", and "If not that one, then the other will do" (*Olmasun Bolsun*). They were either performed in Armenian or Turkish. Most of these operettas had been written by `Aziz `Abdol-Hoseyn Oghlu Haji-Begof (1880-1948) and were quite poular in the Caucasus.[96]

In early 1919, this group was replaced by one led by Arman Aramian and his wife Mme. Daravian, which left Iran at the end of that year. The group returned to Iran in November 1920. It once again staged *Asli and Keram* touted as an Oriental opera. Another member of the group was Mr. Hovanessian who was assisted by Tehrani amateurs. There were solo songs as well as a choir singing of both European and Causasian songs. Sa`id Nafisi wrote a review of this operetta in 1920.[97] It was at that time that Reza Kamal (Shahrezad) wrote a musical comedy in which Armenian girls played an important role.[98] In November 22, 1920 the Aramiyan group once again and for the last time returned to Tehran and performed *Adam and Eve* in the Grand Hotel.[99] At mid-March 1919 the operetta *Ardashir and Astar* was performed in Persian in the Grand Hotel to benefit Jewish educational programs. The group had its own band and at the end Ms. Mary danced.[100] The group

---

[95] Kuhestani-Nezhad, *Gozideh-ye Asnad*, vol. 1, part 2, pp. 18-20.

[96] Kuhestani-Nezhad, *Gozideh-ye Asnad*, vol. 1, part 1, p. 90-94; Malekpur, *Adabiyat*, vol. 2, pp. 98-120; Osku'i, *Pazuheshi*, pp. 106-08 (with a list of his works).

[97] Kuhestani-Nezhad, *Gozideh-ye Asnad*, vol. 1, part 2, pp. 3-7. The group also performed a tragedy (*jenayat-e `eshq*) and a comedy (Adam and Eve) as one evening program in 1920. Ibid., part 2, p. 7.

[98] Rugan, Heyva. *Kusheshha-ye Nafarjam* (Tehran, 1360/1981), pp. 116-17; see also Malekpur, *Adabiyat*, vol. 2, pp. 98-120.

[99] Kuhestani-Nezhad, *Gozideh-ye Asnad*, vol. 1, part 2, p. 7

[100] Kuhestani-Nezhad, *Gozideh-ye Asnad*, vol. 1, part 1, p. 41.

known as *Komedi-ye muzikal* (1919) produced musical shows, which were modeled on shows performed in the Russian Caucasus.[101]

This was not the end of operetta performances in Tehran, because in February
1920 a group led by Mr. Kostanian performed *Arshan Mal Alan* in Tehran. This
was not the first time, for the announcement stated that the cast had been changed
and now only two of the actors spoke in Turkish, the other would perform in Persian. One of his lead actors was the actress Gol Sabah, who was billed as someone
"who danced and sang." In the following days and months other operettas were
staged such as *Mashhadi `Ebad* (in Persian), "Three Suitors and One Bride," "The
50-year old Youth," and, of course, "Asli and Keram," which was performed in
November 1921. We hear once again about this group in March 1922 performing
"Arshin Mal Alan", and later "Mashhadi `Ebad" and "Anush ya Shirin" in June
1922 and again "Mashhadi `Ebad", "Arshin Mal Alan", "Asli and Keram", and
"the 50-year old Youth" in November 1922. In Dcember 1922 it played "One
Bride and Three Suitors."[102]

As of 1920 Iranian artists got involved in making operettas. The first one was
Qowzi performed in November 1920, which was the first operetta in Persian. This
one was followed by "Doktor Riyazidan" written by Mirza Ebrahim Khan and
written by Ahmad Mirza Khosrovani. It was once again performed in December
1920 by the group Komedi-ye Iran.[103] This was followed in May 8, 1921 by the
performance of "Resurrection of the Iranian Kings" (*Rastakhiz-e Salatin-e Iran*)
by Mirzadeh `Eshqi in the Grand Hotel (Tehran), after its premiere in Isfahan
some time prior to that date. `Eshqi wrote that he had spent almost 800 *tuman*s on
the performance in Isfahan and almost 500 *tuman*s on the Tehran performance.
The decors had been made by student of the art school (*madraseh-ye sanaye`ye
mostazrafeh*). It was once again performed in November 7, 1921, July 19, 1922,
November 24, 1922 a sign of its success among the public. `Eshqi also wrote an-
other operetta named "Beloved beggar boy or Dr. Philantropist" (*Bachcheh
gedha-ye ma`shuq va Doktor Nikukar*), which was also staged. At the end of 1923
`Eshqi's position grew precarious because of his political activities. He therefore
published an appeal for help to aid in the production of "Resurrection"
(*Rastakhiz-e Salatin*). One month later the Zoroastrian Reformers Society
(*Hey'at-e Taraqqi-khvahan-e Zartushti*) announced that the operetta would be
performed again under its auspices. `Eshqi was killed in 1924 (allegedly by the
police for political reasons), which put an end to his promising career as a poet,
playwright and politician.[104]

---

[101] Kuhestani-Nezhad, *Gozideh-ye Asnad*, vol. 1, part 2, pp. 190-92.

[102] Kuhestani-Nezhad, *Gozideh-ye Asnad*, vol. 1, part 2, pp. 80-92.

[103] Kuhestani-Nezhad, *Gozideh-ye Asnad*, vol. 1, part 2, p. 29-33 (with a review by a spectator).

[104] Kuhestani-Nezhad, *Gozideh-ye Asnad*, vol. 1, part 2, pp. 68-79; Osku'i, *Pazuheshi*, pp. 132-34.

Reza Kamal (Shahrezad) was another artist who wrote the operetta *Pari Chehri Pari-zad*, which was performed by almost 30 Armenian actors and actresses. It was announced as a historical drama with musical interludes, which had been arranged by a number of musicians. The lead role (*Pari-chehri*) was played by Mme Aqabeyof, who had been trained in Europe, while that of the Shah was played by Mr. Taraban. [?] The first performance took place in December 1921 in Tehran and another show was given in January 1922 and it got a good review from Sa`id Nafisi. It was once again performed in November 1922 and June 1924.[105] In the fall of 1922 the operetta "The Goddess" (*Elaheh*) was staged in Tehran's Grand Hotel. It had been translated by Mojtabi Tabataba'i. It was again played a few months later with some changes and Mme Aqabayof played the lead role, the rest of the cast consisted in both Moslem and Armenian actors and actresses.[106] In June 1921 the operetta "Mirza Morad" was staged, and once again in July and August 1922. One of its attractions were the ballet dances by Suri Khanom and the new tunes from Isfahan. The other actors were Armenian actresses and Moslem amateurs.[107] In June 1921 Gholamreza Sharifzadeh staged the performance of the operetta "Kaveh the Smith" played by more than 60 Caucasian and Iranian actors and actresses. Dances were performed that had not been seen until then on the stage of Tehran, while its songs were exhilarating. The actors all wore historical costumes especially made for this show. This operetta was again performed in April 1922 by Sharifzadeh's group under the direction of Jahangir Mosavver-Rahmani. Sharifzadeh's group together with the *Hey'at-e Aktural-e Opera-ye Azerbaijan* had performed "Leyla and Majnun" in the Grand Hotel some time before.[108] There were some other performances of operettas, and with those mentioned above are confirmation of the growing success of this kind of dramatic performance in Iran. Well-known actors in this genre of theater included Messrs. Kostanian, Armaninak Shahnazarian, and Mardirestan, of which the former also doubled as director. The most famous actress-singer was Mrs. Sa'u Aqabeyof, whose collaboratrices included European actresses such as Ms. Marie, Ms. Victoria, and Ms. Maniya.[109] Mrs. Sa'u Aqabeyof or Aqababiyan, who, because her lead role in Shahrezad's opera, was also known as Pari, was born in 1900 in Tehran to an Armenian family. She went to Europe to study voice and music at the Conservatory of Charlottenburg (Germany). At the outbreak of the First World War she left for Moscow to complete her studies in voice, ballet and theater at the Imperial Conservatory of Moscow,

---

[105] Kuhestani-Nezhad, *Gozideh-ye Asnad*, vol. 1, part 2, pp. 41-57. Reza Kamal also wrote other pieces such as "Khosrow and Shirin."

[106] Kuhestani-Nezhad, *Gozideh-ye Asnad*, vol. 1, part 2, pp. 12-14; Fekri, "Tarikhcheh I," p. 149.

[107] Kuhestani-Nezhad, *Gozideh-ye Asnad*, vol. 1, part 2, pp. 256-57.

[108] Kuhestani-Nezhad, *Gozideh-ye Asnad*, vol. 1, part 2, pp. 247-50, 268. This group also performed the play "Nader Shah Afshar".

[109] Kuhestani-Nezhad, *Gozideh-ye Asnad*, vol. 1, part 2, p. 10-11.

and later also at Paris and Rome. On her return to Iran she became a member of an Armenian theatrical group, where she did the vocal parts.[110]

In 1922 'Ali Naqi Vaziri founded the *Kelub-e Muzikal* together with Kamal Shahrezad, Gholam 'Ali Fekri, Sa'id Nafisi, Moshfeq Kazemi and some Armenian women such as Pari Aqabeyof, Siranush, Beling, and Loretta. Vaziri was the first male European-trained Iranian. The "Club" staged musicals such as "Rosy-cheeked" (*Golrokh*), "Is the lady sleeping?" (*Khanom Khvabandeh*), "Crazy dreams" (*Ru'ya-ye majnun*), "The suspicious husband" (*Shohar-e Badgoman*), "The bald maternal uncle" (*Da'i-ye Kachal*), "Parichehr and Parizad". The cast consisted of Moslem men and Armenian women and launched the half-century careers of Loretta and Fekri. The purpose of the shows was to provide relaxation and amusement, but was in reality the "Club" was also the main meeting point of literary people, intellectuals and politicians. It had so much such success that its performances could easily compete with films. Due to a fire of the locale the "Club" went out of business after two years.[111]

Tabriz

As one would expect, performances of modern theater started in Tabriz before any other city in Iran, because of the proximity of the large "modernized" Moslem communities in the Caucasus, who had been exposed to western theater and played it themselves too. Theatrical groups from Turkey also performed in Tabriz. Some believe that in 1877 the first modern play was staged in Tabriz, but according to the priest Mesrop Papazian it was two years later. In 1879 to collect financing for the relief of the sufferers of a famine in Van the first play was performed by the Armenian School in Tabriz. Mesrop Papazian was the principal of the school, who practiced the performance of "King Ashot" (*Padeshah-e Ashut*) and "The two hungry men" (*Du gorosneh*) with his students. Although there was neither a theater nor a large room, Papazian used a large space behind his school for the play's performance. A large tent was pitched here and a staged was built. Despite support from the Armenian clergy, some of the members of the school board wanted to ban the performance fearing that the Iranian authorities might close down the school due to this innovation. The tent and stage were taken down and Papazian put them up elsewhere, because he had decided to push ahead with the performance of the play. The play was performed three times in 1879 and collected a net income of eight liras for the people of Van. In 1880 and 1881 other plays were staged that had been translated from French and Armenian. Papazian who had seen the "Merchant of Venice" in Russia wrote a play based on that story called "Court of Justice" (*Dadgah-e 'Adl*), which was performed in Tabriz. Papazian also was the first person

---

[110] Kuhestani-Nezhad, *Gozideh-ye Asnad*, vol. 1, part 1, p. fifteen, note 1; part 2, pp. 3, 6, 10-21, 48, 190-91.
[111] Osku'i, *Pazuheshi*, p. 140; Fekri, "Tarikhcheh I," p. 150.

to have a woman perform on stage, in this case his daughter. This caused much talk among the community.

Because there was no theater in Tabriz performances took place in the house of Tigran Goroviyan, who supported theater in any way he could. One of the principal directors was Abraham Panavulian. Some of the plays he staged included Black Soils (*Khakha-ye siyah*), the Court of Justice and Arshak the Second (*Arshak-e Dovvom*). In 1887-88, Avak Avakian formed a theatrical troupe of 12 persons. He staged a few plays in the salon of the Aramian school, some of which were attended by the governor of Azerbaijan. The performance of "Pepu", which had been translated from Armenian into Turkish by Avakian, was a great success.[112]

On December 27, 1888 it was reported that the Armenian community in Tabriz staged every year 2-3 plays in a hall specially designated for that purpose. The net proceeds were used for the Armenian school. In 1888, Mr. Safrazian and his wife Alma had come from Tiflis with other Russian subjects to give a performance of Othello. This is the first time that we learn of the performance by women in Iran, for one of the star actors was Shushanik Tessian, teacher at the Armenian girls school. The troupe from Tiflis also staged a comedy in Turkish entitled "Brother and Sister." That performance was attended by Amir Nezam, the governor-general of Azerbaijan and government officials and notables. The Amir Nezam gave a donation of 80 *tuman*s for the school to show his appreciation for the play as well as a shawl for Mr. Safrazian and his wife and one shawl for the director of the theater. In 1889 the Safrazians returned to Tabriz where they performed several plays in Armenian, several comedies and Othello in Turkish.[113]

From the above it is clear that the Armenians also aimed their performances at the non-Armenian popupation of Tabriz. This was probably because they wanted higher revenues, for the entire proceeds of the performance served to finance the Armenian school. More spectators meant more income. These spectators were males only, for as yet no women were allowed to attend theater performances. This changed in 1891 when for the first time some Armenian women were allowed into the auditorium. In 1892 the female teachers of the school in the Leylabad quarter staged a play for women only, which was the first time that women actually attended a performance. Thereafter it became accepted that women were among the public in the theater. In the 1890s, both Armenian quarters (Qal`eh and Leyalabad) had a theater where plays were regularly performed. As a result, what the public had considered as a joke so far then became to be viewed as an art

---

[112] Hovayan, Andaranik. "Te'atr-e Aramaneh dar Azarbeyjan," *Faslnameh-ye Te'atr* 18-19 (1378/1999), pp. 167-70.
[113] Kuhestani-Nezhad, *Gozideh-ye Asnad*, vol. 1, part 1, p. 98; Havayan, "Te'atr-e Aramaneh dar Azarbeyjan," pp. 170-71.

form. The theater in the Qal`eh quarter was the oldest; the one in Leylabad was built in 1895. In 1900, the theatrically minded of both quarters merged and created the "Club of Theater Amateurs" (*Anjoman-e dustdaran-e te'yatr*). At the same time a similar musical club was created, which later merged with the "Club of Theater Amateurs." In the following years, the "Club" staged several plays such as "`Arusi-ye Kruchinski", "Scapin", "The death of the mouse" (*Marg-e Mush*), "Under the mask of philanthropy" (*Dar zir-e neqab-e nu`-e dusti*), "Criminal family" (*Khanevadeh-ye khinayatkar*), "Dawn" (*Fajr*), "Medea" (Medaya), "Sister Teresa" (*Khvahar-e Tereza*), "Angelo" and (*Anjelu*). The plays continued to change thereafter and often followed the repertoire that prevailed in Tiflis, the cultural Armenian capital at that time. The proceeds of the performances were used for the upkeep of the Armenian school and social works. The price of ticket ranged from 12 to 20 *qeran*s, which was a lot for most people. Despite this problem, each time when there was a performance the theater was full, and this created the belief that theater was for the wealthy. Most plays performed for the various Armenian communities were translated from French, but one of the most popular ones was "Dawn" (*Fajr*), an original Armenian play by Vahram Papazian. It was about an Armenian farmer in Turkey and was performed twice in Tabriz and once in Salmas. In 1903, the *Anahid* group of Tabriz performed *Hekayat* by Ghazaros Aghaian in the Haigazian Tamarian school.[114]

The Armenians were the first who established a theater, known as the Armaniyan, in Tabriz and staged performances together with Moslems as well as with visiting Caucasian troupes. Performances were in Armenian and Azeri Turkish.[115] The *Hey'at-e Aktorha-e Arameneh* performed "For Honor" by Shirvan Boznadeh. An Armenian orchestra also performed.[116] In 1335/1916-17 several groups such as *Jam`iyat-e Kheyriyeh-ye Azerbaijan* and *Jam`iyat-e Nashr-e Ma`aref, Hey'at-e Nashr-e Sanaye`, Hey'at-e Omid-e Taraqqi* and the troupe *Artistha-ye Dramatik-e Azerbeyjan* came into being. These groups staged performances of pieces such as "Nader Shah Afshar" by Nariman Narimanof and "On the Road of Honor" (*Dar Rah-e Sharaf*) by Shirvanzadeh. The Armenian authors and others wrote in Azeri and later also in Iranian for the Armenian stage.[117]

The following theatrical troupes (*aktural*) existed in Tabriz till 1300/1921.

---

[114] Hovayan, "Te'atr-e Aramaneh dar Azarbeyjan," pp.172-75. For short biography of Vahram Papazian see Osku'i, *Pazhuheshi*, pp. 163-67.

[115] Malekpur, *Adabiyat*, vol. 2, p. 58.

[116] Kuhestani-Nezhad, *Gozideh-ye Asnad*, vol. 1, part 2, pp. 180-84 (with a description of the plot).

[117] Aryanpur, *Az Saba*, vol. 2, p. 290; Kuhestani-Nezhad, *Gozideh-ye Asnad*, vol. 1, part 2, p. 184-85, 215-16 (the musical *Asli va Keram*). For a short biography of Narimanof (1870-1925) see Osku'i, *Pazuheshi*, pp. 104-05. For a short appreciation of Shirvanzadeh as well as the English text of his play 'For the Sake of Honor' see Parlakian, Nishan and Cowe, S. Peters eds. *Modern Armenian Drama. An Anthology* (New York, 2001), pp. xvii-xx, 129-84.

i.   *Aktural-e Kheyriyeh* had been created in 1291/1912 by Hajji Khan Chelebi and others. They put up their plays in the Suli cinema. The troupe also had its own stage in their reading room, which only could be used in summer.

ii. *Aktural-e Tabriz* had been created by Reza Khan Qolizadeh in 1296/1917. Its repertoire consisted mainly in musicals.

iii. *Aktural-e Azerbaijan* was established in 1298/1920 by Boyuk Khan Nakhjevani, and was one of the most active troupes in Tabriz. As of 1923 he continued his work under the name of *Aryan* with Mrs. Liza Yusefzadeh, Messrs. `Ala Kan`ani, Hoseyn Mohandes and many others. Boyuk Khan Nakhjevani had come to Iran after the Russian October revolution, and in addition to playing he also staged performances. One of his memorable roles was that of mad Alexander in the play "The Dead." The troupe proba-bly continued to be active after 1925, because Fekri also implies as much.[118]

iv. *Aktural-e Taleshchiyan* was created by M. Mgrdich Taleshchian and mostly staged European pieces. Aryanpur states that he was a Russian émigré, who performed among others Othello as well as some Armenian plays, which he translated into Azeri.[119] Some of his own plays have survived such as "The tyrannical mother-in-law" (*Madar-e zan-e zalem*) and with Aryanpur he translated "Reputation" (*Namus*). His wife also wrote plays that have been translated such as "The Pumpkin Trader" (*Tajer-e Kadu*), "The Illiterate Servant" (*Khadem-e bihush* or *Khadem-e Haj va Vaj*).

v.   *Aktural-e A'ineh-ye `Ebrat* was created in 1921 and was affiliated with the social-democratic party known as *Ejtema`iyun-e `Amiyun*. Among its members were Jabbar Baghchehban, Ja`far Adib, and Halal Naseri.[120] According to Shafi` Javadi this troupe continued to function and perform until 1306/1927.[121]

There were only three locales where performances were held in Tabriz. One was in the Suli cinema, which had been built in 1900 by Catholic missionaries for film projections. The second one was the summer room in the *Kheyriyeh*'s reading room. The third one was the most important one, i.e. the Armenian theater that had been built in 1915 by M. Aramian, himself an actor and translator of plays and which was the only real theater in Tabriz. One of the well-known playwrights was Mirza Hasan Taji Beg, who wrote plays such as "Dervishes," "Siyavosh," and "Key-Khosrow." The latter was performed in 27 Rajab 1337/28 April 1919. Other plays performed included "Sheykh San`an" by Hoseyn Javid and set to stage by

---

[118] Malekpur, *Adabiyat*, vol. 2, p. 58f; "Tarikhcheh-ye si va panj saleh-ye te'atr dar Iran," part II. *Sal-nameh-ye Pars* (Tehran, 1327/1948), p. 76. On Jalil Mohammad Qolizadeh, the playwright of "The dead", see Osku'i, *Pazuheshi*, pp. 109-112; Malekpur, *Adabiyat*, vol. 2, p. 142.

[119] Aryanpur, *Az Saba*, vol. 2, p. 290.

[120] Malekpur, *Adabiyat*, vol. 2, p. 60.

[121] Javadi, *Peyramun*, p. 209.

Aqa Malof, a Russian.[122] In January 1924 the commander of the Northern Army threw a party for the general public during which a theatrical performance was given highlighting the differences between the old and the new army.[123]

Operettas also found their way to the Tabriz stage, of course. In 1920, *Kheyriyeh* staged in its premises "The Fake Marriage" (*Ezdevaj-e dorughi*), played by actors and actresses.[124] Like in other towns in Tabriz also benefit plays were organized for some social worthwhile purpose.[125] In 1925, the *Kelub-e Shuravi* started giving theatrical performances in Russian and Armenian. It got into trouble, because it had not asked the police for permission for the performance. The police drew up a list of the most important Iranians who were among the audience of 100.[126]

Resht

The population of Resht was much more open to new ideas than that of many other towns in Iran due to the presence of European merchants and many Caucasian traders and workers. Also, through its port Enzeli, Resht was the gateway to Europe. Nevertheless modern theater was performed at a much later date than in Tabriz, Tehran and Isfahan. There had been Caucasian groups that reportedly performed in Resht, but the first play known to have been staged in Resht was "Khaju the Broker" (*Khajuy Dallal*). In 1910 it was performed by a group of Armenians. At that time there was as yet no theater and therefore the performance took place in the storage space (*anbar*) of Dr. Stephanos's house. It is also reported that Nariman Narimov's play "Nader Shah" was performed in Resht as well shortly thereafter.[127] In 1910, Mirza Hasan Khan Naser founded the *Majma`-ye Omid va Taraqqi* in Resht, an organization with broad cultural and educational purposes. He and his association also performed plays. Mirza Hasan Khan Naser translated himself Molière's "The Miser," which was the second play performed in Resht. He translated many more pieces, which have never been published. One of the association's main actors and the first theatrical director in Gilan was Mohammad Hoseyn Da'i Namayeshi.[128] Mirza Hasan Khan was also the teacher of French of the state school (*madraseh-ye dowlati*) in Resht and therefore the

---

[122] Malekpur, *Adabiyat*, vol. 2, p. 61.

[123] Kuhestani-Nezhad, *Gozideh-ye Asnad*, vol. 1, part 2, p. 291.

[124] Kuhestani-Nezhad, *Gozideh-ye Asnad*, vol. 1, part 2, pp. 179-80 (with a description of the plot). Because the document referred to bears no date it is also possible that the year of performance is 1919.

[125] Kuhestani-Nezhad, *Gozideh-ye Asnad*, vol. 1, part 1, pp. 119-21.

[126] Kuhestani-Nezhad, *Gozideh-ye Asnad*, vol. 1, part 2, pp. 197-99.

[127] Talebi, Faramarz. "Namayesh dar Gilan," in ed. Ebrahim Eslah-Arabna. *Ketab-e Gilan* 3 vols (Tehran, 1374/1995) vol. 3, p. 712.

[128] `Askari, `Ali Hajj `Ali. *Tarikhcheh-ye Te'atr-e Gilan (1289-1357)* (Tehran, n.d.), pp. 9-18. For a list of the main members of this group see Talebi, "Namayesh," p. 713. There also was *Hey'at-e Namayesh-e Pazhuhan-e Resht* in May 1911. Kuhestani-Nezhad, *Gozideh-ye Asnad*, vol. 1, part 1, p. 21.

school also performed his translation of "The Miser."[129] The *Taraqqi* society continued to perform till 1335/1916-17. Its program usually included adapted pieces by Molière and Labiche. In total Mirza Hasan Khan Naser had translated 20 French plays. The group also performed pieces by Iranian playwrights including two written by Mirza Hasan Khan Naser entitled "The Warning" (`Ebrat*), a play about opium addiction and "The Effects of Alcoholism" (*Natayej-e Moskar*) a play about alcoholism. In August 1913, the group performed a comedy by `Edalat in Persian in the Huraniyans school. It further had built a small theater in 1912 in the Shams school, where Mirza Hasan Khan Naser was head master. The theater sat 200 persons.[130]

Basile Nikitine, the Russian consul in Resht in 1912, wrote that there was no permanent theater in Resht, but whenever people put up a performance he would go there, so as to improve his knowledge of Persian. He found that the acting was competently done, and that men played all the female roles. The plays were translated from French and showed, according to Nikitine, that Iranians liked French plays. It is probably more likely that they did not have any other plays at their disposal, or the required language skills to translate plays from other languages. Furthermore, it shows that plays by Iranian authors were in short supply, even those that had been written and performed in other towns. Nikitine also attended a play by a local author, a young teacher, about the problems of alcoholism, which he sent to V.A. Zhukovskiy, his professor.[131] During its six-year existence the group staged 14 plays that were each performed 30-35 times.[132] Mirza Hasan Khan Naser also put out a newspaper, *Omid-e Taraqqi*, printed in 1911, which, according to Browne, gave "particulars as to the receipts and expenses of certain theatrical performances.[133]

Shortly after the demise of the *Hey'at-e Taraqqi* another theatrical society, *Refah-e Adamiyat*, was founded by Mirza `Abdol-Karim Khan Na'ini. He directed, acted, and also translated French plays that were performed for the benefit of newly established modern local schools such as *Okhuvat*. This society only existed for a short while, however.[134] One of its former members, `Abdol-Majid Khan Farsad, then founded the *Mohammadiyeh* theatrical society in 1916 to support the *Mohammadiyeh* School. Its membership consisted of Azeri Turks from both Azerbaijans and therefore it differed from other similar societies because its plays were performed in Azeri Turkish. The plays included "Arshin Mal Alan", "Mashhadi `Ebad", "Javan-e

---

[129] Qadussi, *Khaterat-e man*, p. 237.

[130] Kuhestani-Nezhad, *Gozideh-ye Asnad*, vol. 1, part 1, pp. 19-20.

[131] Nikitine, Basil. *Irani keh man shenakhte am* (Tehran, 1329/1951), pp. 127-28. This play undoubtedly is that by Mirza Hasan Khan Naser mentioned above.

[132] Talebi, "Namayesh," p. 714.

[133] Browne, *Literary History*, p. 46; on its importance see Fakhra'i, Ebrahim. *Gilan dar Jonbesh-e Mashrituyat* (Tehran, 1353), p. 51. Keshavarz, Karim. "Javanehha-ye Te'yatr-e dar Gilan," *Rudaki* 22 (1353/1974), p. 7.

[134] `Askari, *Tarikhcheh*, p. 19; Talebi, "Namayesh," p. 714.

panjah sal", "Zandat bi zan", "Karbala'i Qobad" written by `Aziz Haji Beg, his brother Dhu'l Feqar Beg, and other Caucasian writers. `Abdol-Majid Khan Farsad also included an actress (Suna Khanom Qafqazi) for the time in his performances, for which audacity he was declared to be an infidel and as a result he was shunned in Resht. The *Mohammadiyeh* society was dissolved in 1921, but it was replaced by the *Aktural-e Azad* that had been founded in 1923 by Jahangir Sartippur. This new society performed comical plays for the benefit of schools and orphans, but it soon fell apart, despite (or because of) its success among the youth of Resht. To attract the public Azad first had given performances free-of-charge during three months. Some other clubs were also founded such as *Okhuvvat, Golshan, Aktural-e Azad-e Iran*, and *Farhang* who performed a variety of plays and were engaged in other cultural activities.[135]

The most important cultural group was the *Farhang* Club that existed in Resht since 1917. It was composed of artisans and workers. They performed plays by Molière, but also *Arshin Mal Alan* and the like. The *Farhang* Club was an off-shoot of and was associated with the *Sharekat-e `Elmiyeh-ye Farhang* of Tehran and had the same objectives.[136] The *Farhang* club in Resht was founded by Hoseyn Jowdat and led by Karim Keshavarz and received a monthly subsidy of 40 *tuman*s from the Russian Legation.[137] According to British intelligence, "20 per cent are said to be Russian subjects, leading spirit is Keshawarz, Munshi Bashi of the Russian Consulate."[138] According to Karim Keshavarz, it not only had a theater, but also a cinema and reading room. The proceeds of the theater were for used for welfare activities. The club's other activities for the public were gratis. Each week one play was performed. Da'i Namayeshi was the stage director and the translator of many plays was Hasan Naser. Da'i Namayeshi was the driving force behind the theater, although Karim Keshavarz also participated in a number of plays. The Club performed amongst others Horace (about patriotism) and Cinna (about politics) by Corneille, which Keshavarz translated.[139] Da'i Namayeshi further directed plays by Molière, Labiche, and Racine, but also plays by Victor Hugo such as Hernani (romantic piece) and Ruy Blas (about the need for political reform). He also staged *Ja`far Khan az Ferang Amadeh* by Hasan Moqaddam. The *Jam`iyat-e Ma`aref-pazhuhan-e Nesvan* was founded by Mrs. Sari Emami in 1923 as part of the *Farhang* Club. This women's club performed on 15

---

[135] `Askari, *Tarikhcheh*, pp. 21-22; Talebi, "Namayesh," pp. 714, 717; Fekri, "Tarikhcheh I," p. 149 (the musical "The Goddess" or *Elaheh* and its actresses and female ballet dancers). There also was a wrestling club (*Anjoman-e Ferdowsi*) in Resht that staged plays to support its athletic activities. This club still performed plays in 1923. Ibid., p. 717.

[136] Aryanpur, *Az Saba*, vol. 2, p. 290. For a picture of some of the members of the *Farhang* club see Fekri, "Tarikhcheh I," p. 150.

[137] PRO, FO 371/13783, f.85.

[138] PRO/FO 461/72, Intelligence Summary nr. 10, March 10, 1923.

[139] Keshavarz, "Javanehha-ye Te'yatr," p. 6-7; `Askari, *Tarikhcheh*, pp. 28-33; Talebi, "Namayesh," p. 716.

March 1925 "Marriage or The Sale of Girls" (`Arusi ya dokhtarforushi`) in the salon of Olus Beg. It was directed and played by women only. On 23 May 1925 the
women's club played "The Mistaken Marriage" (`Arusi-ye eshtebahi`), while plays
performed therafter included "Rastakhiz-e Salatin", "The hairy bride" (`Arusi-ye
pashmin`), "Asli and Keram", "The Bloody marriage" (`arusi-ye khunin`) in both
Resht and Enzeli. "Tartuffe" by Molière was staged by the *Anjoman-e Peyk-e
Sa`adat-e Banuvan* which was another offshoot of the *Farhang* Club.[140] The
Farhang Club was the second theatrical society that allowed women to perform in
its plays. These were Fatemeh Nashuri, Parirokh Vahdat and Banu Khojastegi. It
is not known when and for how long they performed, for women were still not
allowed to visit theaters let alone perform in them. The decision to allow actresses
to play female roles was the logical consequence of the club's objective to uplift
Iranian women from their downtrodden position. For that reason the club had a
special women's branch, as noted above, which continued to function till 1931,
when the *Farhang* Club ceased to exist.[141]

In January 1918, a group of Caucasian artists was sent by the Musavat Committee
of Baku to Resht to give a number of performances to benefit the poor who were
suffering from the famine.[142] There also was a *Hey'at-e Ta'tral-e Gilan* led by
Mirza Hasan Khan Naser, which performed a play in Tehran's Grand Hotel in
February 1921.[143] In 1924, Mohammad Nashuri founded the *Anjoman-e A'in-e
`Ebrat*, which had both male and female members and lasted about 12 years.[144] In
December 1924, the chief of the municipality of Resht made it known that on Friday nights moral plays would be performed free-of-charge for the public so as to
diffuse better behavior and development.[145] It is not known how long this service
to the public lasted, but it is doubtful that it was for a long time. In 1924 the military commander saw to it that a play was performed several times in Resht about
the incorporation of Khuzestan and the fall of Sheykh Khaz`al, the local magnate.
The same play was performed there once again in 1925.[146]

An important member of the artistic community in Gilan was Grigor Yeghagian.
He translated foreign plays into Persian and also wrote new plays in Persian such
as *Anushirvan va Mazdak*, which was performed in 1924 in the Avadis theater in
Resht by *Kanun-e Iran*. This was a progressive club founded by Mohammad `Ali
Javaheri in 1924. It was also performed in 1930 in the Resht city hall. Yeghagian's

[140] Malekpur, *Adabiyat*, vol. 2, p. 67; Talebi, "Namayesh," pp. 717-19. Da'i-ye Namayeshi died in December 4, 1925. For an obituary see Kuhestani-Nezhad, *Gozideh-ye Asnad*, vol. 1, part 2, p. 170.
[141] `Askari, *Tarikhcheh*, pp. 34-43.
[142] Kuhestani-Nezhad, *Gozideh-ye Asnad*, vol. 1, part 1, p. 134.
[143] Kuhestani-Nezhad, *Gozideh-ye Asnad*, vol. 1, part 2, p. 209.
[144] Talebi, "Namayesh," p. 719.
[145] Kuhestani-Nezhad, *Gozideh-ye Asnad*, vol. 1, part 2, p. 295.
[146] Kuhestani-Nezhad, *Gozideh-ye Asnad*, vol. 1, part 2, p. 311 (it was also played in Tabriz).

other plays also were performed in the Avetis Theater. His impact on theater life in Gilan was very influential for he collaborated (acted, directed and wrote) for practically all groups that were in extensence after 1922.[147]

Many of the plays served to raise funds for good works, mainly educational or to help the poor, such as by the *Hey'at-e Taraqqi* for the Armenian School.[148] There also were performances in Gilan by foreign actors such as January 1918 when a group from the Caucasus gave performances for the benefit of the victims of the famine.[149] An interesting case was the performance in Enzeli in December 1921 for the benefit of Russians who had been plundered, although the document does not state where and by whom.[150]

There also were theatrical activities in other towns in Gilan such as in Enzeli, where allegedly in 1904 the first theater was built by `Amid Homayun, the governor of the town.[151] However, there is no report of any theatrical activity in Enzeli until about 1917, when Mohammad Nashuri and his wife performed there in the theater of `Amid Homayun.[152] In 1918 the *Farhakht* Club started its activities. It was an off-shoot of the *Farhang* Club, which kept regular contacts with it. Like its parent the *Farhakht* Club staged plays, was active in the field of adult education, and in general worked to elevate the level of knowledge of its members. It was probably under the auspices of this club that the musical "Goddess" (*Elaheh*) was performed in Enzeli. The club only lasted 20 months.[153] Also active since 1924 was the *Hey'at-e Majma`-ye Omid va Taraqqi*, of which branches (or at least groups with the same name) existed in Resht, Tabriz and Tehran. It staged a play in Enzeli to support local educational programs.[154] In Lahejan the *Hemmat* Club staged theatrical performances since 1917. The main actors were Matavus, Ferdowsi, Mehdi Lahejan. They performed the "Illiterate Teacher" and "Hypocrisy" (*Salus*); the latter also in Enzeli. In April 1924 it performed a play free-of-charge that was attended by more than 1,000 people.[155] In May 1922, the newspaper *Kushesh* reported that the *Majma`-ye Taraqqi-ye Langerud* aimed to support many local social activities,

---

[147] `Askari, *Tarikhcheh*, pp. 43-45; Talebi, "Namayesh," pp. 717-19.

[148] Kuhestani-Nezhad, *Gozideh-ye Asnad*, vol. 1, part 1, pp. 19-21 (another by the *hey'at-e namayesh-e pazhuhan-e Resht*).

[149] Kuhestani-Nezhad, *Gozideh-ye Asnad*, vol. 1, part 1, pp. 134.

[150] Kuhestani-Nezhad, *Gozideh-ye Asnad*, vol. 1, part 2, p. 195.

[151] Javadi, *Peyramun*, p. 211.

[152] Talebi, "Namayesh," p. 726.

[153] Kambakhsh, `Abdol-Samad. *Nazari beh Jonbesh-e Kargari va Komunisti dar Iran* (Stassfurt: Hezb-e Tudeh, 1972), p. 30; Talebi, "Namayesh," p. 726 (with a list of its leading members); Fekri, "Tarikhcheh I," p. 149.

[154] Kuhestani-Nezhad, *Gozideh-ye Asnad*, vol. 1, part 2, p. 215; Talebi, Namayesh," p. 726.

[155] `Askari, *Tarikhcheh*, p. 27; Kuhestani-Nezhad, *Gozideh-ye Asnad*, vol. 1, part 2, p. 212; Talebi, "Namayesh," p. 728. With the title *Salus* usually "Tartuffe" the play by Molière is meant.

amongst which was the staging of moral plays.[156] In January 1925 it was reported that the people of Langerud with assistance from the Ministry of Education had built a theater at a cost of 5,000 *tuman*s. This is an indication of the importance that the people attached to such a cultural institution.[157]

Mashhad

A few Russian merchants were the first to stage theatrical performances in Mashhad. After the second constitutional movement gradually Caucasian theatrical groups came into being and regularly staged pieces. Under influence of what was happening in Tehran and Resht reformers in Mashhad also thought about having a "salon" and a theater group. In 1911 E`tebar al-Saltaneh Ghaffari built an auditorium, which the Caucasian groups used. Reza Adharbakhshi, of the police department, translated a few pieces that he produced himself. Men who played the female roles, of course, had to have a high and sweet voice and be handsome. Messrs. Akbar Kazemeyn, Mozhdeh, and `Ali Akbar Azhdari fit that bill. Later Mme. Siranush and Mrs. Maryam Gorji joined the troupe. The leader was M. Uganof and the director was Qomerlinski. The auditorium built by Ghaffari could hold 300 people, and apart from theater, films were also shown. Because Mashhad had no public electricity they used carbide lights for illumination when staging operettas.[158] In January 1915 a group of youths staged the performance of two plays, one of which was in Turkish, and both had a social message.[159] A second play-house was built in 1297/1918 on the site now constituting the National Park (*Bagh-e Melli*). It was only for performances during the summer, and was mostly used for concerts. The famous poet `Aref Qazvini is said to have staged one of his plays there, before an audience of notables that included Mohmammad Taqi Khan Pesiyan, the commander of the gendarmerie and Iraj Mirza, the famous poet, who was chief of the revenue department of Mashhad at that time.[160] In July 1919 a Moslem group from the Caucasus (Baku), led by Qomarlinski, performed one or more plays in Mashhad, while it also performed some circus acts. One of the plays was "Real Revenge" (*Enteqam-e Haqiqi*).[161] In December 1924 the commander of the Eastern Army staged a play during an official dinner that was followed by fireworks.[162]

---

[156] Kuhestani-Nezhad, *Gozideh-ye Asnad*, vol. 1, part 2, p. 275; Talebi, "Namayesh," p. 726.

[157] Kuhestani-Nezhad, *Gozideh-ye Asnad*, vol. 1, part 2, p. 310.

[158] Malekpur, *Adabiyat*, vol. 2, p. 68 quoting Homayuni, Mansur. *Sargodhasht-e Namayesh dar Mashhad* (Mashhad, Farhang va Honar-e Khorasan, 1348/1969), p. 5.

[159] Kuhestani-Nezhad, *Gozideh-ye Asnad*, vol. 1, part 1, p. 116 (a young man who had studied became the son-in-law of a commoner, and the other was about a Europeanized merchant).

[160] Malekpur, *Adabiyat*, vol. 2, p. 69 quoting Homayuni, Mansur. *Sargodhasht-e Namayesh*, p. 6.

[161] Kuhestani-Nezhad, *Gozideh-ye Asnad*, vol. 1, part 1, pp. 158-59. There also may have been a performance of play in 1923 in Mashhad as such an event was reported by the Shrine Newspaper (*Jarideh-ye Astaneh-Razaviyeh*) without indicating its location.

[162] Kuhestani-Nezhad, *Gozideh-ye Asnad*, vol. 1, part 2, p. 291.

ՆԵՐԿԱՅԱՑՈՒՄ

ՅՕԴՈՒՏ ԲԱՑՖԻ ԳՐԱԴԱՐԱՆ-ԸՆԹԵՐՑԱՐԱՆԻ

ԻՐԱԳԻՐ

ՄԱՐԻՈԼ ՃՐԱԳՆԵՐ

Դրամա երեք գործողութեամբ

Հեղ. Ալ. Աբելեանի

ԳՈՐԾՈՂ ԱՆՁԻՆՔ

ՎԱՐՊԵՏ ՅԱԿՈԲ	Նախկին աշճատաւորՃ	պ. Արմ. Ցառուփիւնեան
ԱՆՆԱ	Սրա կինը	օր. Եղիս. Խառակլեան
ՆԵՐՍԷՍ	Սրանց մեծ որդին (թագախաւոր)	պ. Հ. Տէր Մարտիրոսեան
ՍԵՐՈԲ	» փոքրիկ որդին	պ. Ալեքսի Հախվերդեան
ՄԱՐԹԱ	» աղջիկը	օ. Կատ. Ցառուփիւնեան
ԱԼԵՔՍԱՆԴՐ	Հարուստ եւ ազատորոշական երիտասարդ	պ. Մ. Մարտիրոսեան
ՎԱՐՊԵՏ ՄԻՆԱՍ	Սափրիչ եւ ժողովրդական բժիշկ	պ. Մարգ. Մարգարեան

ԲՌՆԱՍՏԵՂՆ

Կոմրիկ մի տրաբաշով

Հեղ. Փառնակեսի

ԳՈՐԾՈՂ ԱՆՁԻՆՔ

ՄԻՀՐԱՆ	Թեբուս բանասէգՃ	պ. Ալ. Հախվերդեան
ՅՈԼԱԿ	Կիսակերթ խատտաբան	պ. Մ. Մարտիրոսեան
ԴԱԻԹ	Միհրանի ծառան	պ. Մ. Մարգարեան
ԹՈՐՈՍ	Ցոլակի ծառան	պ. Ց. Ընդրուլեան

ԲԻՖԵՏ (կանխիկ վճարով)

Սկիզբն երեկոյեան ժամը 8 ½ -ին:

Figure 42: Pamphlet announcing the performance of a play in Jolfa (1917)

Isfahan

As in Tabriz here also Armenians were the first who started modern theater. In 1888, a group of young Armenians founded the Theater Club (*Bashgah-e Te'yatr*) in Jolfa/Isfahan. They staged plays in the hall of the central school in Jolfa. In 1890 a new priest, Esayi Astuasaturian, became leader of the Armenian community of Jolfa. He opposed the theater performances and as result no plays were performed for seven years. But in 1897 the board and the teachers of the Armenian school blew new life into theater in Jolfa and started performances again. In November 1899 a "Club of the Friends of Theater" (*Anjoman-e dustdaran-e te'yatr*) was formed complete with its own regulations. It was then also for the first time that it was stipulated that women were allowed to act on stage. As a result of which three Armenian women (Hovsana Simonian, Dezaghik Minassian, and Lusaber Darhagopian) started to take an active part in plays staged by the Club. The first play in which they acted was "Pepo" by Gabriel Sundukian. Although the plays that were performed in Jolfa were of course in Armenian, the Theater Club also made an effort to stage plays in Persian. In early 1900, a play in Persian written by Harutiun Hurdanian was performed in the same school hall. The subject of the play was "Hajj `Abdol-Nabi", i.e. not a translated French melo-drama, but a modern play after the Western model in Persian using an Iranian theme that was popular in the *ru-howzi* branch of traditional Iranian theater. This play was the "ancestor" of all subsequent Isfahani plays based on the so-called *hajji* theme. After 1920 Mohammad Mirza Rafi`i was active in staging plays in Isfahani dialect. These plays, modeled on the "Hajj `Abdol-Nabi" play, were a mixture of Western and traditional Iranian elements and were very popular. The Theater Club also supported Armenian schools and welfare activities in Jolfa out of the proceeds of ticket sales. Not only plays in Armenian and Persian were staged by members of the Theater Club, but as of 1900 also four plays in English were shown (The merchant of Venice, and others). Despite the success of the theater in the cultural life of Jolfa, the Theater Club had its ups-and-downs. It was dissolved in early 1900 and reconstituted in August 1900 under the leadership of Mr. and Mrs. Babayan, but when they left Jolfa the Theater Club once again fell apart. In 1905 the Theater Club was started again with a new charter, which, among other things, stated that it also would have a musical section. The new management renovated the theater, expanded its capacity, and added music rooms. In 1913, the Theater Club celebrated its 25-year anniversary noting that during that period it had staged a total of 94 plays. These included "Arshin Mal Alan", "It has to be this not that" (*In bashad an nabashad*), "Black soils" (*Zaminha-ye siyah*), "The useless kid" (*Far-zand-e puch*), "Secret woman" (*zan-e makhfi*), "Othello", "Samson and Delilah", "Si-yavosh and Sudabeh", "For Honor", "The Cruel Family", and "World of the Blind". Not listed were the plays that had been performed for children. The Theater Club continued its theatrical activities during the next decade. Its program in addition to trage-dies and comedies also included musicals.[163]

---

[163] Mamnun, Parviz. *Seyri dar Te'atr-e Mardom-e ye Isfahan* (Tehran, 1356/1977), pp. 14-17; Ku-shan, Naser. *Tarikh-e Te'atr dar Esfahan* (Isfahan, 1379/2000), pp. 82-86. For the text of the `Abdol-

Unlike other towns the Moslem community in Isfahan was rather slow in developing an active interest in modern theater. It is only in 1296/1917 that a group of young members of the Isfahani elite, guided by the Swedish Lt. Folke of the Gendarmerie, founded a *Sharekat-e `Elmiyeh* led by Mozayyen al-Saltaneh. Its purpose was to bring about freedom and modernization and to do good works. The group had several committees, one of which dealt with theater. Its members included Nayeb `Ali Khan Bitar, Nur al-Din Ostevan, Ziya al-Din Janab, and Mostafa Fateh. The purpose of their plays was to show the difference between the new and old educational systems. Their first performance was in the hall of the first hotel across from the *Madraseh-ye Chahar Bagh*. This first play was a comedy and its first part was a pantomime. It showed a school with a teacher with a large dirty beard with a stick in his hand. With threatening gestures of his limbs and looks of his eyes he cowed and rebuked the students. The latter were a bunch of young and old, blind, bald, and blind boys to portray their poverty. The second part showed also a class, but one of the most modern ones, i.e. the Golbahar School. Its teacher, Ziya al-Din Janab, played the role of teacher in the play.[164] At that same year the *Maghzi* theater group was created that existed from 1917 to 1925 near the Dowlat Gate. Mirza `Eshqi had come from Tehran to Isfahan in 1917 and staged the premiere of his plays (*Rastakhiz-e Salatin* and *Seh Tablo-ye Maryam*) in the Maghzi theater. Plays such as "Rostam and Sohrab", "Bizhan and Manizheh", and "Rostam and Ashkebus" were staged in the garden next to the Sahel (now Africa) cinema. The driving force behind these performances was a number of Isfahani intellectuals. In 1925, Ahmad Moshiri Sadri organized theatrical performances such as "The Foolish Old man" (*Pir-e mard-e bu'l-havas*) with the help of Mohammad Mirza Rafi`i in the officers' club. There also was a theater group called *Aryan* that had been created by militant Communist youths about whose activities nothing is known.[165]

The Jewish community in Isfahan also joined the theatrical fray. Students of the *Alliance Israélite*, led by the Frenchman Adolf Brasseur, also performed plays in its school. They staged, for example, Molière's "The imaginary invalid" as well as farcical comedies and a play about "Rostam and Sohrab." It had been written in 1922 by Hoseyn Kazemzadeh Iranshahr and had been published in Berlin as an attachment to the *Iranshahr* journal. Six years later it was performed in Isfahan. It was performed during four consecutive nights in the hall of the *Setareh-ye Solh* building. Women had also been allowed to attend, but separate from the men. The

---

Nabi play see Ibid., pp. 95-106, which was first published in *Faslnameh-ye Te'atr* 16 (1370/1991); Hovayan, Andranik. "Te'yatr-e Armaniyan-e Jolfa-ye Esfahan," *Faslnameh-ye Te'yatr* 1/17 (1377/1998), pp. 196-214 (also with a Persian translation of the various Regulations of the Theater Club).

[164] Government of Iran, *Iran-Shahr* 2 vols. (Tehran: Unesco, 1964), vol. 1, pp. 923-24.
[165] Kushan, *Tarikh*, p. 107; Forughi, Mehdi. "Namayesh", in Government of Iran, *Iran-Shahr* 2 vols. (Tehran: Unesco, 1963), vol. 1, pp. 920-21.

first three nights had been for the men and the fourth night was for women only. Even the ushers and other staff that night were women.[166]

Kermanshah

In Kermanshah, the first modern play was performed through the good offices of `Ali Khan Zahir al-Dowleh when he was its governor in 1326/1907. The proceeds were about 2,000 *tuman*s, which were given to the Scientific Islamic School (*madraseh-ye `elmiyyeh-ye eslamiyyeh*).[167] There is no news about theater in Kermanshah for another decade until October/November 1917, when the British officer Hale, who had just been transferred from Berjand to Kermanshah attended a theatrical performance in his new posting. He wrote:

> Also, I have been to a Persian play-a product of modernity brought out by the democrats in aid of some educational scheme. One or two of the actors had come from Teheran, but the rest were locally-produced amateurs, including a couple of Chaldeans. The play commenced about nine o'clock and went on till after midnight. It was a representation of life in a provincial town some years back, centring round a pleasure-loving, stupid, ignorant, idle and thoughtlessly tyrannical governor and his rapacious and hypocritical satellites, with a sidelight on the superstitious credulity of a family of oppressed villagers, the greed of the tax-collector, and the ruthlessness of an unfeeling village headman. The whole thing was a satire on the old types and manners and the old system, which persists largely in the present day: it was exaggerated and overdone, perhaps, but it contained many telling points, and was remarkably well acted.[168]

Qazvin

In May 1911, a group of reformists organized the performance of pantomime play to benefit a national public school.[169] In Qazvin, there was only one theater that had been built by the Russians. During the first two decades of the twentieth century theatrical groups performed there. One of them was the *Anjoman-e Parvaresh*, which was founded in 1294/1915 by Mirza Yahya Va`ez-e Qazvini, the editor of the newspaper *Nasihat* and like-minded friends, and with the help of members of the *Farhang* Club of Resht. They performed Iranian comedies and historical pieces and also some European ones, but adapted to Iranian needs, such as: "Shah `Abbas", "Nader Shah Afshar", "Thieves of Iran" (*Dozdan-e Iran*) and `Eshqi's "Resurrection" (*Rastakhiz*). The *Farhang* Club not only staged plays, but it was also active in the field of adult education, and in general worked to elevate the level of knowledge

---

[166] Government of Iran, *Iran-Shahr* 2 vols. (Tehran: Unesco, 1964), vol. 1, pp. 923-24.

[167] Soltani, *Joghrafiya*, vol. 1, p. 353.

[168] Hale, *From Persian Uplands*, p. 210.

[169] Kuhestani-Nezhad, *Gozideh-ye Asnad*, vol. 1, part 1, p. 109.

of its members. After the coup d'etat of 1921 the Club ceased its activities.[170] In December 1921 the *Jam'iyat-e Namayesh-e Pazhuhan* announced the performance of a play in Qazvin for the benefit of educational purposes. There is no mention of activities by this group thereafter.[171] The *Anjoman-e Parvaresh* remained idle till 1925 when it resumed its activities. It announced that intended to perform various historical and moral plays such as "Shah 'Abbas"; "Nader Shah"; "Dozdan-e Iran"; "Rastakhiz" and "Shoja' al-Dowleh".[172] However, nothing is heard about its activities anymore, so it is quite likely that the *Parvaresh* Club was discontinued.

Other Towns

In Salmas, it was the Armenian community who organized the first performance of a modern play. In 1894 a theater was built in the village of Haftvan. At that time it was one of the best and most beautiful theaters in Iran. In other Armenian communities large tents were pitched if a play was performed such as in 1900 in the village of Qal'eh-sar. In 1904 such a theater was constructed in the village of Payajuk, and another one in Molham [?] In the year 1904-05 no less than 15 plays were performed in Salmas such as "Window" (*Ruzan*), "Extinguished lights" (*Cheraghha-ye khamush shodeh*), "The criminal man's family" (*Khvanevadeh-ye mard-e khinayatkar*), "The lion's cub" (*Aslan Balasi*), "For the sake of the Crown" (*beh khater-e taj*), and "Noble beggars" (*Gedayan-e ashrafzadeh*). In Orumiyeh the first modern play was performed in 1897. After an intermission of five years performances were restarted in 1902 by a group of theater enthusiasts. These staged two plays, the proceeds of which and some financial help from others served to build a theater. In Khoy, near the Armenian school a small, but adequate theater was built. In Ardabil and Maragheh Armenians staged performances in the school courtyard for many years. In general it may be said that each rural Armenian community in Azerbaijan that had a school also staged theatrical performances in the early 1900s.[173]

Although it took somewhat longer for the Moslem population to initiate modern theatrical activities outside the main cities these finally also found its place there. In July 1915 a group of reformers organized the performance of a play in the Rowshan school in Ardabil, which was also attended by the Russian consul-general, his wife and other Russian officials.[174] In February 1918 a play was performed in Hamadan for the benefit of the gendarmes and educational purposes. In 1923 several plays were performed by school students for social purposes.[175] In

---

[170] Varjavand, *Simay*, vol. 3, pp. 1926-27.

[171] Kuhestani-Nezhad, *Gozideh-ye Asnad*, vol. 1, part 2, pp. 186-87.

[172] Kambakhsh, *Nazari*, p. 30; Varjavand, *Simay*, vol. 3, p. 1926 (with a list of the names of the most important members); Kuhestani-Nezhad, *Gozideh-ye Asnad*, vol. 1, part 2, p. 313.

[173] Hovayan, "Te'atr-e Armaniyan dar Azarbeyjan," pp. 185, 188.

[174] Kuhestani-Nezhad, *Gozideh-ye Asnad*, vol. 1, part 1, p. 116.

[175] Kuhestani-Nezhad, *Gozideh-ye Asnad*, vol. 1, part 1, p. 145; part 2, pp. 286-87.

Astara in June 1922 the theatrical society of Astara (*Hey'at-e Teyatral-e Astara*), which had been created probably around 1917 by a number of graduates from the town's modern school, performed a play to mobilize funds to equip the school and a reading room.[176] In April 1922, to benefit the indigent patients of the hospital in Mazandaran a play was performed. Although no town was specified the performance probably took place in Amol raher than in Barforush. For one year later a number of youths organized the performance of `Eshqi's *Rastakhiz-e Salatin* in Barforush in the karavanserai of Mohammad Esma`il Kolbaba'of. It was the fist time that a theatrical performance had been given in that town.[177] In July 1921, Armanak Eypakian on his way back to Russia stopped in Bandar-e Gaz for one week. With the assistance of Aleksander Huhasian, Maniya Tadarizian and his wife he staged the performance of Schiller's "The Bandits."[178] Undoubtedly more theatrical activities have taken place in these and other towns (given the role of theater in society ascribed to it by the reformers) about which, as far as I know, nothing has been reported. There also were towns where there apparently there were no theatrical performances at all, such as in Bushire and Shiraz.[179]

MAIN CHARACTERSTICS OF THEATRICAL LIFE IN LATE QAJAR IRAN

Theater was alive and kicking in late Qajar Iran. As during the pre-1906 period Armenian actors and actresses dominated theatrical life. Numerous plays and musicals were performed. In Tehran, for example, each year at least 15 plays and other forms of modern theater were offered to the public between 1917 and 1925. The number of actual performances was much higher, because the same play often would be performed more than once in the same month and/or year.[180] The relatively lively theatrical scene in Tehran and elsewhere in Iran prompted a number of writers to translate Europeans plays to be staged by the various troupes. But they also wrote their own original Iranian plays. The most important playwrights of the late Qajar period included Fekri Ershad Mo'ayyad-al-Mamalek (1871-1919), who wrote five plays that focused on social ills and political corruption prevailing in Iran.[181] Other contemporary playwrights included Ahmad Mahmudi Kamal al-Vezareh (1875-1930), who wrote a number of plays, among which Master Nowruz, the Cobbler (*Ostad Nowruz-e Pinehduz*). It was written in 1919 and clearly was modeled after the traditional *baqqal-bazi* farce. It was also the first play that used the argot of southern Tehran. In his Hajj Riya'i, or the Oriental Tartuffe (*Hajji Riai Khan ya*

---

[176] Kuhestani-Nezhad, *Gozideh-ye Asnad*, vol. 1, part 2, p. 211.

[177] Kuhestani-Nezhad, *Gozideh-ye Asnad*, vol. 1, part 2, p. 75, 269.

[178] Hovayan, "Te'atr-e Armaniyan dar Azarbeyjan," p. 202.

[179] Kuhestani-Nezhad, *Gozideh-ye Asnad*, vol. 1, part 2, p. 267; Hudi, Rahim. "Pishineh-ye Te'yatr-e Novin-e Shiraz ta sal-e 1359," in Homayuni, Sadeq ed. *Yaran* (Shiraz: Navid, 1384/2005), pp. 232-44.

[180] Kuhestani-Nezhad, *Gozideh-ye Asnad*, vol. 1, part 2, pp. 220-62.

[181] Amjad, *Teyatr*, pp. 179-286. For a short biography of Ershad and a list of his works see Osku'i, *Pazuheshi*, pp. 115-16.

Tartuf-e Sharqi; Tehran, 1918) Khan Kamal al-Vezareh presented an Iranian Tartuffe.[182] Hasan Moqaddam (1898-1925) published, under the pseudonym `Ali Nowruz, his "Ja`far Khan Has returned from Europe" (*Ja`far Khan az Ferang Amadeh*). This successful comedy ridicules the Europeanized Iranians that put on European airs and speak Persian with French words to project an image of a modern man.[183] Its first performance at the Grand Hotel, Tehran, on 23 March 1922, was an important event in the history of the modern theater in Iran. Another important playwright was the poet Mohammad Reza Mirzadeh `Eshqi (1894-1924), who used drama as a literary genre in several of his works such as "Ideal" (*Idi'al*), "Black Shroud" (*Kafan-e siyah*) and the musical drama "The resurrection of the Iranian kings" (*Rastakiz-e salatin-e Iran*; Tehran, 1916), which conjured up the spirits of the pre-Islamic Achemenian kings of Iran.[184]

Actors were mainly amateurs, although professional actors and actresses from the Caucasus and even some from Europe also performed in Tehran. This interaction improved, of course, the acting skills of the amateurs. There also were a few professional Iranian actors and even an Iranian actress/vocalist. Armenian artists had paved and shown the way for and to modern theater, and other Iranian actors followed. At first the Armenian community kept to its own, but after the 1907 Constitutional Revolution there was increasing direct co-operation. However, Armenian artists continued to lead with innovations, which was facilitated by the fact that they had easy access to the fully-developed artistic scene in the Caucasus in particular and Russia and Europe in general. The lack of home-grown professional artists was felt by all groups. In 1922 graduates of the Armenian co-ed school of Tehran established a Club of its graduates. Ardu Tarian organized for those interested in theater a Dramatic Studio. This was the first attempt to create a permanent training center for dramatic art in Iran.[185]

Comedy was one of the main preferences of the public and especially many French plays were performed over and over again. Slowly plays from other countries (Russia, UK) also became part of the repertory, but these remained marginal as compared to the French plays. Historical tragedies, especially evoking episodes of the history of Iran, were also very popular. The musical/operetta had also enormous appeal and they would remain part of the variety of theatrical fare offered to the public. To satisfy the demand a great many Iranian playwrights started

---

[182] Amjad, *Teyatr*, pp. 287-372. For a short biography of Kamal al-Vozareh see Osku'i, *Pazuheshi*, pp. 117-18.

[183] Javadi, Hasan ed. *Hasan Moqaddam va Ja`far Khan az Ferang Amadeh* (Oakland, 1984) with a French translation by Hasan Moqaddam himself; Browne, *Literary History*, vol. 4, p. 463. Kuhestani-Nezhad, *Gozideh-ye Asnad*, vol. 1, part 1, pp. 31-40; part 2, pp. 100-163; Osku'i, *Pazuheshi*, pp. 140.

[184] For other plays and a discussion thereof see Javadi, *Satire*, pp. 261-67; Kuhestani-Nezhad, *Gozideh-ye Asnad*, vol. 1, part 2, pp. 59-79.

[185] Huyan, "Te'atr-e Armaniyan dar Tehran," p. 204.

writing a substantial number of comedies, moral plays, tragedies and musicals, many of which became part of the regular repertory. Iranian playwrights made use of, among other things, current affairs to convey their message such as a play about the bandits Na'eb Hoseyn and Masha' Allah Khan Kashani that was performed in December 1919 in Tehran.[186] Comedies also made fun of existing conditions such as "Uncle Rajab has become a child" (`Amu Rajab bachcheh shodeh) that poked fun at dentists and chemists.[187]

Attendance data are lacking for most performances, but in 1909, 100 people attended two comedies performed in Azeri in Tehran. This was not just a play to laugh, but also had a moral message. Also, at the end of the play one of the actors held a detailed talk about constitutionalism and freedom. Some 250 people attended the performance of a play in Armenian at the Hasanabad School.[188] At the attendance of another play the crowd was so large that people pushed to get in, the more so because more tickets had been sold than there were chairs. Many people therefore had to stand to attend the performance. A contributing factor to the confusion inside the theater was that the tickets were not peculiar to a numbered seat, but only to a class of seat. These usually include first, second and third class (darajeh). The best seats in the house (loge and the first row) usually were reserved for notables. The performances were stopped for regular pauses, so that the actors could take a rest and the audience also could drink a cup of tea.[189] In case of plays for women the latter were asked to leave their small children at home. Only children of 10 years of age and above were allowed to attend.[190] Although women attended some of the theatrical performances they would do so completely veiled. It is not clear how the various actresses were dressed when they did their performances; either acting, singing and/or dancing. Since most of them were non-Moslem and non-Iranian it may be that some measure of liberty as to their veiling was accepted, as is implied in a letter to the editor of the Shafaq-e Sorkh newspaper. However, none of the texts that I have consulted for this study say anything about this issue.[191] The matter is not made much clearer either by the organization of the first masked ball by Iranians in Tehran on June 11, 1925. Such an event implies that [a] women were present and [b] that they wore no veil, but nothing of the kind is revealed by the document that contains this information.[192] It seems unlikely, because the government of Reza Khan became much more restrictive with regard to foreigners, in particular foreign female artists. It opposed the com-

---

[186] Kuhestani-Nezhad, Gozideh-ye Asnad, vol. 1, part 2, p. 229.

[187] Kuhestani-Nezhad, Gozideh-ye Asnad, vol. 1, part 2, p. 299.

[188] Kuhestani-Nezhad, Gozideh-ye Asnad, vol. 1, part 1, pp. 105-06.

[189] Kuhestani-Nezhad, Gozideh-ye Asnad, vol. 1, part 1, pp. 25, 31-32.

[190] Kuhestani-Nezhad, Gozideh-ye Asnad, vol. 1, part 1, p. 107.

[191] Kuhestani-Nezhad, Gozideh-ye Asnad, vol. 1, part 2, pp. 277-78, 280 (another letter to the editor states that the rumor that Persian women participated unveiled in plays in the American school were not true; also because no plays had been perfomed at the school).

[192] Kuhestani-Nezhad, Gozideh-ye Asnad, vol. 1, part 2, p. 300.

ing to Iran of a non-Moslem female artist and her troupe from Baku, unless she only would play for a female public.[193]

Despite a lively theatrical life in Tehran, and for that matter in the major provincial capitals, there was no dedicated theater in Tehran other than the hall of the Armenian school in Hasanabad, which was the center of Armenian cultural activities. The auditorium of the *Dar al-Fonun* was not available for unknown reasons and therefore the Hasanabad hall was of great importance. It was the only non-governmental location where theater could and was performed regularly in Tehran. Other locations also were used, such as the hall Zahir al-Dowleh's house, the hall in Atabeg Park, the hall in Mas`udiyyeh Park, Rusi Khan's cinema and other private locations, but these were indicental rather than permanent solutions to the problem of the lack of a fixed theater in Tehran. As 1911, plays were also performed in a room above the Farus press in Lalehzar Street, and as of about 1919 in the hall of the Grand Hotel in the same street. The latter auditorium also was referred to as the Baqerof Theater after the name of the owner of the Grand Hotel.[194] As I have mentioned when discussing theater in the various provincial towns the situation was not much different there and the actors made do with halls and locales that were available to them.

The success of modern theater did not escape the notice of the fiscal authorities either. As of February 1918 a 5% tax was imposed on ticket sales. Because so many, in fact practically all, performances were staged to benefit some social objective some of the social groups affected by the fiscal imposition asked and received a tax waiver. In fact, in 1921 the government decided to use part of the revenues from the tax on theaters for educational purposes. It is not know how long this regulation remained in effect.[195]

Although permission had to be asked to perform a play censorship was relatively light during the late Qajar period (1907-25). Plays were not allowed to be performed during Moharram and Safar, the two holy months of mourning.[196] Similarly when the British suppressed the Islamic 'revolt' in Iraq in August 1923 the government ordered the halt of all theatrical performances for one week.[197] From the few remaining documents relating to supervisory activities by the government of Iran as to the contents of the plays it would seem that officials looked at political sensitivity and morality. These officials of the publications office (*edareh-ye entaba`at*) were attached to the Ministry of Education and policical bureau (*sha`beh-ye politiki*) of

---

[193] Kuhestani-Nezhad, *Gozideh-ye Asnad*, vol. 1, part 2, pp. 300-05.

[194] Kuhestani-Nezhad, *Gozideh-ye Asnad*, vol. 1, part 1, pp. 8, 10, 14, 15, 22, 44-45, 75, 103-06, 111, 135, 129, 147, 152.

[195] Kuhestani-Nezhad, *Gozideh-ye Asnad*, vol. 1, part 1, pp. 144, 156; part 2, pp. 251-55.

[196] Kuhestani-Nezhad, *Gozideh-ye Asnad*, vol. 1, part 2, p. 237.

[197] Kuhestani-Nezhad, *Gozideh-ye Asnad*, vol. 1, part 2, p. 288.

the Police, of which the former was the responsible political body. On December 31, 1921 the government laid down rules to regularize the supervistory process. (1) two copies of each play had to be submitted; one to be kept in the National Library; (2) the text had to be written in a legible hand; (3) the text of the play has to be submitted at least 15 days pior to its performance date; (4) text in a foreign language had to be submitted with a Persian translation (two copies); and (5) the name of the author or translator as well as the names of the actors have to be written on the back. In addition to the government imposed the use of Persian terms instead of European ones such as: *Namayesh* instead of *te'atr* [theater]; *sahneh* instead of *sen* [scène]; *bazigar* instead of *actor* [actor]; *san`atgar* instead of *artist*; *qat`eh* instead of *piyes* [*pièce*]; and *taghazzali* instead of *lirik* [lyrical].[198]

The government was also convinced of the educational value of theater. In 1924, A`lam al-Dowleh, an official of the Ministry of Education proposed to create a school of dramatic arts in each town based on the model of the Paris Conservatory. He referred to the fact that a similar proposal had been made 30 years before in Tehran, i.e. to include such a subject within the musical program of the *Dar al-Fonun*. Although the proposal was considered to be an important and necessary one it was not acted upon, also because the Minister wanted to create such an institution in the *Negarestan*, where already an art school existed.[199]

Reza Shah Period (1925–1941)

The relative freedom that people had enjoyed after the Constitutional Revolution came to an end with the establishment of the Pahlavi regime in 1925. The new ruler, Reza Shah, did not tolerate any dissent; he only wanted support for his drive toward modernization of the country. This meant that he wanted to portray the country as a modernizing state to the outside world. In chapter three I have discussed the ban or discouragement of the performance of many of the traditional theatrical performances, because these did not fit Reza Shah's image of modern Iran. Modern theater suffered from a similar attitude. Galunov reported that the main police department of Iran was very strict promoting government policy and applied censorship very diligently. The police opposed anything that it considered to be vulgar. For example, gramophone disks had been released with the performance of "two Persian plays concerning the Anderun, in particular 'The Wheat Flower' (*Gandom Gol-e Gandom*) ... They were very popular and widely distributed. The police banned further recording of such plays finding the theme vulgar and discrediting art in the eyes of Europeans."[200] Satire was not tolerated, unless it was aimed at the backward previous Qajar dynasty, and because each play had to

---

[198] Kuhestani-Nezhad, *Gozideh-ye Asnad*, vol. 1, part 2, pp. 60-61, 219-25.
[199] Kuhestani-Nezhad, *Gozideh-ye Asnad*, vol. 1, part 2, pp. 296-97. The art school was the one founded by Kamal al-Molk, which was housed in the *Negarestan*.
[200] Galunov, "Neskolk'ko slov," p. 310.

be cleared by the censors, drama found an outlet in the writing and performance of patriotic and historical dramas eulolizing the glories of the past.

As in the late Qajar period, authors had to submit their script to the government, i.e. the Ministry of Education, Foundations and Fine Arts (*vezarat-e ma`aref va owqaf va sanaye`-ye mosta`rafeh*). One of the reasons that plays did not pass censorship was that there was a high turnover of censors (*momayyez*), who each had their own agenda. The published government documents of this period do not provide evidence that there existed a clear detailed policy and guidelines what was permissible. The personal opinion of the censor therefore played a major role in the decision to allow performance. Usually three criteria were applied: (i) artistic value (*fanni*), (ii) moral value (*akhlaqi*), and (iii) appropriateness (*moqtaziyat*) and the decisive comments were quite succinct such as in one case: (i) artisitic value: no good; (ii) moral value: medium; and (iii) appropriateness: good. This particular play was allowed to be performed, because it was only for a school. Even after permission had been received to perform a play, the theatrical group needed to adhere to a number of rules such as to inform the Ministry in writing five days prior to performance.[201]

In 1927 there came an end to theater in the Armenian language. For in that year the government closed all parochial schools such as Armenian schools and banned theater performances in Armenian. Of the Armenian theatrical groups only *Zowj-e Gustiniyan* continued to perform, but in Persian. Until that year some seven such groups had existed.[202]

The continued amateur nature of much of the theater world is evident from the fact that many plays still were performed for the benefit of some public group such as the Tehran football club, the women's reading room and library, the Golestan newspaper, uniform clothing (*lebas-e motahhed al-shekl*) for the poor, and the Red Lion and Sun hospital.[203] Also, theater was still mainly an affair of the elite and not of the population in general. The majority of the population was poor and could not afford the luxury of the price of a ticket to benefit the football club and other elite institutions. This is clear from where the plays were staged as well as from the outlets for the sale of the tickets were clearly not locations frequented by the poor. They consisted of, for example, chemistry shops, bookstores, barbershops, newspaper offices, libraries, cultural clubs, merchant offices, and many

---

[201] Mir-Ansari, `Ali and Ziya'i, Sayyed Mehrdad eds. *Gozideh-ye Asnad-e Namayesh dar Iran* 2 vols. (Tehran, 1381/2002), vol. 2, pp. xv-xvi, 97, 202-03, 219 (two tickets had to be reserved for officials of the Ministry; not later than two days after the performance a report had to be submitted to the Ministry), 226, 228-29; see also Osku'i, *Pazhuheshi*, pp. 157-58.

[202] Hovayan, "Te'atr-e Armaniyan dar Tehan," p. 209.

[203] Mir-Ansari and Ziya'i, *Gozideh-ye Asnad*, vol. 2, pp. xvii-xviii.

modern stores (*maghazeh*). In total some 75 of these outlets were mentioned in the published documents of this period.[204]

Despite the difficulties under which theater had to operate no less than 40 different locations in Tehran were listed where plays were performed, while some 20 different theatrical groups were active during the Reza Shah period.[205] This indicates a high level of activity and of public interest, which is also implied by the high number of ticket sales points in Tehran. To respond to this interest a large number of playwrights wrote new Iranian or translated existing European plays. Data from published government's files show that some 320 plays had been submitted to it for review during the 1925-41 period, or an average of 20 plays per year, which is quite a considerable output. These plays were written by some 112 playwrights who are mentioned by name in the same documents.[206] Government documents further list a total of 110 artists related to modern theater in Tehran. These included directors, actors, singers, conductors, dancers and musicians, which shows that theater during this period consisted of more than the performance of a play, as is also clear from contemporary descriptions.[207] Most of the aspiring playwrights were not experienced in their craft, and although familiar with Western plays, from a literary, artistic, and theatrical point of view many of their plays were immature. It has been suggested that apart from experience and schooling in this craft that the heavy censorship constrained their ability to properly express themselves. This seems to be a weak argument, for the same shortcomings were also evident in the plays written about acceptable themes (to both the government and the reformers) such as the need to improve social and educational conditions. Iranian critics took their playwrights to task for not adhering to traditional literary standards.[208] Indeed Hoseyn Qoli Mosta`san, an active playwright and director, in an article written in 1935 listed ten problems under which theatrical life in Iran suffered and which had to be overcome, he argued, before it would become a viable force for both educational and entertainment purposes. The ten problems included: (1) need for sufficient funds; (2) knowledgeable playwrights with psychological insight; (3) trained and experienced directors; (4) competent actors; (5) properly equipped theaters; (6) public interest as a result of the previous five items; (7) foundation of theatrical clubs and troupes whose aim should not solely be financial; (8) special laws regulating the behavior of actors. Mosta`san admitted that there were of course some good directors and actors, but there were not enough of them and they were handicapped by the other constraints mentioned to develop new talent and good performances. Because he saw art in general and theater in particular as a non-commercial occupa-

---

[204] Mir-Ansari and Ziya'i, *Gozideh-ye Asnad*, vol. 2, pp. xvii, Index 12.

[205] Mir-Ansari and Ziya'i, *Gozideh-ye Asnad*, vol. 2, Indices 10 and 11.

[206] Mir-Ansari and Ziya'i, *Gozideh-ye Asnad*, vol. 2, Indices 2 and 5.

[207] Mir-Ansari and Ziya'i, *Gozideh-ye Asnad*, vol. 2, Index 1.

[208] Mir-Ansari and Ziya'i, *Gozideh-ye Asnad*, vol. 2, pp. xix, xxi, Index 3 (list of theater 'critics' and summaries of their pieces).

tion, he therefore pleaded for government support to resolve all these shortcomings, so that theater might flourish in Iran.[209]

Hasan Javadi distinguishes three 'types' of plays during the Reza Shah period. First there were historical ones, second, romantic musical plays and finally, didactic social comedies. Sadeq Hedayat and many others wrote plays on episodes from the history of Iran. The former, Iran's foremost author wrote, for example, two plays *Parvin Dokhtar-e Sasan* (Parvin, the daughter of Sasan, 1928) and *Mazyar* (1933), both plays nationalistic in tone and having as their theme the Arab invasion of Iran by the Arabs in 640 CE. Romantic musical plays such as "'Abbaseh, Amir's sister" (*`Abbaseh khvahar-e Amir*) were written, for example, by Reza Kamal "Shahrezad", who wrote many more of that type. And, finally there were didactic social comedies that basically supported the new regime's modernizing efforts (women's emancipation, hygiene, education), while contrasting them with the backwardness of the past. Sayyed `Ali Nasr, who later was hailed as the father of modern Iranian theater, wrote many of those plays such as *`Arusi-ye Hoseyn Aqa* (1939). Another playwright was Dhabih Behruz (1891-1971) whose satirical and comical play *Jijak `Ali Shah* criticized social conditions.[210] Less well-known now, but quite successful in the 1930s were playwrights such as Qodrat Mansur, Rasam Arzhangi, Ahmad Gorji, Baharmast, Mohtasham and Mohammad Khan who wrote a large number of plays, which were also regularly performed.[211]

Thus, it would appear that despite the constraint of censorship modern theater was alive and well in Iran. Mrs. Merrit-Hawkes who toured Iran in 1934 took the time to get acquainted with Iranian theater. While in Shiraz she was staying in a hotel where a theatrical troupe from Tehran also had taken up residence. She had discussions with the actors and became interested in their show. Merrit-Hawkes sent for a ticket, but a soon as it had been brought she was offered a complimentary seat. Because so little is known about the actual performance of theater in Iran during the 1930s I quote her observations about her theater visit.

> When I arrived all the seats were taken, so I was put into a niche at the end of the hall called a box, where the balustrade was broken and the floor covered deep with nutshells and cigarette ends."

> "The actors had come down from Tehran as a temporary touring company, doing a mixed show of dancing, singing, music and acting. Most of

---

[209] Mosta`san, Hoseyn Qoli. "Namayesh dar Iran va `Elal-e Enhetat-e An," *Salnameh-ye Pars* 1314/1935, pp. 128-143.

[210] Javadi, *Satire*, pp. 267-68 (with short characterizations of each play). It was published as *Jijak `Ali Shah ya Owza`-ye sabeq-e darbar-e Iran* (Piedmont: Jahan Books, 1985). For a similar classification see Osku'i, *Pazhuheshi*, pp. 155-56, who also provides a short biography of Reza Kamal Shahrezad (Ibid,, pp. 153-54).

[211] Fekri, "Tarikhcheh II," pp. 73-75 (with a partial list of their most successful plays).

the men were handsome, but the women were rather heavy and stodgy. … The occasion was historic, for it was the first time that women had appeared on the stage at Shiraz, all their parts up to that point having been taken by men. Special permission for this innovation had been obtained, with great difficulty, for Shiraz had passed through a period of controversy with regard to women." "The show took place in one of the local cinemas. In front of the ordinary seats were placed a row of French drawing-room chairs on which the great and the very greatest sat. The very greatest was the local head of the army." […] "*Kalemkars* were draped in front of the stage." […] "The men sat on the left, the women on the right, whether the greatest or the cheapest, so the women's side, as everyone wore the black *chadar*, was somber except for a few children under twelve who wore very gay modern clothes." [there also was a man who sold ice-cream, tea and lemon juice] "The show began with a solo dance, a European affair with a few Eastern gestures thrown in; the girl was graceful, although too abdominal for our taste, but not charming, for her blue knickers looked as if they might have come from Woolworth's and the skirt had been made from the curtain of Miss Aspidistra's front parlour. How the house did enjoy the very carefully arranged splits. But she had lovely eyes. […]

The second time was a woman singing to the accompaniment of a piano, the kind that in England is forgotten in the nursery, with the bottom front knocked out, two violins and the *tar*. The first violinist was a clever, delightful player and a most charming man. The singer sat in an arm-chair, behind a table covered with a white tea-cloth, on which were two pots of flowering stocks. […] Her singing was purely Persian, little lip movement, but much use of her mouth as a resonator. […] She stood up in recognition of the applause, never smiling." […] "Then followed several plays, selected scenes from Molière and plays written by a few actors. The acting was excellent, showing strong Russian influence. It was curious, in that cinema in a little Persian town, to feel one was back in the Arts Theatre at Moscow. There was laughter at old men's animosity and cupidity, there was rejoicing when a woman kissed the man she loved and not the one who had bought her, there were jibes at the chadar [veil]. A recurrent and much-loved joke was:

'So you are a father once again?'

'Yes; unfortunately it is one's duty to sleep with one's wife sometimes.'

The man who wrote the plays wanted a changed Persia.

The actors were an intelligent group of men, who were keen about their profession, although, as yet, acting is much looked down upon in Persia. But
they had hope of a great future as the country became more enlightened.[212]

Although quasi-profesional acting troupes as the one seen by Mrs. Merritt-
Hawkes gave performances also in other towns, the Reza Shah period was not a
very encouraging context for theater to thrive in. Professional theatrical groups
did not really exist yet.

Tehran

Some 20 theatrical groups existed during 1925-41 in Tehran,[213] but in reality only
a few groups were able to stage regular performances. The most important ones
are listed in Table 2.

Table 2: Name and year of founder and founding of leading theater groups in Tehran

Name group	Year of founding	Name founder
Komedi-ye Iran	1296/1917	Sayed `Ali Nasr
Kelub-e Muzikal	1301/1922	`Ali Naqi Vaziri
Komedi-ye Akhvan	1302/1923	Mahmud Zahir al-Dini
Jame`eh-ye Borbad	1305/1926	Esma`il Mehrtash
Sirus	1308/1929	Aradashes Nazarian
Nakisa	1307/1928	Aflatun Shahrokh
Estudiyu-ye Deram-e Kermanshah	1309/1930	Mir Seyf al-Din Kermanshahi
Markazi	1310/1931	Aflatun Shahrokh and Kheyrkhvah
Iran-e Javan	1311/1932	Shahrezad and Aqabeyof
Kanun-e San`ati	1311/1932	Fekri, Nushin, Loretta and Kheyrkhvah

Source: Osku'i, *Pazuheshi*, p. 146.

Komedi-ye Iran was a holdover from the Qajar period having started in 1917 (see
above). In 1924 it had even performed before Reza Khan, who was then Minister of
War and one year later the new Shah of Iran. In 1925 the group ceased its activities
due to `Ali Nasr's travel to Europe, but on his return in 1926 the Komedi-ye Iran
was back in business again. The new cast of actors included Hoseyn Kheyrkhvah,
Asghar Garmsiri, Sadeq Bahrami and the first Moslem women, Moluk-e Hoseyni
and Shekufeh. The group was the most active one, for it gave two to three performances per month. It staged many translated European plays, in particular those by
Molière as well as the plays written by Nasr himself. Komedi-ye Iran stopped performing in 1930 due to stricter censorship, financial problems and Nasr's support of

---

[212] Merritt-Hawkes, O. A. *Persia—Romance & Reality* (London: Nicholson & Watson, 1935), pp. 59-
63. Not all of the male visitors went to see the play, however, for according to Mrs. Merritt-Hawkes,
p. 129, "Although the Persians go to Julfa to dance, to see plays, to watch the girls at the cinema." The
most well-known actresses in 1931 were Loretta and Varto Tariyan, both Iranian Armenians. Jahed,
Salnameh-ye Pars 1310/1930-31, p. 101.

[213] Mir-Ansari and Ziya'i, *Gozideh-ye Asnad*, vol. 2, Index 12.

the Pahlavi regime.[214] Published government documents further mention new groups such as the *Kanun-e San'ati*, *Terup-e Pari*, *Iran-e Javan*, and *Kelub-e Fer-dowsi* and that in an intermittent fashion only. It also happened that a company of foreign actors was invited to Iran at the expense of a philanthropic society to put up shows for their benefit.[215] Other theatrical groups that are mentioned, but not listed in the published government documents, included that of the *Barbod Society*, started in 1926 by Esma'il Mehrtash, a musician. *Jame'eh-ye Barbod* was founded in 1926 inspired by the success of *Kelub-e Muzikal*. Mehrtash attracted a number of promising youths such as Moluk Zarrabi, Abu'l-Hasan Saba, Daryabegi, Javad Torbati, Fazlollah Bayegan and 'Abdol-Hoseyn Nushin. The group staged plays such as "Leyla and Majnun" and Khosrow and Shirin" by Javad Torbati, which had been adapted as musicals. The group existed for eight years till 1934 and was later revived in 1946.[216] Another theatrical group not mentioned in the published government documents is the *Cyrus Studio*, which started in 1929. This may be the same as *Te'atr-e Sirus* (or *Te'atr-e Melli-ye Iran*). In 1927-28, the permanent theater *Nakisa* was founded by Arbab Aflatun Shahrokh, which is not mentioned in the published government documents either. It was a collaborative operation between the *Tamasha-khaneh-ye Zartushtiyan* and the *Komedi-ye Akhavan*. Performances were given in the old auditorium of the Zoroastrian community. Among the collaborators the 'usual suspects' were present such as Loretta, Zahir al-Dini, Fekri, Kheyrkhvah, Mosiri [?] and other old actors of *Komedi-ye Akhavan*. It was only in 1932 that the group adopted the name *Nakisa* and by that time they performed in the auditoriums of the Grand Hotel, Niku'i and Sepah. Although, according to Fekri, most of the plays that the Nakisa group performed had a commercial objective they also produced serious plays such as "The Merchant of Venice", "Nader Shah", and "Abu Moslem Khorasani" by Aflatun Shahokh and "Ghayath-e Kheshtmal" by Ebrahim Khan Nahid.[217]

In 1930, Mir Seyf al-Din Kermanshahi founded the Kermanshahi Drama Studio (*Estudiyu-ye Deram-e Kermanshahi*). He had learned the theater trade, in particular that of making decors, in Moscow, Tiflis and Baku. After the death of his wife Boyuk Khan Nakhjevani invited him to Tabriz where he worked for the "Sun and Lion Theater." Then he was hired by *Jame'eh-ye Barbod* and after some time he worked for *Nakisa* and other theater groups in Tehran. Finally, he began to work as an independent. Kermanshahi introduced the use of the term "studio" in Iran and also the making of attractive professional decors. The "Studio" worked among others with Mohammad 'Ali Soltani, Rahim Namvar, 'Ali Adhari, and the

---

[214] Osku'i, *Pazuheshi*, pp. 144-45; Fekri, "Tarikhcheh II," pp. 79-80.
[215] Mohammadi, Ahmad. "Negahi beh Tarikh-e Namayesh-e Iran," *Honar va Mardom* 129-130 (1352/1973), p. 24.
[216] Osku'i, *Pazuheshi*, p. 147; Fekri, "Tarikhcheh I," p. 151.
[217] Mohammadi, "Negahi beh Tarikh," pp. 23-24; Fekri, "Tarikhcheh I," p. 151 (with a photo of some of its members); Fekri, "Tarikhcheh II," p. 80.

actresses Iran Daftari, Helen and Maryam Nuri and Niktaj Sabri. The group went out of business due to a variety of other reasons such as financial, artisitic, organizational, locational and not to forget the competition. For example, when "Studio" staged its play *Leyla and Majnun* in secret its competitors were rehearsing the same play at the same time. Although probably unrelated to this event, Kermanshahi committed suicide in 1932.[218]

In that same year Reza Shahrezad, Fekri, Habib Ettehadiyeh, Eskandaripur and Mohammad Shams founded the "Acting Club" (*Kanun-e San`ati*). They collaborated with Messrs. Nushin and Mohtashem and actresses Loretta and Maryam Nuri who earlier (1928) had founded "The Theatrical Society of Iran" (*Hey'at-e Te'atral-e Iran*). They performed various plays such as "`Aziz and `Azizeh and `Abbaseh" by Shahrezad, "Whimsical" (*Hardam bil*) by Fekri, "The Imitators" (*Mardom-e Eqtebas*) by Nushin, "Turandot" (*Turandokht*) by Rahim Namvar as well as "People" (*Mardom*) and "Leyla and Majnun." In 1934 they performed Othello benefiting from the presence of the Russian actor Papaziyan in Tehran in the *Palace* Theater.[219] For the occasion of the millenary of the poet Ferdowsi Messrs. Fekri, Ahmad Dehqan and Ahmad Gorji in collaboration with Mrs. Pari Aqababof and Mr. Garmsiri founded the *Kelub-e Ferdowsi*. They staged a performance of "Rostam and Sohrab" written for the occasion by Fekri based on the story from Ferdowsi's epos. The performance in the Niku auditorium was followed by performances of plays written by Forughi and based on others stories from the *Shahnameh*.[220]

In 1936 and 1937 a number of new Iranian plays were performed by other groups. The most outstanding one was *Fereshteh* by Hoseyn Qoli Mosta`san with songs and music by Amir Jahed.[221] It is not clear whether in cabarets also theater performances were given, for in Tehran in 1936, "there are numerous cabarets, with Hungarian, Roumenian and White Russian artistes, all competing at different restaurants."[222]

Some 30 locations in Tehran are known where plays have been performed, but these were not all regular performance halls. Twelve were high schools, eight were theaters, four were cinemas, two were cafes, two were hotels, and four were educational institutes. The most important location was Lalehzar Street, where at least four venues existed where performances were given. Of these thirty locations only the following performance halls are mentioned numerous times: *Salon-e Zardushtan, Kanun-e Banuvan, Gerand Hotel* (Lalehzar), *Namayeshgah-e Markazi-ye Lalehzar*, and *Honarestan-e Pishegi*. The other locations are only mentioned once or some at most five times. What is of some import is that women groups and minorities (Armenians,

---

[218] Osku'i, *Pazuheshi*, pp. 146-52; Fekri, "Tarikhcheh I," p. 152; Fekri, "Tarikhcheh II," pp. 80-81.
[219] Fekri, "Tarikhcheh I," pp. 152-53; Fekri, "Tarikhcheh II," p. 81.
[220] Fekri, "Tarikhcheh I," p. 153.
[221] Fekri, "Tarikhcheh I," p. 153 (with a photo of the group).
[222] Emanuel, *The Wild Asses*, p. 272.

Zorastrians) were strongly represented.[223] Despite the ban on performances in Armenian, theater life in the Armenian community remained strong. In January 1931 Margo Kostanian staged and directed a play named "The Terrible Woman" (*Zan-e Makhuf*). She was the second Armenian Iranian woman to do so. Misha Kostanian founded that same year a theater group known as the theater group of Armenian Artists (*Goruh-e Te'yatr-e Honarpishegan-e Deramatik-e Armani*). With this group he performed plays such as "The Roman Emeror" and "Othello" in the Armenian Club. In 1932 Kostanian continued to perform plays and operettas in Persian and in Armenian, which had been allowed again as a performance language. Other Armenian theatrical groups also came into being that year and staged performances.[224]

Robert Byron may have seen the Kostanian performance. He reported that he attended on January 22, 1934 a theater performance. "To increase the tedium, there has been a performance of Othello in Armenian. The chief part was taken by Papatzian, a Moscow star, who certainly upheld the Muscovite reputation for finished acting. The rest were local amateurs, and knowing no other models of our bygone costumes, had dressed themselves after the Europeans in the frescoes at Isfahan."[225] According to a contemporary, the *Kanun-e Banuvan*, which had been created in 1935, only occasionally staged theatrical performances. This means that at the other locations performances most likely were even less frequent.

Because there are so few descriptions of actual performances in Iranian theaters I therefore reproduce here one by Janet Miller about her visit to a theater in Tehran in 1932. This and her other description of a play not only gives a view of the acting, the costumes, and the outlay of the theater, but also of the décor, the stage props, and the popularity of theater in Iran at that time. It further shows that female actors were a fixed part of the cast and that female spectators, be it veiled, also visited these theaters showing modern plays.

> We went to a Persian theater last night. We had tickets for the same performance the night before, but Mr. Benfeld, one of the young Americans in Tehran, and I were later than the rest of the party in reaching the, and we found the doors closed. The manager told us that it was the last scheduled performance, but, because so many people had been disappointed, the play would be repeated the following night and urged us to come back.
> Last night we arrived just at the moment when a Persian mob—having been refused entrance—was tearing down the wall enclosing the open-air theater. We flattened ourselves against another wall to watch this disgraceful per-

[223] Fekri, "Tarikhcheh I," pp. 152-53; Mir-Ansari and Ziya'i, *Gozideh-ye Asnad*, vol. 2, Index 13. The high incidence of the listing of these locations is also reflected in that of their parent organizations. Ibid., Index 12.
[224] Huyan, "Te'atr-e Armaniyan dar Tehran," p. 210.
[225] Byron, Robert. *The Road to Oxiania* (London, n.d. [1937]), p. 143. Byron's Papatzian probably is Vahram Papazian, who indeed played this role see Osku'i, *Pazuheshi*, p. 167.

formance. Suddenly we heard a sound which was a cross between the roar of a lion and the bellow of a hippo. [It was a policeman who cleared the place with blows and kicks. The policeman ordered the theater to be opened because] he wanted to see the play that had created this battle royal.

Curiously enough, it was about Joseph and his brothers. Joseph is the Mohammadan ideal of manly perfection. The first scene showed him being sold into slavery. It was, without doubt, the most realistic piece of acting I ever saw. Joseph was not so convincing—probably because he was not wearing his coat of many colors, but a white-and-black *abba*. He made a long, but very fine, speech to his brothers just before he was carried to Egypt. This was dramatic and well done. One of the brothers wept, but the other paid no attention, being busily engaged in quarreling over the money.

Pharao's audience-hall was next show—on a revolving stage. Pharao was not so true to life as the brothers. The drapery which covered the furst step of the throne became disarranged, early in the scene, and disclosed a rough plank resting on two boxes. No one took the trouble to replace it. Naturally this detracted from the general effect. The father of Joseph was a splendid old patriarch.

The Koran version of the story differs slightly from that in the Bible. In the last scene the heroice became blind. Just who she was or what connection she had with the rest of the play, I never knew; but Joseph summoned an angel from heaven to heal her. The stage was darkened and a small dark green angel appeared, with round featherless wings and en electric-light bulb in her hair. She healed the blind lady. Then Joseph—who was supposed to be in love with her—gave her a half-heartened embrace, and kissed her as if she were a hot brick, and the curtain went down and the performance was finished.

The play began at seven-thirty and lasted three hours and thirty minutes.[226]

Between 1933-38 the *Alliance Française* was also active in promoting theater with the help of a few Iranians and a number of French diplomats, such as Mrs. Godard, Messrs. Brasseur and Molinari. The plays were performed in French in the building of the Alliance in the Mokhber al-Dowleh Street. One of their successful plays was that of "The girl who sold chocolate", which had already been performed by regular Iranian theatrical troupes.[227]

---

[226] Miller, Janet. *Camel-Bells of Baghdad* (Boston-New York, 1934), pp. 235-37.
[227] Fekri, "Tarikhcheh II," p. 73.

اولین تئاتر دائمی ملی ایران

" سیروس "

بنابتقاضای جمعی از خانمها محترمه و آقایان محترم برای دومین دفعه

در روز پنجشنبه ٥ دیماه ١٣٠٨ ساعت شش و نیم بعدازظهر

ماهپار

با

یك قربانی دیگر

درام اجتماعی در سه پرده - بقلم آقای علی اكبر سیاسی

تحت نظر صنعتی آقای ٢. آ. آریزاد -

باشتراك :

مادام لالا ــ (ماهپار)

سوفلور اقای شاهپریان   مادام د. گیور گیان - (فیروزبخت)   اقای ٠٠. - (ثمیر علیخان)
آقای ص. فرامند ــ (فرامند)   آقای ح. خیرخواه ــ (معین)   اقای م. صفامنش ــ (مشهدی قربان)
آقای کیوان فر ــ (دکتر)   آقای ص. بهرامی - (مستشیر دیوان)   اقای طایفت ــ (فراش پست)

گذارشات ماهپار مربوط به پانزده سال قبل میباشد

قیمت بلیط از سه قران تا سی قران ——

تماشاجیان محترم باید بلیط خود را درتمام مدت نمایش برای ارائه بمفتشین نگاه دارند

محل فروش بلیط

شعبه بلیط فروشی تئاتر سیروس مغازه بن ار خیابان لاله زار نمره تلفن ١٣

روز نمایش از ٢ ساعت بعد از ظهر در بلیط فروشی تئاتر سیروس

درب ورود چهار راه قوام السلطنه ــ کوچه شامرخ

Figure 43: Pamphlet announcing a performance by Cyrus, the first permanent national
theater of Iran (1929)

Tabriz

According to Shafi` Javadi, there was very little theater activity in Tabriz until 1941. Published government documents mention performances at the National Park (*Bagh-e Melli*) and the Hall of the Red Lion and Crescent organization.[228] Other than that, performances appear to have been limited to a few plays by school clubs in the Persian language. The problem was the actors were not fluent in Persian and therefore they mostly played comedy pieces. Also, because most people did not yet appreciate the value of theater and many considered it a joke.[229] There were, however, musical performances in the modern hotel of Tabriz. It had an orchestra that played a limited repertoire of European music, mostly Strauss waltzes. One of its actors had a good tenor voice.[230]

Resht

The vibrant theater life in Resht suffered a serious downturn after 1925 due to increased censorship that discouraged directors, actors and playwrights. Some performances took place in City Hall and the Royal Theater (*Baladiyeh*; *Te'atr-e Shahenshahi*). Official oppression became even more pronounced when in 1928 some of them were banished to other parts of Iran, which finally led to the dissolution of the *Farhang* Club in 1931.[231] During the entire 1931-41 period there was little theatrical activity in Resht. Some of the actors of the previous period occasionally staged performances. In particular `Ebadollah Khan Ranjbar with his daughter and son-in-law were active in this regard (Mehdi Komod). Another group was the *Anjoman-e A'in-e `Ebrat* that had existed since 1925 and was led by Mohammad Nashur. In 1929 he produced "Who is right?" (*Haqq ba kist?*) from Yeghikian. Most of the plays they staged were comedies and musicals or a combination thereof. When Ranjbar finally gave up theater, due to the very strict censorship, Nashur continued to stage a few plays till 1936. There also was the occasional from professional troupes from Tehran such as *Kanun-e San`ati* in 1933. However, despite these activities theater life in Resht was all but dead.[232]

Qazvin

With the opening of the cinema in Qazvin in 1307/1928, theatrical groups also used it to perform plays. The cinema owner, Arbab-e Barzu hired a man known as "the little brother of Ahmad Lister" at 100 *tuman*s per month to make the scenes and decors. `Abbas Mo'asses and his group, among others, performed in this theater. There also were performances in the salon of the Armenian school, in particular after Ostad

---

[228] Mir-Ansari and Ziya'i, *Gozideh-ye Asnad*, vol. 2, pp. 17, 29.

[229] Javadi, *Peyramun*, pp. 209-11.

[230] Koelz, *Persian Diary*, p. 168.

[231] `Askari, *Tarikhcheh*, p. 45; Mir-Ansari and Ziya'i, *Gozideh-ye Asnad*, vol. 2, pp. 20-21.

[232] `Askari, *Tarikhcheh*, pp. 55-57; Talebi, "Namayesh," p. 719; Fekri, "Tarikhcheh II," p. 75.

Janbaziyah, who had been expelled from Russia, became its director. There also were occasional performances in the basement of the Municipality building in the 1930s, including the "opera" `Omar Khayyam.[233]

Ardabil

In a conservative town like Ardabil there was no modern theater. However, even there theater finally arrived in 1929 when Mirza Gholam Torkpur and Reza Aqa Sheykh al-Eslami organized the performance of a modern play. Out of fear of the reaction of the religious conservatives the female roles were played by young men dressed up as women. The performances did not last long due to lack of interest. When the Russians came in 1941 some plays once again were performed by, for example, people like Hasan Artist to benefit teachers who were without school supplies.[234]

Kermanshah

Another name connected with the beginning of theater performances in Kermanshah is that of Mir Seyf al-Din. He returned to Tabriz from Tiflis in 1309/1930. He then moved to Tehran where he came into contact with the first attempts of theater. There he learnt the trade and then put on a performance of "Leyla and Majnun" and later one of "Khosrow and Shirin" with Daryabegi and Ms. Moluk Zarrabi. Mir Seyf al-Din then decided to work on his own and opened his own theater. He did various plays such as "Yusef and Zoleykha," "Mashhadi `Abbas," and "`Aiziz and `Azizeh" which had professional decors. On July 26, 1933 he performed "*Arshin Mal Alan*" that had been translated at his request. He died two days later; he had just been told by the government either to abandon theater or to leave Iran.

However, Mir Seyf al-Din was not the first to organize a theater in Kermanshah, but a group known as *Hey'at-e Te'atral-e Aramaneh* led by Mirza Taqi Khan. They performed at the opening of the first normal school in Kermanshah. The school's hall also served for later performances. They also wrote pieces and taught acting to those interested. The group became serious when GholamReza Parsa took over its management. One of the plays that he put on was "Napoleon." The group continued to perform till 1320/1941. In 1323/1944 they started to rehearse for "The doctor in spite of himself" and later also staged plays such as "The Merchant of Venice." Parsa also used Armenian women for female roles for the first time in Kermanshah. There also were other groups that put on performances in the 1940s.[235]

---

[233] Varjavand, *Simay*, vol. 3, p. 1926-27.
[234] Safar, *Ardabil*, vol. 3, p. 258.
[235] Soltani, *Joghrafiya*, vol. 1, p. 353-54.

**Figure 44: Announcement of the performance of the play "Ghayath the Brickmaker"
in Jolfa (1936)**

Isfahan

On the occasion of the inauguration of the Sa`di high school in 1927 in the presence
of the Minister of Education, `Ali Asghar Hekmat, the musical "Good and Evil" by

Nezami was performed. The Sa`di high school remained a center of theatrical activities led by Mohammad Mirza Rafi`i. Other plays performed at the school included "Zal and Rudabeh", "Sham` and Parvaneh" that were performed as musicals. The music was arranged and performed by `Abdol-Hoseyn Barazandeh.[236] There also were other theatrical activities in Isfahan. Janet Miller attended what she called a theater-party in Isfahan in 1932 and gave the following description of her experience of what probably was a performance of "Nader Shah Afshar".

> Arriving at the theater, we went through a gate, past the box-office, and through another gate into a large park. At the far end was the open-air theater. A tea-garden occupied the rest of the park.

> Many small tables were placed on the four sides of two large pools of water. Swimming on the surface were a number of swans. Willow-trees drooped over the pols. It was cool and delightful there. We sat at a table and ordered refreshments. The swans came out of the water and associated with the humans in a fraternal manner, like a flock of geese.

> The Persian orchestra kept up a continual squeaking that set my teeth on edge. Some Mohammadan women hurried past the tables with their veils closely drawn over their faces, and took their seats at a place far to one side of the stage, especially reserved for them. It rejoiced my heart to see them in a place of amusement.

> Finally the gong sounded and we took our seats before the curtained stage. Never in any theater have I seen more georgeous costuming than I saw in that Persian theater.

> The play opened with a scene in Delhi. It was the story of the Koh-i-Nur which is pre-eminently the greatest diamond of romance and history in the world. The dazzling magnificence of an East-Indian Court was shown in the first act. The peacock Throne was there, in which thr Koh-i-Nur was originally set to form one of the eyes.
> The second scene showed Nadir Shah obtaining from a woman of Emperor's Mohammad's harem the secret that the Emperor wore the diamond concealed in his turban. ... This was a beautiful scene. The Persian conquerer was wearing a robe so covered with gems that it dazzled the eyes. Toward the end of the scene he removed his headdress and handed it to the Emperor, idicatign that an exchange of turbans was expected. The moment was intrensely dramatic and was well acted. Not by so much as a flicker of an eyelid did the Emperor betray his emotion, but with a deep salaam presented his turban to Nadir Shah.

---

[236] Kushan, *Tarikh*, pp. 110-11.

The last scene showed Nadir Shah in his georgeous tent with his court round him. It showed the dancing-girls and the musicians and all the regal splendor in which he lived. Thye scene was beautiful, but it was tremendously drawn out, while we sat there devoured by the desire to know whether or not the turban contained the diamond, and frantically hoping that the extremely good-looking Mogul Emperor had managed to remove it.

At last Nadir Shah was alone and unfolding the turban he found the diamond as he expected. With raptire he held it high above his head and exclaimed: 'Koh-i-Nur! Koh-i-Nur! and the curtain descended amid the wildly enthusiastic applause of the Persians and the disappointment of the Americans. ... It was one o'clock when we reached the hotel.[237]

The Armenian community also continued its theatrical performances, although at a much lower level of frequency than before. Performances took place in the hall of the Armenian school of Jolfa (*Salon-e Madraseh-ye Aramaneh*). The year 1936, when all Armenian schools were closed in Iran and the performance of plays in all languages other than Persian was banned, meant the end of Armenian theater in Isfahan for the time being.[238] When Reza Shah visited Isfahan in 1935 he attended a theatrical performance at the Sa`di school that included both poetry declamation and dramatic performances. In 1939, Molière's "The Miser" was performed, which was translated and directed by Hoseyn `Arizi.[239]

Mashhad

Between 1935 and 1938 theater was mainly organized by Abu'l-Hasan Amir Ebrahimi, with the help of Mrs. Siranush and Messrs. Azhdari and Zarinfar had founded the Artists Group (*Goruh-e Honarmandan*). They staged their plays in the hall of the Lion and Sun Society, the best building in Mashhad. Some of the plays they performed included "The Locksmith" (*Chelengar*) by Amir Ebrahimi and others. They benefited from occasional visits by Fekri and a number of good actors to Mashhad. In 1939 the hall was lost to fire, but after it had been rebuilt by the municipality once again plays were performed there.[240] There also were a limited number of performances by the students of the High School, initially in the *Salon-e Bagh-e Naderi* and later in the hall of the *Arkan-e Hezb* in Mashhad.[241] There were also other forms of theatrical entertainment in Mashhad during that period. In 1939, the modern hotel in Mashhad had "an entertaining cabaret of dancers and singers. One

---

[237] Miller, *Camel-Bells*, pp. 169-71.

[238] Mir-Ansari and Ziya'i, *Gozideh-ye Asnad*, vol. 2, p. 72 (Jolfa); Hovayan, "Te'yatr-e Armaniyan-e Jolfa-ye Esfahan," pp. 215-16; Merritt-Hawkes, *Persia*, p. 129.

[239] Kushan, *Tarikh*, p. 111. There also was the occasional visit by professional troupes from Tehran by 1940 and thereafter. Fekri, "Tarikhcheh II," p. 79.

[240] Fekri, "Tarikhcheh II," p. 78.

[241] Mir-Ansari and Ziya'i, *Gozideh-ye Asnad*, vol. 2, p. 40.

of the performers is a huge girl who executes Russian-looking dances very well, and one is a mute girl who does clever dances in pantomime."[242]

Shiraz

There seems to have been theater in Shiraz prior to 1925, because Fekri mentions that the English during World War cut short most theatrical performances. It was only after their departure that theater came alive again. With the help of enthusiastic officers of the Iranian army Hasan Aqa Vafa'i staged `Eshqi's "Rastakhiz" and a comedy "Qorban `Ali Kashi." Some times later he performed the popular "Arshin Mal Alan". Thereafter, the organization of theatrical performances was taken over by Messrs. Mo`addel, Hosam al-Din `Arefi, Reshtizadeh Mohammad `Ali Akhlaqi and some others. They staged amongst others the play "Soldier without choice" (*Sarbaz-e ejbari*). Also, active was Colonel Akhgar Adib and Sayyed Taqi Taqavi (a.k.a. Sayyed Golestan of the paper of the same name).[243] They may have also staged an unnamed play that was performed in January 1929 by a number of ladies. This play had so much success that it was performed again during two consecutive evenings.[244] By that time Messrs. Akhlaqi, Nowdhari, Zahed and Tajalli were the main theatrical force in Shiraz. They usually staged plays in Cinema Mayak or the auditorium of the high school. Their performances were enlived with music and poetry.[245] In 1932 or 1933 the play "The elephant and the elephant keeper" (*Fil va Filban*) was staged in the Hafez school. In 1935 the play *Ardashir Babakan* was played in the Shahpur school, and in 1937 "Dervish on the mountain" (*Darvish-e Kuhneshin*) (by Mohammad Javad Torbati). These plays were all directed by `Ataollah Zahed. There also was a performance at the *Mokhadarat* school in 1939. In 1934 a professional theater troupe from Tehran played in the cinema of Shiraz, and it may well be that in subsequent years other similar performances took place there, for Fekri states as much.[246]

Other Towns

Theatrical performances of modern drama also took place in other cities about which no further information is available. Government documents mention performances at Masjed-e Soleyman (*Bashgah-e Iran*), Ahvaz (*Daneshsara-ye Ahvaz*), Qom (*Dabirestan-e Hakim Nezami*), Kerman (*Salon-e Madraseh-ye Pahlavi*) and Barforush (*Kelub-e Shilat*). Apart from Masjed-e Soleyman and Barforush, where respectively the cultural societies of the oil company and the fishing company were involved, in all the other towns the performances took

---

[242] Koelz, *Persian Diary*, p. 119.
[243] Fekri, "Tarikhcheh II," p. 81.
[244] *Setareh-ye Jahan* Year 1, number 6 (21/1/1929).
[245] Fekri, "Tarikhcheh II," p. 78.
[246] Hudi, "Pithiniyeh-ye te'yatr," p. 232; Mir-Ansari and Ziya'i, *Gozideh-ye Asnad*, vol. 2, pp. 283-84 (Shiraz); Merritt-Hawkes, *Persia*, pp. 59-63; Fekri, "Tarikhcheh II," p. 78.

place at high schools.[247] Given the dominant role of educational institutions in the occasional performance of drama it is quite likely that at other towns that I have not mentioned also theatrical performances also took place.

Despite censorship of the theater under the Pahlavi regime, Reza Shah did much for theater and he liked it personally, according to Sayyed `Ali Nasr (d. 1961), the founder of Komedi-ye Iran and one of the founding fathers of modern theater in Iran. Reza Shah also allowed and even urged women to attend theater and perform in plays. After his visit to Turkey, Reza Shah gave orders to construct an opera building in Tehran. Work started, but in 1941 the building was still unfinished. In 1318/1939, modern theater for the first time received official recognition as an important section of modern Iranian culture. With the encouragement of Reza Shah the *Honarestan-e Honar-e Pishegi-ye Tehran* was created to ensure the training of actors and directors so that theaters and plays be started with a view to educate and amuse people. For theater was considered to be the best means to educate people about social, child rearing, and hygienic matters.[248] The latter was no surprise, because those had been the objective of all early twentieth century reformers and hence the themes of most of Sayyed `Ali Nasr's plays, while it was also one that the government wanted to promote. The creation of the *Honarestan* had been a long cherished goal of the small group of actors, directors, and playwrights, who felt that to become really good they had to take a more professional approach to the art. Up till that time the only organization that provided formal training to aspiring actors, directors, and theater decorators was that of *Estudiyo-ye Deram-e Kermanshahi*, which had been established about 1931. In 1936, the Tehran Municipality also had organized and financed a series of theater training classes. These were given by `Ali Daryabegi, who had studied drama in Germany. He was assisted by a number of others who taught ballet, music, acrobatics, gymnastics, scene painting, and make-up. Daryabegi and his team not only taught theater, they also had their students performs plays such as "Leyla and Majnun," "Salomé" (Oscar Wilde) and 'The fifteen-year feast" (Chekhov).[249] In this connection, Mrs. Merritt-Hawkes's remarks are of interest:

> Persians have considerable natural dramatic ability and when given adequate opportunities will be fine actors. Their present inability to unite is a constant drawback. Tehran has several dramatic groups which work in

---

[247] Mir-Ansari and Ziya'i, *Gozideh-ye Asnad*, vol. 2, pp. 17, 306-07 (Masjed-e Soleyman), Ahvaz (250), 312 (Qom), 17, 29 (Tabriz), 72 (Jolfa), 40 (Kerman), 26 (Barforush). There also was a club of the British consulate-general, which probably also staged performances. Ibid., p. 44.

[248] Nasr, "Honar-e Te'atr," p. 311. Within the *Sazman-e Parvaresh-e Afkar* there existed a theater office (*edareh-ye te'atr*) and at the urgings of the members of this office the *Honarestan* was created. Mohammadi, "Negahi beh Tarikh," p. 24; Osku'i, *Pazhuheshi*, p. 171; Fekri, "Tarikhcheh I," p. 153 (in 1940 it had its first graduate who was awarded a role in free plays staged in the auditorium of the *Dar al-Fonun*, *Bagh-e Ferdowsi* and the *Kanun-e Banuvan*).

[249] Mohammadi, "Negahi beh Tarikh," pp. 23-24; Fekri, "Tarikhcheh II," p. 73.

opposition to one another. If they would unite, good professional standards would result. One day I watched an actress being taught her lines,
for, although quite nineteen, she could not read. She and her teacher sat
at a rough table in a little courtyard while, time after time, he repeated
the words. A few evenings later she gave a very good show at the open-
air theatre.[250]

The *Honarestan* thus was the first drama school in Iran and its teaching program
was modeled after that of the Conservatory in Paris. It continued to function until
1958 when the Anahita Drama School replaced it. Nasr had arranged for the construction of a small theater at the *Honarestan*, which sat 70 people. At first once a
week, later twice a week performances were given and thus a permanent theater
came into being in Iran. In 1940, the *Namayesh-khaneh-ye Tehran* was begun by
Seyyed `Ali Nasr and Ahmad Dehqan, which later was renamed *Te'atr-e Dehqan*
to honor Dehqan after his death. With this new organization the dispersed and an-
tagonistic field of theater 'professionals' became more convivial and gave new
energy to theater life in Iran.[251]

From the foregoing it is clear that modern theater was a labor of love, because
everybody involved, whether actor, playwright, director or stagehand was an amateur. Each theatrical group consisted of like-minded people, often even friends,
with a common interest that often when beyond that of theater. Politics and theater
often went together in the early days as well as later. For that reason, strong censorship was exercised under Reza Shah (1925-41), which had a dampening effect
on theatrical life. Each group usually had one or more "strong man" who was the
driving force behind the theatrical activities and who kept the group together.
When he left, usually the group dissolved. These theatrical forces of nature often
were playwright, translator, actor, director, manager, bookkeeper, and stagehand
rolled into one. The members of the group worked during the day and put up their
performances at night. Sometimes their enthusiasm and cohesion was such that
they stayed together for an extended period of time, which allowed them to perform also in other cities. There were not many theaters, and those often were used
for other functions such as cinema. Often performances took place at schools, at
private homes and in gardens. The plays were mostly translated Western ones,
mainly French, in particular Molière. Both translators and actors took liberty with
the text. The translators assimilated the drama to the contemporary Iranian context, while the actors were allowed to improvise, which was in line with the tradition of Iranian comic drama as discussed in chapter four. What is remarkable is
that apparently the same foreign plays were translated over and over again, for

---

[250] Merritt-Hawkes, *Persia*, p. 306.
[251] Mohammadi, "Negahi beh Tarikh," p. 24; Osku'i, *Pazhuheshi*, p. 173; Fekri, "Tarikhcheh I," p. 153. Nasr was also a prolific translator and by 1945 he had translated as many as 260 mostly French plays. Ibid., p. 155.

due to communication difficulties theatrical groups either did not know about already existing translations in other towns and/or were not able to get them. It is, of course, also possible that the so-called translations were in reality adaptations or brush-ups of the older translations, which seems more likely. For it is hard to believe that the original French edition was more accessible in Iran than the printed Persian translations thereof.[252]

Mohammad Reza Shah Period (1941–1979)

During the Second World War theater thrived as never before. Reza Shah had abdicated in 1941; his son Mohammad Reza Shah sat on a shaky throne, while the foreign occupying powers (Soviet Union, USA, and United Kingdom) did not mind strong criticism in theater as long as it was not aimed against them. Many playwrights wrote plays and others made many translations, for translated plays continued to hold their important place in the repertoire of the Iranian companies. Among the new Iranian plays stood out *Tup-e Lastik* (the rubber ball) by Sadeq Chubak, which was a satire of Reza Shah's police state and was published in 1949.[253] The Allies (United Kingdom and the Soviet Union) were also involved in the support of theatrical activities to curb favor with the public.

Mashhad

In Mashhad the so-called Mashhad Amateur Dramatic Society (M.A.D.S.) existed, in the founding of which Lady Skrine, the wife of the Britsh consul had played a leading role. "She persuaded some of our younger Persian friends of both sexes not only to act but to translate English, French and even Russian plays into Persian for her to produce in the Red Lion and Sun Hall." The production of Chekhov's "The Proposal" even made it to the pages of the *Pravda*, because it was the first time that Chekhov had been performed in Iran. Another, and even more successful performance, was that of "Charley's Aunt." This performance almost was cancelled when one of the lead actors informed the director that he would not play, because his father had not been given a seat among the VIPs on the first row. These kinds of problems were a recurrent headache for the theatrical producer, one of which occurred in March 1944.

> Tomorrow is the first night of the play D. [Lady Skrine] is producing for the M.A.D.S., a French piece called 'Amours'. The seats are priced at 10 tomans (13/6), 5 tomans and 3 tomans. Now they find they can't sell any but 1-toman seats for the first night because the Ostandar [governor] is

---

[252] Bertel's, E. "Persidskii teatr," *Vostotsnyj teatr* IV (Leningrad, 1924), pp. 72f., 80-82; Cejpek, "Iranian Folk-Literature," p. 678

[253] Javadi, *Satire*, pp. 268-70 for a discussion of this play.

taking a party to it, and they can't sell any but 3-toman seats for the second night because he isn't![254]

There also were other theatrical groups in Mashhad, one of which was 'sponsored' by the commander of the Iranian garrison, who was theatrically minded. He asked M.A.D.S. for help to stage a play "illustrating the fighting spirit of the Army." The consul's wife experienced that producing a play for the Army had its own kind of problems.

> Last night D. attended a rehearsal of Colonel Kh-'s play. All went well, she says, and she was able to give the cast some tips, but it was rather difficult when the gallant Colonel went on to the stage in the middle of the scene as he did several times. On these occasions, as he was in uniform, the actors had to salute every time he addressed them and, in accordance with regulations, remain at the salute all the time, whether acting or not![255]

With the end of the Second World War the Allies lost interest in supporting local cultural activities. There may have been other theatrical activities in Mashhad thereafter, but I have not been able to find any information about them.

Tabriz

After the Allied invasion of Iran in 1941 theater became more popular. Actors banded together and formed small troupes. The Russian-Iranian Cultural Relations Society (VOKS) of Tabriz put a troupe together and performed plays, even going so far as to use actors from Russian Azerbaijan or elsewhere. The *Ferqeh-ye Democrat* government also promoted Azerbaijani theater in Azeri and when it had access to broadcast radio the government broadcasted plays in Azeri as well. After the ouster of the *Ferqeh* government the theater troupes fell apart. Theater once again was limited to school plays or to radio, but now in Persian.[256] The year 1944 was very important for Armenian theater because it staged 10 performances in that year, mostly on Sundays. The performances were announced by wall posters. Apart from one headline in Persian the remainder of the text was in Armenian.[257]

Resht

In 1941 'Ebadolah Khan Ranjbar, one the actors of the first-hour in Gilan immediately started a group called *Darakhshan* in honor of his friend and fellow-artist Ahmad Darakhshan. However, this group after a few sessions fell apart. At the

---

[254] Skrine, Clarmont. *World War in Iran* (London, 1962), pp. 194-95 (the translator of Chekhov's piece was Dr. Mahmud Ziya'i, a well-known surgeon and later *Majles* deputy).

[255] Skrine, *World War*, p. 195.

[256] Javadi, *Peyramun*, pp. 209-11.

[257] Hovayan, "Te'atr-e Aramaneh dar Azarbeyjan," p.176 translation of such a poster; 177 facsimile. They also staged an operetta "Sus va Vartitr."

same time another group started theatrical activities. Mrs. Nashuri, one of the first actresses in Gilan, appeared for the last time on the stage in the plays organized by this group. The Russian occupation authorities took advantage of this situation by sending Caucasian troupes to Gilan. Mrs. Suriya Qajar managed the Russian department store in Resht and also rented the theater hall in City Hall where plays and films (in the East cinema) were shown.[258] In this situation came a radical change in 1944 when the Joint-Stock Art Company (*Sharekat-e sehami-ye honar*) was founded by Mehdi Gerami. Its artistic director was Mir `Ali Naqi Mir-Kiya, who also occasionally received assistance from his teacher and actor of the first-hour `Ali Daryabegi. The Company staged two plays: "Richard Darlington" and "The Barber of Seville." After these two performances the Company went out of business. Right at that time three men (Messrs. Afshar, Shoja`i and Tabash) decided to start the Future Club (*Kanun-e a'ineh*); its stage director was Akbar Afshar. Their first play was "Volpone" by Ben Johnson, which they had translated from English into Persian. However, the public demanded superficial and comical plays reason why mostly foreign plays were performed. Because of these and other problems the leading men, in particular the two stage directors, of the Company and the Future Club met on 8 Shahrivar 1323/1944 and decided to merge their groups into a new one called Drama Studio Gilan (*Estudiyu-ye Deram-e Gilan*). One of the objectives of the Drama Studio was to provide training classes for actors and directors. The first play the new group staged was "Chicago Farmer" by Mark Twain, which had been translated by Karim Keshavarz. Its second performance was that of "The Lost Ring or Marriage" by Gogol. It had been translated by Ms. Jeanne Godard, the daughter of the Russian director of the Sepah Bank in Resht. Godard also helped in staging he play and by arranging the help of a director from Baku to study the play. In 1945 the group staged Gogol's Inspector-General for the benefit of the members of the Red Army. Thereafter "Mahkum Biganeh" and "Nafrin Khiyanatgar" and "Nader Shah Afshar" (by Narimanof) were performed. After the performance of this last play differences arose between the managers, reinforced by a negative balance sheet, which led to Studio's demise. Some of its actors then decided to stage two plays (*Qezavat-e Donya* by Barchegadof and "Marriage" by Gogol), which they performed in all towns of Gilan and for the workers of the various textile factories in the province. After they returned from Mazandaran where they had staged the same two plays their effort to continue the Studio came to a formal end. The actors did not yet give up and performed Mazyar in the theater of City Hall.[259] Encouraged by the public's reaction these actors then in Aban 1325/1946 decided to found the Art Club (*Kanun-e honar-e pishegan-e peyruz*). The Art Club staged three plays

---

[258] Talebi, "Namayesh", p. 719.

[259] Until 1940 most of the plays had been performed in the Avadis Theater. But when General Ayram observed that this theater did not have enough chique for the reception of foreign ambassadors he ordered the construction of a theater attached to City Hall. The Russians had rented that theater, but neglected maintenance so that in 1949 it was a ruin and was destroyed. `Askari, *Tarikhcheh*, p. 64; Fekri, "Tarikhcheh II," pp. 75-76.

as variety shows in the Avadis Theater. However, due to opposition from Mehdi
Gerami, then the provincial chief of the Art Council the performances were stopped
in 1946, after a few months of success. One of the leading members of the Art Club,
Mohammad Ra'iszadeh, then contacted the Tudeh Party Club with whose collaboration he founded the Victorious Workers Club (*Kanun-e pishegan-e peyruz*). This
new club staged a few plays, but ceased to exist when the Tudeh Party Club was
closed down in Adhar 1345/1946. Ra'iszadeh and some other like-minded actors
then staged a few plays on their own during the next months, but then they could
not continue due to lack of means.[260] In that same years some other actors
(Mohammad E`tedalkhu, Shahpur Darakhshani, Rahim Rowshani) decided that
they wanted a permanent theater in Resht. To that end they started preparatory activities including the performance of a number of plays. They staged among other
things *Mordeh bad jang* and *Khiyanat va Vafa*. In 1948 they performed "The cess-
pool of misery" (*Manjalab-e badbakhti*) by Fereydun Nowzad and in 1949 (*Naziya*)
by the same author, which was their last act.[261]

When the Drama Studio went out of business the founder of the Company, Mehdi
Gerami, with some backers founded the Gilan Theater (*Tamasha-khaneh-ye Gilan*) in Mehr 1224/1945. The new group was too much of a competitor for other
groups to surive, and all their actors finally joined the Gilan Theater. The latter
staged many plays, but after a few successful years the Gilan Theater went out-of-
business in the second half of 1337/1958 due to not having playwright and good
translators that resulted in repeating the same plays, not having good actors, and
the final blow cinema, especially dubbed films. Ironically on the site of its theater
built the Abshar Cinema.[262] There also were theatrical activities elsewhere in Gilan notably in Fumen, where since 1941 plays were performed in a theater that
later became the town's City Hall. This situation lasted till 1969 when Amir Quy-
del started a new phase of theater with the novel play by Gohar Morad, followed
by "In the presence of the wind" (*Dar hozur-e bad*) by Bahram Beyza'i. Thereafter other plays by modern Iranian authors were staged.[263]

Isfahan

With the assistance of the British consulate the *Peyruzi* theater group had been established in the early 1940s. The group mostly performed comedies and with the end of
World War II its activities came to an end. In 1945 Victor Hugo's "The Orphans" was
performed at the Sa`di school.[264] In 1941 Mehdi Rowshan-Zamir a.k.a. Kargari estab-
lished in the garden behind the *Jahan* Hotel a theater with the help of two recent

---

[260] `Askari, *Tarikhcheh*, pp. 58-81; Talebi, Namayesh," p. 720.
[261] Talebi, Namayesh," p. 720.
[262] `Askari, *Tarikhcheh*, pp. 58-81; Talebi, Namayesh," p. 721.
[263] Talebi, Namayesh," p. 728 (with name sof the plays and their playwrights)
[264] Kushan, *Tarikh*, p. 111-12.

graduates of Tehran's school of dramatic arts, Naser Farahmand and Karim Ghaffari-yan. They called it the *Olymp Theater*, because the space it occupied was part of the Olymp Athletic Club. They staged plays such as "the One-Day Caliph', by Mehdi Mizan in which Arham-e Sadr played the role of Harun al-Rashid. The next play was "The Bad Friend" which was very popular among the public. The *Olymp Theater* then was dissolved due to differences among its members. Rowshan-Zamir left for Tehran and was able to convince some well-known Tehrani actors (Amir Hoseyn Fazli, `Abbas Hemmat Azad and his wife, Jahangir Foruhar and his wife) to come to Isfahan. Rowshan-Zamir formally separated from the Olymp Club and called his new theater *Setareh-ye Sobh*. However, once again internal difficulties proved too much and the new theatrical group came to an early end. Its actors joined the *Sepahan* Theater and later the *Isfahan* Theater.

The *Sepahan* Theater was founded by `Ali Sadri who sold his truck to convert a hostelry into a theater. The hostelry had been made available by Mohammad Kazeruni, a local factory owner and theater-lover. The theater opened its doors in 1944 and it staged one play per week. Sadri also invited actors from Tehran to his theater to increase the quality of the performances. The theater proved to be quite successful, for its theatrical performances lasted 20 years when, due to a conflict between Sadri and his actors, the Sepahan Theater was not viable anymore. It was transformed into the Moulin Rouge cinema. The cinema was burnt during the Islamic Revolution and is still in ruins.[265] Despite its success already in 1947 Naser Farahmand, the artistic director of the *Sepahan* Theater broke with `Ali Sadri over a financial issue. Some of the best actors followed him when he founded the *Isfahan Theater*. Farahband was also helped by a factory owner who loved theater (Mahmudiyeh), who turned a garage into a theater for him. This theater also was quite successful and staged a large number of different plays, both Iranian and European. According to Parviz Mamnun, the *Isfahan Theater* did even better than the *Sepahan* Theater, because it had the better actors and it had more actresses. Sadri started to have problems wit his actors in 1951 after he had introduced singing and dancing attractions to attract spectators. As a result of these differences the *Isfahan Theater* went finally bankrupt.[266] In 1946-47 the Post and Telegraph Theater was established in that organization's compound near the Dowlat Gate in Isfahan (now the Peyruzi Hotel). The indefatiguable Mohammad Mirza Rafi`i was, of course, involved in staging comedies performed in Isfahani dialect. Major actors included Reshtizadeh whose performance as 'the servant' made a great impression on Arham-e Sadr, who later became one of the great actors of Isfahan.[267] Methqali, an Isfahani capitalist, financed the establishment of the *Ferdowsi* Theater. Its target audience were the factory workers of Isfahan, of whom there were many. Consequently, the plays

---

[265] Kushan, *Tarikh*, p. 113-15 (which also lists all the major actors and the major plays that were performed), 120-21.
[266] Kushan, *Tarikh*, p. 117-20.
[267] Kushan, *Tarikh*, p. 119.

were light-hearted and aimed to please the taste of its public. This theater only existed a few years when Methqali closed it.[268]

In 1944, as in other towns, Armenian theater also was revived. Several plays were staged in subsequent years. Between the years 1950-60 the number of performances was on the decline, while theatrical life also had lost some of its zest. Things changed for the better during the period 1960-80. Two groups staged performances, viz. the Club of Art lovers (*Anjoman-e dustdaran-e honar*) (as of 1960) and the Cultural Club of Jolfa-Isfahan (*Anjoman-e farhangi-ye Jolfa-ye Esfahan*) (as of 1962). The director of the former was Harvig Alahverdian who produced 10 plays during two years (*Gedayan-e moyakhasses*; *Yezdan-e kohan*, *Anhushiz*, *Tavallod-e du bareh*, and *Cheraghha-ye khamush shavandeh*). The Cultural Club gave performances till 1967 amongst which were "The killed pigeon" (*Kabutar koshteh shodeh*), "The led-astray" (*Monharefin*), "The Leader" (*Pishva*) and "Adam and Eve". In the 1970s also some of the well-known Armenian artists from Tehran came to give performances in Isfahan. The remaining rural Armenian communities in Chahar Mahall and Faridan also had a theater where in collaboration with the Armenian school teachers plays were performed. Sometimes actors from Jolfa would also come and give performances.[269]

Shiraz

There apparently was a greater appeal for theater in Shiraz than in preceding years, for `Ataollah Zahed started a small theater in a converted garage in 1943 where he directed plays such as *Rostam and Sohrab* and *Nader Shah Afshar*. This endeavor only lasted one year, although thereafter occasionally theater performances were given in Cinema *Mayak* and Cinema *Khorshid*. In subsequent years there continued to be performances of plays, often written by local playwrights such as by Rahim Hudi. However, until 1958 it remained a marginal affair that was kept alive by enthusiastic amateurs. Although theater received a boost in 1958 with the creation of the *Kanun-e Deramatik-e Fars* and the participation of actors from Tehran, it nevertheless was a financially nonsustainable activity. Even with the help of the local educational authorities, who organized visits of teachers-in-training to the theater at half priced tickets could not save the theater in Shiraz. That there nevertheless continued to be performances was due to the passion, energy and conviction of the theatrical amateurs.[270]

Hamadan

In 1945 a permanent theater was opened in Hamadan under the name of 'The Ekbatana Theater" (*Tamasha-khaneh-ye Ekbatan*) with the assistance of Messrs. Abu'l-

---

[268] Kushan, *Tarikh*, p. 107.
[269] Hovayan, "Te'yatr-e Armaniyan-e Jolfa-ye Esfahan," pp. 216-20.
[270] Hudi, "Pithinuyeh-ye Te'yatr," pp. 232-38; Fekri, "Tarikhcheh II," pp. 81-82.

Qasem Nasuni [?], Vali Sedq and Seyfollah Majir. The leading actors included Mrs. Parivash Zandi and Klara as well as Messrs. Kohanmu'i and Roshdi. They performed plays such as "The Miser", "Ali Baba", and "Harun al-Rashid." They also benefited from the visit that a group of actors from Tehran made to Hamadan to give a performance in that town.[271]

TEHRAN

In addition to *Te'atr-e Tehran* and *Jame`eh-ye Barbod*, some additional theaters came into being such as *Tamasha-khaneh-ye Honar*, *Te'atr-e Giti*, *Te'atr-e Ferdowsi*, *Te'atr-e Bahar*, and *Te'atr-e Farhang*. The latter theater in particular became well-known for its productions of amongst others "Volpone" and "People" (*Mardom*) during the years 1943-1947. It had been founded by Nushin, Loretta, Kheyrkhvah and Mehrzad.[272] The Armenian community also developed theater activities. In 1945 two new theater groups were added to the existing ones, to wit: *Goruh-e Te'yatr-e Anjoman-e Farhangi-ye Javanan-e Tehran* and the *Goruh-e Te'yatr-e Shant*. Manul Marutian rented the Naderi Cinema, which after repairs, was ready for plays. In that same year Mgrdich Tashjian came to Tehran and on July 5 performed "Spring flood" (*Silab-e bahari*) and on September 6 "The surpise of divorce" (*Surpariz-e talaq*), and in mid-December *Kuradu* [?]. In 1945-46 the Armenian theater groups mostly staged plays for children. There was even a Children's Theater group (*Goruh-e Te'yatr-e Kudakan*) led by Ataian and Aghasian, and another *Te'atr-e Kakh-e Kudakan* led by Sarvarian. In 1947, the Sundukian theater group was formed.[273]

Once again, political parties realized the usefulness of theater as a political tool to make propaganda for a political message. *Te'atr-e* or *Tamasha-khaneh-ye Tehran* led by Nasr was politically pro-shah. It nevertheless included among its collaborators Dehqan, Fekri and Mosiri. [?] The main actresses were Badri Hurfar, Jahanbakhsh, Safavi, daftari, Niktaj, and Kivanfar as well as the actors Garmsiri, Mofid, Naqshineh, Bahrami, Sheybani and Kivanfar. Its repertoire reflected a conservative leaning. After a while Ahmad Dehqan took over the management from Nasr. *Tamasha-khaneh-ye Honar* was founded in 1942 and pursued an apolitical and purely artistic objective. It was an initiative of graduates of the Arts School (*Honar-e pishegi*) such as Pur Zanjani, Vothuq, Amini, Zahedi and Safi and because of the need to have each week a different play and lack of funds they were seldom able to

---

[271] Fekri, "Tarikhcheh II," pp. 78-79.
[272] Mohammadi, "Negahi beh Tarikh," pp. 24-25; Osku'i, *Pazhuheshi*, pp. 177, 189; Fekri, "Tarikhcheh I," p. 154. One of the established playwrights in 1946 was Dhabih Behruz, author of *Jijak `Alishah*, *Banu-ye Arman* and *Shab-e Ferdowsi*. An up and coming author was `Ali Jalali who wrote *Shah `Abbas*, "Ramazan Tragedy" (*Faje`eh-ye Ramazan*) and "The constitutional revolution" (*Enqelab-e mashrutiyat*). A prolific translator was the actor and playwright Gholam `Ali Fekri, who had translated about 60 plays. Ibid., p. 155
[273] Hovayan, "Te'yatr-e Armaniyan-e Tehran," pp. 212. "Theater Shant" may have named after the Armenian playwright Lewon Shant (1869-51).

produce quality plays. In addition to plays in Persian they also performed some plays in Azeri.[274] In 1947, `Abdol-Hosayn Nushin (1901-71) an active member of the *Tudeh* party, with the help of a few actors, started to translate Western dramas by Sartre, Maeterlinck and Hamilton and perform them. His initial success convinced a private investor to fund the *Ferdowsi* Theater, where Nushin continued to stage translated Western dramas. His first production was Priestly's "An Inspector Calls." The *Ferdowsi* Theater went out of business when in 1948 the *Tudeh* party was banned and Nushin was jailed.[275] After 1951 some other theaters were opened in Tehran. Among them was the *Sa`di* Theater that had been started by friends of Nushin. Their production of Western theater reportedly met with success. The *Sa`di* Theater was burned during the coup d'etat of 1953 and some of its actors were jailed. In addition to the Sa`di other theaters were also closed, including *Tamasha-khaneh-ye Tehran*, which had defended the coup d'etat.[276]

Given the new freedoms and possibilities, Western-style dramatic art for the first time became one performed by professionals instead of amateurs. One of the leading personalities of the theater in Iran during the 1950s was `Abd al-Hoseyn Naseriyan (1905-70) who was active as a director as well as a translator of foreign drama; he also wrote the handbook *Honar-e Te'atr* (1952). The other was Mostafa Osku'i who founded *Anahita* Theater and introduced modern acting training to Iran. `Ali Naseri-yan and `Abbas Javanmard started producing plays with a small company called the National Art Group (*Goruh-e Honar-e Melli*) that had been created by Shahin Sark-isiyan (1912-66). The latter also created *Te'yatr-e Arman* in 1960, which was an Armenian group. It performed many plays in the cultural and sports club Ararat throughout the 1960s and 1970s. Some other troupes were also established and plays were staged, and people were interested. However, there was hardly any support from the state or municipality and thus these efforts died a natural death. No new artistically or otherwise significant plays were written either.[277] Osku'i also ascribes the lack of progress due to heavy government taxation and the absence of any kind of government support. The Municipality, for example, demanded 25% to 50% of the net revenues, except in the oil-producing regions. When acting outside Tehran *Anahita* asked the mayors and/or governors for a waiver of these taxes. Another problem was obtaining good plays that could pass the censor.[278]

---

[274] Osku'i, *Pazhuheshi*, pp. 178-84, 189; Fekri, "Tarikhcheh U," pp. 153-54 (they performed "Abu Moslem Khorasani", "For Honor" and "The Ideal" by `Eshqi).

[275] Osku'i, *Pazhuheshi*, pp. 185-97 with a short biography of Nushin (pp. 198-208), Loretta (p. 217) and Hoseyn Kheyrkhvah (p. 218). Nushin also staged plays by Sadeq Hedayat such as "The Legitimator" (*Mohallel*) and "The Ghouls" (*Mordeh-khurha*). Ibid., p. 226.

[276] Mohammadi, "Negahi beh Tarikh," pp. 24-25; Osku'i, *Pazhuheshi*, pp. 209-16, 219.

[277] Nasr, "Honar-e Te'atr," p. 311; Mohammadi, "Negahi beh Tarikh," p. 25; Javadi, *Peyramun*, p. 211. Hovayan, "Te'atr-e Armaniyan dar Tehan," pp. 213-16 (with lists of the names of the plays). Osku'i, *Pazhuheshi*, p. 227, implies that Naseriyan and Javanmard had sold out to the government and thus stifled the group's artistic spirit; they ousted Sarkisiyan in 1957.

[278] Osku'i, *Pazhuheshi*, p. 253.

In the 1950s, theater moreover received competition from radio broadcasts, which started to offer radio plays, first in Tehran, later in a larger number of cities and finally throughout Iran. The nature of these plays was not the kind that was performed in high-brow theater halls, but rather belonged to the tradition of *ru-howzi*. Yarshater wrote:

> A number of these playwrights continued the broad farcical tradition: their characters achieved humor through exaggerated attitudes, comical dialects, and affected speech. Whereas plays of ideas were rare, maudlin plays abounded. The Broadcasting Service did offer, however, valuable opportunities for actors and playwrights to exercise their talent. In recent years, radio playwrights have managed to broaden their range of subjects and improve their technique.[279]

As a result, Iranian theater was moribund by the mid-1950s. Theaters in Lalehzar Street therefore tried to attract the public by offering "girlie-shows", acrobats and singing prior to their normal theatrical performance. This trend, which had been initiated by *Tamasha-khaneh-ye Tehran*, was also imitated in the few existing provincial theaters with so-called comical pre-curtain singing acts (*pish-pardeh khvani*).[280] Although much bewailed by the theater purists such as Osku'i, this was in fact nothing new, because modern theater from the very beginning had been introduced and/or concluded with music playing and singing to attract audiences (see above).

To counter this anti-cultural trend in theater as well as government efforts to "run" the world of theater Mostafa Osku'i created *Te'atr-e Anahita* on March 17, 1958 to the amazement, if not dismay, of the reactionaries. The new group started to stage old and avant-guarde European plays. Its first performance was that of Othello to much public acclaim. Anahita's initial success also drew the government's attention. Pahlbod, the Minister of Culture came to see for himself one of the performances with 100 of his staff the play "Eight and Five Minutes." The next day the Minister praised the quality of Anahita's artistry. In addition to lengthy serious plays Anahita also staged short plays by, for example, Chekhov, Dostoyevski, Cervantes and Goldoni. Many of these were offered live on Iranian television in the early 1960s. The government finally decided to exempt Anahita from paying income tax and in addition to grant it a subsidy of 50,000 rials per month. Pahlbod held up this agreement and made it conditional on Anahita becoming affiliated with

---

[279] Yarshater, Ehsan. "Development of Persian Drama," in Yarshater, Ehsan. ed., *Iran Faces the Seventies* (New York, Washington and London: Praeger Publishers, 1977), p. 32

[280] Echo of Iran, *Iran Almanac* 1973, p. 453; Kushan, *Tarikh*, pp. 85-90 (with some text examples of *pish-pardeh khvani* from Gilan), 120; Osku'i, *Pazhuheshi*, pp. 219, 233 (he added that many of the real artists in that group then left. Of two of them, `Ali Asghar Garmsiri and Mohammad `Ali Ja`far, he provides short biographies on pp. 175, 220-22).

his Ministry. In reality it came down to Anahita giving up its artistic independence in change for the monthly payment, finally leading to its demise.[281]

Osku'i not only was the leader and founder of Anahita Theater he also founded the Anahita Arts Training College. Here Osku'i introduced the teaching of the Stanislavski system into Iran for the first time.[282] Osku'i had been trained in Moscow and therefore was thoroughly familiar with this method.[283] This training program was an important step which was the government considered a challenge to its own efforts to 'guide' theater.

Acting, directing and writing was still in its infancy in Iran despite intermittent short periods of sometimes vibrant theatrical activities during the previous five decades. Also, there was not one respectable theater in Tehran given the size of its population. The Grand Hotel had burnt down in the late 1940s and the other locations where plays were performed were not optimal. The Pahlavi government, which had tried to 'run' modern theater activities from the very beginning of its existence, took steps to keep it alive in the mid-1950s. In 1950 a Fine Arts Department had been created to encourage artists of various hues (painting, theater, and film) in developing their art. Until 1961 the department was part of the Prime Minister's Office, when it was transferred to the Ministry of Education. After the split of this Ministry in December 1964 all non-educational matters became the responsibility of the newly created Ministry of Art and Culture.[284] To ensure that dramatic theater became known among people as well as to improve the theater scene for actors and theatergoers the government took a series of steps amongst which the broadcasting of dramatic serials on the radio. With the rise of TV in 1960 plays were also broadcast via this medium, which meant more work for actors and playwrights and technically broadened the scope for dramatic arts.[285]

As of 1955, Tehran University had started to give introductory drama classes for students with the help of three American professors, who were staying in Tehran. Modern European plays were translated and put on stage as were some

---

[281] Osku'i, *Pazhuheshi*, pp. 234-53.

[282] Konstantin Sergeyevich (Alexeyev) Stanislavski (1863-1938) developed a system of training wherein actors would research the situation created by the script, break down the text according to their character's motivations and recall their own experiences, thereby causing actions and reactions according to these motivations. The actor would ideally make his motivations for acting identical to those of the character in the script. He could then replay these emotions and experiences in the role of the character in order to achieve a more genuine performance. The "Stanislavski Method", was the catalyst for method acting and arguably the most influential acting system on the modern stage and screen.

[283] Osku'i, *Pazhuheshi*, p. 256.

[284] Echo of Iran, *Iran Almanac* 1973, p. 453.

[285] Osku'i, *Pazhuheshi*, p. 255; Echo of Iran, *Iran Almanac* 1963, p. 470.

Iranian plays.[286] The School of Dramatic Arts (*Daneshkadeh-ye honar*) was established in 1959 to popularize theater and to train actors. It published a fortnightly magazine of the Dramatic Arts Section of the Fine Arts Administration. In 1965, Tehran University established a theater section in its Faculty for Fine Arts.[287] By that time Anahita Theater and the Anahita Arts Training College did not exist anymore. According to Osku'i, these new government institutions were incompetent and only served to extend government control over the artists and their work. In fact, Osku'i argued that not the lack of an audience, but rather government policy was the real reason why theater life was moribund in Iran.[288]

Table 3: Number of students attending the School of Dramatic Arts (1960-63)

	1959-60	1960-61	1961-62	1962-63
No. of students in dialogue class	19	15	28	41
Successful candidates	–	9	5	Session not finished
No. of students in class for playwriting	11	13	12	11
Successful students	–	5	4	Session not finished
No. of students in acting class	14	30	25	26
Successful students	6	14	7	Session not finished
No. of students in class for stage setting and decoration	–	–	9	16
Successful canddiates	–	–	–	Session not finished

Source: Echo of Iran, *Iran Almanac* 1963, pp. 470-71.

The Ministry also provided support to amateur groups such as in Isfahan where in 1967 some 49 drama classes were taught over a six-month period by `Ali Naseriyan and Bahram Beyza'i. This activity led to the creation of the *Hatef* Group that staged at least one play each year. Teaching classes for amateurs were repeated in early 1970s this time by Parviz Meymun. The Ministry also had created a Cultural Center in Isfahan that aimed to interest youth in drama by having them perform in small venues and for small groups.[289] Similar activities were also sponsored by the Ministry in other provinces such as in Gilan where in 1970 with the help of the Ministry the Theater Teaching Center (*Markaz-e Amuzesh-e Te'atr*) was established, which was led by Parviz Khezra'i.[290]

---

[286] Osku'i, *Pazhuheshi*, pp. 223-25 (with details about the teaching program and methods, American and Persian teachers and plays.

[287] Mohammadi, "Negahi beh Tarikh," p. 25; Echo of Iran, *Iran Almanac* 1963, p. 470. For the activities of the theater section at the University of Isfahan as of 1961 see Kushan, *Tarikh*, p. 132.

[288] Osku'i, *Pazhuheshi*, p. 267-71.

[289] Kushan, *Tarikh*, pp. 129-31.

[290] Talebi, "Namayesh," p. 726 (the center's student also staged plays). Teaching classes were also organized in Shiraz. Hudi "Pithinuyeh-ye Te'yatr," pp. 239-40.

288HISTORY OF THEATRE IN IRAN

To further improve the quality of acting the government made it also possible for Iranian actors to be exposed to professional acting in Europe. The National Art troupe, for example, took part in the World Festival of Theater in Paris in 1960 with a piece called "The Wandering Nightingale" (*Bolbol-e sargashteh*). It is based on an Iranian folktale and is the first Iranian play performed abroad.[291] Furthermore, French theatrical groups visited Tehran in 1963 and 1964, and group of the *Comédie française* performed five plays at the *Nasr* Theater.[292] A theatrical troupe also participated in 1965 in the Theater of Nations Festival in Paris where they performed Sunset in a Strange Land (*Ghorub dar Didyari Gharib*) by Beyza'i.[293] To stimulate theater life in Iran the government established in 1961 the National Center for Iranian Theater (*Markaz-e melli-ye te'atr*), which was affiliated with UNESCO. It provided an official link with the world of theater elsewhere on the planet. Since it creation the National Center celebrated its birthday every year in March 27, which corresponded with the World Theater Day. During that day a play would be staged, meritorious persons would be honored and discussions would take place relating to all theater-related activities.[294]

To ensure that actors could stage their performance under better conditions the Ministry also built a number of theaters in Tehran and in the provincial capitals over the next 15 years. Without theaters actors and modern theater could not exist. An artistically well-known theater in Tehran was the *Anahita* (from 1958), which was operated by Mostafa Osku'i. In 1960, it was taken over by the Fine Arts Administration, because Anahita was financially insolvent. In May 1962, the need for government action was once again brought home to Mr. Osku'i. In that year he appealed for financial assistance from the public to build a cinema-theater. Although many sent contributions it was not sufficient. Since then the *Anahita* group staged performances on the TV organized by the Fine Arts Administration.[295]

By 1965, there were only four seasonal theaters in Tehran (*Kasra, Nasr, Anahita, Jame`eh-ye Barbod*). *Kasra* had been just created in that same year. Its members included young actors as well as Loretta, who had returned from the Soviet Union and other old hands from the *Sa`di* Theater (Ja`far, Mehrzad, Mina, etc.). However, despite government support *Kasra* lasted barely one year. There were also several amateur theatrical groups of the Jewish and Armenian minorities, and of the English, French, and German speaking foreign residents. Of the latter the "Little Theater" (English) and the *Deutsche Kleine Theater* (German) were the most active ones.[296] Foreign cultural centers also staged performances such as the

---

[291] Echo of Iran, *Iran Almanac* 1965, 642.
[292] Echo of Iran, *Iran Almanac* 1965, 642.
[293] Echo of Iran, *Iran Almanac* 1966, p. 674.
[294] Mohammadi, "Negahi beh Tarikh," p. 25; Echo of Iran, *Iran Almanac* 1972, p. 637.
[295] Echo of Iran, *Iran Almanac* 1963, p. 470; Osku'i, *Pazhuheshi*, pp. 257-78.
[296] Echo of Iran, *Iran Almanac* 1965, p. 642; Osku'i, *Pazhuheshi*, pp. 257-58, 277-78.

French-Iran cultural society and the Iran-America society.[297] In the provinces Isfahan was the only town that had a permanent one-show theater. As of 1966, Arham-e Sadr, after the break with *Te'atr-e Sepahan*, founded his own theater that had shows almost every evening. The repertory consisted of two-hour comedies with mild social criticism expressed with humor and innuendos in Isfahani dialect. His program was so popular that many came from outside Isfahan to attend. Likewise, a mumber of theaters were also established in other provincial towns, where despite the problems theater enthusiasts had to overcome theater still was very much alive.[298] In 1966 a new theater, called the *25th of Sharivar*, was added to the ones already extant in Tehran. It was for the use of the groups supported by the Ministry of Arts and Culture. Thus, there were in total six theaters in Tehran with seating for 3,457 visitors. In 1968, Rudaki Hall (*Talar-e Rudaki*) was opened, but it was mostly used for opera and music performances. The new *25th of Shahrivar* theater had the reputation of offering the best performances, but Osku'i has a rather low opinion of its repertoire. As of 1969 the new hall of the *Iran Bastan Museum*, or the *Talar-e Muzeh* also was used to stage serious translated foreign plays.[299] The new theaters served to (i) portray the government's interest to promote culture and in particular theater and (ii) extend government control over theatrical life in all its aspects (actors, directors, repertory).

Table 4: Most important theaters in Tehran in 1968—their capacity and date of opening

Name theater	Number of seats	Date of opening
Dehqan	800	1926
Jame`eh-ye Barbod	420	1928
Pars	444	1944
Hafez-e Now	110	1953
Yas-e Now	180	1960
25th of Shahrivar	381	1965
Rudaki	1122	1968

Source: Echo of Iran, *Iran Almanac* 1971, p. 637.

Major Performers and Playwrights

The number of theatrical troupes was still limited and they were of varying quality. In addition to Osku'i's Anahita group there was that of Ja`fari with Mrs. Shahla. They usually performed in the *Barbod* theater. The troupe of Amir Shirvan usually performed

[297] Echo of Iran, *Iran Almanac* 1963, p. 470-71; Ibid., 1971, p. 637.
[298] Echo of Iran, *Iran Almanac* 1971, p. 637; Kushan, *Tarikh*, pp. 125-28. For the situation of theater in Gilan between 1958 and 1979 see Talebi, "Namayesh," pp. 725-26. For the situation in Shiraz were, albeit with the help of the Ministry of Fine Arts, ten different theater groups (Pars, Melli, Arya, Aryu, Talash, Zharf, Sapid, Azad, `Arusaki, Shahr) performed some 66 plays between 1969 and 1980. Many of these plays were written Iranian playwrights, but the *Geruh-e Te'yatr-e Shahr*, for example, mainly performed plays by Berthold Brecht. Hudi, "Pithinuyeh-ye Te'yatr," pp. 240-43.
[299] Echo of Iran, *Iran Almanac* 1971, p. 637; Ibid., 1970, p. 620; Osku'i, *Pazhuheshi*, pp. 268-71.

in the *Nasr* Theater (the former *Tamasha-khaneh-ye Tehran*).[300] In 1963, these were the only theatrical activities in Tehran apart from those on the TV and the radio. Amir Shirvan's troupe performed with much success "The Tea House and the August Moon." Radio Iran broadcast every night a popular program under the direction of Bahrami, an old actor. Other well-known actors were Turan Mehrzad, Taji Ahmadi, Messrs. Satomi, `Ali Mahmudi Sarang, and others. On TV, under the aegis of the Fine Arts Administration, the Maqsudi troupe performed led by `Ali Nasiriyan and `Ezzatollah Entezami. They were also gradually improving theater technique in Iran.[301]

The leading actors/actresses by the mid-1960s included Mr. and Mrs. Osku'i, Ms. Jaleh, Ms. Mehrzad, Mr. Ja`fari, Mr. Vahdat, Mr. Qadakchiyan, Mr. Mohtasham, Mr. Bahrami, Ms. Azar Hekmat-Sho`ar and Mr. Amir-Sherman; they also all played in films. There was the perception that the troupe trained by the Fine Arts Administration was the best of all groups of actors. It performed weekly on TV with Hoshang Entezami, Mashayekhi, Ms. Khurvash, `Abbas Javanmard, `Ali Nasiriyan, and Davud Rashidi. Other well-known troupes were those of Paris Saberi and Khojasteh Kis.[302]

The number of playwrights for theater grew significantly during the 1960s as the result of incentives provided by the government. There were three trends. One that based its plays on modern Iranian literature, the other that took its inspiration from popular dramatic Iranian tradition and the third one that was influenced by European avant-garde theater. The leading playwrights of the 1960s and 1970s included: Gholam Hoseyn Sa`edi, Bahram Beyza'i, Akbar Radi, `Ali Nasiriyan, Bahman Forsi, Bizhan Mofid, Esma`il Khalaj, Parviz Sayyad, Arsalan Purya, `Abbas Na`lbandiyan, Parviz Kardan, Sa`id Soltanpur, Mahmud Dowlatabadi, Mohsen Yalfani, Ebrahim Makki, Nader Ebrahimi, Mostafa Rahimi, Naser Shahinpar, and Naser Irani. This group of new playwrights would dominate Iranian theater till 1979. Bahram Beyza'i and Gholam Hoseyn Sa`edi (under the penname of Gowhar Morad) also wrote for film. The former wrote a "History of Theater in Iran" and the latter also wrote sociological studies. The leading stage directors were: Mohammad `Ali Ja`far of *Te'atr-e Emruz*, `Ezzatollah Entezami, `Ali Nasiriyan, Arbi Ovanessiyan, Ja`far Vali, Davud Rashidi, `Abbas Javanmard of *Goruh-e Honar-e Melli*.[303]
Experimentation was encouraged by the government so as to enable Iranian theater to compete with Western theater output and quality. However, playwrights who went too far were censored and even jailed. During the late 1960s, continuing in the 1970s, censorship increased and playwrights became increasingly introvert. Theater there-

[300] Sayyed `Ali Nasr died in February 14, 1962. He was called the "Father of Iranian Theater" because of his services to dramatic arts. The Tehran Theater was renamed *Nasr* Theater to honor him. Echo of Iran, *Iran Almanac* 1963, p. 470.
[301] Echo of Iran, *Iran Almanac* 1963, p. 470.
[302] Echo of Iran, *Iran Almanac* 1965, pp. 642-43.
[303] Javadi, *Satire*, pp. 271-76; Echo of Iran, *Iran Almanac* 1974, p. 134; Ibid., 1970, p. 620; Osku'i, *Pazhuheshi*, pp. 278-83.

fore focused on foreign plays ranging from classical Greek authors like Sophocles and Euripides to Shakespeare, Goethe, and Schiller. More importantly were the plays of modern authors such as by Shaw, Wilde, Ibsen, Gogol, Chekhov, Brecht, Frisch, Dürrenmatt, Beckett, Ionesco, Genet, Pinter, Osborne, Tennessee Williams, and Böll. Iranian playwrights joined the world-wide avant-guarde movement in their plays, or they became representative of the realist movement, and/or they took their inspiration from *ru-howzi* tradition. I wrote and/or, because sometimes an author would borrow from more than one artistic tradition and current. Not being allowed to voice certain ideas and critcism, playwrights therefore sought an outlet in experimentation with technique. Those Iranian writers who chose to express themselves in forms of symbolism were often difficult to follow, let alone understand. Forsi was one of the first to play with symbolism and language in his play "The Vase" (*Goldan*). Others such as Na`lbandiyan took the road of absurdist theater. Even Gholam-Hoseyn Sa`edi could not escape this absurdist tinge, in, for example, his play "Honey Moon" (*Mah-e `Asal*). Not all of his plays were written in that style, for most of them were charazterized by what Hasan Javadi calls "black humor." His "The Clubwielders of Varazil" (*Chub-beh-dastha-ye Varazil*) is a story of betrayal. Hunters who are welcomed by villagers threaten them; the villagers seek refuge in an Islamic shrine that also fails them. His play "Workaholics in the trenches" (*Karbafakha dar Sangar*) is about the conflicts caused by rapid industrialization and belongs more to the realistic trend in playwriting.

Other writers, just like many modern Iranian painters, resisted the appeal of foreign models and sought their inspiration in Iranian dramatic tradition and popular stories. The realists such as Akbar Radi also wrote about the clash between the old and new Iran, while he included colloquial language from his home province of Gilan. His "Descent" (*Oful*) and "The Fishermen" (*Sayyadan*) published in 1964 and 1969 made his name. Khalaj chose as his theme urban marginal life of the poor, addicts, whores and their pimps. His "Hangout" (*Patugh*) is situated in the red-light district of Tehran and portrays unrequited love and deception. This and his other plays, such as "Goldun Khanom," were an indirect criticism of existing social conditions. `Ali Nasiriyan's play "Black" (*Siyah*), is the story of the sadness of the black-faced clown of *ru-howzi* theater as is his "The theatrical agency—A *takht-howzi* show in two parts" (*Bongah-e Te'atral—Nemayesh-e takht-howzi dar do bakhsh*), which is a modernized version of a *ru-howzi* play. Both addressed social issues, in particular the tension between the old and the new.[304] The mix of modern and traditional, symbolism and realism, foreign influence and social ills remained the main menu that the theatergoer was offered until the end of the Pahlavi regime. In addition,

---

[304] Javadi, *Satire*, p. 271, 276; Echo of Iran, *Iran Almanac* 1975, p. 467; Osku'i, *Pazhuheshi*, pp. 278-83.

there was the less literary form of theater, which was more popular in nature and close to *ru-howzi* that continued to enjoy great popularity.[305]

Theatrical Festivals

Another stimulant for modern theater were the various festivals that the government organized, because it gave opportunities to actors and playwrights to show their art, to experiment, to compete and to learn. It brought leading foreign stage directors to Iran, where they staged experimental theater of the most advanced kind. However, Osku'i and others have argued that the Festivals were a waste of money that could have been better spent on the development of indigenous Iranian theater. However, given the liberal if not leftist tendencies of many of the Iranian artists (actors, playwrights, students) such a development was the last thing the Pahlavi regime wanted. It therefore tried to dominate the world of theater through the targeted use of funding and censorship.[306]

Whatever the truth of the matter, the government festivals had an impact on theatrical life in Iran, whether it was one that one wanted or not. It started with the Festival of Iranian Drama that was held in the *25th Sharivar* Theater. It was the biggest theatrical event of the year in 1965 in cooperation with the Ministry of Art and Culture. The following plays were performed: "Amir Arsalan," written and directed by `Ali Nasiriyan; "The Club Wielders of Varazil" and "The best daddy in the world" both by Gholam Hoseyn Sa`edi; "The Golden Coach" by Khalil Delmaqami; "The Iranian Collection" (specimens of traditional Iranian drama form) directed by Parviz Sayyad; "Pahlavan Akbar Dies" by Bahram Beyza'i and "Cyrus the son of Madana" by `Abbas Salahshur.[307] Otherwise the world of theater was rather listless in the mid-1960s. The exception was theater life in Isfahan, which was almost entirely due to one man, Arham-e Sadr, an actor and producer. He had his own theater where he performed plays that were considered to be of a low theatrical standard, but it was popular with the common man. The secret of his success was that he performed plays in the *ru-howzi* tradition commenting wittily on current affairs. To that end he translated successful European satirical comedies and adapted them to Iranian realities.[308] In Tehran, the *25th Shahrivar* Theater continued to promote Iranian plays thus encouraging Iranian playwrights. Other theaters staged "Antigone" and some other foreign plays.[309] In collaboration with the Iranian TV and supported by the queen the Ministry of Arts and Culture organized the Shiraz Arts Festival in 1967 where only one Iranian play was staged, a production of a religious drama. But in 1968 Shiraz Festival five Iranian plays were performed that had been selected from 57 submissions: "A

---

[305] For a partially annotated catalogue of all the plays published in Persian, either translated or original Iranian plays, see Sho`a`i, Hamid. *Namayeshnameh va Filmnameh dar Iran* (Tehran, 2535/1977) which also has pictures of scenes of performances, artists and posters.
[306] Osku'i, *Pazhuheshi*, pp. 302, 308.
[307] Echo of Iran, *Iran Almanac* 1966, p. 673-74.
[308] Echo of Iran, *Iran Almanac* 1968, p. 642; Javadi, *Satire*, p. 270.
[309] Echo of Iran, *Iran Almanac* 1968, p. 642

Man with Two Trays and Dog in the Manger" by Nosratollah; "Fossils" by `Abbas Na`lbandiyan; "A Garden of Shades" by Tahmineh Mirmirani; "The City of Tales" by Bizhan Mofid and "Lunch" by Mahin Jahanbaghi.[310]

The year 1968 was an exciting year for Iranian theater because of the staging of two new plays. The first one was a kind of musical play "The City of Tales" (*Shahr-e Qesseh*) by Bizhan Mofid, the winner of the Iranian TV prize at the Shiraz Arts festival. It was so popular that it ran for three months, and was repeated every year thereafter. It is a social satire inspired by popular stories and written in traditional rhythmic verse of children's stories, and put on stage with the use of animal masks; it was performed by unknown actors. The other play was "Research on the Fossils of the 25th Geological Era" by `Abbas Na`lbandiyan, a high school student; this ran for about one month. The 1969 Shiraz Arts Festival also had organized a dramatists' competition; some 67 playwrights participated, but none was good enough to get the first prize. However, since most of them showed promise it was decided to organize a training class for them.[311]

In 1968, it was also decided to organize each year a Culture and Art festival (held in October/November), in addition to the Shiraz Arts Festival (which was always held in September). The first Art Festival was mainly an affair of foreign music and ballet, but with the second one it became a purely Iranian affair, and since then the emphasis has been on folk art and music. Amateur drama companies and young playwrights got a chance to show their stuff. As a result several training centers came into being in Tabriz, Mashhad, Ahvaz, Abadan, Qazvin, and Kermanshah. These were small schools, often without a permanent home. The festival also helped to keep alive traditional forms of art such as story telling (*naqqali*), passion play (*shabih-khvani*), and improvisatory comedy (*ru-howzi*). Thereafter, many traditional groups traveled throughout the year performing in towns and villages, to which end the newly created cultural houses served. Normally the Arts Festival was held at Tehran, but as of 1970 various parts, performed by four troupes, were also shown in 155 provincial towns and 200 villages.[312]

The most important plays performed in 1970 were "The Thunderbolt" by the Russian playwright Ostrovsky, "A View from the bridge" by Arthur Miller, "The One who says yes and the one who says no" by Brecht and "Tale of a Spell, Fine Silk and Fishermen" by `Ali Hatami, "Soltan Mar" by Bahram Beyza'i, "The man who was unaware he was dead" by Parviz Sayyad, "Present from Abroad" (*Soghat-e*

---

[310] Echo of Iran, *Iran Almanac* 1968, p. 642; Ibid., 1971, p. 637 (The Ministry of Arts and Culture also supported a number of theatrical troupes that performed on TV, while the Information Ministry supported some groups that did radio plays.).

[311] Echo of Iran, *Iran Almanac* 1969, p. 618. For a discussion of "The City of Tales" see Javadi, *Satire*, pp. 274-76. In 1969 the artists also formed a syndicate.

[312] Echo of Iran, *Iran Almanac* 1972, p. 633.

Ferang) by the Arya Theatrical Group of Isfahan, "The black man" (*Siyah-e zangi*), "The European" (*Mardi-ye ferangi*), "The dulcimer" (*Dayereh-ye zangi*) by `Abbas Maghfuriyan, "Striptease" and Parvarbandan" by Gohar Morad, which was also staged in the provinces. Iran Television also showed many plays, the most important being "The Group of the condemned" and "Five Days" by Zeiger.[313] During 1969-70, the total number of theater tickets sold at Tehran was 689,000, of which the *25th of Shahrivar* sold 56,400 and *Dehqan*, *Nasr*, and *Barbod* theaters sold 600,000. This situation remained unchanged in 1970-71.[314]

Theater at Death's Door

Reading the above as well as authors who deal with literature one gets the impression that theater in Iran was progressing well. According to Hasan Javadi, "the upsurge of the Iranian economy in the 1960s served as another impetus for the advancement of Iranian drama," while Hans de Bruijn opined "the theatre … took off in the 1960s and continued until the revolutionary turmoil began about a decade later."[315] However, reality looked a bit different. The growth in the output of new plays had not resulted in a growing public interest for theater. In fact, despite all the new theatrical activities and incentives given, theater hovered at death's door around 1970, for there was no significant development of the world of theater. The spread of the cinema really hurt theater, the more so, when Persian language or dubbed foreign films were shown. The introduction of TV and its growing audience also severely constrained theater its development.[316] Theater was much less popular than cinema, because of its less versatile technique, limited production budget, and inferior artistic talent. The cinema was also cheaper and easier fare to appreciate for the average spectator. It was not because most plays that were performed were mostly translated foreign pieces, for Iranian plays did not enjoy much popularity either.[317] The growing popularity of TV and cinema emptied the theaters so that by 1970 only the theater in Lalehzar Street (Tehran) and two independent theaters in the provinces were still in operation that were able to survive by performing popular plays. In 1970 student and non-students therefore came together and started in Tehran a new theater known as *Te'atr-e Shahr* that was affiliated with Iranian TV. Finally, the *Molavi* Theater affiliated with the University also gave hope for the future.[318]

---

[313] Echo of Iran, *Iran Almanac* 1970, pp. 620-21 (the actors group of the Ministry of Arts and Culture performed 40 programs. In the provinces during the Shiraz Arts Festival)

[314] Echo of Iran, *Iran Almanac* 1971, p. 637.

[315] Javadi, *Satire*, p. 271; de Bruijn, J. Th. P. "Masrah," *Encyclopedia of Islam²*.

[316] Nasr, "Honar-e Te'atr," p. 311; Javadi, *Peyramun*, p. 211; Echo of Iran, *Iran Almanac* 1971, p. 637.

[317] Echo of Iran, *Iran Almanac* 1965, p. 642; Ibid., 1972, p. 637.

[318] Mohammadi, "Negahi beh Tarikh," p. 25.

Table 5: The number of plays staged in 1968-69

25ᵗʰ Sharivar	4
Nasr	16
Dehqan	16
Barbod Society	16
Yas	15
Golshan (Mashhad)	30
Isfahan theater	12

Source: Echo of Iran, *Iran Almanac* 1970, p. 620.

Without the support of the Ministry of Arts and Culture, Radio and Television of Iran modern theater might have died a quiet death. However, the Shiraz Festival, the Iran Art Festival and some radio and television programs kept it alive. `Abbas Javanmard wrote in the *Ettela`at* newspaper of November 22, 1971,

> Everybody has forgotten theatre these days. Lack of space, lack of government protection, not even to the extent of books and libraries, lack of aid from municipalities (it pays only Rials 50,000 to the Theatre of Tehran); disinterestedness of the private sector in building theatre halls (they are interested in construction of cinema halls only), cinema and television competition, have jointly deprived theatre of its popularity in Iran."[319]

His reference to the municipalities had to do with the fact that a few years earlier a law had been passed for the protection of theater, which obliged municipalities to pay 10% of their municipal income to theater, but it was not implemented. Theater artists and aficionados opined that the government should do more. Students at the arts faculty of the University of Tehran complained, "they had no amphitheatre, no library and no theatre accessories, but that they loved theatre.[320]

Despite the many complaints that the government did not do enough, that there were not enough theaters or that public interest in theater was too weak objective facts seem to have belied them, if we can trust the official data. In 1970-71 the number of theaters in Tehran had risen to seven, while Abadan also had acquired a theater and Mashhad added a second one.[321] The best-equipped theater in Tehran was the newly opened City Theater (*Teyatr-e Shahr*), the biggest in Iran with 700 seats. Next in importance was Arham-e Sadr's theater in Isfahan with a large popular audience, especially after the opening of a second modern theater there around 1970. As a result, there were 13 modern theaters in Iran by 1972 with about one million visitors.[322]

---

[319] Echo of Iran, *Iran Almanac* 1972, p. 637 (*Ettela`at* 14 December 1971).
[320] Echo of Iran, *Iran Almanac* 1972, p. 637 (*Ettela`at* 14 December 1971).
[321] Echo of Iran, *Iran Almanac* 1972, p. 638.
[322] Echo of Iran, *Iran Almanac* 1973, p. 133.

Table 6: Number of theaters in selected cities and the size of their audience (1971)

City	No. of theaters	Number of theatrer goers
Tehran	6	711,400
Rezayeh	1	25,000
Isfahan	2	152,525
Mashhad	1	90,000

Source: Echo of Iran, *Iran Almanac* 1972, p. 637.

Clearly everything was not well in theater land, for in July 1972 the Ministry of Culture issued new rules and those troupes that adhered to them would qualify for government support. The best performances were at the *25ᵗʰ Shahrivar* and *Shahr* Theaters. The standard also reportedly was improving at Tehran University. Modern theaters also receive support via the Theater Workshop (*Kargah-e Namayesh*) and Iranian TV and Radio. There was still a dearth of Iranian playwrights, which explains the large number of foreign plays that were staged. In the second-category theater and in the provinces where the audience liked Iranian plays most the actors "often improvise their parts with extempore lines." The revival of *ru-howzi* (comedy) and *ta`ziyeh* also received much attention. On the 300ᵗʰ year of Molière's death some of his plays were shown on TV and round tables were held to discuss his work.[323]

Te'atr-e Shahr had its first anniversary in January 1974, it had 70,000 theatergoers during that first year and many international concerts. Apart from Beyza'i's *Sunset in a Strange Land* and *A Tale of a Hidden Moon* with 17,544 spectators most of the 11 plays were from the Theater Workshop.[324] An indication how much theater was the government's business was the fact that it was reported that during the Fourth Development Plan (1968-72) there had been 300 theater programs and 42 story-telling (*naqqali*) ones, with 9 art festivals (in Tehran and in the provinces). During the Fifth Plan the existing theatrical groups would be completed and 30 other art centers established. Also, 12 urban cultural centers were to be established in the provincial centers.[325] In the provinces, such as Isfahan and Resht, theater was alive and even kicking in Isfahan. In Resht there was a sequence of theatrical groups that followed one after the other, but nevertheless kept theater alive in Gilan.[326]

---

[323] Echo of Iran, *Iran Almanac* 1973, p. 133.
[324] Echo of Iran, *Iran Almanac* 1974, p. 134.
[325] Echo of Iran, *Iran Almanac* 1975, p. 465.
[326] Kushan, *Tarikh*, p. 129-31; `Askari, *Tarikhcheh*, pp. 121-38.

Table 7: Number of theaters and theatergoers in selected cities (1969-74)

City	1969-70		1970-71	1973-74
	No. of theaters	No. of theatergoers	No. of theaters	No. of theaters
Tehran	6	711,400	7	7
Shiraz	-	-	2	2
Isfahan	2	152,525	2	2
Mashhad	1	90,000	2	2
Rezayeh	1	25,000	1	1
Abadan	-	-	1	1
Tabriz	-	-	-	1
Total	10	978,925	15	16

Source: Echo of Iran, *Iran Almanac* 1973, p. 133; Ibid., 1974, p. 134

THEATER DURING THE ISLAMIC REPUBLIC (1979–_)

Just when theater in Iran seemed to on the road to revival the Islamic Revolution took place in 1979. Initially scores of theatrical groups were formed and plays, both new and old, were staged in all major towns of Iran. Most notable were the plays "The Law" (*Qanun*) by Mahmud Rahbar and "Barracks in the Evening" (*Padegan dar Shamgah*) by Faramarz Talebi both portraying how the Pahlavi regime turned good people into bad through its immoral policies. However, this Tehran spring lasted not longer than one year and theater, like other expressions of opinion, was suppressed. The newly established Islamic Republic did not care much for theater, epecially the kind that was imbued with Western tradition. Many leading artists and playwrights such as Gholam Hoseyn Sa`edi and Bizhan Mofid fled the country, fearing arrest and worse because of their political conviction. "Mofid's *City of Tales* was the most popular play ever written in Persian, running for seven years in Tehran before the revolution and broadcast by fans in protest from the rooftops of Tehran when the revolution turned sour. It was the satirical portrait of a mullah in this musical play that led to Mofid's exile."[327] Theater was socially, religiously, and, above all, politically suspect and hence was relegated to the sidelines. Those who insisted on their fundamental right of the freedom of expression found themselves quickly muzzled. One of them, the playwright and poet Sa`id Soltanpur (1940-81) was even executed because of his political activities. Therafter gradually all theater performances were all but discontinued. With the start of the Iran-Iraq war in 1980 the government imposed strict censorship. However, contrary to expectations the Islamic government did not ban theater. In fact, after a while it realized the importance of theater as a political propaganda tool. Apart from the occasional *ta`ziyeh-khvani* performance few plays were staged for some time. These were mostly so-called Islamic theater, i.e. theater that praised the achievements of the Revolution.[328]

---

[327] Osku'i, *Pazuheshi*, pp. 319-30; [http://www.wordswithoutborders.org/article.php?lab=Irantheater].
[328] Javadi, *Satire*, p. 276. Soltanpur wrote the play "'Abbas Aqa, worker of the Iran National Company" (`*Abbas Aqa, kargar-e Iran nasiyunal*). For a short biography of Soltanpur see Osku'i, *Pazuheshi*, pp. 333-34.

After this initially difficult period theater in Iran returned to the stage and with a vengeance. The change started at the end of the Iran-Iraq war in 1988, when the country could focus once again on living rather than dying. Nothing had changed in the context of art world, but for once thing, viz. the enormous demand and enthusiasm for theater in Iran and that there was more of everything than before. Also, the drama schools at all major universities were re-opened as well as private drama training institutions and both have large number of students. Most importantly, the Islamic government and its various institutions have adopted theater as a means of politically correct expression. As in the Reza Shah period those plays that support the objectives of the regime are supported through the organizations affiliated with the Ministry of Culture and Islamic Guidance.[329]

As a result of the government's positive attitude toward theater, the First International Congress in Islamic Dramatic Art took place in 1991, while in 1993 the First Congress on Ta`ziyeh was organized. This was followed by the First Congress on Children Theater in 1994 and the Tehran International Puppet Festival Congress in 1996. All these conferences continue to be held at regular intervals. In addition, an increasing number of theater-related festivals were organized. There was the Fajr Theater festival, which was part of the larger Fajr Festival that since 1981 has been organized every year to commemorate the victory of the Islamic revolution. Other festivals included the annual commemoratation of World Theater Day as well as some incidental events such as the Khvarazmi and Roshdi Festival. During the first five festivals each year 25 groups and about 500 people participated in theatrical activities. Thereafter with government support participation increased. During the first decade the most important playwrights were Reza Saberi, Mohammad Ahmadi, Nosrat Siyahi, Hoseyn Nuri, Mostafa Qalandari, Parviz Gharib and a few others.[330] There are furthermore organizations such as the Iranian Board of the National Theater, the Iranian Theater Artistic Association and a number of journals delaing with the dramatic arts. Even the Martyr's Foundation has now an Artistic Affairs office.[331] Similarly, as during the Pahlavi period, there is an actors' guild with compulsory membership.[332] This had led to the joining of strange bedfellows and hence funny interaction among its members.

> Honourable actors and actresses of the stage announced their anger and
> doubts about actors and actresses who end up going over to TV, and obviously make more money, and still call themselves *theater* actors and
> actresses. We had debates to determine whether to recognize them as

---

[329] Osku'i, Pazuheshi, p. 340 describing the ups-and-downs of the Anahita group noted that 1971-78 was a period of forced inactivity; the years 1978-86 were a perod of limited performance of plays and training, but as of 1987 a new period of activity began. For the situation in Gilan after 1979 see Talebi, "Namayesh," pp. 728-29.

[330] Osku'i, Pazuheshi, pp. 341-50 (with a list of their plays), 385ff.

[331] [http://www.qoqnoos.com/body/arosak/vafadari.y/resume.htm]

[332] Osku'i, Pazuheshi, pp. 351-57, 373-84.

competitors or colleagues. Whether they were sell-outs? How to regard actors and actresses in cheap comedy-musicals? Finally, the question amounted to: Is anybody an actor or actress, except us?[333]

Playwrights continued writing about the same themes as under the Pahlavi regime. Although experimentation remained an important characteristic of playwriting more recourse was had to traditional models such as story telling (*naqqali*) and improvisatory comedy (*ru-howzi*). Hamid-Reza A`zam's "The last technique" *(Shegerd-e akhar)* written in 1986 is played by a story teller, who, although famous for his epic tales, regales his audience with the heroic deeds of Iranian soldiers at the front. It is nationalistic and patriotic in tone and aims to rally the audience around the flag. Salman Farsi Salehzehi's play "Water, wind, land" (*Ab, bad, khak*) deals with conflicts between peasants and landlords. In addition to new playwrights some of the old ones continued to write as well such as Beyza'i, whose "The death of Yazdegerd" (*Marg-e Yazdegerd*) draws a parallel with the demise of the last Sasanid shah and that of Mohammad Reza Shah Pahlavi. Radi's "Slowly with the rose" (*Ahesteh ba gol-e sorkh*) was produced in 1988 and portrays the problems of an Iranian family deals with the rapid changes in Iranian society.

The world of theater is fully aware that the more things supposedly change the more they stay the same. Sayyed Mehrdad Ziya'i wrote in 2003:

> Whether we like it or not, our theater is state-run. This has been the case in its 120-year history in Iran. Officials prune to approve a play. Then theater groups can refurbish it for stage. Next is the ordeal of finding a place to set up the play. Finally, it is not easy to get necessary equipment, stage props, and costumes. Honourable members of supervisory boards will monitor your play before, during, and after rehearsals, not to mention at the time of live performance, private or public. Despite all these, last year many valuable plays were able to clear the hurdles and attract drama fans.[334]

The dark and difficult war years (1980-88) and of the elimination of the leftist opposition (1981-83) with the suppression of freedom of expression may explain the enormous popularity theater now enjoys in Iran when both socio-economic and political conditions have improved. European performers comment on the incredible enthusiasm their performances receive, so unlike the more subdued atmosphere in Europe.[335] There is something like a "theater boom." In this seeemingly neutral activity, the government gave the people what it wanted and it increased its support to cultural activities as well as higher subsidies to facilitate theater visits. In fact, the subsidies increased by 1000% between 1997 and 2001. There are about 1,000 free

---

[333] [[http://www.tehranavenue.com/ec_yir_theater.htm]]
[334] [www.tehranavenue.com/ec_yir_theater.htm]]
[335] [www.iran-today.net/article.php?sid=676] November 2004

theatrical workshops in Iran, of which 200 in Tehran alone. Each year some 1,000 students complete their studies at the Fine Arts Colleges at the universities or the 50 private theater schools most of them only can hope to get a role in TV or film projects. The annual *Fajr* theater festival, which is international in scope since 1999, experiences a record number of visitors each year. In 2002 more than 200,000 tickets were sold during the 12-day Festival, which is a singular phenomenon for an Islamic country. Theater performers try to push the limits of censorship and both playwright and actors are very inventive. Although female actors are allowed to perform their hair and bodies must be covered. Male skin may not touch female skin on stage. Actors therefore wear gloves and looks speak tomes. European directors in particular had to find their way about, because the interpretation of the rules changed all the time. Can a woman slap a man on stage, can they dance together? Iranian actors use kerchiefs, gestures and other props to symbolize bodily relationships. This demands much refined acting from the actors and actresses and a public of connoisseurs. Furthermore, playwrights write and directors select plays that indirectly provide a sometimes critical if not satirical view of conditions in contemporary Iran. It is therefore no surprise that many of the plays receive standing ovations.[336] When abroad Iranian troupes are less observant where censorship rules are concerned and during their performances men and women touch, dance, and a headscarf is not immediately correctly put back when it accidently reveals too much hair. One of the leading groups is that of Narges-e Siyah.[337] Another one is the "Acting Theater" or *Bazi Te'ater* (Attila Pesiyani, Setareh Pesiyani, and Fatemeh Naghavi), which performed a play about contemporary life in Iran in pantomime, thus borrowing both from Iran's theatrical tradition (*taqlid*) as well as European techniques.[338] According to Zara Houshmand a writer and theater artist,

> Jafari's work, like that of Pessyani and so many Iranian directors, owes a huge debt to Jerzy Grotowski, Peter Brook, Tadeusz Kantor, and other leading lights of the European avant-garde who accepted invitations to the Shiraz Festival before the revolution. That their influence remains powerful after a generation and a revolution speaks not only to the continuity of this lineage among Iranian theatre artists, but also perhaps to a special cultural fit.[339]

The 22nd International *Fajr* Theater Festival was held in Tehran in February 2003. During the ten-day event, not less than 117 theater groups had 365 performances

[336] [www.freitag.de/1999/08/99081501.htm] For such a play of social criticism see, for example, *Sleeping in an Empty Cup* that was staged in the Qashqa'i Hall of Tehran's City Theater in May and June 2003 (Playwright Naghmeh Samini; director Gayomarth Moradi [www.tehranavenue.com/ws_theater_cup.htm] According to Sayyed Mehrdad Ziya'i: "Our critics last year were just as saucy as those found in any other part of the world." [www.tehranavenue.com/ec_yir_theater.htm]]
[337] [www.ifa.de/zfk/magazin/akp/dmarcus.htm]
[338] [www.debalie.nl/artikel.jsp?podiumid=theater&articleid=5782]
[339] [http://www.wordswithoutborders.org/article.php?lab=Irantheater]

in 27 sites in six sectors of the festival including in competitions, out of competitions, international sector, reviews, open-air performances and religious plays. Nine plays from Switzerland, Germany, Italy, Great Britain, and Spain as well as a joint work by Romanian and Portuguese artists were performed during the festival. During the closing ceremony, the top artists in different theater fields received awards and two of the theater artists, Fahimeh Rastkar and Khosrow Khorshidi, were paid tribute for their life-long achievements in this area.[340] Although these festivals certainly help to keep theater alive it is, like under the Pahlavi regime, part of the government's cultural and even foreign policy. An artist and afficianado of Iranian theater Sayyed Mehrdad Ziya'i therefore could not fail but make some funny remarks about that part of the festival cycle.

> But these festivals showed us at least one thing: that we have thousands of officials in service of the arts, many more so than there are theatergoers. Festivals ranged from traditional to environmental, recreational, pastoral, experimental, occasional, international, intra-national, provincial, continental, oceanic, and comic. It is nonetheless puzzling how outfits like CNN or BBC can invade our homes on a daily basis with only a few hundred personnel. Perhaps they need to learn a thing or two from our officials, who are excellent at creating job opportunities.[341]

It is no wonder because the Center for Dramatic Arts that organizes the *Fajr* and other festivals is a large organization with many other responsibilities. According to its charter, it has the responsibility for the management, planning, and promotion of theater (both professional and amateur) in Iran. This means not only managing theaters, artists, and troupes, but also overseeing (a euphemism for censorship) all performances throughout Iran. Contacts with foreign theatrical troupes and organization also fall within its bailiwick. In Tehran the Center manages the City Theater Complex, which includes five auditoriums, *Vahdat* Hall (formerly Rudaki), *Honar* Hall that is devoted to children's theater, *Sanglaj* Hall and the *Khaneh-ye Namayesh*. The availability of these auditoriums makes it possible to stage plays throughout the year. The priorities of the Center are not necessarily those of the artists. One of them wrote:

> One official did the most last year to open several small venues for theater performance, but only in and around the City Theater in central Tehran. Theater people like to mock him by saying that he has built so many halls that the City Theater now looks more like the Tower of Babel. In other cities of Iran, many theater halls, amphitheaters, coliseums, aquariums, and gymnasiums were built to cater to the dramatic needs of the art-loving people of Iran. Honourable officials, from governors to MPs and local council members, would attend the opening ceremonies with or without the presence of

---

[340] [www.payvand.com/news/04/feb/1020.htm]
[341] [[http://www.tehranavenue.com/ec_yir_theater.htm]]

the honourable representatives of the National Radio and Television. Several attempts were also made to restore abandoned buildings—army barracks and caravansaries—but lack of budge did not permit the completion of sanitary systems (read toilets and modern bowls) and heating/cooling systems (oil furnaces and electric fans). Meanwhile, in Tehran, and given the fact that Iranians are hounded by proper appearances, last year, millions were spent to face-lift Vahdat Hall. This hall, once called Rudaki after Iran's pioneering poet, is the only venue in which gala performances can take place. We needed that face-lift no doubt.[342]

The Center therefore boasts of a Planning & Program Office, a Publication Unit, a Public Relations office, and the Secretariat for the Festivals. The latter organizes every year a number of festivals, some of which are international in scope. These include the International *Fajr* Theater Festival, in which professional, provincial and street groups participate as well as foreign groups. Further, the International Puppet Theater Festival is held bi-annually since 1989, with participation of both national and foreign groups. Other festivals are the festival of Traditional and Ritualistic Performances (since 1989), the Kurdish Theater Festival (since 1999 and in Kurdish), the Tribal Theater Festival (since 1997 and held in one of the provinces), the Youth and Children's Theater Festival (since 1990, held in one of the provinces), the Regional and Provincial Festivals (since 1990). The best productions of the latter are invited to participate in the *Fajr* Festival. Finally, the Center supports festivals organized by other entities such as the Students Theater Festival and the Holy Detense Theater festival. The center has other departments such as the Center of Ritualistic and Traditional Performances. It supports those performances and provides training, research and information. The Center of Street Theater exists since 1997 and supports these activities throughout the country, which have become so important that they also participate in the major national festivals. Finally, the UNIMA office is affiliated with UNESCO with which it organizes the international puppet theater festival.[343] In addition to the Center, there is also Theater House, which has the responsibility of producing and performing plays as well as providing insurance coverage and other services to artists. It also shares with the Center the responsibility of, for example, the organization of the commemoration of World Theater Day.[344]

Despite this overwhelming government hold (both financially and otherwise) on the theater world, there are also some independent organizations such as the Iranian Women's Center, which was established in 1985 under the name "Women's Theatrical Unit" managed directly by the Center for Dramatic Arts. In 1988 the latter continued its activities as a semi-governmental organization. The "Iranians's

---

[342] [[http://www.tehranavenue.com/ec_yir_theater.htm]]
[343] [www.irannamayesh.com/english/about.asp]
[344] [www.iran-daily.com] April 15, 2003.

Women's Theater Center" continued its work independently without any support of the Theatrical Association and is the only supporter of women's theater in the country. The center is active in three areas: production, education and culture. Its educational unit admits some students twice a year in: make-up, costume design, graphics, painting, acting, writing screen plays, and doll-making. It aims at identifying talents in women, by themselves and hence directing them to artistic centers for training. Its producion unit has produced valuable plays in the last eight years in which women were main actresses.[345] There also are independent troupes, which were established with the financial support of art-loving private investors. However, their lifespan is usually short, as investors are risk-averse by nature.[346]

Figure 45: Modern play with ancient masked dancers (Fajr Festival 2004)

Not everybody is pleased with the way cultural life in Iran has been developing in recent years. There are two major groups of criticial opponents: the conservatives inside the country and the Iranian exiles abroad. Both express their opinion on this issue, sometimes forcefully. For example, fifty activists from the hardline *Ansar-e Hezbollah* party burst into a theater in Mashhad on 27 July, 2001 to disrupt the show, *Iran's Mr Bean*, starring the well-known Iranian comic Hami Reza Mahisefat. An Iranian court sentenced two of the thugs to flogging and jail terms.[347] The Iranian community in exile is rather vociferous in the expression of its negative opinion

---

[345] [http://www.salamiran.org/Women/Organisations/iwtc.html]
[346] [[http://www.tehranavenue.com/ec_yir_theater.htm]
[347] [http://www.corpun.com/irj00109.htm]

about the Islamic Republic in all the media available to it. As far as drama is concerned this has led to the production of many serious plays, which, among other things criticize the socio-political values of the Islamic republic of Iran.[348]

---

[348] For those interested in this exile theater see Javadi, *Satire*, pp. 276-77 and Ghanoonparvar, M.R. "Drama," *Encyclopaedia Iranica.*

APPENDIX 1

PAHLAVAN KACHAL

What follows is a partial translation of Y.N. Marr, "Koje-chto o Pehlevan Kechel i drygikh vidakh narodnogo teatre v Persii." *Iran* II, pp. 75-84. For easy reference the page numbers have been inserted at the end of each page between brackets. Pages 84-88 contain a short description of a puppet play of which the main characters may be seen at figure 13. They are (1) *Pahlavan Kachal*, (2) *Mobarak* his servant; (3) *Mashshaq*, the music teacher, an Armenian whose nickname is *Korapet*; (4) *Khvajeh Zad o Bord*, the thief; (5) *Hakim Molla Soleyman*, a Jewish doctor from Jubareh (a quarter of Isfahan); 6. *Sarv-e Naz Khanom*, a girl; (7) *Zardab Div*; (8) *Bachcheh* or the baby.

—·—

One November evening in 1925 in Isfahan I was invited to a children's party, which was called by our consul general, W.G. Tardov and his wife, E. O. Tardova. During this evening the main types of folk entertainment were nicely represented. In this article I just tell what I saw at that party. The first number was the storyteller, who can be seen most often in a coffeehouse or in the street in front of a coffeehouse. Usually he sits on a bench (*takhteh*) and talks and around him also on a bench or on the ground on small carpets are listeners. They sit, listen, smoke their water pipe, or their ceramic pipe, which is cheaper, and drink tea from small glasses.

Access to such crowded coffeehouses is sometimes difficult for Europeans. One of the local writers said to me, today you can go with a European hat, tomorrow the priest will tell the owner to close down the coffeehouse because you were there. To prevent this, the owner will have to pay an amount that is higher than he will get from you.

The storyteller was a middle-aged man wearing a green turban (*chelmeh*) and a cloak (`aba); he had huge a beard. He sat on a chair and before he started storytelling he told how it was done in coffeehouses; he praised the prophet and the imams, and the last sentence of this praise was repeated by the audience. He was telling the story in a very low bass voice; it was an episode of Rostam and Askibu. It was in prose and he used more details than in the Shahnameh. During the high points he used various facial expressions and body gestures.

After the storyteller, there were two dervishes, one young who sang some *ghazal*s, the old one recited the *Bostan* of Sa'di. The repertoire off such singing dervishes is very diverse as well as the conditions where they perform. I am not going to describe that having done that often elsewhere.

The next number is this snake charmer. The dervish-*margir* [i.e. snake-catcher] does important folk entertainment. I saw one of these dervishes in the beginning of May 1925 at the house of our military attaché. The dervish brought him a marten. He was dressed in a white large shirt, and white loose pants, and cotton shoes (*giveh*s). He was not wearing a belt and, and on his head he wore a small hat (*taj*), which was rolled in white cloth. On his neck he wore a piece of leather with wavy writing. This piece of leather looks like a sunshade. He was holding a cage with a rodent in his hands and a crooked dagger without a sheath. Also a small stick longer than one ell; one end of it was shaped like a fish head (*sar-e mahi*). He had carved it himself and on one side of the head where the eye should be he had put a nail with a white head. He had long hair, which was divided into locks, and he was very suntanned and had no upper front teeth, no beard and looked very young. He said that he was dervish Hoseyn. I asked him "what is your dervish order [*selseleh*]?" He said, [76] "I am from the 'Ajam (*ma az tudeh-ye 'Ajam hastim*]. I am from Persia, but we dervishes are all the same. There are *Ne'matollahi*s and *Khaksar*, but it does not matter." And then he stopped talking about himself. He had a sack on his shoulder with two boxes in it, a small one with scorpions, the big one with snakes. He took two snakes out, one male and one female. They call them *mar-e ja'fari*. He let them free and when one of them would turn oneway, that is, was trying to flee, he caught it and tapped it on its head with a finger and it would curl up, so that the head would be in the middle of the curl. This snake would immediately fall asleep. The dervish repeated this several times.

Then he showed his scorpions, one black and the others yellow. He would take them by the tail and put them in his palm. Sometimes, and they would hit him with their tails but this did not harm him. He explained to me how to catch scorpions and to make them harmless. The big black ones are found in kitchens (*ashpazkhaneh*), where they like to walk on the blackened ceiling. The small yellow ones live in the rocks and near water sources. They are caught as follows; the dervish and his apprentice would find a hole and make sure there is a scorpion it; then he makes the hole wider, and takes the scorpion out by the tail with tongs (*anbur*) and put it in the box. Then the training starts. The dervish used his nail to rub and dull the sting of the scorpions. He also keeps the scorpions on a diet. The black scorpion dies of hunger in 10 days, the yellow ones, depending on the kind, die in three to five days. The dervish feeds them raw meat, which they suck (*mimaked*). He does not give them any food if they are not obedient. The big black scorpion is called *parrareh*, the small very poisonous yellow one is called *jarrar* or *jarrareh*. He showed me the most poisonous one from his collection, [77] while the black one was as long as his palm, the poisonous yellow one, even with its tail straight, would fit in a matchbox.

The dervish also said that he catches and trains sand dogs [*mush-e dupa*], mountain cats [*gorbeh-ye kuhi*], cheetahs [*yuz*], wolves, and foxes.

Then there was the dervish with the snakes. I had not met him in the squares in Isfahan where he would perform with an assistant who was not the dervish. On his head, he had the usual hat (*taj*) covered with white cloth. His long dark, almost black locks and beard made him look vicious. This performance was not complicated. He would hold one or more snakes by the tail, let them go, call them back, and put them on his neck, and he would tell them while doing all is what to do. Sometimes he had an assistant with whom he would play a very primitive boring scene. For example, he would scare him with the snakes, and threaten him that the most poisonous snake would like him and that he would die. The assistant, very unsuccessfully, tried to show terror.

Then there was a magician. I will talk about him at the end of the article. There also was music and short comedies. The following instruments are used.

(1) *Da'ereh* or *dayereh* is a tambourine.
(2) *Ney* or flute.
(3) *Tar*, kind of a guitar.
(4) *Kamancheh*, which is like the balailaika. [78]
(5) *Org* or organ.
(6) *Tombak* or drum.
(7) Castagnettes.
(8) *Mothalath* or triangle.

The musicians played well, they played popular tunes as well as Isfahani tunes. They also played some pieces of Caucasian music. The orchestra played alone or accompanied the performers including dancers.

Some words about the play. The genre of old traditional Persian comedy where actors wear masks is disappearing. Instead European style drama is replacing it. This is already played on a stage where there is a curtain, and where they have tables and chairs. They still keep some of the old comedy, for example, in the manner how characters are treated in a stereotyped way; lazy servants, an old loser in love, the nagging shrew. In Enzeli I saw the drama of the new type of where there was a servant without mask, but his face was like a mask, because it did not move and was expressionless, his brows were raised, he had wide open eyes that are rolling frantically all the time, a large mustache and his mouth open to his ears. [If women were allowed in the theater they were seated higher up and during intermission separated by a curtain; women were not allowed to attend in Isfahan]. Amazement and indignation [79] he would express by raising his brows even more, rolling his eyes even more, and by pursing his lips. He would put a besom in his belt and walk with big unnatural steps and every time he came on to the stage the audience would laugh.

In the play that I saw in Isfahan, *Mashti `Ebad*, there was an unlucky groom. This groom is an old man with long red beard, hair, and face. He is ugly, a miser and he wants to marry a young girl. He is cheated, laughed at and they beat him. These two characters seem to have been taken from the old masked comedy. These comedies are still played by special actors. In the comedy I saw at the Tardov's not everybody was wearing masks; as stage props there were only two chairs, and later a bed, which was just a mattress and a blanket.

Cast of characters:
A young handsome officer, without mask.
His valet, a Turk, a comical type with mask.
An old feeble man, with mask.
The wife of the officer, without mask.

The rest of the characters did not have time to appear because the first part was interrupted. The main intrigue was extremely simple. A young officer receives a note from a lady in which he is interested. She wants to come to him. The officer is very happy, but he cannot be alone and call her to come to him, for he is constantly interrupted. This is the background against which the intrigues develop. There are two comical characters. One is an officer's valet, who is big and silly. He cannot sit still on a chair, and cannot lie on a bed, etc. the other one is a feeble, the good-humored old man with fluffy white beard. He is deaf and can hardly walk. So when he needs the Turk [80] he always loses and falls on the ground. This old man probably is the petitioner, but because he is deaf and the valet stupid the petition remains unknown and the valet thinks the old man is the father of the officer. During the play the consul-general understood that a very improper scene was coming and that it was unavoidable. He went to the next room and asked one of the actors to change the play. The actor went out on to the stage, killed one of the characters, and the play was over. The actors playing this comedy were also musicians in the orchestra. That is why there were never more than two and sometimes only one actor on the stage. They took turns in performing. At the end of the playing there was one young man dressed like a woman with dark glasses (pincenez), who danced very passionately.

In Isfahan, *Pahlavan-Kachal*, puppet theater and conjury is done by one person. His name is *Sayyed-e Habib-e Hoqqehbaz*, I cannot tell whether he was alone, but I did not see any other like him in Isfahan. I often saw him performing in the square. I saw him once at the consul-general and twice in my own house. He was middle-aged, thin and wore a tall head, and a worn out coat. He worked with an assistant. The assistant makes masks and the magician knows how to make puppets. Heads are made from cardboard, both for puppets on a string and glove puppets. Together they carry everything needed for the performance. For the magician's tricks all is in a small sack that Sayyed Habib has on his shoulder. In it are various sticks, cotton wool, paper, thread etc. The puppets are put in a box (*sanduq*). The figures for *Pahlavan Kachal* are in a small box. Finally, the very important prop for the performance of screens for *Pahlavan Kachal*, [81] and if marionettes are shown then a tent, which is useful for both performances.

When the magician came to my house and gave a full performance he started with tricks and then continued with the puppet show and in the end performed *Pahlavan Kachal*. I do not know if it is done in the same order when he performs in the street. I think he does one thing at the time. In any case, I had never seen marionettes in the square or the streets. He started his performance with a long praise of God. He sat crossed legged (*bedu zanu*) on a small carpet and took out of his sack the puppets he needed. During the performance he repeated verses of a famous Isfahan poet, especially the following;

> Open the eyes of your heart to see the unseeable.

He recites this poem always in a quick manner to really show thereafter the unseeable things. To give you on approximate idea I describe the tricks for you:

1. Four small balls and four metal cups. The balls are made of dark wax or of bread. When the magician tells the balls to go from one cup to the other their number increases or decreases. The four cups are named after four cities.
2. He fills a glass with clear water and puts a tin cover over it. When the cover is lifted there is coal in the glass. Another manipulation with the cover and there are live scorpions in it. At the end, the glass is filled with flower petals.
3. He swallows and then pushes with a stick into his throat a huge quantity of cotton wool. He puts a stick in his mouth, and starts rolling it in his palms and then he takes it out of his mouth and moves it like a spindle and an endless thread comes out of his mouth by blowing.
4. He takes a big book out of his bag; he holds it with one hand at the cover and with the other he flips through the pages in front of the audience. The book is either completely blank or there is text. After

magicking it is all of a sudden full of flowers, then with demons, animals, or people.

5. Then he performs as a juggler, i.e. with big metal rings that have no opening. Suddenly they are joined in various ways.
6. He shows a small tin vessel with water; when he orders something water comes out of several holes; after the next order it stops leaking.
7. He pierces his tongue.

He shows many other tricks in addition. These examples are sufficient. They are not all based on the dexterity of the hand, for some require props even if they are simple. The magician plays both types of puppet theater. Puppets for *Pahlavan Kachal* consist of a head, made of cardboard and the robe. The head is put on the index finger or on the index and middle finger. The big and ring finger are put into the sleeves. During the performance Sayyed Habib is outside; his apprentice (*shagerd*) sits in the tent and shows the puppets from behind a screen. This performance is called *Pahlavan Kachal* or *Kheymahgar*. (footnote: the term *panj* I have not heard)

The other puppet show is different in that all the puppets are partly of wood, partly of cardboard and are moved by strings. The screen for these puppets is bigger and at the bottom of the screen there is an opening of 35 cm off the ground. Behind the screen (*sherm*) and the flat screen (*akram*) there is another, behind which the assistant stands. The puppets are on strings; the assistant sitting inside make them sit, lie, but very few can move one arm. However, there is an interesting puppet named Ghoul. It is a monster with a round body, which can be extracted so that the head goes outside the stage or it can be compressed. Usually there are several dozen of these puppets. I am just noting what I saw. On the dark background of the internal screen appears a man's figure in a blue overcoat (*qaba*). He brings two chairs and he falls down. Another male figure appears with a broom. They start arguing and then fight. One of them falls down and then comes a water carrier, a soldier with a cannon, then a shah in an armchair drives by, the queen walks, a dancer entertains the shah, the executioner comes, a ghoul, and many others. This is called *shab-bazi* [84].

APPENDIX 2

THE VIZIER OF THE KHAN OF LENKORAN

These are two pages from Thalasso's article on theater in Qajar Iran that describe the career and works of Mirza Fath `Ali Akhundzadeh (see pages 221-222) as well as the first-ever performance of one of his plays entitled "The Vizier of the Khan of Lenkoran." The play was staged in 1900 at the Paris home of Mme Jane Dieulafoy, who had accompanied her husband Marcel Dieulafoy to Shushtar to start the first French archeological excavations there in 1881. On her return to Paris she wrote two informative and beautifully illustrated travel accounts of their experiences in Iran.

LA COMÉDIE DE MIRZA FETH ALI

❖

Le dialecte *Azéri* qui se parle au Caucase russe et dans la Perse septentrionale, est aux langues turque et persane ce que l'idiome provençal est au français et à l'italien. Écrit dans ce dialecte, le théâtre de Mirza Feth Ali — quoique ne relevant pas directement de l'art dramatique persan — se rattache plus à lui, cependant, qu'à l'art dramatique turc, tant à cause de l'idiome dans lequel il a été composé que pour la traduction persane dont il a eu les honneurs.

Mirza Feth Ali nous a été présenté, dans la *Revue Critique* du 19 mars 1883, par le directeur actuel de notre Ecole des Langues Orientales, M. A. Barbier de Meynard.

C'est à l'étude documentée du savant orientaliste que nous puisons les détails ayant trait à la biographie de notre auteur dramatique.

Le Vizir du Khân de Lênkêrân (Scène de la Marmite).
M⁰⁰ X...   M. G. Soulier   M⁰⁰ Léon
(Niça Hanum).   (Le Vizir).   (Péri Hanum).

Le Vizir du Khân de Lênkêrân.
M. Gustave Soulier (le Vizir).

Mirza Feth Ali Akhond Zadé (Zadé signifie enfant, rejeton) ainsi que son nom l'indique, était fils d'un akhond. Natif de Karadjah-Dagh, la Montagne-Noire, en Mésopotamie, il entra, jeune encore, au service de la Russie. Il ne tarda guère à être promu capitaine. Une mutation suivit ce grade et l'officier fut envoyé à Tiflis. Il y devint tout de suite un des habitués du théâtre que le Gouverneur général de cette ville, Woronsow, avait fait construire en 1850. On y jouait les pièces du répertoire russe et souvent des troupes françaises et italiennes de passage y donnaient des représentations. Cette communion journalière d'ouvrages dramatiques révéla à Mirza Feth Ali sa vocation. Elle ne fut pas longue à s'affirmer. Coup sur coup, notre auteur écrivit les sept comédies dont les titres suivent 1° *l'Alchimiste* ou *Mollah-Ibrahim* ; 2° *Monsieur Jourdan, le botaniste* et le derviche *Mest-Ali-Chah, le célèbre enchanteur* ; 3° *le Divan-Beyi* ; 4° *l'Avare* ; 5° *le Vizir du Khân de Serab*, qui devint plus tard le *Vizir du Khân de Lênkêrân* ; 6° *les Procureurs* ; 7° une scène historique dialoguée, qui se passe sous le règne de Chah-Abbas.

Toutes ces comédies parurent en *azéri*, en 1858, et furent imprimées à Tiflis. De cette édition originale, extrêmement rare et fort recherchée, l'Europe ne possède que deux exemplaires dont l'un se trouve dans la bibliothèque de M. A. Barbier de Meynard.

Un des envois d'auteur avait été fait au prince Djelal-Ed-Din Mirza, historien très prisé en Perse, en retour de son *Livre des Rois* adressé à Akhond Zadé. Dans la dédicace de cet envoi, nous apprend une lettre de Sidney Churchill à la Société Asiatique de Londres, l'auteur *azéri* exprimait au prince le désir de voir ses comédies traduites en persan. Pendant de nombreuses années, ces comédies restèrent enfouies au fond d'une bibliothèque. En 1871, Mirza Dja-Fer, secrétaire de Djelal-Ed-Din, les découvrit, les lut et, charmé de leur esprit, voulut déférer au vœu de leur auteur.

Les comédies parurent à Téhéran, au fur et à mesure de leurs traductions. En 1874, elles furent recueillies en un volume presque aussi rare, paraît-il, que l'original de Tiflis. Malheureusement l'édition lithographique persane est si peu lisible et si pleine de fautes d'orthographe que M. A. Barbier de Meynard n'hésita pas, avec la collaboration de Stanislas Guyard à faire publier, à Paris, en 1886, d'après l'édition de Téhéran, les trois meilleures comédies de Mirza Feth Ali : *L'Alchimiste, Le Vizir du Khân de Lênkêrân et Les Procureurs*, suivies de notes et d'un glossaire.

Le Vizir du Khân de Lênkêrân.
M. Henri Derras (Timour).

Non content de nous avoir fait connaître la belle traduction de Mirza-Dja-Fer, M. A. Barbier de Meynard publia dans le *Journal Asiatique* de janvier 1886, le texte *azéri* de *l'Alchimiste*, avec la traduction française de cette comédie.

Deux années plus tard, M. Alphonse Cillière, alors attaché au Ministère des Affaires étrangères, aujourd'hui consul de France à Constantinople, faisait paraître chez Ernest Leroux la traduction des deux œuvres maîtresses de Mirza Feth Ali : *Le Vizir du Khân de Lênkêrân et Les Procureurs*, précédées d'une introduction aussi raisonnée que savante sur le théâtre d'Akhond Zadé. Il est un point, cependant, où nous ne partageons pas sa façon de voir. M. Cillière préfère de beaucoup *Le Vizir*

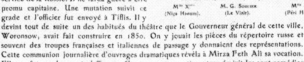

Le Vizir du Khân de Lênkêrân.
M⁰⁰ Buisson (Cho'lé Hanum).

Photographies inédites de M. Marcel DIEULAFOY.

Le Vizir du Khân de Lénkérân. (Scène de la Querelle).
M. Pierre Thesmar   Mᵐᵉ Buisson
(Ziba Hanum).   (Cho'lé Hanum).

du *Khân de Lènkèrân* aux *Procureurs.* Tel n'est pas notre humble avis. Malgré de brillantes qualités, le *Vizir du Khân de Lènkèrân* procède directement de Scribe : tout y est arbitraire, jusqu'au dénouement, jusqu'au titre qui n'a été changé qu'à cause de ce dénouement. Cette comédie est loin de respirer le souffle puissant de vie qui passe au travers des *Procureurs,* les anime, et — malgré quelques inexpériences et des inégalités — les rend autrement humains que les fantoches du *Vizir.*

De toutes ces comédies, aucune n'a été représentée, pas plus en Perse qu'en Turquie. Et cela se conçoit. Soumis aux lois de l'Islam, aucun de ces pays ne tolérerait une attaque directe faite à leurs mœurs et à leurs coutumes. Le croirait-on ? C'est Paris qui, le premier, mit à la scène Mirza Feth Ali. Tout l'honneur de cette initiative revient à Mᵐᵉ Dieulafoy qui, en 1900, fit donner chez elle, la « Première » des quatre actes du *Vizir du Khân de Lènkèrân,* sans retouches, sans tripatouillages, dans la belle traduction littérale, littéraire et intégrale de M. A. Cillière. La soirée avait commencé par une charmante causerie de M. A. Barbier de Meynard sur le théâtre de Mirza Feth Ali. Ceux qui ont assisté à cette représentation ont encore présent à leur mémoire le franc éclat de rire qui l'accueillit et le succès que remporta M. Pierre Thesmar, *un homme,* dans le rôle de Ziba Hanum, la *vieille femme* du Vizir.

Le théâtre de Mirza Feth Ali puise, directement, son inspiration aux sources de notre scène. La formule européenne est adaptée avec un art infini aux mœurs et coutumes orientales. L'écriture en est alerte et vive, et

Le Vizir du Khân de Lènkèrân.
M. Gustave Soulier (le Vizir).

les caractères, finement observés, humainement décrits ne procèdent en aucune façon, pas plus pour leur esprit que pour leur langage, des personnages de *Ketchel* et de la *Temaschâ.*

Dans une étude spécialement consacrée aux autres scènes de l'Asie, nous nous étendrons plus à loisir sur le *Théâtre Azéri* et sur Mirza-Feth-Ali, dont les trois comédies citées plus haut, méritent chacune un examen approfondi, une minutieuse analyse et la reproduction de nombreux extraits.

Si pour la documentation de notre étude nous avons pris plaisir à signaler ce théâtre, notre cadre même nous enjoint à ne pas pénétrer plus avant dans une scène, ramifiée, il est vrai, aux arts dramatiques turc et persan, mais qui n'est, à proprement parler, pas plus iranienne qu'ottomane.

Nous ne saurions trop recommander, cependant, à tous ceux qui veulent connaître ce théâtre, de lire les traductions de MM. A. Barbier de Meynard et A. Cillière, colla-tionnées sur le texte Azéri et les deux textes persans.

Ils se feront une idée, aussi exacte que pos-sible, du génie de Mirza Feth Ali, qui a su se tailler une place bien à part et très caractéristique dans le « Théâtre Oriental ».

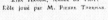

Grâce à l'obligeance extrême de M. Marcel Dieulafoy —— que nous remercions vivement —— nous avons pu avoir les photographies des prota-gonistes du *Vizir du Khân de Lènkèrân.* Nos lecteurs y verront aussi celles des deux princi-pales situations de la comédie : la curieuse *Scène de la querelle* entre la vieille et la jeune femme du vizir : Ziba et Cho'lé Hanum, et celle si originale de *La Marmite,* où Niça et Peri Hanum couvrent d'un récipient la tête du vizir pour permettre à

Le Vizir du Khân de Lénkérân.
Ziba Hanum, femme du Vizir.
Rôle joué par M. Pierre Thesmar.

l'amoureux Timour Agha de s'esquiver sans être vu.

Le Vizir du Khân de Lénkérân.
Mᵐᵉ Buisson
(Cho'lé Hanum, la jeune femme du Vizir).

BIBLIOGRAPHY

Abu'l-Hasan Khan, Mirza. A Persian at the court of King George 1809-10. The Journal of Mirza Abul Hassan Khan. translated and edited by Margaret Morris Cloake (London: Barrie & Jenkins, 1988).

Adamiyat, Fereydun. *Amir Kabir* (Tehran: Khvarezmi, 1348/1969).

Adams, Isaac. *Persia by a Persian* (n.p., 1900), p. 419.

Afshar, Hasan `Ali Khan. *Safarnameh-ye Lorestan va Khuzestan* ed. Hamid-Reza Dalvand (Tehran,1382/2003).

Afshari, Mehran ed. *Haft Lashkar ya Shahnameh-ye Naqqalan* (Tehran: Ketab-e Haftom, 1369/1990).

____, *Ayin-e Qalandari* with Mir `Abedini (Tehran: Fararavan, 1374/1995).

____, "Ferqeh-ye `Ajam va Sokhanvari," *Hasti* 3/1 (1374/1995), pp. 142-152.

Ahmad Bey, "La Société persane: le Théâtre et ses Fêtes," *La Nouvelle Revue* 14/77 (1892), pp. 524-38.

Alberts, Robert Charles. *Social Structure and Culture Change in an Iranian Village* 2 vols. (unpublished dissertation; University of Wisconsin, 1963).

Amanat, Abbas. *Pivot of the Universe* (Berkeley, 1997).

Amin, Ahmad. "Iran dar sal-e 1311 AH," translated by Gharavi, Mohammad. *Barrasiha-ye Tarikhi* 9/4 (1353/1974), pp. 75-100.

Amjad, Hamid. *Teyatr-e Qarn-e Sizdahom* (Tehran, 1378/1999).

`Anasari, Jaber. "Mo`arrefi-ye barkhi az noskh-e tarafeh-ye shabih-khvani (beh zaban-e Azeri)," *Ganjineh-ye Asnad* 5/3-4, nrs. 19-20 (1374/1995), pp. 7-11.

____, "Asnad va madarek-e vizheh-ye shabiyeh-khvani dar Takiyeh-ye Dowlat," *Ganjineh-ye Asnad* 5/4, nr. 16 (1374/1995), pp. 6-10.

And, Metin. *A History of Theatre and Popular Entertainment in Turkey* (Ankara, 1963-64).

Anjavi Shirazi, Sayyed Abu'l-Qasem. *Baziha-ye Namayeshi* (Tehran: Amir Kabir, 1973).

____, *Jashnehha va Adab va Mo`tadiqat-e Zamestan* (Tehran: Amir Kabir, 1973).

Anonymous. *A Chronicle of the Carmelites in Persia and the Papal Mission of the Seventeenth and Eighteenth Centuries*, 2 vols. (London, 1939).

Anonymous, *Histoire des Decouvertes faites par divers savans voyageurs* 6 vols. (Lausanne: Heubach, 1784).

Anonymous, "Die Passionsspiele der schiitischen Mohammedaner," *Globus. Illustrierte Zeitschrift für Länder- und Völkerkunde*, vol. XVI/23 (1870), p. 353-59.

Arabshah, Ahmed ibn. *Tamerlane or Timur the Great Amir* translated by J.H. Sanders (Lahore, n.d.).

Arbab, Mohammad Taqi Beg. "Ketabcheh-ye Tafsil-e Halat va Nofus va Amlak-e Dar al-Iman-e Qom," ed. Hoseyn Modarresi Tabataba'i, in *Farhang-e Iran-Zamin* 22 (2536/1977), pp. 151-206.

Ardakani, Hoseyn Mahbubi, *Tarikh-e Mo'assesat-e Tamaddon-e Jadid dar Iran* 3 vols. (Tehran: Daneshgah, 1368/1989).

Arnold, A. *Through Persia by Caravan* (New York: Harper & Brothers, 1877).

Aryanpur, Yahya. *Az Saba ta Nima*, 2 vols. (Tehran, 1357/1978).

Asaf, Mohammad Hashem. "Rostam al-Hokoma," *Rostam al-Tavarikh*, ed. Mohammad Moshiri (Tehran, 1348/1969).

`Askari, `Ali Hajj `Ali. *Tarikhcheh-ye Te'atr-e Gilan (1289-1357)* (Tehran, n.d.).

`Ata'i, Abu'l-Qasem Jannati. *Bonyad-e Namayesh dar Iran* (Tehran: Mihan, 1333/1954).

Atabay, Badri. *Fehrest-e Ketabkhaneh-ye Saltanati, fehrest-e tarikh, safarnameh, siyahatnameh*, etc. (Tehran 2537/1977).

`Attar. *Osthornameh* ed. Mahdi Mohaqqeq (Tehran, 1962).

Aubin, Eugène. *La Perse d'aujourd'hui* (Perse, 1908).

Athenaeus of Naucratis, *The Deipnosophists*, translated by Charles Burton Gulick (Cambridge: Harvard UP, 1926-57).

Babayan, Kathryn. *The Waning of the Qizilbash: The Spiritual and the Temporal in Seventeenth Century Iran* (unpublished dissertation, Princeton University, 1993).

Bafqi, Mohammad Mofid Mostowfi-ye. *Jame`-ye Mofidi*. 3 vols. ed. Iraj Afshar (Tehran 1340/1961).

Bahar, Mohammad Taqi. *Bahar va Adab-e Farsi*. ed. Mohammad Golbon (Tehran, 1351/1972)

____, *Sabkshenasi ya tarikh-e tattavor-e nathr-e farsi* 3 vols. (Tehran, 1331/1952).

____, ed. *Mojmal al-Tawarikh*, partially tr. by Jules Mohl, as "Extraits du *Modj-mel al-Tewarikh*, relatifs à l'histoire de la Perse," *Journal Asiatique*, 1841, pp. 479-536.

Bamdad,Mehdi. *Tarikh-e Rejal-e Iran qorun-e 12-13-14*. 6 vols. (Tehran, 1347/1968).

Başgöz, Ilhan. "Marasem-e tamanay-e baran va baran-sazi dar Iran," *Ketab-e Jom`eh* 1/19 (29 Adhar 1358), pp. 130-41.

Basir al-Molk Sheybani. *Ruznameh-ye Khaterat*. eds. Iraj Afshar and Mohammad Rasul Daryagasht (Tehran: Donya-ye Ketab, 1374/1995).

Basset, James. *Persia, the Land of the Imams* (New York: Charles Scribner's Sons, 1886).

Bedik, Petro. *Cehil Sutun seu explicatio utriusque celeberrisimi, ac pretiosissimi theatri quadriginta columnarum in Perside Orientis* (Vienna, 1678).

Benjamin, S. G. W. *Persia and the Persians* (London: John Murray, 1887).

Bent, Theodore ed. *Early voyages and travels in the Levant. I. The diary of Master Thomas Dallam, 1599-1600. II. Extracts from the diaries of Dr. John Covel, 1670-1679. With some account of the Levant company of Turkey merchants* (London: Hakluyt Society, 1893).

Bertel's, E. "Persidskii teatr," *Vostotsnyj teatr* IV (Leningrad, 1924).

Beyza'i, Bahram. *Namayesh dar Iran* (Tehran, 1345/1966).

Binder, Henry. *Au Kurdistan* (Paris: Quantin, 1887).

Binning, R.B. M. *A Journal of Two Years' Travel in Persia, Ceylon, etc*. 2 vols. (London: Wm. H. Allen & Co, 1857).

Bird, Isabella (Mrs. Bishop). *Journeys in Persia and Kurdistan*, 2 vols. (London, 1891 [London, 1988]).

Biruni, Abu Reyhan. *Al-Tafhim li ava'il sana`at al-tanjim* ed. Jalal Homa'i (Tehran, 1362/1983).

Bolukbashi, `Ali. "Namayeshha-ye shadi-avar-e zananeh dar Tehran," *Honar va Mardom* 27 (1343/1964), pp. 26-28.

Boratav, P. N. "Qaragöz," *Encyclopedia of Islam*[2].

Boyce, Mary. "The Parthian gosan professional singer and the Iranian Minstrel Tradition" *Journal of the Royal Asiatic Society*, 1957, vol. Pt 1 & 2," pp. 10-45.

____, "Some Remarks on the Transmission of the Kayanian Heroic Cycle," *Serta Cantabrigensia*, Studies presented to the XXIII International Congress of Orientalists, Mainz 1954, pp. 45-52.

____, "Zariadres and Zarer," *BSOAS* 17/4 (1955), pp. 463-77.

Browne, E.G. *A Literary History of Persia*. 4 vols. (Cambridge, 1959).

____, *The press and poetry of modern Persia* (Cambridge, 1914).

____, *A Year Amongst the Persians* (London: A. & C. Black, 1970).

Brugsch, Heinrich. *Die Reise der K.K. Gesandtschaft nach Persien 1861-1862*, 2 vols. (Berlin: J.C. Hinrichs, 1863).

Buckingham, J.S. *Travels in Assyria, Media and Persia* (London, 1829 [Westmead: Gregg Int., 1971]).

Burnes, Alexander. *Travels into Bokhara*. 3 vols. (New Delhi: Asia Educational Services, 1992 [London, 1834]).

Busse, Heribert. *Chalif und Grosskönig; die Buyiden im Iraq (945-1055)* (Beirut, 1969).

Byron, Robert. *The Road to Oxiania* (London, n.d. [1937]).

Calmard, Jean. "Les Rituels Shiites et le Pouvoir. L'imposition du shiisme safavide: eulogies et maledictions canoniques," in Jean Calmard ed. *Etudes Safavides* (Pars-Tehran, 1993), pp. 109-50.

Calmard, Jean. "Le mécénat des representations de ta`zie. I," *Le Monde Iranien et l'Islam* 2 (1974), pp. 73-126.

____, "Le mécénat des representations de ta`ziye. II," *Le Monde Iranien et l'Islam* 4 (1976-77), pp. 133-62.

____, "Les rituals shiites et le pouvoir. L'imposition du shiisme safavide: eulogies et maledictions canoniques," in Jean Calmard ed. *Etudes Safavides* (Paris/Tehran, 1993), pp. 109-50.

Castanheda, Fernão Lopes. *História do descobrimento e conquista da India peolos Portugueses*, 4 vols. Ed. Pedro de Azevedo (Coimbre, 1924-33).

Cejpek, Jiři. "Iranian Folk-Tales and Problems Arising From Them," in Jan Rypka ed. *History of Iranian Literature* (Dodrecht, 1986), pp. 607-710.

Chardin, Jean. *Voyages*, ed. L. Langlès, 10 vols., (Paris, 1811).

Chardin, Sir John. *Travels in Persia 1673-1677* (London, 1927).

Chelkowski, Peter. "Dramatic and Literary Aspects of Ta'zieh-Khani—an Iranian Passion Play," *Review of National Literatures*: Iran 2 (Spring, 1971), pp. 120-25.

____, ed. *Ta`ziyeh: Ritual and Drama in Iran* (New York, 1979).

Chodzko, Aleksander B. *Théatre Persan. Choix de Tèaziès* (Tehran, 1976).

Conolly, Arthur. *Journey to the North of India*. 2 vols. (London: Richard Bentley, 1834).

Curzon, G.N. *Persia and the Persian Question* 2 vols. (London, 1892 [London, 1966]).

D'Allemagne, H. *Du Khorasan au Pays de Bakhtyaris*, 4 vols. (Paris, 1911).

De Clavijo, Ruy Gonzalez. *Narrative of the Embassy of Ruy Gonzalez de Clavijo to the Court of Timour at Samarcand A.D. 1403-06* translated by Clements R. Markham (London, 1859)

De Bruijn, J. Th. P. "Masrah," *Encyclopedia of Islam*[2].

De Gobineau, A. *Trois Ans en Asie* 2 vols. (Paris, 1923).

____, *Les religions et les philosophies dans l'Asie Centrale* 2 vols. (Paris, 1923).

Della Valle, Pietro. "Extract of the Travels of Della Valle," in John Pinkerton, *A General Collection of Voyages and Travels*, (London, 1811), vol. 9.

____, *Les Fameux Voyages* 4 vols. (Paris: Gervais Clouzier, 1664).

De Lorey, Eustace & Sladen, Douglas. *Queer Things About Persia* (Philadelphia-London: J.B. Lippincot Co, 1907).

____, *The Moon of the Fourteenth Night: Being the Private Life of an Unmarried Diplomat in Persia during the Revolution* (London: Hurst & Blacket, 1910).

Dhabihi, Masih ed.. *Astarabadnameh*, (Tehran, 1348/1969).

Dhoka, Yahya. *Tarikhcheh-ye Sakhtemanha-ye Arg-e Saltanati-ye Tehran* (Tehran, 1349/1970).

al-Dinawari, Abu Hanifa. *Kitab al-Akhbar* ed. W. Guirgass (Leiden, 1888).

Donaldson, Bess Allen. *The Wild Rue* (London, 1938).

Drouville, Gaspard. *Voyage en Perse pendant les années 1812 et 1813*. 2 vols. (Paris, 1819 [reprint Tehran: Imp. Org. f. Social Services, 1976).

Du Mans, Raphael. *Estat de la Perse*. ed. Ch. Schefer (Paris: Leroux, 1890).

Dwight, H.D. *Persian Miniatures* (New York: Doubleday, Page & Company, 1917).

Eastwick, Edward B. *Journal of a Diplomate's Three Years' Residence in Persia*. 2 vols. (London, 1864 [Tehran: Imp. Org. f. Soc. Services, 1976]).

Echo of Iran, *Iran Almanac* 1961-1977.

Eichwald, Eduard. *Reise auf dem Caspischen Meere und in den Caucasus Unternommen in den Jahren 1825-1826*. 2 vols. (Stuttgart und Tübingen: J.G. Cotta, 1834).

Ekhtiar, Maryam Dorreh. *The Dar al-Funun: Educational Reform and Cultural Development in Qajar Iran* (unpublished thesis, New York University 1994).

Eliade, Mircea. *Traité d'Histoire des Réligions* (Paris, 1964).

Ellwell-Sutton, L.P. "The Literary Sourcs of the Ta`ziyeh," in Chelkowski, *Ta`ziyeh*, pp. 167-81.

`Emad al-Din Dhakariya Mahmud Qazvini, `*Aja'eb al-makhluqat va ghara'eb al-mowjudat* (Lucknow, 1912).

Emanuel, W.V. *The Wild Asses, a Journey through Persia* (London, 1939).

Ende, Werner. "The Flagellations of Muharram and the Shi'ite `Ulama," *Der Islam* 55/1 (1978), pp. 19-36.

Eqbal, `Abbas et alii, *She`r va Musiqi dar Iran* (Tehran, 1366/1987).

E`temad al-Saltaneh, *Athar va'l-Ma'ather* (Tehran, 1306/1889).

E`temad al-Saltaneh, Mohammad Hasan Khan.*Ruznameh-ye Khaterat*. ed. Iraj Afshar (Tehran: Amir Kabir, 1345/1967).

E`tesam al-Molk, *Safarnameh-ye Mirza Khanlar Khan E`tesam al-Molk*. ed. Manuchehr Mahmudi (Tehran, 1351/1972).

Ettinghausen, R. "The dance with zoomorphic masks," in G. Makdisi, ed., *Arabic and Islamic studies in honour of H. A. R. Gibb* (Leiden 1965), pp. 211-24.

`Eyn al-Saltaneh, Qahraman Mirza Salur. *Ruznameh-ye Khaterat*. 10 vols. eds. Mas`ud Salur and Iraj Afshar (Tehran: Asatir, 1376/1997).

Falsafi, Nasrollah. "Tarikh-e Qahveh va Qahvehkhanrh dar Iran" in Ibid., *Chand Maqaleh-ye Tarikhi va Adabi* (Tehran 1342/1963), pp. 269-83.

____, *Zendigani-ye Shah `Abbas Avval*. 5 vols. (Tehran 1344/1966).

Faramarz Fils de Khodadad. *Samak-e Ayyar* translated by Razavi, Frédérique (Paris: Maisonneuve, 1972).

Fekri, Gholam `Ali. "Tarikhcheh-ye si va panj saleh-ye te'atr dar Iran,"part I. *Salnameh-ye Pars* (Tehran, 1325/1946), pp. 147-55.

____, "Tarikhcheh-ye si va panj saleh-ye te'atr dar Iran," part II. *Salnameh-ye Pars* (Tehran, 1327/1948), pp. 73-81.

Felix de Jesus, "Chronica da Ordem de S. Augustinho nas Indias Orientais," *Analecta Augustiniana* 30 (1967), pp. 5-147.

Feuvrier, J.B.: *Trois ans à la Cour de Perse*. (Paris: F. Juven, 1900).

Flandin, E. and Coste, P. *Voyage en Perse ... 1840-41* 2 vols. (Paris, 1851).

Floor, Willem. "The Lutis, a social phenomenon in Qajar Persia," *Die Welt des Islams* 13 (1971), pp. 103-120.

____, "The political role of the lutis in Qajar Iran," in: G. Schweizer ed., *Interdisziplinaere Iran-Forschung, Beitrage aus Kulturgeographie, Ethnologie, Soziologie und Neuerer Geschichte*, (Beihefte zum Tuebinger Atlas, reihe B, no. 40) (Wiesbaden: Reichert, 1978), pp. 179-88.

____, "The political role of the lutis in Iran," in: *Modern Iran, the dialectics of continuity and change*, M.E. Bonine & N.R. Keddie eds. (Albany: SUNY, 1981), pp. 83-95.

____, *Hokumat-e Nader Shah* (Tehran: Tus, 1367/1988), translated by Abu'l-Qasem Serri.

____, "The Secular Judicial System in Safavid Persia," *Studia Iranica* 29 (2000), pp. 9-60.

____, "Tea Consumption and Imports into Qajar Iran," *Studia Iranica* 33/2004, pp. 47-111.

Forugh, Mehdi. "Takiyeh-ye Dowlat," *Honar va Mardom* 29 (1343/1964), pp. 7-10.

____, "Namayesh," in Government of Iran, *Iran-Shahr* 2 vols. (Tehran: Unesco, 1964), vol. 1, pp. 899-939.

Fowler, George. *Three Years in Persia* 2 vols. (London: Colburn, 1841).

Francklin, William. *Observations made on a tour from Bengal to Persia in the years 1786-7* (London 1790 [Tehran: Imp. Org. f. Soc. Services, 1976]).

Fraser, J.B. *A Winter's Journey from Constantinople to Teheran*, 2 vols. in one (London, 1838 [New York: Arno, 1973]).

Frye, Richard N. *The Heritage of Persia* (Cleveland, 1963).

Fryer, John. *A New Account of East India and Persia Being Nine Years' Travels, 1672-1681*, 3 vols. (London: Hakluyt, 1909-15).

Fullerton, Alice. *To Persia for Flowers* (Oxford: OUP, 1938).

Fumeni, `Abd al-Fattah. *Tarikh-e Gilan dar vaqaye`-ye salha 923-1038 hejri qamari*, ed. Manuchehr Setudeh (Tehran 1349/1970).

Galunov, R.A. "Pakhlavan Kachal- persidskii teatr petrushki," *IRAN* II (1928, Leningrad), pp. 26-27.

____, "Neskol'ko slov o perspektivakh sobirania materialov po fol'klory i teatr v Persii *Dokladie Akademii Nauk* 17 (Leningrad, 1929), pp. 307-12.

____, "Kheyme shab bazi—persidskii teatr marionetok," *Iran* III (1929), pp. 1-50.

____, "Ma`rikeh giri," *Iran* III (1929), pp. 940-1006.

____, "Narodniy Teatr Irana," *Sovietskaia Etnografiya* 4-5 (1936), pp. 55-83.

Gemelli-Careri, Gio Francesco. *Giro del Mondo* 6 vols. (Napoli: Giuseppe Roselli, 1699).

Genet, *Le Martyre d'Ali Akbar—Drame Persan* (Liege-Paris, Droz, 1947).

Ghanoonparvar, M.R. "Drama," *Encyclopaedia Iranica*.

Ghirshman, Roman. *Iran* (Hammondsworth: Penguin, 1961).

____, *Parthes et Sassanides* (Paris: Gallimard, 1962).

Gmelin, S.G. *Reise durch Russland*, 4 vols. (St. Petersburg, 1774).

Goyan, Georges. *Teyatr Sovietskogo Armenii* 2 vols. (Moscow, 1952).

Gramlich, Richard. *Die Schiitischen Derwischorden Persiens* 3 vols. (Wiesbaden, 1981).

Grothe, Hugo. *Wanderungen in Persien* (Berlin, Alg. Verein f. Deutsche Literatur, 1910).

Hafez-e Shirazi, Khvajeh Shams al-Din. *Lesan al-Gheyb* ed. Pazhman Bakhtiyari (Tehran, 1362/1983).

Hale, F. *From Persian Uplands* (New York: E.P.Dutton, n.d.).

Hamadani, Hajji `Abdollah Khan Qaraguzlu Amir-e Nezam. *Majmu`eh-ye Athar* ed. `Enayatollah Majidi (Tehran, 1383/2003).

Hanaway, William L. "Formal Elements in the Persian Popular Romances," in *Review of National Literatures—Iran*, vol. 2/1 (1971), pp. 142-49.

____, "Stereotyped Imagery in the Ta`ziyeh," in Chelkowski, *Ta`ziyeh*, pp. 182-92.

____, "Marthiya," *Encyclopedia of Islam*[2].

Haqani, Musa. "Moharram az negah-e tarikh va tasvir," *Tarikh-e Mo`aser-e Iran* 6/21-22 (1381/2002), pp. 493-574.

Haqiqat. Asnad-e Tarikhi. Jonbesh-e kargari-ye sosoyal demokrasi va komunisti-ye Iran. vol. 7 (Florence: Mazdak, 1978).

Hasuri, `Ali. *Siyavoshan* (Tehran: Cheshmeh, 1378/1999).

Hovayan, Andaranik. "Te'atr-e Armaniyan dar Tehran," *Faslnameh-ye Te'atr* 4-5 (1378/1999), pp. 183-217.

____, "Te'atr-e Aramaneh dar Azarbeyjan," *Faslnameh-ye Te'atr* 18-19 (1378/1999), pp. 165-70.

____, "Te'yatr-e Armaniyan-e Jolfa-ye Esfahan," *Faslnameh-ye Te'yatr* 1/17 (1377/1998), pp. 196-214.

Hedayatollah Afushteh-ye. *Naqavat al-athar fi dhekr al-akhyar*, ed. Ehsan Eshraqi. (Tehran, 1350/1971).

Heinrich, Gerd. *Auf Panthersuche durch Persien* (Berlin: Reimer/Vohsen, 1933).

Hodgson, Marshall G.S. *The Venture of Islam: conscience and history in a world civilization.* 3 vols. (Chicago, 1974).

Holmes, W.R. *Sketches on the Shores of the Caspian, Descriptive and Pictorial.* (London: Richard Bentley, 1845).

Höltzer, Ernst. *Persien vor 113 Jahren* ed. Mohammad Assemi (Tehran: Vezarat-e Farhang va Honar, 2535/1976).

Homayuni, Mansur. *Sargodhasht-e Namayesh dar Mashhad* (Mashhad, Farhang va Honar-e Khorasan, 1348/1969) [not seen]

Homayuni, Sadeq. *Ta`ziyeh dar Iran* (Shiraz, 1368/1989).

Howard, R. W. *A Merry Mountaineer. The Story of Clifford Harris of Persia* (London: CMS, 1931).

Huan, Ma. *Ying-yai Sheng-lan: The Overall Survey of the Ocean's Shores [1443]* (trans. & ed. by J.V.G. Mills (Cambridge, 1970).

Humayuni, Sadeq. "An Analysis of the Ta`ziyeh of Qasem" Peter J. Chelkowski, *Ta`ziyeh: Ritual and Drama in Iran* (New York, 1979), pp. 12-23.

Hommaire de Hell, X. *Voyage en Turquie et en Perse.* 2 vols. (Paris: P. Bertrand, 1856).

Heribert Horst, *Die Staatsverwaltung der Grossseljuqen und der Khorazmshahs (1038-1231)* (Wiesbaden: Steiner, 1964).

Hudi, Rahim. "Pishineh-ye Te'yatr-e Novin-e Shiraz ta sal-e 1359," in Homayuni, Sadeq ed. *Yaran* (1384/2005), pp. 232-44.

Ivanow, W. *An Abbreviated Version of the Diwan-e Khaki* (Bombay, 1933).

Jacob, Georg. *Geschichte des Schattentheater* (Berlin, 1907).

____, *Die Herkunft der Silhouettenkunst (ojmadschylyk) aus Persien* (Berlin, 1913)

Ja`fariyan, Rasul. "Molla Hoseyn Va`ez Kashefi va Ketab va Rowzat al-Shohada," in Rasul Ja`fariyan, *Maqalat-e Tarikhi* 5 vols. (Qom, 1376/1987), vol. 1, pp. 168-210.

____, "Naqsh-e Qessehpardazan dar Tarikh-e Eslam," *Keyhan-e Andisheh* 30 (Khordad-Tir 1369/1990), pp. 121-44.

____, "Qesseh-khvani dar Iran `asr-e Safaviyyeh," in Ibid., *Safaviyyeh dar `arseh-ye din, farhangi va siyasat.* 3 vols. (Qom, 1379/2000), vol. 2, pp. 858-78.

Javadi, Hasan. *Satire in Persian Literature* (Cranbury, 1988).

Javadi, Shafi`. *Tabriz va Peyramun* (Tabriz: Bonyad-e Farhang-e Reza Pahlavi, 1350/1971)

Jenati `Ata'i, Abu'l-Qasem. *Bonyad-e Namayesh dar Iran* (Tehran, 1334/1955).

Jewett, Mary. *My Life in Persia* (Cedar Rapids, 1909).

Juvaini, `Ata-Malik. *The History of the World-Conquerer*. Translated by John Andrew Boyle 2 vols. (Manchester, 1958).

Kaempfer, Engelbert. *Am Hofe des persischen Grosskönigs (1684-85). Das erste Buch der Amoenitates exoticae in deutscher Bearbeitung*, hrsg. v. Walter Hinz. (Leipzig 1940).

Kambakhsh, `Abdol-Samad. *Nazari beh Jonbesh-e Kargari va Komunisti dar Iran* (Stassfurt: Hezb-e Tudeh, 1972).

Kashefi, Hoseyn Va`ez. *Fotovvatnameh-ye Soltani* ed. Mohammad Mahjub (Tehran, 1340/1971) translated by Jay R. Crook as *The Royal Book of Spiritual Chivalry* (Chicago, 2000).

Kazemi, Moshtaq. *Ruzgarva Andisheh* 3 vols. (Tehran, 1350/1971).

Kellermann, *Auf Persiens Karawanenstrassen* (Berlin: S. Fischer, 1928).

Keshavarz, Karim. "Javanehha-ye Te'yatr-e dar Gilan," *Rudaki* 22 (1353/1974), pp. 6-12.

Keyvani, Mehdi. *Artisans and Guild Life in the later Safavid period* (Berlin 1982).

Khalaj, Mansur. *Tarikhcheh-ye Namayesh dar Kermanshah* (Tehran, 1364/1985) [not seen]

Khanlari, Parviz Natel. "Teyatr va Adabiyyat," *Sokhan* 23 (1352/1973), pp. 141-45.

Khorenats'i, Moses. *History of the Armenians*. Translated by Robert W. Thomson (London-Cambridge: Harvard UP, 1978).

Koelz, Walter N. *Persian Diary, 1939-1941* (Ann Arbor, Michigan, 1983).

Korf F. *Pro'ezd' chrez' Zakavkaskii krai* (St. Petersburg, 1838) translated into Persian by Eskander Dhabihan as Kurf, Barun Fyudur. *Safarnameh* (Tehran: Fekr-e Ruz, 1372/1993).

Kotov, F.A. *Khozhenie kuptsa Fedota Kotova* ed. N.A. Kuznetsova (Moscow 1958) translated by Kemp, P.M. as *Russian Travellers to India and Persia [1624-1798] Kotov-Yefremov-Danibegov* (Delhi 1959).

Kovalenko, Anatoly. *Le Martyre de Husayn dans la poésie populaire d'Iraq* (Thesis University of Geneva, 1979).

Krymskij, A. *Pers'kii Teatr* (Kiev, 1925).

Kuhestani-Nezhad, Mas`us. *Gozideh-ye Asnad-e Namayesh dar Iran* 2 vols. (Tehran, 1381/2002).

Kushan, Naser. *Tarikh-e Te'atr dar Esfahan* (Isfahan, 1379/2000).

Laessø, Agnate. *Fra Persien* (Copenhagen, 1881).

Landau, J.M., "Khayal al-Zill," *Encyclopedia of Islam*[2]

Le Bruyn, Cornelius. *Travels into Moscovy, Persia and part of the East-Indies*, 2 vols. (London, 1737).

Lerch, Johann Jacob. "Auszug aus dem Tagesbuch von einer Reise … von 1733 bis 1735 aus Moscau nach Astrachan, und in die auf der Westseite des caspischen Sees belegene Länder, gethan hat", in *Büschings Magazin* III (Hamburg 1769).

Lerch, Johann Jacob. *Lebens- und Reise-Geschichte von ihm selbst beschrieben* (Halle: Curtts Witwe, 1791).

Levy, Reuben (translator). *A Mirror for Princes.* The Qabus Nama by Kai Ka'us Ibn Iskandar, Prince of Gurgan (New York, 1951).

Lewis, Bernard "`Ashiq," *Encyclopedia of Islam*[2].

Litvinsky, B. A., Guang-da, Zhang and Samghabadi, R. Shabani eds. *History of the Civilizations of Central Asia, Volume III: The Crossroads of Civilizations: A.D. 250 to 750.* (Paris: UNESCO Publishing, 1996).

Ma`ani, Ahmad Golchin. *Shahr-e Ashub dar she`r-e farsi* (Tehran, 1346/1967).

_____, *Karvan-e Hend* (Mashhad, 1369/1991)

MacKenzie, Charles Francis. *Safarnameh-ye Shomal* tr. Mansureh Ettehadiyeh (Nezam-Mafi) (Tehran: Gostareh, 1359/1980).

Mahjub, Mohammad. Ja`far. "Sokhanvari," *Sokhan* 6 (1333/1954), pp. 530-35; vol. 7, pp. 631-37, and vol. 8, pp. 779-86.

Mahjub, Muhammad Ja`far. "The Effect of European Theatre and the Influence of its Theatrical Methods Upon Ta`ziyeh," in Peter J. Chelkowski, *Ta`ziyeh: Ritual and Drama in Iran* (New York, 1979), pp. 137-53.

Malcolm, John. *The History of Persia.* 2 vols. (London, 1820 [Tehran: Imp. Org. f. Soc. Services, 1976]).

Malcolm, Napier. *Five Years in a Persian Town* (London: John Murray, 1905).

Malekpur, Jamshid. *Adabiyyat-e Namayeshi dar Iran* 2 vols. (Tehran, 1363/1994).

Mallah, Hoseyn`Ali. *Hafez va Musiqi* (Tehran, 1351/1972).

_____, *Manuchehri Damghani va Musiqi* (Tehran, 1363/1984).

Mamnoun, P. Ta`zija, *Schi'itisch-Persisches Passionsspiel* (Vienna, 1967).

Mamnun, Parviz. *Seyri dar Te'atr-e Mardom-e ye Isfahan* (Tehran, 1356/1977).

Maqrizi, Ahmad b. `Ali. *Kitab al-Khitat al-Maqriziyah* 3 vols. (1959).

Marr, Y.N. "Koje-shto Pehlevan Kechel i drygikh vidakh narodnogo teatre v Persii." *IRAN* II (Leningrad, 1928), pp. 75-80.

Massé, Henri. *Croyances et Coutumes Persanes* 2 vols. (Paris: Maisonneuve, 1938).

Massé, Henri. "Epigraphy. B. Persian Inscriptions," Pope, Arthur and Ackerman, Phyllis, *A Survey of Persian Art* (Oxford, 1939), vol. 2, p. 1797-98.

Mas`ud Sa`d-e Salman *Divan*, ed. Rashid Yasimi (Tehran 1339/1960).

Mehrabadi, Abu'l-Qasem Rafi`i. *Athar-e Melli-ye Esfahan* (Tehran, 1352/1973).

Meier, Fritz and Gramlich, Richard. "Drei moderne Texte zum Persischen Wettreden" *ZDMG* 23 (1961), pp. 289-327.

Meisami, Julie Scott. *The Sea of Virtues (Bahr al-Fava'id) A Medieval Islamic Mirror for Princes* (Salt Lake City: Utah UP, 1991).

Melgunof, Gregorii Valerianovich. *Das südliche Ufer des Kaspischen Meeres oder die Nordprovinzen Persiens* translated by J. Th. Zenker (Leipzig, 1868).

Membré, Michele. *Relazione*, ed. G.C. Scarcia (Rome, 1969). English translation by A.H. Morton as *Mission to the Lord Sophy of Persia (1539-1542)* (London: SOAS, 1993).

Menzel, Theodor. *Meddah, Schattentheater und Orta Ojunu* (Prague, 1941).

Merritt-Hawkes, O. A. *Persia—Romance & Reality* (London: Nicholson & Watson, 1935).

Meskub, Shahrokh. *Sug-e Siyavosh: dar marg va rastakhiz* (Tehran: Khvarezmi, 1350/1971).

Mez, A. *Die Renaissance des Islams* (Heidelberg, 1922).

Miller, Janet. *Camel-Bells of Baghdad* (Boston-New York, 1934).

Millingen, Frederick. *Wild Life Among The Koords* (London: Hurst and Blackett, 1870).

Mir-Ansari, `Ali and Ziya'i, Sayyed Mehrdad eds. *Gozideh-ye Asnad-e Namayesh dar Iran* 2 vols. (Tehran, 1381/2002).

Mir Shokra'i, Mohammad. Paygah-e ejtema`i-ye namayeshha-ye `amiyaneh dar Mazandaran va Gilan," *Honar va Mardom* 129-130 (1358/1979), pp. 52-65.

Mirza Rafi`a, *Dastur al-Moluk*. ed. Mohammad Taqi Daneshpazhuh. Zamimeh-ye shomareh-ye 5 va 6 sal-e 16 Majalleh-ye Daneshkadeh-ye Adabiyat va `Olum-e Ensani (Tehran 1347/1967).

Mirza Sami`a. *The Tadhkirat al-Muluk, A Manual of Safavid Administration*. Edited and translated by Vladimir Minorsky (Cambridge, 1980).

Mitford, Edward Ledwich. *A Land March from England to Ceylon Forty Years Ago*. 2 vols. (London: Allen & Co, 1884).

Mo`ayyer al-Mamalek, Dust `Ali. *Yaddashtha'i az Zendegani-ye Khosusi-ye Naser al-Din Shah* (Tehran, 1351/1972).

Mohammadi, Ahmad. "Negahi beh Tarikh-e Namayesh-e Iran," *Honar va Mardom* 129-130 (1352/1973), pp. 19-25.

Mo`in al-Dowleh. *Khaterat* ed. Sirus Sa`dvandiyan (Tehran: Zarrin, 1380/2001).

Momtahen al-Dowleh, *Khaterat*. ed. Hoseynqoli Khan-Shaqaqi (Tehran: Amir Kabir, 1353/1974).

Monajjem, Molla Jalal al-Din. *Ruznameh-ye `Abbasi ya Ruznameh-ye Molla Jalal*, ed. Seyfollah Vahidniya (Tehran 1366/1967).

Monchi-zadeh, Davoud. *Ta`ziya. Das Persische Passionsspiel* (Stockholm, 1967).

Monshi, Eskander Beg. *Tarikh-e `Alamara-ye `Abbasi*. Iraj Afshar ed. 2 vols. (Tehran, 1350/1971).

Monshi-bashi-ye Nahid, "Valedeh-ye Te'atr Mireh." *Nahid* nr. 47, 11 Dey 1307, pp. 1-2.

Moore, Benjamin Burges. From *Moscow to the Persian Gulf* . (New York: G.P. Putnam's Sons, 1915).

Moqaddasi, Mohammad b. Ahmad. *Ahsan al-Taqasim fi ma`rifat al-aqalim* (Leiden, 1967).

Morier, James. *A Journey through Persia, Armenia and Asia Minor in the Years 1808 and 1809* (London: Longman, Hurst, Rees, Orme, and Brown, 1812).

Morier, James. *A Second Journey through Persia, Armenia, and Asia Minor ... between the years 1810 and 1816* (London: Longman, Hurst, Rees, Orme, and Brown, 1818).

Morony, Michael G. *Iraq After the Muslim Conquest* (Princeton, 1984).

Mostafavi, Sayyed Mohammad Taqi. *Athar-e Tarikihi-ye Tehran* 2 vols. ed. Mir Hashem Mohaddeth (Tehran, 1361/1982).

Mosta`san, Hoseyn Qoli. "Namayesh dar Iran va `Elal-e Enhetat-e An," *Salnameh-ye Pars* 1314/1935, pp. 128-143.

Mostowfi, `Abdollah. *Sharh-e Zendegani-ye Man* 3 vols. (Tehran: Zavvar, n.d.).

Mounsey, Augustus H. *A Journey through the Caucasus and the Interior of Persia* (London: Smith, Elder & Co, 1872).

Mu`in al-Dowleh. *Khatirat* ed. Sirus Sa`dvandiyan (Tehran: Zarrin, 1380/2001).

Müller, Hildegard. *Studien zum persischen Passionsspiel* (Freiburg i. Breisgau, 1966).

Al-Nadim. *The Fihrist of al-Nadim. A Tenth Century Survey of Muslim Culture.* Translated by B. Dodge 2 vols. (New York: Columbia UP, 1970).

Najmi, Naser. *Dar al-Khelafeh* (Tehran: Amir Kabir, 2536/1977).

Naqib al-Mamalek, Mohammad `Ali. *Amir Arsalan* (Tehran, 1966).

Narsakhi, *The History of Bukhara.* Translated by Richard N. Frye (Cambridge, 1954).

Nasiri, Mohammad Ebrahim b. Zeyn al-`Abedin, *Dastur-e Shahriyan.* ed. Mohammad Nader Nasiri Moqaddam (Tehran 1373/1995).

Nasr, Sayyed `Ali Khan. "Honar-e Te'atr va Namayeshnameh-nevisi dar Iran," *Rahnameh-ye Ketab* 4/4 (1340/1961), pp. 310-13.

Nasrabadi, Mirza Mohammad Taher. *Tadhkereh-ye Nasrabadi.* Ed. Vahid Dastgerdi (Tehran 1361/1982).

Natanzi, Mahmud b. Hedayatollah Afushteh-ye. *Naqavat al-athar fi dhekr al-akhyar*, ed. Ehsan Eshraqi. (Tehran, 1350/1971).

Nevill, Ralph. *Unconventional Memories. Europe-Persia-Japan* (New York: George Doran, 1923).

Nezam al-Saltaneh-Mafi, Hoseyn Qoli Khan. *Khaterat va Asnad.* 2 vols. eds. Mansureh Ettehadiyeh (Nezam-Mafi) and Hamid Ram-Pisheh (Tehran, 1361/1982).

Nezami Ganjavi, *Nameh-ye Makhzan al-Asrar* (Tehran, 1955).

Nezami al-Samarqandi. *Ketab-e Chahar Maqaleh* ed. Mohammad Qazvini (Berlin: Iranschär, 1927).

Niebuhr, Carsten. *Reisebeschreibung nach Arabien und andern umliegende Ländern* (Zürich, 1992).

Nikitine, Basile P. *Irani keh man shenakhteh am* (Tehran, 1329/1951).

_____, *Les Kurdes, étude sociologique et historique* (Paris, 1956).

Norden, Hermann. *Under Persian Skies* (Philadelphia: McCrea Smith, n.d.).

Nurbakhsh, Hoseyn. *Delqakha-ye mashur-e darbari va maskharahha-ye dowrehgerd* (Tehran, 1354/1975).

O'Donovan, Edmond. *The Merv Oasis*. 2 vols. (London: Smith, Elder & Co, 1882).

Olearius, Adam. *Vermehrte newe Beschreibung der moscowitischen und persischen Reyse*, ed. D. Lohmeier (Schleswig, 1656 [Tübingen, 1971]).

Orsolle, E. *Le Caucase et La Perse* (Paris: Plon, Nourrit et Cie., 1885).

Orta Rebelo, N. de. *Un voyageur portugais en Perse au debut du XVII siecle* ed. J. Verissimo Serrao (Lisbon 1972).

Osku'i, Mostafa. *Pazhuheshi dar tarikh-e te'atr-e Iran* (Moscow, 1992).

Ouseley, W. *Travels in various countries of the East: more particularly Persia*, 3 vols. (London, 1819-23).

Papazian, V. "Teatr v Persii: Iz vospominanij V. Paziana," *Kavkazskij Vestnik* 3/8-9 (Tiflis, 1902), pp. 152-60.

Pavlovich, M. *Enqelab-e Mashrutuyat-e Iran* translated by M. Hushyar (Tehran, 1330/1951).

Pelly, Lewis. "Remarks on a recent Journey from Bushire to Shirauz," *Transactions of the Bombay Geographical Society* 17 (1865), p. 156, note. [pp. 141-74.]

Perkins, J. *A Residence of Eight Years in Persia* (Andover, 1843).

Perlin, L. "Ozherk zapadnoi Persii (pis'mo iz Kermanshaxa)," *Novyi Vostok* III (1923), 443-45.

Pirzadeh, Mohammad `Ali. *Safarnameh-ye Hajji Pirzadeh*. ed. Hafez Farmanfarma'iyan 2 vols. (Tehran, 1342/1963).

Plutarch, *Lifes* (many editions).

Ponafidine, Pierre. *Life in the Moslem East* (New York, 1911).

Price, William. *Journal of the British Embassy to Persia*. 2 vols. in one (London: Thomas Thorpe, 1832).

Qaddusi, Hasan A`zam. *Khaterat-e Man* 2 vols. (Tehran, 1349/1970).

Qazvini, Mohammad. "Mir-e Nowruzi," *Yadgar* 1/3 (1323/1944), pp. 13-16.

____, "Shahedi-ye digar baraye 'Mir-e Nowruzi'," *Yadgar* 1/10 (1323/1944), pp. 57-66.

Qazvini Razi, Sheikh `Abdol-Jalil. *Ketab al-Naqz ma`ruf beh Ba`z Mathalib al-Navasib fi Naqz ba`z Faza'ah al-Ravafiz* (Tehran, 1358/1980).

Querry, "Rouz-e Qatl," *Revue de l'Orient* III (1856), p. 371-80.

Rabino, H. L. "Les provinces Caspiennes de la Perse: La Guilan," *Revue du Monde Musulmane* 29 (1915-16).

_____, *Mazandaran and Astarabad* (London: Luzac, 1928).

Rapin, Claude. *Fouilles d'Aï Khanoum*, VIII: La trésorerie du palais hellénistique d'Aï Khanoum. Mémoires de la Délégation archéologique française en Afghanistan XXXIII. (Paris, 1992).

Rashid al-Din, *The Successors of Genghis Khan*. Tr, John Andrew Boyle (New York: Columbia UP, 1971).

Rezvani, M. *Le théâtre et la danse en Iran* (Paris, 1962).

Rice, Clara. *Persian Women and Their Ways* (London: Seeley, Service & Co, 1923).

Rice, W.A. *Mary Bird in Persia* (London, 1916).

Roemer, Hans Robert. *Staatsschreiben der Timuridenzeit. Das Sharafnama des `Abdallah Marwarid in kritischer Auswertung* (Wiesbaden 1952).

Rugan, Heyva. *Kusheshha-ye Nafarjam* (Tehran, 1360/1981).

Rumlu, Hoseiy Beg. *Ahsan al-Tavarikh*. ed. `Abdol-Hoseyn Nava'i (Tehran 1357/1978).

Ruznameh-ye Ettefaqiyeh-ye Vaqaye` 4 vols. (Tehran: Ketabkhaneh- Melli, 1373-74/1994-95).

Sabar, Yona. *The Folk Literature of the Kurdistani Jews: An Anthology* (New Haven, 1982).

Sackville-West, V. *Passenger to Teheran* (London, 1926 [New York, 1990]).

Sadr, Mohsen, *Khaterat-e Sadr al-Ashraf* (Tehran, 1364/1985).

Sadvandian, Cyrus. "The Inhabitants of Meydan-Gusfand", *The Journal of the Middle East Studies Society at Columbia University* 1 (1987), pp. 39-54.

Safa, Fathollah. *Tarikh-e Adabbiyat dar Iran* 3 vols. (Tehran: Ebn Sina, 1339/1960).

Safa al-Saltaneh, Mirza `Ali Khan Na'ini. *Safarnameh-ye Safa al-Saltaneh* ed. Mohammad Golbon (Tehran, 1382/2003).

Safa'i, Ebrahim. *Rahbaran-e Mashruteh* 2 vols. (Tehran: Javidan, 1344/1965).

Safar, Baba. *Ardabil dar Godhargah-e Tarikh* 3 vols. (Tehran, 1350-62/1971-83).

Safinezhad, Javad. *Talebabad* (Tehran, 2535/1976).

Salmon, Th. Van Goch M. *Hedendaagsche Historie of Tegenwoordige Staat van Alle Volkeren. IV. Deel Behelzende den tegenwoordige Staat van Persia, Arabia, en het Asiatisch Tartaryen* (Amsterdam: Isaak Tririon, 1732).

San Bernardino, Gaspar de. *Itinerario da India por terra ate a ilha de Chipre* (Lisboa, 1842).

Sanson, N. *The Present State of Persia* (London, 1695).

Sasan Khan Malek, *Siyasatgaran-e dowreh-ye Qajar.* 2 vols. (Tehran, 1338/1959).

Savory, R.M. *History of Shah `Abbas the Great* (translation of Monshi) 2 vols. (Boulder 1978).

Schafer, Edward H. *The Golden Peaches of Samarkand* (Berkeley, 1953 [1962]).

Serena, C. *Hommes et Choses en Perse* (Paris: G. Charpentier, 1883).

Setudeh, Manuchehr. "Namayesh-e `arusi dar jangal," *Yadgar* 1/8 (1324/1945), pp. 41-43.

Seystani, Malek Shah Hoseyn b. Malek Ghayath al-Din Mohammad b. Shah Mahmud. *Ehya al-Moluk.* ed. Manuchehr Setudeh (Tehran 1344/1966).

Shahri, Ja`far. *Tarikh-e ejtema`i -Tehran dar qarn-e sizdahom*, 6 vols. (Tehran: Farhang-Rasa, 1368/1989).

Shahri, Ja`far. *Tehran-e Qadim.* 5 vols. (Tehran: Mo`in, 1377/1999).

Sharaf (1300-1309 Q) and *Sharafat* (1314-1321 Q) reprint Tehran (2535/1976).

Shari`ati, `Ali Akbar, "Sargarmiha va Baziha-ye Pishin-e Yazd," in Afshar, Iraj ed. *Yazdnameh.* 2 vols. (Tehran, 1371/1992), vol. 1, pp. 506-11.

Sheil, Lady. *Glimpses of Life and Manners in Persia* (London, 1856 [New York: Arno, 1973]).

Sheykh-Reza'i, Ensiyeh and Azari, Shahla ed. *Gozareshha-ye Nazmiyyeh az Mahallat-e Tehran* (Tehran: Sazman-e Asnad-e Melli, 1377/1998).

Sho`a`i, Hamid. *Namayeshnameh va Filmnameh dar Iran* (Tehran, 2535/1977).

Shoemaker, Michael Myers. *The Heart of the Orient* (New York: G.P. Putnam's Sons, 1904).

Skrine, Clarmont. *World War in Iran* (London, 1962).

Smirnov, K. *Persy, otcherk religii Persii* (Tiflis, 1916).

Soltani, Mohammad `Ali. *Joghrafiya-ye Tarikhi va Tarikh-e Mofassal-e Kermanshahan.* 3 vols. (Tehran, 1370/1991).

Speaight, George. *The History of the English Puppet Theatre* (London, 1955).

Spuler, Berthold. *Iran in früh-Islamischer Zeit* (Wiesbaden, 1952).

Strauszens, J. J. *Reisen durch Griechenland, Moscau, Tartarey, Ostindien, und andere Theile der Welt* (Amsterdam, 1678).

Stuart, Lt. Colonel. *Journal of Residence in Northern Persia* (London: Richard Bentley, 1854).

Sykes, Percy M. *Ten Thousand Miles in Persia or Eight Years in Iran* (New York: Charles Scribner's Sons, 1902).

Sykes, Ella. *Through Persia on a Side-Saddle* (London: MacQueen, 1901).

____, *Persia and its People* (London: MacMillan, 1910).

Tabataba'i, Sayyed Hoseyn Modarresi. *Bargi az Tarikh-e Qazvin* (Qom, 1361/1982).

Tahvildar, Mirza Hoseyn Khan. *Joghrafiya-ye Isfahan*, ed. M. Setudeh. (Tehran: Daneshgah, 1342/1963).

Talebi, Faramarz. "Namayesh dar Gilan," in ed. Ebrahim Eslah-Arabna. *Ketab-e Gilan* 3 vols (Tehran, 1374/1995) vol. 3, p. 705-52.

Tancoigne, J. M. *A Narrative of a Journey into Persia* (London: William Wright, 1820).

Tarbiyat, nakhostin nashriyeh-ye ruzaneh va gheyr dowlati-ye Iran. 4 vols. (Tehran, 1376/1997).

Tate, G. P. *The Frontiers of Baluchistan. Travels on the borders of Persia and Afghanistan* (London 1909 [Lahore: East & West Publishing Comp, 1976]).

Tavernier, Jean-Baptiste. *Les six voyages ... en Turquie, en Perse et aux Indes*. 2 vols. (Amsterdam, 1678)

Tenreiro, António. *Viagens por terra da India a Portugal* Neves Aguas ed. (Lisbon 1991).

Texier, C. *Description de l'Armenie, la Perse et la Mesopotamie* (Paris, 1852).

Thalasso, M.A. "Le Théatre Persan," *La Revue Théatrale* (1905), pp. 865-88.

Titley, Norah M. *Miniatures from Persian Manuscripts* (London, 1977)

Ussher, John. *Journey from London to Persepolis* (London: Hurst & Blackett, 1865).

Varjavand, Parviz. *Simay-e Tarikh va Farhang-e Qazvin*. 3 vols. (Tehran, 1377/1998).

Vasefi, Zeyn al-Din Mahmud. *Badaye` al-Vaqaye`* 2 vols. ed. A. N. Boldyreva, (Moscow, 1961).

Waring, Edward Scott. *A Tour to Sheeraz*. (London 1807 [New York, 1973]).

Wegener, Walther. *Syrien, Irak, Iran* (Leipzig, 1943).

Werner, Christopher, *An Iranian Town in Transition* (Wiesbaden: Harrassowitz, 2000).

Wilbraham, Richard. *Travels in the Transcaucasian Provinces of Russia* (London: John Murray, 1839).

Wills, C. J. *Persia As It Is* (London, 1886).

Wills, C. J. *In the Land of the Lion and the Sun.* 2nd edition (London: Ward, Lock & Bowden, 1893).

Wilson, S.G. *Persian Life and Customs* (New York: Fleming. H. Revell, 1895).

Wishard, John G. *Twenty Years in Persia. A Narrative of Life under the Last Three Shahs* (New York: Fleming H. Revell, 1908).

Xenophon. Xenophon's Symposium, with notes by Samuel Ross Winans (Boston, 1881).

_____, *Anabasis*, Book VI, section 1.

Yarshater, Ehsan. "The Modern Literary Idiom," in Yarshater, Ehsan. ed., *Iran Faces the Seventies* (New York, Washington and London: Praeger Publishers, 1977), pp. 284-320.

___, "Ta`ziyeh and Pre-Islamic Mourning Rites in Iran," Peter J. Chelkowski, *Ta`ziyeh: Ritual and Drama in Iran* (New York, 1979), pp. 88-94.

Yate, C .E. *Khurasan and Sistan* (London: William Blackwood & Sons, 1900).

Yamamoto, Kumiko. *The Oral Background of Persian Epics: Storytelling and Poetry* (Leiden: Brill, 2003).

Zarrinkub, `Abdol-Hoseyn. *Donbaleh-ye josteju dar tasavvof dar Iran* (Tehran, 1357/1978).

Zoveyri, Mahjub. *Abu Moslemnameh va naqsh-e an dar tarikh-e ejtema`i-ye `asr-e Safavi* (Tehran, 1382/2003).

INDEX

OTHER MAGE PUBLISHERS TITLES

Agriculture in Qajar Iran
Willem Floor

Public Health in Qajar Iran
Willem Floor

Crowning Anguish: Taj Al-Saltana
Memoirs of a Persian Princess
Introduction by Abbas Amanat / Translated by Anna Vanzan

New Food of Life: Ancient Persian and
Modern Iranian Cooking and Ceremonies
Najmieh Batmanglij

Persian Cooking For A Healthy Kitchen
Najmieh Batmanglij

A Taste of Persia: An Introduction to Persian Cooking
Najmieh Batmanglij

Silk Road Cooking: A Vegetarian Journey
Najmieh Batmanglij

The Lion and the Throne:
Stories from the Shahnameh of Ferdowsi, Volume I
Translated by Dick Davis

Fathers and Sons:
Stories from the Shahnameh of Ferdowsi, Volume II
Translated by Dick Davis

Sunset of Empire:
Stories from the Shahnameh of Ferdowsi, Volume III
Translated by Dick Davis

My Uncle Napoleon
Iraj Pezeshkzad / Translated by Dick Davis

Inside Iran: Women's Lives
Jane Howard

CPSIA information can be obtained
at www.ICGtesting.com
Printed in the USA
LVHW050517161222
735312LV00008B/556

9 780934 211291